ETHICS FOR BIOENGINEERING SCIENTISTS

ETHICS FOR BIOENGINEERING SCIENTISTS
Treating Data as Clients

Howard Winet

CRC Press
Taylor & Francis Group
Boca Raton London New York

CRC Press is an imprint of the
Taylor & Francis Group, an **informa** business

First edition published 2022
by CRC Press
6000 Broken Sound Parkway NW, Suite 300, Boca Raton, FL 33487-2742

and by CRC Press
2 Park Square, Milton Park, Abingdon, Oxon, OX14 4RN

© 2022 Howard Winet

CRC Press is an imprint of Taylor & Francis Group, LLC

Reasonable efforts have been made to publish reliable data and information, but the author and publisher cannot assume responsibility for the validity of all materials or the consequences of their use. The authors and publishers have attempted to trace the copyright holders of all material reproduced in this publication and apologize to copyright holders if permission to publish in this form has not been obtained. If any copyright material has not been acknowledged please write and let us know so we may rectify in any future reprint.

Except as permitted under U.S. Copyright Law, no part of this book may be reprinted, reproduced, transmitted, or utilized in any form by any electronic, mechanical, or other means, now known or hereafter invented, including photocopying, microfilming, and recording, or in any information storage or retrieval system, without written permission from the publishers.

For permission to photocopy or use material electronically from this work, access www.copyright.com or contact the Copyright Clearance Center, Inc. (CCC), 222 Rosewood Drive, Danvers, MA 01923, 978-750-8400. For works that are not available on CCC please contact mpkbookspermissions@tandf.co.uk

Trademark notice: Product or corporate names may be trademarks or registered trademarks and are used only for identification and explanation without intent to infringe.

Library of Congress Cataloging-in-Publication Data
Names: Winet, Howard, author.
Title: Ethics for bioengineering scientists : treating data as clients / Howard Winet.
Description: First edition. I Boca Raton, FL : CRC Press, 2022. I Includes bibliographical references and index. I
Summary: "This book introduces bioengineers who must generate and/or report scientific data to the ethical challenges they will face in preserving the integrity of their data. It provides the perspective of reaching ethical decisions via pathways that treat data as clients to whom they owe a responsibility"-- Provided by publisher.
Identifiers: LCCN 2021032695 (print) I LCCN 2021032696 (ebook) I ISBN 9781032052359 (hardback) I ISBN 9781032053547 (paperback) I ISBN 9781003197218 (ebook)
Subjects: LCSH: Bioengineering--Moral and ethical aspects.
Classification: LCC QH332 .W56 2022 (print) I LCC QH332 (ebook) I DDC 174.2--dc23
LC record available at https://lccn.loc.gov/2021032695
LC ebook record available at https://lccn.loc.gov/2021032696

ISBN: 978-1-032-05235-9 (hbk)
ISBN: 978-1-032-05354-7 (pbk)
ISBN: 978-1-003-19721-8 (ebk)

DOI: 10.1201/9781003197218

Typeset in Times
by MPS Limited, Dehradun

Dedication

This work is dedicated to two of my mentors, Theodore Y. Wu who taught me that "arrogant scientist" is an oxymoron and Richard P. Feynman who taught me that data trumps all theory and its integrity is the measure of its reporter; and my wife Carol, who made my composition readable and the effort enlightening.

Contents

Preface..xiii

Acknowledgments..xvii

Introduction..xix

Author Biography..xxi

Acronyms..xxiii

Chapter 1   Bioengineering and Ethics 1

    1.1   Bioengineering as an Interdisciplinary Profession 1

    1.2   What BEs May Do 1

    1.3   Basis for Value Conflict between Bio and Engineering 2

    1.4   The Ancient Period and First Western Societies 2

    1.5   The Classical Period—Mythos and Logos 4

    1.6   Decline of the Latin World and Rise of the Islamic World 8

    1.7   The 12th-century Rise of the Universities (800–1400) 10

    1.8   The Italian Renaissance (1400–1650)................................12

    1.9   Emergence of Science from Philosophy—The Enlightenment (1650–1750) 17

    1.10   The Industrial Revolution—Determinism and Reductionism 18

    1.11   The Industrial Revolution—Causalism and Empiricism in Science..20

    1.12   The Second Industrial Revolution—Darwin Changes Human Concept of Self in the 19th Century 23

    1.13   The Path to Bioengineering from 1927 28

    1.14   The Advent of Bioengineering..30

    1.15   Bioengineering and Epidemiology......................................31

Chapter 2   Ethics Biology: Are There Ethical Genomes? 33

    2.1   Some Definitions 33

    2.2   The Unethical Experiment...33

    2.3   Can We Infer a Genetic Basis for Altruistic Behavior from Psychology? 34

    2.4   A Partial Substitute for the Human Experiment: Evolutionary Psychology...35

    2.5   Ethical/Moral Behavior in NonHuman Primates (from de Waal 1997)...38

    2.6   The Key to Ethical Motivation Is That Which Is Valued 39

    2.7   The Biological Structure of Moral/Ethical Behavior 40

vii

viii   Contents

| | 2.8 | Classical Case Supporting a Biological Basis for Morality/Ethical Behavior .... 42 |
| | 2.9 | Evolutionary Psychology and Social Darwinism .... 43 |

Chapter 3   Philosophical Basis for Moral Analysis 45

	3.1	The Eugenics Movement, a General Case Study Illustrating the Need for Ethical Analysis 45
	3.2	Macroethics vs. Microethics (Herkert 2005) 46
	3.3	The Concept of Moral Theory 46
	3.4	Motivation for Applying Moral Theories 47
	3.5	Overview of Moral Theories Used in This Book 48
	3.6	Consequentialism—General and Specific-type Utilitarianism 48
	3.7	Nonconsequentialism—Deontology 52
	3.8	Kantian Deontology 53
	3.9	Rossian Deontology 55
	3.10	Contractarianism 56
	3.11	Virtue Ethics 58
	3.12	Feminist Ethics—The Ethics of Care 60
	3.13	Critiques of the Five Moral Theories 63

Chapter 4   Moral Analysis: Deriving a Moral Decision 67

	4.1	Recognizing that an Ethical Problem Exists 67
	4.2	Kinds of Moral Challenges 68
	4.3	Commitment to Implementing a Solution 69
	4.4	Basic Strategy for Moral/ethical Analysis 69
	4.5	Example Case (Adapted From Rowan and Zinaich 2003) 70
	4.6	Actual Case Example, *John Moore v. Regents*, University of California et al. (Supreme Court of California No. S006987) 75
	4.7	A Word about Applications of Moral Analysis in this Chapter 80
	4.8	How Will You Apply a Moral Analysis? 81

Chapter 5   Separating Professional from Lay Ethics 83

	5.1	Ethics and Professional Responsibility 83
	5.2	Lay Ethics of Employee–Employee and Supervisor– Employee Interactions 84
	5.3	Professionals as Employees and Supervisors 86
	5.4	Professionals and Clients 87
	5.5	Individual Goals that Should Be Accomplished (Adapted from Faber 2003) 88

Contents

	5.6	Level/Form of Participation in Decision-Making and Implementation (Adapted from Faber 2003)	89
	5.7	Prima Facie Obligations of All Professionals: Confidentiality, Client Autonomy	94
	5.8	When Obligations Conflict: Conflict of Interest	97
	5.9	Coworkers and Clients	97

Chapter 6 Engineering Ethics 103

	6.1	The Engineer's Client	104
	6.2	The Classic Engineering Ethics Case—Monetary Value of a Human Life	105
	6.3	Engineering Codes of Ethics	109
	6.4	The BART Case—Unprotected Whistleblowing by Engineers	110
	6.5	The Challenger Case—Failure to Blow the Whistle	112
	6.6	Basic Engineering Business Ethics	113
	6.7	Cultural Variation in Business Ethics	113
	6.8	Intellectual Property	114
	6.9	The Key Lessons	114

Chapter 7 Medical Ethics 117

	7.1	The Physician's Client	118
	7.2	The Standard of Care	118
	7.3	Autonomy as It Relates to the Health Professions	119
	7.4	Example of Autonomy in Action	119
	7.5	The Components of Autonomy	120
	7.6	Two Interpretations of Autonomy	121
	7.7	Deciding If the Patient Has True Autonomy	122
	7.8	Physician Role in Autonomy	124
	7.9	Physician Role in Confidentiality	125
	7.10	Physician Guidelines When Patient Information Must Be Shared	126
	7.11	Physician's Code of Ethics	126
	7.12	Conflict of Interest in the Health Profession	127
	7.13	The Impact of Science on the Physician–Patient Relationship	129
	7.14	The Hospital IRB as the Patient's Local Watchdog	130
	7.15	The Advanced Health-care Directive	130
	7.16	Ethical Issues Associated with Treatment	131
	7.17	The Physician, a Life of Diagnosis and Treatment	132

Chapter 8 Bioengineering Scientist Ethics 137

	8.1	Bioengineers as Scientists	137

	8.2	Bioengineering Scientists Cannot Be Truth Professionals	137
	8.3	The Scientific Investigation	139
	8.4	Data, the Scientists' Clients	141
	8.5	Science Profession Code of Ethics	141
	8.6	Funding and Government Regulation of Scientific Ethics	142
	8.7	Scientific Misconduct	143
	8.8	Government Decreed Scientific Ethics	144
	8.9	Evidentiary Requirements for Findings of Research Misconduct	144
	8.10	Populations Where Scientific Misconduct Occurs	145
	8.11	Scientific Misconduct Cases	152
	8.12	The Bioengineering Scientist as a Professional	155

Chapter 9 Ethics of Research with Non-Human Animals 157

	9.1	History of Animal Use by Humans	157
	9.2	Changes in Human Link with Domestic Animals	158
	9.3	The Animal Rights Movement	159
	9.4	The Scientific Basis for Humane Treatment of Laboratory Animals	162
	9.5	Development of Animal Research Regulations	162

Chapter 10 Health Professionals and Historic Human Research Ethics 169

	10.1	The Tradition of Experimenting on Humans	169
	10.2	The Tuskegee Syphilis Study	170
	10.3	Nazi Use of Human Experimental Subjects	172
	10.4	Japanese Army Experiments Using Chinese Civilians in Ping Fan	174
	10.5	Development of First Conventions Regulating Experiments Using Human Subjects	175
	10.6	The Nuremberg Code	176
	10.7	The Helsinki Declaration and OPRR	178
	10.8	The National Research Act and the Belmont Report	178
	10.9	Humans Being Humans	179

Chapter 11 Health Professionals and Modern Human Research Ethics 181

	11.1	The Industrial Revolution Creates a Drug Industry	181
	11.2	Science, Medicine, and Technology Come Together after 1945	182
	11.3	Medical Research in University and Pharmaceutical Laboratories	183
	11.4	Science and Technology Create Biomedical Physicians	184

Contents

11.5	What Is Pre-clinical Research?	185
11.6	What Is Clinical Research?	185
11.7	Case Study: Hyman v. Jewish Chronic Disease Hospital (JCDH) of New York and Informed Consent—Vulnerable Patients	187
11.8	Clinical Research and the Practice of Medicine	188
11.9	Impact of the "Heyday of Drug Development" on Medical Practice	189
11.10	Case Study: Possible Conflict of Interest in Research Using Human Subjects	191
11.11	Non-medical Scientific Research Using Human Subjects	191
11.12	Naming the Third Pharmaceutical Epoch	192
11.13	Physicians in Practice and the FDA in the Third Pharmaceutical Epoch	193
11.14	Imaginary Case Study: Financial Conflict of Interest	194
11.15	Financial Conflict of Interest and the Grassley-Kohl Sunshine Act	195
11.16	*Human Subject Disregard for Science* (Based on an Account from Murphy 2004)	196
11.17	The FDA as a Regulator of Research with Human Subjects	197

Chapter 12 Ethics of Medical Product Development 199

12.1	The Bioengineer as a Product Developer	199
12.2	Bioengineer, Engineer and Physician: The Medical Product Development Team	199
12.3	The Public and the Government Place Limits on Medical Products	200
12.4	A History of the FDA	201
12.5	FDA Device Classification	204
12.6	Preclinical Testing	208
12.7	Publishing Pre-clinical Test Results	209
12.8	Considerations that Enhance Success of Clinical Trials	211
12.9	Clinical Trials	212
12.10	Protecting a Device or Drug as Intellectual Property	214
12.11	CRISPR Patent Case: Regents, University of California v. Broad Institute, Inc.	216
12.12	The Brave New World of Genomic Technology Clinical Research	217

Chapter 13 Ethics of Product Failure and the Courts 219

13.1	Phase III Monitoring of an FDA-approved Device Has No End Date	220

xii   Contents

13.2	Enter the Lawyers	220
13.3	How Does a Device Failure Become a Court Case?	222
13.4	*Intrauterine Device (IUD) The Dalkon Shield Case (1971)* (after Mayesh and Scranton 2004)	223
13.5	*The Artificial Heart Valve Cases* (after Mayesh and Scranton 2004)	225
13.6	*Metal-on-Metal ASR Case* (after Cohen 2011)	226
13.7	*Silicone Breast Implant Cases* (after Schleiter 2010, and Hooper 2001)	229
13.8	*Expert Witnessing and the Federal Rules of Evidence: Daubert v. Merrill Dow Pharmaceuticals (after SKAPP 2003)*	232
13.9	Can the FDA Be Sued?	233
13.10	The Future of Data Care	234

References 237

Glossary 245

Appendix A Suggested Format for Class Debates 269

Appendix B Informed Consent 271

Appendix C Advance Health Care Directive Example 277

Appendix D Research Misconduct Policy Example 285

Appendix E Significant Events in the History of Experimentation With Human Subjects 297

Appendix F Examples for Safe Medical Devices Act Report Incidents 305

Index 311

Preface

This textbook is an introduction to ethical challenges that students trained as bioengineers may face. Its stress is those challenges that arise when a bioengineer, whether in industry, government, or academia, has to report data to others, or is a scientist responsible for generating them. The discourse will provide perspective and authentic simulations, as well as theoretical bases for ethical analysis. It will follow a practical approach that defines the limits that government regulation imposes on moral decisions. It will remain general, that is, cover multiple professions, in order to allow those bioengineers not headed for the sciences (particularly pre-meds and pre-engineers) to relate to the subject.

Chapter 1 introduces bioengineering as a profession with a wide range of approaches to research, from trial-and-error engineering to basic science. It then contrasts the objectivity of scientific studies (that are limited to the natural world) with the subjectivity of moral theory application. In this way, the groundwork is laid for encouraging students to explore moral visions as part of their quest to develop their own.

Chapter 2 reviews organic evolution of the brain from a structure incapable of thinking ethically, to one capable of proto-ethical motivation, and, finally one capable of understanding moral theories. Key questions are, "What is ethical/moral behavior?", "How much is ethical behavior determined genetically?", and "How much is molded by experience?" The implied question of this chapter is "How natural is it for humans to act ethically/morally?"

Chapter 3 addresses the question, "If I decide to behave ethically in a particular situation, what choices do I have to guide me?". There is variation in moral visions that leads people to apply different ethical theories in deciding how to behave when there appear to be choices. We avoid making a one-size-fits-all choice. Ethics is not a science and ethicists will tailor a proposed action for the circumstance. To illustrate the variety of moral visions that can be used to guide one's choice of ethical behavior, we examine five moral theories. They are traditional in professional ethics texts.

Chapter 4 proposes a procedure for applying the five moral theories to the moral decision-making process. The end result of the application is shown to be a judgment of which behavioral choice is "good" vs. "bad" or "right" vs. "wrong". The concept of autonomy is more deeply explored here, using the classic case *Moore vs. Regents, University of California.*

Chapter 5 examines how moral theories operate in specific professions; first, by defining a profession, and then explaining how professional ethics must differ from lay ethics. Lay ethics is presented to reiterate that a bioengineering (BE) scientist is a citizen, and is, therefore, expected to follow the same social contract rules as all other citizens. The model case presented explores the question of perceived harassment from the point of view of professional employer and employee.

Chapter 6 addresses the unique ethical considerations faced by engineers who are not engaged in bioengineering. This chapter explores the interaction between risk and ethics. Its model case is *Grimshaw v. Ford Motor Co.* where the concept of monetary value of a human life is addressed.

xiii

Chapter 7 is for those bioengineers who will work with physicians and for pre-meds. In parallel with the focus of Chapter 6, this chapter examines a profession, medicine, that is not bioengineering. Its emphasis is the client-health professional relationship. A comparison between clients as people and clients as data is presented. Chapter 7 sets the stage for discussion of potential conflict in moral visions, as it relates to their clients, between the bioengineering scientist and physician that is discussed in succeeding chapters. The Health Insurance Portability and Accountability Act (HIPAA) government guidelines are introduced, and related to confidentiality and autonomy. Confidentiality is further explored in the model case Tarasoff v. University of California Regents.

Chapter 8 addresses the profession of bioengineer scientist. The question "What are data and what constitutes scientific treatment of them?" is discussed. The process of collecting data, insuring their integrity, analyzing and reporting them, is reviewed. Scientific misconduct, as defined by the National Institutes of Health (NIH), is discussed and related to scientific codes of conduct. The model data fabrication case of Andrew Wakefield is explored. Graduate studies involving research and publication are examined, covering such topics as authorship, plagiarism, and predatory publishers.

Chapter 9 investigates nonhuman animal research from the point of view of constructive advocacy. FDA requirements for pre-clinical research are introduced. The history of animal rights vs. animal welfare polemics is presented. The work of Institutional Animal Care and Use Committees is explained.

Chapter 10 begins the final portion of the textbook that is devoted to research involving human subjects. This chapter reviews the history of research using humans. A number of classic cases that have become traditional models in bioethics are presented, including the Tuskegee study, Nazi concentration camp experiments, and Ping Fan experiments.

Chapter 11 presents more recent case models of research involving human subjects as they contributed to the evolution of the FDA. *Hyman v. Jewish Chronic Disease Hospital* (JCDH) of New York is one of the classic case models discussed. Particular importance of the integrity of data gathered from human subjects is illustrated by discussion of the consequences of lack of valid data from testing in the United States during early stages of the 2020 COVID-19 pandemic. The Bradford Hill considerations for causality in clinical research are introduced as part of a discussion of statistical correlation in clinical data.

Chapter 12 examines the role of the FDA in biomedical product development and the practical value of treating data as clients. Emphasis is on the law as executed by the FDA and enforced by the Department of Justice. Protection of intellectual property, and the right to market developed biomedical products via patents is described. The case of the legal battle over the CRISPR patent is presented.

Chapter 13 focuses on the dynamics of biomedical product failure. The structure of the court system is outlined to differentiate federal and state jurisdictions. The nature of liability is explained with particular attention to the role of the FDA in limiting liability. Classical and contemporary cases are presented. Expert witnessing is explored with particular attention paid to examples of violations of data integrity in testimony.

Preface

The students I taught bioengineering ethics for ten years were generally smart and motivated. Most of them went on to careers in product development or academic research. However, they were naive about the competitive aspects of these occupations that put them under pressure to generate either a product or other target result. One potential outcome of this pressure is skewed and biased data that fit a corporate goal. There is no science if data have no integrity. The way to ensure such integrity is to treat data as clients. The ethical goal of this textbook is the motivation of the bioengineering student to respect and adopt this moral vison. Rarely did a student enter my classroom with a concept of what a moral vision is, or how to apply it as a foundational job element. The chapters on moral theories are presented to give the student practice in formal moral analysis that may be applied to the vocation of bioengineering. Further, since bioengineers often work with health professionals, ethical conflicts can arise. There may be ethical conflicts between BE scientists and physicians. The bioengineering student needs to know the source of such conflicts, and their mitigation. Consequently, medical ethics are discussed in Chapter 7. Medical research ethics, a more common arena in which bioengineers and health professionals interact, is discussed in Chapters 10 and 11. Representatives from industry have decried that bioengineering students know too little about the FDA. Therefore, the FDA structure and function are covered in Chapters 12 and 13. Product failure is a fact of life in industry. It is rarely discussed in ethics textbooks. In this book it is discussed in the context of the FDA and liability. In support of the learning experience, enrichment activities are included at the end of each chapter. These include subjects for debate, essay, and oral committee reports. A suggested debate format for use in the classroom is presented in the appendix.

Acknowledgments

It is doubtful that this book would have been conceived without the aid of the following two groups:

1. The lecturers for Bioengineering Ethics, UCLA BE165, leaders in their fields, who volunteered their expertise, some making special trips:

Andrea Scott, LLB, the devoted patient advocate lawyer, James O'Callahan, LLB, the steadfast product liability lawyer, Arthur Hsieh, Ph.D., LLB, the best doctoral student, and a Silicon Valley bioengineer/patent lawyer, James Rosen, M.D., the spine surgeon focused on conflict-of-interest of orthopaedic surgeons, Lynne Jones, Ph.D., the science trainer of orthopaedic surgeons, and model for clinical research ethics, David Thordarson, M.D. and Mark Hoffer, M.D., the models for medical ethics, and Ken Pickar, Ph.D. the model for engineering and industry ethics.

2. Two colleagues, both oral surgeon scientists, much-awarded leaders in their fields, who nurtured and ardently pressed the author:

Ben Wu, D.D.S., Ph.D., who in his devotion to developing the highest quality bioengineering department, saw a need for a Bioengineering Ethics course. His steadfast support and leadership were crucial, and their quality will be confirmed by the scrutiny of history.

Jeffrey O. Hollinger, D.D.S., Ph.D., who's enthusiasm drove him from retirement to become an implicit editor of the book. His gift for clarity turned many wandering paragraphs into clear paths. Any quotable lines are surely traceable to him. All errors result from the author straying from the path.

Introduction

Why another book that preaches "bioethics" to a bioscientist? Firstly, because this is not another book on bioethics. It is about "data"-ethics, because bioengineers who become scientists, or otherwise involved in bioproduct development, usually handle nothing more important than data produced by scientific research. Data ethics is a requirement for ethical bioengineering. What all this means to bioengineering students will be clearly described in this textbook through examples and exercises.

When the research is clinical, the range of ethical concern broadens to include bioethical behavior. The reader will learn that data are always at the core of the work of bioengineering scientists, and commitment to the integrity of these data determines, as for any scientist, their professional value. The elevation of data to a level of something being owed care equivalent to that of biological subjects, may seem curious to the reader. As a student in an ethics course, however, the reader will learn, through discussion, case examples, and debates, that clinical data often determine lives, and a habit of safeguarding data integrity at all times will protect, not only patients, but the career of the bioengineering scientist.

The bioengineering student, using this book as a textbook, or the general scientist reader, using it as a resource, will be led to realize that their career as a scientist cannot survive if they cannot be depended on to maintain data integrity. We define data integrity as trustworthiness that observation documentation is as truthful, verifiable, and scientifically analyzable as is possible. Development of integrity begins with experimental design, which is defined, and discussed in Chapter 8.

Observations result from execution of experimental design, and become data when documented. Truthfulness is honesty of documentation. Accuracy to the point of certainty is not possible in science, but precision to the point of confidence that an observation is repeatable, is. An observation that tests the validity of a hypothesis cannot prove it, but can disprove its converse. The disproof is evaluated by repetition of the observation a sufficient number of times to have confidence that exactness has been achieved as well as is realistic.

The chapters in this text are thematic to data integrity, data as clients, and the application of moral theory to ethical encounters. In Chapter 8, students are cautioned that science is not certain, and scientists can at best estimate the risk that their understanding of nature is wrong. In this context, statistical tools and quantities (e.g. sample size, significance) for generating estimates for risk of rejecting a hypothesis are discussed. There is an extensive discussion of empirical vs. causal association. The difference between correlation and causality is presented in the context of studies by Bradford Hill who linked smoking and lung cancer.

A primary theme of the book is the conviction that data are the bioengineering scientist's clients. Readers are made to realize that just as professionals who serve living clients (e.g. engineers, physicians, dentists, veterinarians) are no longer professional when violating the welfare of their customers, so bioengineering scientists, when violating the "welfare" of their clients have abandoned their profession. A bioengineering scientist may be considered to have violated a professional–client contract if the integrity of the data they report was intentionally violated. That is, reported data were biased or manipulated to underscore a nonexperimental outcome, or, in fact, were fictional: not derived from experimentation. When the violation is the result of incompetence, the violator may be dismissed as a scientist too unskilled to be taken seriously. When the violation is intentional, the violator has committed an unethical act, according to the codes of ethics of all professional scientific societies.

A secondary book theme, is the subjectivity of ethics. A given moral theory does not always provide the "best" ethical solution to a dilemma of choosing between action choices of a moral challenge. The reader is provided with five distinctly different moral theories to apply to the problem via moral analysis, and thereby generate reasonable arguments for how to behave. The reader's moral vision will guide selection of the path to a final choice. The cases presented are meant to show the consequences of this path being a challenge to data integrity.

Chapters on bioethics of human client-based professions, Engineering, and Medicine are included for comparison and contrast with bioengineering ethics. Students using the book as a textbook, some of whom are pre-health profession, will learn that trustworthiness is also at the core of these vocations.

Because they are crucial to clinical product development, the FDA and product failure are also discussed extensively. Thus, readers of this textbook will learn about moral theories, data ethics, their role in ethical bioengineering science practice and clinical product development, and their contribution to clinical product improvement.

Author Biography

Howard Winet, Ph.D. is an Adjunct Professor, Orthopaedic Surgery and Bioengineering, recall at University of California, Los Angeles. He is also an Emeritus Research Staff and former Director, Bone Chamber Laboratory, Orthopaedic Hospital. His research areas are bone microcirculation as it relates to bone wound healing, tissue engineering, ischemic osteonecrosis, biocompatibility of bone implants, and exercise and external stimulation modalities such as electromagnetic fields, ultrasound and hyperbaric oxygen. He has taught Bioengineering Ethics for ten years at UCLA.

Acronyms

AAES	American Association of Engineering Societies
AALAS	American Association for Laboratory Animal Science
ACC	Anterior cingulate cortex
ACP	Animal Care Panel
AHCD	Advance Health Care Directive
AIDS	Acquired Immune Deficiency Syndrome
ALF	Animal Liberation Front
AMA	American Medical Association
ANOVA	ANalysis Of VAriance
ASPCA	American Society for the Prevention of Cruelty to Animals
ASR	Advanced Surface Replacement
ASTM	American Society for Testing Materials
ATC	Automatic Train Control (system)
CDC	Centers for Disease Control and prevention
COX	Cyclo-Oxygenase (enzyme)
CRISPR	Clustered Regularly Interspaced Short Palindromic Repeats
DOJ	Department of Justice (U.S.)
ECPD	Engineers' Council for Professional Development
ELF	Earth Liberation Front
FAA	Federal Aviation Administration
FD&CA	Food, Drug And Cosmetics Act
FDA	Food and Drug Administration
GMP	Good Manufacturing Processes
GNP	Gross National Product
HHS	Health and Human Services
HIPAA	Health Information Portability and Accountability Act
HIV	Human Immunodeficiency Virus
HMO	Health Maintenance Organization
IACUC	Institute Animal Care and Use Committee
IDE	Investigational Device Exemption
IEEE	Institute of Electrical and Electronic Engineers
ILAR	Institute for Laboratory Animal Resources
IP	Intellectual Property
IRB	Institutional Review Board
IUD	Intra-Uterine Device
MDA	Medical Devices Amendments
MDR	Medical Device Report
MDUFA	Medical Device User Fee Amendment
MDUFMA	Medical Device User Fee and Modernization Act
NCPHSBBR	National Commission for the Protection of human Subjects of Biomedical and Behavioral Research
NHTSA	National Highway Traffic Safety Administration

NIH	National Institutes of Health
NSF	National Science Foundation
OPRR	Office for Protection from Research Risks
ORI	Office of Research Integrity (of the NIH)
PAM	Protospacer Adjacent Motif
PDMS	PolyDiMethylSiloxane
PDR	Physicians Desk Reference
PETA	People for the Ethical Treatment of Animals
PI	Principal Investigator
PMA	Pre-Marketing Approval
PMAA	Pre-Marketing Approval Application
PMMA	PolyMethylMethAcrylate
PSDA	Patient Self-Determination Act
PTAB	Patent Trial and Appeal Board
SMDA	Safe Medical Devices Amendments
WWHWWEW	WhoWhatHowWhenWhereExtenuatingWhy
U.S.S.R.	Union of Soviet Socialist Republics (now Russia)
UHCIA	Uniform Health-Care Information Act
USDA	U.S. Department of Agriculture
USPHS	U.S. Public Health Service

1 Bioengineering and Ethics

1.1 BIOENGINEERING AS AN INTERDISCIPLINARY PROFESSION

The term "bioengineer" (BE) is used in this text for all engineers trained to work on biological/medical problems. By definition, a BE is both a biologist and an engineer. Biologists are scientists who study organisms. Engineers, traditionally, are empiricists; people rooted in trial-and-error. Prior to the 1960s, BE did not exist as a specialty. The process of a biologist working with an engineer either to maintain lab equipment or build models of a biological phenomenon was coined as bioengineering. The engineer was uninvolved in the scientific aspects of the biological investigation (Britannica 2016). However, when collaboration between biologists and engineers became more frequent and complex, the discipline of bioengineering grew, and sub-groups, such as fields like biomaterials, emerged. As is common in growing professions, a need arose to incorporate an ethical component in bioengineering. The need became more acute as its "bio" component spread into medicine and agriculture. Today, bioengineering ethics (BEE) spans three professions: biology, engineering, and medicine. Accordingly, the ethical problems it addresses cover a broad range.

1.2 WHAT BEs MAY DO

The BE neither designs bridges nor bandages a wound. However, a BE may develop a neurologically controlled device that would allow an engineer to construct a bridge robotically. As a health scientist, he/she may develop a controlled-release "bandage" that directs wound healing. As a biologist, a BE may develop implantable transmitters that allow researchers to monitor behavior of an animal in nature. Since these are all forms of intervention in the life of a living being, they raise general concerns about the welfare of that being, and the ethical problems associated with invading its life. As a scientist, a BE is typically involved in research that produces data, which leads to a different kind of concern—the integrity of those data. If the data result in production of a medical product that fails, the government agency that approved it, the Food and Drug Administration (FDA), will ask "why?" If the answer includes a violation of data integrity, the FDA will assign the Department of Justice (DOJ) to investigate. What follows would be a nightmare for the company, and, by extension, the responsible BE. In parallel, data integrity may be compromised in a noncommercial setting. In these cases, investigations rarely lead to formal trials. But, careers may be ended by the institute involved.

DOI: 10.1201/9781003197218-1

1.3 BASIS FOR VALUE CONFLICT BETWEEN BIO AND ENGINEERING

When you became curious about the world outside your crib, you began to investigate it. A couple of pokes with a pin taught you painfully to avoid sharp things. When you touched a lighted bulb, you learned that there is a heat threshold, which, when crossed, leads to pain. You were learning empirically about the natural world, and the facts, evidence, or data you gathered led you to empirical conclusions we call "truths". If the truths that attracted you as you matured were solutions to problems, you were leaning toward an interest in a profession, like engineering or medicine, that solved problems. We refer to members of such professions as "truth professionals" because each solution to a problem ends their quest for its truth.

But isn't science also based on drawing conclusions from facts, data? Yes, it is, but the ultimate goal of a scientist is not to stop at solving problems. It is to understand the natural world. A truth professional may discover the longest lasting implant by empirically testing many candidates. A scientist would try to understand how the tissue needing the implant works, and how it became compromised so as to need the implant. A scientist may solve a problem, but understanding the mechanism or cause underlying the problem opens the door to solutions for similar problems. If the implant failed, a scientist would want to understand the pathophysiological and biomaterial mechanisms underlying that implant's failure. In fact, failure is a scientist's best teacher. To a truth professional, failure is often a catastrophe.

The line between science and truth professions is not rigid. Empirical and clinical science exist in the world of investigation between the extremes of causal science and trial-and-error empiricism. The nature of clinical science will be discussed in Chapter 11, where we describe the approach of Bradford Hill used epidemiology to causally link smoking and lung cancer. Bioengineering research encompasses all these investigative approaches.

Our first challenge to understanding the roles of empiricism and science in the development of bioengineering is to put the truth and causal fields of endeavor into perspective through their histories. We shall hit only the highlights, to avoid getting sidetracked into historical arguments. It will be necessary to limit the location of cultures for our story to the fertile crescent, because, as Diamond has maintained, technological and scientific advancement had different histories elsewhere (Diamond 1999).

1.4 THE ANCIENT PERIOD AND FIRST WESTERN SOCIETIES

1.4.1 GENERAL

We begin with the first agricultural societies, some 15,000 or so years ago. These have been supposed to have all transitioned from hunter-gatherers. But there is evidence from Göbekli Tepi in Turkey contradicting this conclusion (Harari 2015). Agricultural societies depended on "simply serendipity" (Aslaksen 2013) or trial-and-error experience, empiricism, for solving survival problems (Diamond 1999; Harari 2015). Domestication of plants and animals for food, clothing, and shelter

Bioengineering and Ethics

TABLE 1.1

Adjusted Timetable of Historical Periods from One Engineer's Point of View

Period	Approximate Duration
Ancient	13,000 B.C.–500 B.C.
Classical	500 B.C.–400 A.D.
Medieval	400–1400
Renaissance	1400–1650
Enlightenment	1650–1750
Industrial Revolution	1750–1850
Second Industrial Revolution	1850–c.1920

(Diamond 1999); the use of trephines in paleomedicine (Ackerknecht 2016); and by about 10,000 years ago "engineering activities" (Aslaksen 2013) were taking place in some regions. The individuals who performed such "engineering activities" are identified by Aslaksen, as "craftsmen". Here (Table 1.1) is his timetable with some modification (last two rows replaced by row from Parodi (Parodi et al. 2006)).

Until the invention of writing, in about 3,500 B.C. (Ackerknecht 2016), accounts of inventions or innovations that solved each problem were passed to succeeding generations by oral tradition alone. For anthropologists, then, evidence for such solutions had to come from resulting constructions and tools, that is, the technology (e.g. flintstones) that craftsmen left behind (Ackerknecht 2016). The segment of time under discussion, from prehistory to about 500 B.C., has been called the "Ancient" Period (Aslaksen 2013). It included, near its end, rise of the Mesopotamian, Egyptian, and early Greek civilizations (Principe 2002).

1.4.2 MEDICINE

Cuneiform writing from Sumeria and Babylonia 5,300 years ago indicated that illness was caused by spirits and could be cured by sorcery (Parker 2019). The medical practitioners who could perform the sorcery were called "ashipus". Alternative treaters, who were information reservoirs for practical treatments, such as herbal potions, were called "asus" (Parker 2019). In any group, one man stood out as a healer, shaman, or medicine man. Fractures and skin wounds could be treated. Teeth could be drilled. In Egypt, 2,500 years later, physicians were hailed as priests—one of the most famous being Imhotep who was treated as a demigod (Parker 2019). The Egyptians learned anatomy from their experiences with mummification. Imhotep's following in Ancient Greece continued to revere him in the form of Asclepios (Parker 2019). In all these societies, medicine was a mixture of spiritualism and empiricism.

1.4.3 ENGINEERING

Near its end, the Ancient Period was characterized by reorganization of craftsmen from members of small groups that fashioned tools for building rafts, boats, and simple houses, bridges, and irrigation canals, to larger workgroups that built government structures requiring designers and managers (Aslaksen 2013). Craftsman skills that were needed included not only the physical ability to process and work with copper, bronze, iron, and glass, but also, starting with the Babylonians (Mesopotamians), mathematics and accounting skills (Principe 2002). The Egyptians further advanced metalworking and glassmaking (Principe 2002).

1.4.4 SCIENCE

Judging from surviving documents, attempts to understand the natural world beyond empirical application or religious interpretation were "quite limited" in pre-Greek civilizations (Principe 2002). The acknowledged first philosopher, who moved beyond empiricism toward an understanding of the natural world, was the Greek, Thales of Miletus (whose lifetime fell between the interval 624–545 B.C.; Britannica 2009,Principe 2002). Thales marks the end of Aslaksen's Ancient period of craftsmen and the beginning of his Classical Period (500 B.C.–400 A.D.; Aslaksen 2013).

1.5 THE CLASSICAL PERIOD—MYTHOS AND LOGOS

1.5.1 GENERAL

Intellectual development in the Classical Period was dominated by Greek and Roman philosophers. They built the foundation of the enlightenment that produced science (Principe 2002) and, eventually, bioengineering. We shall not detail their writings. Instead, we shall highlight concepts they developed that are crucial for gaining insight into concepts of truth and causal thinking as it evolved in society.

The first crucial concept is the difference between *mythos* and *logos* ways of thinking. While a number of Greek philosophers have argued over the meaning of this difference (Bottici 2008), a case can be made (Principe 2002) that Plato (428–347 B.C.), in his *Republic* (Shorey and Plato 1953), settled on mythos as a belief or "sacred narrative explaining how the world and man came to be" (Orfanos 2006). In contrast to mythos thinking, logos thinking develops a narrative explaining the world, based on reason and following the rules of logic.

What separates the philosophers of the Classical Period from thinkers that preceded them is the way they organized their thoughts to transform reason into logic. The scheme, traceable to Plato (Principe 2002), may be found in a traditional

Introduction to Philosophy book (Rosen et al. 2018). The formal thinking that follows this scheme employs the following three kinds of statements:

A. Logical/formal/analytical: Declarations of relationships or states of existence true by definition (e.g. There must be a force—call it gravity—that attracts objects toward the earth.).
B. Factual/empirical: Declarations of relationships or states of existence confirmable by observation (e.g. Whenever a ball is struck off its center, it travels at an angle different from that of the strike path.).
C. Normative: Declarations of value judgments (which, as we shall see, are outside the realm of science) (e.g. One should not drop a heavy ball on a sibling.).

These statements are traditionally incorporated into a three-component philosophy (Rosen et al. 2018):

1. Ontology—the study of reality, the nature of the universe
2. Epistemology—the study of how we know reality and
3. Axiology—the study of what we should value and what we ought to do to preserve it

1.5.2 MEDICINE

Davis defines a profession as a "number of individuals in the same occupation voluntarily organized to earn a living by openly serving a moral ideal in a morally-permissible way beyond what law, market, morality and public opinion would otherwise require" (Davis 2009). During the Classical Period, medicine became a profession as one result of the development of writing (Dean-Jones 2003). Writing increased the transfer of information about internal medicine, and the existence of shared information increased esteem for those who possessed it (Dean-Jones 2003), allowing greater public acceptance of physicians as professionals. Notwithstanding their acceptance, physicians in Greece were not formally trained in any school. They passed down their practice within families. Most followed a practice heavily influenced by the philosophy of either Plato or Aristotle (Supady 2020). Platonists, in accordance with their more mythos orientation, based their medicine on reasoning rather than observation. They were called Dogmatics. Aristotelians, in accordance with their more logos orientation, based their medicine on observation, and considered the effects of their treatment the most important component of their labor (Supady 2020). They were called Empiricists, and fit the designation "truth profession" quite well. A third group, that challenged the possibility of thoroughly solving any medical problem, were called the Skeptics (Supady 2020). There were a few other minor groups.

FIGURE 1.1 Aristotle. Greek philosopher who viewed matter as potential and developed Virtue Moral Theory. Image by MidoSemsem, courtesy of Shutterstock.

The Greece that was absorbed by the Romans, had a more developed medical profession than did its conquering culture. Unfortunately, Greek physicians were viewed with disgust by Roman aristocracy (Supady 2020). This attitude was probably due to an influx of charlatans into the Greek medical establishment, following the dissemination of writing (Dean-Jones 2003). The charlatans selected techniques from works on internal medicine and built practices around them, without bothering to learn from thoroughly trained physicians how to use them properly (Dean-Jones 2003). When they learned how to avoid the charlatans, the Romans gravitated toward competent Greek physicians (Supady 2020) like Galen (129–200). Galen combined aspects of Hippocrates, Plato, and Aristotle in his writings so effectively, that his influence on medical practice could still be detected 20 centuries later (Bynum et al. 1981).

1.5.3 Engineering

Neither Greek nor Roman classical engineers were as independent as their medical counterparts, so their professionalism was not fully developed (Aslaksen 2013). Both

Bioengineering and Ethics 7

were employed, mainly by the military, to develop weapons, or municipalities, to develop urban infrastructure. The model practitioner for the Greek engineer was still Archimedes, a physicist adept with mathematical theory, who implemented an epistêmê-oriented mechanical engineering approach. He is well-known for developing catapults and water pumps (Aslaksen 2013). The corresponding model for Roman engineers was Marcus Vitruvius (75–25 B.C., approx.). He was a military engineer who specialized in architecture and excelled in applying effective building materials. He stressed practical application, technê over epistêmê. Roman engineers tended to operate in large groups that shared information preserved in writings, a practice that served to move their occupation toward professionalism (Aslaksen 2013).

1.5.4 SCIENCE

The second crucial concept is the difference between *technê* and *epistêmê* areas of endeavor. Its chief Greek philosophical proponent was Aristotle (384–322 B.C.). Technê is knowledge of the craftsman, the "how to" of solving a problem. Epistêmê is the "how come" of solving a problem. In its ultimate state, it is causal knowledge (Principe 2002), the end point of understanding nature; and it is referred to by most historians as *natural philosophy* (it did not really become "science" until after the 17th century). Aristotle obviously classifies natural philosophers as proponents of epistêmê thought. But where do the Classical Period "designers and managers", who guided craftsmen, or physicians belong? May one claim that they adhered to logos because their reasoning was more complex than that of craftsmen? There were individuals who did not conform to just one category. The philosopher Archimedes (287–212 B.C.), for example, solved many mechanical problems.

The logic that directed Aristotle's philosophical approach was deductive. Deductive reasoning requires a transcendent truth that can be "deduced from" to form conclusions that explain nature. For example: (Table 1.2).

TABLE 1.2
Example of Aristotle's Deductive Reasoning

Transcendent Truth	Only a God Is Immortal
Observation	Man is not a god.
Conclusion	Man is not immortal.

The reality Aristotle chose was a God reminiscent of his mentor Plato's demiurge (Principe 2002). However, Plato's demiurge was much closer to mythos than was Aristotle's God (Menn 1992). But even for Plato this supernatural entity could not be interacted with physically (Shorey and Plato 1953). Aristotle's God was an ideal, but not a real goal toward which the real world strives (Perl 1998). The real world provides the data/facts/evidence that allow us to extrapolate the nature of God. But we do not have access to God, and must therefore depend on our observations for attaining a sufficient understanding of nature to explain reality (Waterlow 1982).

But what is the path from observing a natural object or event and fitting our observations into the knowledge base we call our understanding of nature? This path is the subject of epistemology or "how we know". We begin on the path with a kind of faith; the faith that the path is not encumbered enough to prevent us from "seeing" reality. Consequently, we see reality as it is, and the perceived pictures we gain from our seeing—the functioning of our epistemological organ—are believable (Waterlow 1982). It may seem to the reader that a discussion of God is superfluous to the question of what Aristotle contributed to the development of scientific thinking. As we shall see, Aristotle's God allowed him to be accepted by the church in the Middle Ages.

1.6 DECLINE OF THE LATIN WORLD AND RISE OF THE ISLAMIC WORLD

The Medieval period (400–1400; Aslaksen 2013) was marked by the fall of the Roman Empire just before the year 500, followed by stagnation in its medicine (Parker 2019), engineering (Gimpel 1978), and natural philosophy (Principe 2002). The period started with the rise of Christianity whose adherents initially rejected Greek philosophy as pagan (Principe 2002). As more educated Romans and Greeks converted, a movement to reexamine philosophical thinking arose, culminating in the birth of Christian theology (= religion + philosophy) under St. Augustine of Hippo (354–430; Principe 2002). Augustine saw God in Plato's demiurge and agreed with the latter's admonition to obtain scientific knowledge. The Platonic meaning of scientific knowledge, unlike the Aristotelian meaning, stressed interpreting nature rather than gathering data (Principe 2002). Augustine's theology stressed that study of nature would reveal the goodness and power of God (Principe 2002). Functioning under church jurisdiction, physicians had to credit God as the ultimate cause of cures (Parker 2019). By the same token, treatment failure was a punishment from God. Engineers, meanwhile, turned from designing new devices involved in manufacturing and agriculture, to surveying and architecture, predominately of churches (Aslaksen 2013).

FIGURE 1.2 St. Augustine of Hippo. Philosopher who developed Christian philosophy to create theology. Formed foundation for scholasticism. Image by Digital Version Vectors, courtesy of Getty Images.

Bioengineering and Ethics

To characterize the Middle Ages as "Dark", however, is to ignore the contributions followers of Islam made to the growth of Western civilization. Islam began in the first quarter of the 7th century. Its reach eventually spread from the Arabian Peninsula, west to Spain, and east to the borders of China, making natural philosophy—at least the Islamic version—for the first time in history, an "international enterprise" (Bynum et al. 1981). There were Muslim philosophers, but the first stage in their empire's development of medicine, engineering, and natural philosophy, was the "translation movement", which lasted from about 750 to 1000 (Principe 2002). They learned from the Chinese how to make paper and set about translating into Arabic the accumulated written knowledge of the Greeks, Persians, Indian, and other developed cultures (Principe 2002). The translation movement gave way to a period of consolidation and creativity (Bynum et al. 1981) for medicine and natural philosophy.

1.6.1 MEDICINE

One notable Muslim physician who incorporated Greek, Chinese, and Indian medicine into his writings and practice was the silk road city Bukhara's Ibn Sina (Avicenna, in Latin, as he was later known to European scholars; c. 980–1057; Parker 2019). Ibn Sina's masterpiece *The Canon of Medicine* was translated from Arabic and influenced medicine in the fertile crescent for five centuries (Parker 2019).

1.6.2 ENGINEERING

Engineering did not fare as well as did medicine in the Islamic Empire. Engineers concentrated mainly on architecture, as applied for the building of mosques and palaces, and mechanical engineering, as applied to agriculture for the development of pumps and mills until the latter part of the period (Aslaksen 2013).

1.6.3 SCIENCE

Arab Muslims dominated the advancement of natural philosophy in the Islamic Empire of the Middle Ages (Principe 2002). They applied the Indian number system (that we call "Arabic numerals"), defining zero, and developed algebra. They named and developed an astrolabe to measure distances and objects in the night sky (Principe 2002). Ibn al-Haytham (Alhazan, in Latin, as he was later known to European scholars; c. 965–1039) developed a theory of optics based on rays of light being emitted by objects being viewed; his formulation is much like that used today (Principe 2002). Another major scientific advance by the Arabic investigators was laying the foundations for the development of chemistry

10 Ethics for Bioengineering Scientists

through alchemy (an Arabic word; Principe 2002). Interest in alchemy was driven, in part, by belief in transmutation, the ability for elements to transform into one another. Ibn-Sina, already noted earlier for his contribution to medicine, was also an alchemist, but did not accept transmutation (Principe 2002). He produced *Book of Remedy* that proposed that metals were combinations of just two underground exhalations. The Muslims conquered Spain in 711 and were finally driven out in 1492. But decline of their civilization was already evident by 1258 when the Mongols destroyed Baghdad (Principe 2002). By this time, Latin Europe, encouraged by the Christian church, had already started conquering the Middle East.

1.7 THE 12TH CENTURY RISE OF THE UNIVERSITIES (800–1400)

1.7.1 GENERAL

Of the three cultures—the Greek West, the Arabic West, and the Latin West—that dominated human civilizations' West of India from the Classical Period to the end of the Industrial Revolution (Principe 2002), the Latin West's ascendance was the last, and of longest duration. In fact, it came to dominate the entire world. Its rise began in the church that had survived the 5th-century collapse of Rome. A warming of climate in Europe, starting around 750, called the "little climatic optimum" (Gimpel 1978), probably was responsible for enhanced crop and associated population growth until about 1215 (Principe 2002). Along with the favorable climate, the spark that turned remaining Christian monasteries and cathedrals into centers of learning, was the appointment of Charlemagne (742–814), King of the Franks to Holy Roman Emperor in 800 (Principe 2002). The movement he started, grew, and led to demand for classical works in Latin. So many of these had been lost during the Middle Ages that the only viable source for most was Arabic translation of Greek works. A European translation movement (1125–1200) commenced, to supply to the developing centers of learning with Latin translations of Arabic translations of Greek writing (Principe 2002). The local schools that Charlemagne set in motion were at first extensions of monasteries or Cathedrals. In urban settings, however, these small schools grew into universities by the end of the 12th century (Principe 2002). Bologna, Paris, and Oxford were prime examples of such universities. The University of Paris, for example, had four faculties: Arts, Law, Medicine, and Theology.

Bioengineering and Ethics 11

FIGURE 1.3 Holy Roman Emperor Charlemagne. Who developed monastic and cathedral schools that became the first universities. Image by Digital Vision Vectors, courtesy of Getty Images.

1.7.2 Medicine

The medical schools with the greatest impact were, however, in Italy; with Salerno the 11th-century model, joined in the 12th by Bologna and Padua (Parker 2019). Training of physicians was highly organized and well-connected with the works of Hippocrates, Galen, and Arab physicians, such as Ibn-Sina/Avicenna. Not only physicians, but also surgeons, healers, and apothecaries gained certificates that attested to their learning (Parker 2019). Training methods, including dissection from Bologna in about 1200, were exported to other medical schools (Parker 2019). Improvements in understanding of anatomy continued to enhance medical learning, but the "black death", or bubonic plague, that appeared in 1346, and killed about 20% of the population (Parker 2019) hampered the spread of education.

1.7.3 Engineering

The universities did not include engineering in their curriculum, so there was no educational path to certification and official establishment of a profession in this period. There was, however, some appreciation of the potential for technology. Roger Bacon (c. 1219–1292), a Franciscan monk, in his *De secretis operibus* predicted a future with machines that were not moved by beasts, and could even fly (Aslaksen 2013).

1.7.4 Science

It can be argued that the major education advance that led eventually to the science of bioengineering, was the application of scholasticism as the fundamental form of university teaching. The argument goes as follows: By developing Christian theology, St. Augustine opened a door in religious education for philosophical debates about the church's interpretation of secular ideas. Scholasticism was the method for conducting these debates in a classroom setting. The accumulating translations of Aristotle from Arabic provided ample subject matter for scholasticism by the second half of the 13th century (Principe 2002). Accompanying the translations, were commentaries by Muslim philosophers such as Avicenna (Lindberg 2002). The method proceeded as follows: Students were presented a point of view (often Aristotelean) in a lecture. A yes/no question would then be posed by the master to commence a *disputation*. A *responden* student would answer the question at length. An *opponen* student would critique the answer. Finally, the issue would be resolved by the *praeses*, a master teacher (Principe 2002). The format was repeated in written assignments. Faculty members ranged from "radical Aristotelians" (Lindberg 2002) to fundamentalist conservatives. It was inevitable that challenges to church doctrine, like Aristotle's claim that the world is eternal, would sound alarms in Rome. Reports were accumulated by a conservative Spanish scholar and submitted to the bishop of Paris, who composed the Condemnation of 1277, citing 219 propositions attributed to Aristotle or other secular philosophers, that could not be accepted as true, because they conflicted with Christian theology (Principe 2002). The follow-up action by the church did not eliminate scholasticism or the teaching of Aristotle from the universities. It eliminated the more extreme elements of the secular faculty, and forced the remaining scholars to become creative in their teaching of the 219 propositions. The church continued its support of the universities (Lindberg 2002). Creative forms of Aristotelianism and other secular philosophies continued to develop, making the church, to whom the universities were responsible, a "patron of natural philosophy" (Lindberg 2002).

1.8 THE ITALIAN RENAISSANCE (1400–1650)

1.8.1 General

In 1400, the printing press was invented, and Europe entered what is often considered the official Italian Renaissance (Aslaksen 2013). A humanist movement that challenged the liberal proponents of scholasticism, and stressed human unity with nature, in a religious sense (Blackburn 1994), was in full swing (Principe 2002). During the period,

Bioengineering and Ethics

voyages of discovery to foreign lands were exposing new cultures, animals, and plants that were not described by classical literature. The Protestant Reformation challenged the Catholic Church in 1517 and the latter responded with a Counter Reformation by about 1563. There were inquisitions by both Catholics and Protestants. Art flourished, and private industry began (Aslaksen 2013).

1.8.2 Medicine

Recovery from the bubonic plague continued, enhancing the number and quality of medical schools. Faculty insisted on high levels of "scholarship" and "unblemished morality" (Parker 2019). Students were offered a broad range of translated classical and Islamic medical works. Inevitably, errors in the conclusions of the ancients were uncovered by new observations. The anatomical drawings of Galen, up to then sacrosanct, were challenged by Padua Medical School's Andreas Vesalius (1514–1564), who first produced a revised version of Galen's *Institutiones Anatomicae* in 1541, and then his own work *De Humani Corporis Fabrica* in 1543 (Parker 2019). Through this tome and his follow-up compendium, Vesalius presented accurate anatomical data, and thus "created the modern science of anatomy" (Nordenskiöld 1928). Vesalius, who had extraordinary dissection skill, supported his findings with demonstrations before skeptical physicians (Parker 2019). This defense of the integrity of anatomical data was a perfect example of treating data as clients. The 1543 publication of his tome was a fitting harbinger to The Enlightenment.

FIGURE 1.4 Andreas Vesalius. Anatomist whose work replaced that of Galen as the authority on human anatomy. Image by Digital Vision Vectors, courtesy of Getty Images.

1.8.3 ENGINEERING

Engineering, like medicine, flourished during the Italian Renaissance. Inventors like Leonardo da Vinci (1452–1519) and Johannes Gutenberg, and architectural engineers like Fillipo Brunelleschi (1377–1446) flourished. Major developments included:

1. *more accuracy and precision in time and length scales of manufacturing processes.*
2. *the beginning of standardization of parts.*
3. *manufacture of production machines that reduced variation between manufactured parts.*
4. *application of mechanics to improve machines such as pumps.*
5. *industrialization of mining with the help of explosives, ore transporters and water pumps*
6. *printing was used to produce engineering textbooks, particularly for mining*
(Aslaksen 2013)

The division of the world of technê into craftsmen, and engineers, who worked on government projects (effectively "civil engineers"; Aslaksen 2013), became more evident during the Renaissance. Craftsmen formed guilds and monitored work performance quality through training programs, such as apprenticeships. Engineers designed and managed public works and were involved in product manufacturing. Yet, while they applied some physics concepts, they were limited in scope by a lack of formal engineering education (Aslaksen 2013).

1.8.4 SCIENCE

Crucial groundwork for the scientific enlightenment of Western Civilization was laid during this period. The specific areas of advance were (1) mathematics, (2) methodology, and (3) instrumentation. It should be noted, for perspective, that all of the individuals described here were either Catholic or Protestant, and often took great care to separate mythos from logos.

While the Vesalius' defense of his data was slowly making its way into the medical curriculum, Nicolas Copernicus' (1473–1543) posthumous publication of *De Revolutionibus Orbium Coelestium*, which postulated a heliocentric solar system, convinced hardly a dozen scholars for the following 50 years (Principe 2002). Three reasons for this delay appear to be (1) his absence, (2) his defense of the concept was based on humanistic, rather than natural philosophy grounds, and (3) the work lacked confirming data (Principe 2002). In short, Copernicus' data had insufficient integrity to qualify as clients.

Bioengineering and Ethics

The data Copernicus needed was gathered with great integrity by Tycho Brahe (1546–1601), who was not inclined to challenge the church, and was satisfied to merely make adjustments to the geocentric system of Ptolemy (Principe 2002). Johannes Kepler (1571–1630) sympathized with the humanist devotion to Plato's belief that mathematics was the key to understanding nature through reason. He was a mathematician, not an experimentalist, but he understood and accepted the Copernican model, with reservations (particularly about the circular shape of his orbits). His genius lay in his ability to induce three laws of planetary motion from Brahe's data (Smith 1972). He started publication of them with the first law in *Astronomia nova* (1609).

Galileo Galilei (1564–1642) made significant advances in astronomy instrumentation with his telescopes. He made his advances in mechanics with his methodology, performing a number of experiments. His observational astronomical data, published in *Dialogue on the Two Chief Systems of the World* (1632; written in Italian to reach the largest audience; Smith 1972), were not of Brahe quality, but he saw so much with his self-made telescopes that the observations were new. They confirmed the Copernican model, albeit without the elliptical orbit correction of Kepler's laws (Smith 1972). His well-documented problems with the Catholic Church left a church-science dispute that was not formally settled until the 20th century (Blackwell 2002). His physics featured extensive experimentation and conclusions, including the Laws of Inertia. But he did not connect his mechanics conclusions with those from his astronomy (Smith 1972).

Francis Bacon (1561–1626) proposed that the gathering of data in a controlled systematic way—by performing experiments—was the only trustworthy path to learning the truth about nature. His *Novum Organum* (1620) described a methodology by which inductive logic can take a body of empirical data, and build it into a general theory that explains a natural phenomenon (Smith 1972). Theories ("axioms" as he called them) were themselves testable by performing further experiments. Bacon maintained that by learning directly from the natural world without invoking scholasticism thought filters, mankind would be able to solve real problems, by finding their natural causes (Blackburn 1994). Bacon ensured that no supernatural filters threatened data integrity in his method, but he lacked the expertise to incorporate a mathematical component in his description of the handling of data (Smith 1972). So, he had no quantitative safeguard to guarantee reproducibility of experimental results. René Descartes (1596–1650), a mathematician and natural philosopher, provided the missing safeguard with works like *La Géométrie* (1637); developing a coordinate system and a means for performing calculations within it. His philosophy was deductive; being based on a mathematical approach.

FIGURE 1.5 Francis Bacon. Natural philosopher who developed an inductive logic approach to formulating conclusions about natural world observations. Image by Science Museum Library, courtesy of Science Museum Library.

One can build a scientific method from the contributions of these last three natural philosophers: (1) Galileo, the observer, designs the experiment and gathers its data, (2) Descartes, the mathematician, formats the data into quantitative statements, (3) Bacon, the inductive logician, constructs conclusions that state causal relations between steps of data processing, and (4) Descartes (or Galileo), the deductive logician, makes predictions for further experiments suggested by Bacon's conclusions (Smith 1972).

During this period, tools were invented to provide reproducible measurements that would allow comparison of data from different experiments. The new instruments (some improvements of older versions) included thermometers, barometers, pendulum clocks, air pumps (to make vacuums), telescopes, and microscopes.

Bioengineering and Ethics

1.9 EMERGENCE OF SCIENCE FROM PHILOSOPHY—THE ENLIGHTENMENT (1650–1750)

1.9.1 GENERAL

In medicine, engineering, and science, *the enlightenment* was dominated by the work of Isaac Newton (1642–1727). Indeed, it has been claimed that the 18th and 19th centuries were pre-occupied with confirming Newton's Laws in all fields impacted by his physics (Smith 1972).

1.9.2 MEDICINE

What Vesalius did for anatomy, William Harvey (1578–1657) did for physiology (Parker 2019). From delicate experiments with live animals and careful cadaver dissection, without the benefit of a microscope, Harvey was able to collect data leading to the conclusion that veins and arteries were connected by capillaries to complete vertebrate blood circulation. He published his work in *De Motu Cordis et Saguinis* (1628). Taken together, the work of Vesalius and Harvey substantially ended the hold of Galen on medicine (Smith 1972).

1.9.3 ENGINEERING

As natural philosopher understanding of nature grew in the Italian Renaissance, and scientific societies began to influence the governments of the West, confidence in human intellectual ability, as well as the belief in individual value, percolated down to tradesmen (Aslaksen 2013). Where experience alone was insufficient to solve an engineering problem, judgment that had depended on empiricism and lore was supplemented or replaced by science and mathematics. As a result, separation between engineers and the tradesmen grew. Craftsmen demanded more accurate and effective instruments to assure the quality of their work and engineers demanded more education to increase their sophistication about potential applications of the new instruments and other products (Aslaksen 2013). Demand fueled industry and capitalism, preparing the way for an industrial revolution in the West.

1.9.4 SCIENCE

Communication between natural philosophers was stimulated by development of the printing press and outpouring of scholarly works during the Italian Renaissance. Rather than wait for private publication or posting of their works, many scholars decided to organize societies that would provide for discussion and publication, for dissemination of news from their field. Two of the first few societies were the *Royal Society* of London (1660) and the *Académie Royale des Sciences* of Paris (1666). Their journals are still published today.

The genius of Isaac Newton was essentially a combination of Galileo, Bacon, and Descartes (Smith 1972). A countryman of Bacon, this "father of the 'age of reason'" (Blackburn 1994), developed a "new paradigm of scientific method"

18   Ethics for Bioengineering Scientists

(Blackburn 1994) that according to the philosopher David Hume (1711–1776; Hume 1748), was, nevertheless, limited to placing "the events of nature into lawlike orders and patterns" (Blackburn 1994). Newton's *Philosophiae Natarulis Principia Mathematica* (1687) summarized his work, which included the development of The Calculus, his three laws of motion and optics.

1.10 THE INDUSTRIAL REVOLUTION—DETERMINISM AND REDUCTIONISM

1.10.1 GENERAL

By naming the force that attracted planets "gravity", Newton established the existence of a cause around which hypotheses predicting its effects could be constructed. He did not explain its properties, beyond its ability to act through space instantaneously; affected only by distance and the mass of the interacting objects. His approach dictated the kind of data that needed be collected to test the predictions of each law of motion. But because the predictions were in the form of mathematical equations, the data had to be quantitative, meaning their utility depended to a great extent on the accuracy of the device measuring them. He assumed gravity's existence, and its action through space without having any idea of its true nature or how it was transmitted through space. In essence, he asked other natural philosophers to believe in a cause he could not describe beyond its effects. For Newton, who was a religious man, and, ultimately, a deist, the existence of gravity was part of the logos created by God. He felt no obligation to explain it beyond this (Smith 1972). As it turned out, attempts to understand the cause itself were fruitless until Einstein described gravity in his General Theory of Relativity over 200 years later. Einstein's predicted "gravity waves" were not detected for another 100+ years.

But, what does it mean to "understand" gravity waves? Can you see them or touch them? They appear as a "signature", that is, an effect on a laser beam reflection detected by a Laser Interferometry Gravitational-Wave Observation (LIGO) interferometer. But, do observations of the instrument's output constitute understanding gravity? One can pose this kind of question for any phenomenon observed by scientists. The philosopher Emmanuel Kant (1724–1804) in his *Kritique der reinen Vernuft* (*Critique of Pure Reason*; 1781; Kant 1998) exposed this flaw in causality by describing total understanding of a natural phenomenon as knowing or being certain one "knows" a "thing in itself" ("ding an sich" in the original German).

1.10.2 MEDICINE

The confidence spawned by reductionism (see later) made it seem as if science would eventually explain all human function. Physicians, often in competition with other specialists for patient trust, would at times promote their treatments as being "scientific". A famous example that exposed such "overselling" was the case of Francis Mesmer. He claimed that a device he developed that generated an electromagnetic field (EMF) he called "animal magnetism", was based on scientific principles and was curative for a number of ailments (Parker 2019). Benjamin Franklin (1706–1790), who had some understanding of EMFs, was skeptical and challenged Mesmer to corroborate

Bioengineering and Ethics

his claim under laboratory conditions. The great experiment took place just outside Paris in 1791 where Franklin introduced the concept of a controlled experiment. Two groups of patients with appropriate ailments were treated with true and sham generators that appeared to act the same. The subjects were blinded to the condition of the generators, and their responses were random, disproving Mesmer's claim (Lopez 1993).

1.10.3 ENGINEERING

The impetus for the Industrial Revolution in 1750 and the demands on engineering resulting from it were generated in England (Aslaksen 2013). Its prime customer at this time was America (after its revolution, The United States of America). Engineering's growth as a profession was spurred not only by a growing market for England's products, but by "the best patent system in the world" (Aslaksen 2013). The Society of Civil Engineers was formed in London in 1771. Engineering education was not formalized, however, until late in the 19th century.

1.10.4 SCIENCE

The success of Newton's models persuaded most natural philosophers in the 18th century—becoming more like scientists with each generation—that the concerns of Kant were not critical for their success. They now had more ability to predict reality, using inductive logic and analytical models, in the form of equations, like those of Newton, than they had ever had before. Their conviction grew (Smith 1972) that determinism, every effect had a cause (Blackburn 1994), ruled nature. When they successfully applied the laws of physics and chemistry to industrial problems, their confidence as problem solvers also grew. There was significant progress in thermodynamics, with the work of H. Helmoltz (1821–1894, *Conservation of Energy*—1847) and J. Joule (1818–1889, *Mechanical Theory of Heat*—1840).

As a rule, living things are more complex and variable than are the nonliving. Consequently, while accurate measurements were relatively easy to obtain in physical science research, they were more difficult to obtain in biological research without endangering the living subject. Data from a biological experiment could be rather scattered. Notwithstanding these challenges to precision, biologists began to believe that life processes would eventually be completely explained in physical and chemical terms, an outlook, known as "reductionism" (Bynum et al. 1981). The problem of biological data scatter was eventually addressed by the biometricians Francis Galton (1822–1911), W.F.R. Weldon (1860–1906), and Karl Pearson (1857–1936), who established modern statistics applied to biology (Bynum et al. 1981; Millar et al. 1996).

As the popularity of determinism and reductionism grew, many emerging scientists became convinced that there was no place for mythos in the natural world and, therefore, science. They are known as "positivists" (Blackburn 1994). Some went so far as to claim that mythos had no existence in any world. They are known as "logical positivists". Richard Dawkins is a famous member of the latter group. A scientist functions professionally as a logical positivist. We assume that the

20   Ethics for Bioengineering Scientists

scientist, toward whom this book is directed, is a positivist and need not be a logical positivist.

1.11 THE INDUSTRIAL REVOLUTION—CAUSALISM AND EMPIRICISM IN SCIENCE

The image of a modern "scientist" begins to emerge during the Industrial Revolution, particularly the 19th century. The term "scientist" as applied to a natural philosopher, became official in 1834 (Stevenson 2010; Ross 1962). Since determinism is such an important part of this image, we need to take a closer look at causalism to be sure we understand it before we can appreciate the challenges to it that appear in the 20th century.

1.11.1 CAUSALISM AND THE THREE PROFESSIONS

During the Industrial Revolution, physicians and engineers secured their positions as problem solvers with human clients. They did not perform laboratory experiments to serve their clients, although some "moonlighted" as scientists (Nordenskiöld 1928) Some others, like Mesmer, identified themselves as "scientific" in order to enhance their appeal. None spent their energies replacing their problem-solving functions with quests to find the cause of the problem for which their clients were paying them. They were functioning as empiricists. When an empiricist reaches the solution of a problem, she has achieved a truth and has no need to continue the investigation. Accordingly, we refer to engineers and physicians as "truth professionals". As long as they suppose no supernatural cause is involved in the problem, they are also "positivists". If they are interested in learning the cause, they are causalists. If they perform investigations that apply methodologies in agreement with how scientific philosophy defines a scientific method, they are causal scientists. When a causal scientist completes an investigation, she always discovers that there is more to be understood about the mechanism in question; this is particularly true if the investigation failed. Indeed, failure drives science because it teaches more than does success. But it is the ultimate failure, the inability to know a *ding an sich* that forces us to the conclusion that there are no final answers, that is, proofs, in science. Discovery of a natural law is the closest a scientist can approach a final answer. Most scientists are satisfied to discover a mechanism that explains their observations. We refer to scientists seeking the level of natural law as causal or basic scientists, and those seeking the level of an explaining mechanism as empirical scientists.

We propose, then, for the purposes of this text, to define three kinds of professionals who develop and handle data.

1. Truth professionals: Those who solve real-world problems using data empirically. Not committed to finding causal relationships. Usually have human clients. Traditional physicians and engineers, for example.
2. Empirical scientists: Those who solve real-world problems by detecting causal relationships, but are not concerned with understanding their

Bioengineering and Ethics

connection with the rest of the natural world. Their clients are data, but they may have an alternative life as a truth professional (M.D., Ph.D.s). Most scientists working in industry, medical schools, and engineering schools.

3. Causal (or basic) scientists: Those who seek to better understand the natural world by detecting causal relationships. Their clients are data, exclusively. These are usually biologists, physicists, geologists, chemists, astronomers, etc., who work in nonprofit institutions.

Scientists investigate the natural world using two general styles based on how much access they have to the source of data as summarized in the following table (Table 1.3).

TABLE 1.3
Investigative Styles of Science

General Approach	Observational	Experimental
Specific approach	Epidemiological	Laboratory
	Instrumental	Human (e.g. clinical) groups
	Historical	Environmental

Epidemiological observations are usually the only way to study human phenomena requiring large populations, because most countries have laws restricting laboratory experimentation on people. In order to determine safety and efficacy of health products, however, patients become experimental subjects. Historical events like quasar pulsations cannot be practically tested in a laboratory for obvious reasons.

How one applies logic to the data gathered will also vary depending on whether a problem-solving truth or a causal relationship is the goal.

The following table compares the role of logic in causal and empirical investigations (Table 1.4).

TABLE 1.4
Application of Logic to Empirical vs. Causal Investigations

Investigative Orientation	Approach	Reasoning
Causalism: experimental	Laboratory research	Combination of inductive and deductive reasoning using data and
	Controlled population research	
Causalism: observational	Observation outside laboratory	models
Empiricism: testing	Trial-and-error, experience	Deductive reasoning referenced to
Empiricism: observational	Statistical correlation—risk assessment (epidemiology)	specific goal

1.11.1.1 Causalism vs. Empiricism in Ethical Decisions—The Ebola Case Example (from WHO Website (WHO 2014)

A dramatic example of the difference between empirical and causal approaches may be found in real-world events. The Ebola virus is a compelling real-world challenge. It was identified near the Ebola river in Africa in 1976. It is a virulent pathogen with a 25% to 90% fatality rate. It is spread by human-to-human contact.

The latest Ebola epidemic was in Guinea in March 2014 and killed more than 2,000 by September. There was no vaccine that had been scientifically tested. The truly scientific test would have consisted of at least two groups of subjects that were initially disease-free. Both groups would have been given the disease, and only one, the experimental group, would have received the vaccine. The control group would have gotten a placebo, dispensed the same way as the vaccine. In a more-complete investigation, a third group without the disease would have received the vaccine in order to assess its side effects. The "subjects" referred to here would be nonhuman primates that support the disease. Any experiment in which a human is infected on purpose would be unlawful in nearly all countries. In 2015, Zmapp, a triple antibody drug made by Mapp Biopharmaceutical, showed promise in tests on macaque monkeys. But these investigations would have not run long enough to assess long-term effects. Since the disease posed a high risk of spreading throughout Africa and beyond, authorities turned to empirical approaches to find a cure or some method of arresting spread of the disease. One approach was to try Zmapp on patients immediately. Two such patients were treated at Emory university and have been declared "disease free". Another approach was to use the antibodies assumed to have developed in response to the disease in patients who had survived it. The quickest way to administer such antibodies was by blood transfusion. This approach was applied. In both of these empirical approaches, the effectiveness of a specific group of antibodies against Ebola was taken as a truth. From this truth, a *deduction* was made that the ineffectiveness of the victim's immune system against the virus would have been compensated for by supplementary antibodies that had been effective against the virus.

Note the role of risk assessment in making these decisions. Often the risk of a deadly epidemic raises fear to a level that pushes aside the benefits of taking time to learn more about how the detailed mechanism (pathophysiology) by which the course of the disease (its etiology) takes place. Consequently, the more we understand about the mechanism, the more we can effectively predict the treatment design most likely to control pathophysiology without significant side effects.

1.11.2 STATISTICS AND SCIENCE

Thirty-three years before Kant published *Critique of Pure Reason*, David Hume published *An Enquiry Concerning Human Understanding* (1748) in which he challenged the ability for humans to infer a cause without directly experiencing it. The Hume–Kant "partnership" has been a philosophical challenge to scientific certainty since their century. It has been replaced by a "probability" method for assessment of the likelihood of a causal connection between two phenomena that

Bioengineering and Ethics

we call "statistics". The need for statistics could have come as no surprise to the experimentalists, particularly in biology. Their experiments probably suffered from data scatter that presented challenges for predicting tendencies. There was some help from C.F. Gauss, who (1787–1855) developed the statistical method of "least squares" (1809) that facilitated curve-fitting (Millar et al. 1996).

At least a laboratory experimentalist had some control over the source of data. What recourse is left to investigators who cannot carry out lab experiments to obtain data? Examples include astronomy and public health. It is not possible to perform lab experiments on distant planets and unlawful in most cases to perform them on human populations. One must gather data from large groups of humans (epidemiologically) or using special instruments (e.g. Viking space probe) while disturbing their subjects minimally. Historical data is past being tested, although one can make models that mimic past events and test them (e.g. earthquake models of a quake that occurred 200 years ago). Evolution of galaxies or organisms falls into this category.

Experimental scientific investigation produces the most reliable and precise data when carried out competently in a laboratory. Here, one can set up a baseline group of subjects called "controls" and group(s) to which the agent being studied is applied, called "experimentals". Ideally, both groups are identical except for the treatment. Statistical conditions are imposed to assess whether differences between data from controls and experimental are significant. Experiments "in the field", such as tests involving animals treated in some fashion and then released into the wild have less precision, being outside the confines of a lab. But they are crucial for understanding ecological relationships and environmental effects.

Research involving humans is a challenge because it usually cannot be performed in a laboratory, with control and experimental groups that are totally monitored, to avoid extraneous data. In one of the first human investigations, P.C.A. Louis in 1835 collected data evaluating the ability of bloodletting to reduce the incidence of pneumonia in patients. He evaluated the daily course of the disease in 175 patients divided into subgroups, dividing the results into tables. He concluded that the procedure had no significant effect on the course of the disease (Parodi et al. 2006). In spite of Louis' report, this practice lasted until the late 19th century (Parker 2019). The reader may wonder what lawyers were doing during this period. Suffice it to say, malpractice suits were not yet a concern of lawyers.

1.12 THE SECOND INDUSTRIAL REVOLUTION—DARWIN CHANGES HUMAN CONCEPT OF SELF IN THE 19TH CENTURY

1.12.1 GENERAL

The course of science, and the relationship of science to the rest of society, was drastically changed in mid-19th century, by what some consider the most important scientific conclusion ever reached (Watson 2005). In 1859, Charles Darwin, using thousands of observations of living and extinct organisms, theorized that the history of life on earth was causally connected (i.e. had evolved) by a process he called "natural selection". The resulting organic evolution included humans. He published his conclusions in *On The Origin Of Species* (1859).

As the 19th century ended, the Industrial Revolution was being witnessed by 7.6 million (U.S. Census) Americans who had, if they were white males, a life expectancy of 47.8 years; an increase of 7.8–20.8 from the 20–40 years reported for the Ancient Period populations (Aslaksen 2013). By the end of the 20th century, that value had increased another 40 years. Such a jump was launched, to a great extent, by the industrialization of chemistry, during what is called the "second industrial revolution" (Pickstone 2011). The Dalton model for molecules had demonstrated that complex organic—even physiological—molecules were made of the same elements as were inorganic molecules (Leicester 1956). Science was being redirected from being philosophically driven—as it was by natural philosophers—to being driven by application—as by industry. The Germ Theory of Disease motivated development of antisepsis and vaccines (Parker 2019). The idea that humans were at the center of the universe, diminished by Galileo's heliocentric model, was now made irrelevant by Darwin's discoveries. Humans were now just *Homo sapiens*, a primate of the class Mammalia. But the connection of humans to other animals made reductionism more plausible. There were problems with the theory that Darwin himself pointed out (Darwin 1859). Chief among them was the lack of a mechanism for genetic variation. Darwin was not aware of the work of Mendel.

"Darwinism", as the implications of natural selection came to be called, altered societies' concept of the basis for human behavior (Hofstadter 1944). Consequently, the aspect of behavior having to do with values and resulting moral orientation was seen as somehow connected with human ancestry. Another important effect of Darwinism was emergence of the acceptance that one could extrapolate data from lab animal models to humans.

1.12.2 MEDICINE

There were many successful adaptations of 18th- and 19th-century scientific advances to the practice of medicine. Surgery and childbirth were made safer and endurable by antisepsis and anesthesia, with minimal side effects. Robert Koch (1843–1910) and Louis Pasteur (1822–1895) confirmed the germ theory of disease and used it to develop vaccines and sterilization treatments. Pasteur scientifically demonstrated the germ theory of disease by infecting lab animals with cultures isolated from carriers of the microorganisms. Koch formulated a procedure for scientifically demonstrating a causal relationship between a specific organism and a disease. The procedure, known as "Koch's postulates" established a standard for pathology, and may be summarized as follows: (1) Show that the suspect organism is consistently present in diseased tissue in a characteristic state. (2) Isolate and grow the organism in laboratory cultures. (3) Experimentally induce the disease by injecting pure cultures of it in a subjects susceptible to it (Walker et al. 2006).

Another area of medicine that grew significantly in this century was its connection with statistics. The connection began with empiricism. John Snow (1813–1858) applied statistics to data from a 1854 cholera epidemic, and so originated epidemiology (Parker 2019). Physicians needed to be able to predict the risk of epidemics spreading to specific locations, and emerging insurance companies needed to calculate the risk of success for insured constructions and other ventures.

Bioengineering and Ethics

Epidemiology grew from the study of infectious epidemics to include the study of incidence, rise and spread of all human diseases. Focus was now on all factors associated with the disease in question. This included not only those highly correlated with coming down with the disease—risk factors—but those correlated with resistance to the disease—protective factors. This tool was used also to show that a disease was not caused by a germ. Joseph Goldberger in 1923 showed that pellagra was more highly correlated with diet than conditions for spread of disease. Niacin deficiency, the cause of the condition, was not discovered until 1937.

Walter Reed used Panama Canal construction workers in 1901 to test the hypothesis that mosquitoes were necessary for yellow fever to be spread. He corroborated his hypothesis but did not discover the causative virus carried by the mosquitos or how the vector transmitted it.

One of the greatest catastrophes for which we still lack data, was the H1N1 influenza epidemic of 1918 (Barry 2005). Some 675,000 people died in the United States (30 million worldwide) before the virus ran out of susceptible victims. Most decedents were young "fit" people. No treatment worked. Even though the virus' RNA has been sequenced, its origin is still not clear (Morens et al. 2010).

1.12.3 ENGINEERING

By the end of the 19th century, engineering had somewhat matured as a truth profession. Industrialization of product manufacturing was a major driver that attracted prospective engineers to training institutions (Aslaksen 2013). The path from Newton's laws to engineering mechanics of building construction was relatively obvious. Nevertheless, when the U.S. Congress considered the question of funding the first university engineering programs in the 1870s, a fight broke out over the question of whether to consider engineers as professionals or craftsmen (Reynolds 1991a).

Engineers began using statistics to calculate the odds of a catastrophe, based on experience. As they connected increasingly with science, forward-looking engineers wanted to base predictions on more than correlations. For example, the French companies insuring construction of the Panama Canal had only their experience of the Suez Canal to guide them on risk assessment. The geology of Panama was dramatically different from that of Egypt and it was important to know how the difference affected speed of completion. As it turned out, the lack of geology data contributed significantly to the French failure in Panama (McCullough 1977).

1.12.4 SCIENCE

A number of physical laws were developed in the 1800s. J.C. Maxwell (1831–1879) developed a unified theory of electromagnetism, which was supported by the experimental data of M. Faraday (1791–1869). It is said that the impact of this pair on physics was almost as great as the impact of the astronomical observations of Galileo and Newton's Laws of Motion (Millar et al. 1996). John Dalton (1766–1844) proposed in *A New System of Chemical Philosophy* (1808, 1810) that (1) atoms were the smallest components of each element, (2) atoms were unchangeable, (3) a "compound atom" may be formed by combining two or more

26   Ethics for Bioengineering Scientists

atoms, (4) the identity of an atom in a compound atom does not change, and (5) mass is conserved in a chemical reaction (Holton 1952).

In Geology, Charles Lyell (1797–1875) in his *Principles of Geology* (1830) firmly established Hutton's principle of uniformitarianism, postulating that most (nontectonic) geologic changes occurred slowly over time. Darwin used Lyell's data in his natural selection model.

One of the social consequences of Darwin's theory was the incorporation of it into the philosopher Herbert Spencer's notion that society's leaders reflected the results of competition in nature, such that only the "fittest" succeeded. The new name for his philosophy became "social Darwinism" (Hofstadter 1944). Adherents of social Darwinism (that did not include Darwin) were motivated to find evidence supporting it. Francis Galton, a cousin of Darwin, began gathering data to support the idea. Mendel's Laws of Heredity had not yet been sufficiently disseminated to provide Galton with a mechanism for predicting genetic trends. He gathered data, but had no way to show how the values he measured related to relatives of the subjects. Finally, he derived the correlation coefficient (Millar et al. 1996). This was an indicator of a human population tendency, an epidemiological tool. But here it was not used to indicate spread of disease.

With the discovery of Gregor Mendel's 1866 paper in 1900, a mechanism for transmitting Darwin's "variations" was finally in place. By 1903, microscopic techniques developed since 1866 helped reveal chromosomes, and the "gene" was named in 1909 (Millar et al. 1996). The Neo-Darwinism era had begun. It was concluded that it was the "natural selection" of this structure by the environment that drove biological evolution. When examined at the level of whole societies, population genetics could be applied to evolution. Natural selection began to be seen as a statistical problem in which risk and protective (from disease, etc.) factors had genetic determinants. Variation within a population can be considerable. Accordingly, the only way to conclude that a particular action had to be taken to stop agent A from reaching the population at large was to be "confident" about the correlation between the undesirable effect and agent A. A similar procedure needs to be followed in deciding if society would benefit from administering agent B to the population. Statistical methods for arriving at the required levels of confidence can be quite sophisticated. The techniques of previous statisticians like Galton were "modernized" by Karl Pearson (1857–1936) who developed the chi-square test (Millar et al. 1996). Pearson is considered a founder of 20th-century biological statistics (Millar et al. 1996).

While Darwin was being reborn, Newton was being redefined. Albert Einstein's two papers (1905, 1915) replaced a mysterious Newtonian force of gravity with curvature of space in his special and general theories of relativity. In a 1905 paper on photoelectric effect, he provided crucial evidence for light quanta and quantum theory of the atom. In another paper that same year, he provided direct evidence from calculations of Brownian motion for the existence of molecules. Evidence that the atom was not indivisible was provided by J.J. Thompson (1897) and E. Rutherford (1898). The work of these pioneers led to development of the fields of the smallest, nuclear, and the largest, space, physics. We shall spend no more of our history on space physics, although BEs interested in space-related careers will want to pursue the subject. Erwin Schrödinger (1887–1961) developed wave mechanics,

Bioengineering and Ethics

the mathematical equations that predict the behavior of subatomic particles using wave equations (Millar et al. 1996).

Werner K. Heisenberg (1901–1976) developed quantum mechanics, which turned out to be another approach to the same method as Schrödinger's wave mechanics. He rejected visual models of the atom in favor of measurable qualities. Applying this approach led him to his principle of indeterminacy *Über den anschulichen Inhalt der quantentheoretischen Kinematik und Mechanik* (1927), which concluded that an atomic particle's position and speed could not be determined simultaneously (Millar et al. 1996). This viewpoint is the physicists equivalent of denying that one can know a "ding an sich". Quantum and wave mechanics had confirmed Kant and determinism was disproved. Causalism was replaced by uncertainty and science could not claim to have a path to empirical truth. It could not be a truth profession because there could be no causal endpoint to mark the complete understanding of any natural phenomenon. By the same token, reductionism, which depended upon physics to carry biology to its own complete understandings had lost its ticket on the trip to ultimate reality. Scientific philosophers have not found a way out of this conundrum (Goldman 2006).

FIGURE 1.6 Werner K. Heisenberg. Physicist who derived the Principle of Indeterminacy that disproved the certainty of knowing a deterministic cause. Image by Daily Herald Archive, courtesy of Science Museum Library.

1.13 THE PATH TO BIOENGINEERING FROM 1927

In 1927, the United States was the major power in the world. It had survived the First World War in which chemistry had been weaponized, an influenza pandemic that had been allowed to run its course without any program to stop it, and the loss of assurance that it could eventually understand the natural world through science. During the next 40 years, until the development of bioengineering, it would face another World War, the application of nuclear power, and a transformation from small science to Big Science.

In *Logik der Forschung* (1935), Karl Popper (Popper 1959) restored some of the loss of confidence in causality. He concluded that induction, saddled with the deterministic conviction that enough data can be gathered to lead to ultimate truth, was not a valid starting point for understanding the natural world. Instead, one should start with what we already understand about the natural world and deductively use it to formulate falsifiable hypotheses. In other words, although in science one could not prove that results of an experiment had confirmed the hypothesis being tested, one could disprove its converse (Popper 1959). An example of a falsifiable hypothesis would be: "The erosion of a polylactide-polyglycolide implant produces an insignificant pH change in a 1 ml volume of surrounding tissue". Popper proposed that one could actually quantify a level of confidence that the falsifiable hypothesis had been disproved using statistical tools such as the p value of Ronald Fisher (1890–1962). It followed that this level of confidence was an indicator of the degree to which the opposite—the hypothesis advocated by the experimenter—had been corroborated (i.e. that the pH change was significant). "Corroborate" became one of the scientifically acceptable replacements for "prove" in 1927.

FIGURE 1.7 Karl R. Popper. Philosopher of Science who blunted the effects of the Principle of Indeterminacy on science research by developing a falsifiable hypothesis approach. Image by Sueddeutsche Zeitung Photo, courtesy of ALAMY.

Bioengineering and Ethics

Prior to WWII scientific research was conducted either in larger product producing companies like those of Bell Telephone and General Electric, or at universities. Funding for the latter came from the private sector or a research branch of a government agency such as the Department of the Navy (Hiltzik 2015). Principal investigators (the individuals who took responsibility for the research) worked as individuals with assistants or graduate students to help. (Postdoctoral fellowships did not exist.)

Just prior to the war medical research was funded by a single National Institute of Health (formed in 1930) or the National Cancer Institute. Funding recipients were employed by the institutes or universities. The funding footprint of government in university laboratories was relatively small (Lassman 2005).

In 1939, a group of physicists convinced President Roosevelt to organize a research project to develop an atom bomb. The group convinced him that Germany had nuclear physicists capable of developing the weapon. If they succeeded, the balance of power between Ally and Axis nations would shift toward the latter. The resulting "Manhattan Project" employed several hundred scientists and over 100,000 workers. It was overseen by the Army Dept. A number of scientific discoveries resulted. It marked the birth of "Big Science", which is characterized by multiple laboratories working on the same research project and invariably government funded because of the cost (Hiltzik 2015). The NIH did not yet engage in Big Science. It focused, during the war, on war-related technical projects like investigating exposure of war industry workers to munitions toxins and preparation of vaccines for soldiers fighting in the tropics (Swain 1962).

In 1944, Congress passed the Public Health Service Act that converted the NIH of the PHS (which became today's U.S. Department of Health and Human Services) into a medical research granting agency. At first, the agency focused on nonclinical research that could be carried out in university laboratories or otherwise under the control of nonclinical academics. Causal research was a priority. One of the reasons behind this limitation was an official stand by the American Medical Association against socialized medicine. Since clinical research involving patients would have to be conducted in hospital settings, the federal government would have to regulate their treatment as part of oversight of any project. Congress was lobbied successfully by the AMA to place restrictions on the National Institutes of Health (NIH) to block such research (Fox 1987). Political pressure came in the opposite direction from patients through voluntary health organizations. They saw success of the NCI in having its own institute as giving cancer patients an "unfair" advantage in the struggle for research funding (Mukherjee 2011). They lobbied congress and by 1949 there were seven institutes under the newly named NIH. By 1970, this number had increased to 15. In 1953, a hospital was built on the NIH campus to provide a controllable site where clinical research could be conducted in close proximity to the other institutes. The NIH had to make repeated assurances to the medical profession that this hospital was not a starting point for any socialized medicine movement.

By 1970, funding of the NIH had reached the billions of dollars and, increasingly, researchers outside traditional causal research faculty were attracted to the agency as a source of funding. Physicians and engineers, collaborating with physiologists, biochemists, and biologists, applied in increasing numbers. Hospitals on university campuses increasingly became models of the NIH hospital and university medical faculty became counterparts to NIH research faculty. The production of Ph.D.'s increased as did their employment by medical schools. By 1970, it had become common for a Ph.D. in a medically related field to join a lab specializing in a health-related problem, and, after 1–3 years of postdoctoral research, move into an academic faculty or health industry position.

Unfortunately, for continued growth of this tendency, the U.S. economy slowed in the late 1960s. Funding allocation from Congress was reduced and an employment crisis developed in the academic sciences. Competition for NIH funding intensified. Positions that had been funded by NIH grants (graduate students, postdoctoral fellowships, and even tenure track faculty) could no longer be supported. Pressure on principal investigators to produce grant-winning results increased accordingly. Hiring by universities decreased and it became common for postdoctoral fellows to either continue beyond the usual three-year limit or move to industry. For new Ph.D.'s whose goal had been industry, these ex-postdocs were unexpected competition. State money for public universities shrunk as well. As a result of all these pressures, tuition rose. Today, the NIH has 21 on-campus research and external research funding institutes including the National Institute of Biomedical Imaging and Bioengineering. These are supported by eight centers.

In 1950, an agency to complement the NIH was founded. The National Science Foundation was established to fund "fundamental" (as it is called by the NSF) research in all scientific and engineering disciplines. The intent of Congress in creating this agency was to extend government funding to the sciences beyond the health sciences. Inclusion of engineering was recognition of (1) the crucial role of instrumentation necessary for making scientific observations and (2) potential for new technologies for all truth professions (Swain 1962). NSF funding has always been much less than that for NIH. But the same economic downturns affecting NIH have similarly impacted NSF.

1.14 THE ADVENT OF BIOENGINEERING

The science of bioengineering began to take form in the late 1950s and early 1960s. Most individuals trained as "BEs" at this time were in fact engineers who serviced medical instruments. They interacted with patients only peripherally and were even less involved in science per se (Requena-Carrión and Leder 2009). Academic programs in response to increased interest in NIH funding for bioengineering (at this time usually called "Biomedical Engineering"—BME—to reflect the medical goal of much of the research) research were developed at Johns Hopkins University, the University of Pennsylvania, and the University of Rochester. In 1966, the first University of California bioengineering department started at UCSD (Chien 2011). One of the notable pioneers of this new discipline was Y.C. Fung who is considered the father of modern biomechanics. These programs enriched with government and industry funding grew to take bioengineering from a profession almost exclusively populated by electrical engineers specializing in instrumentation to an interdisciplinary science mixing engineers, biologists, physicians, physicists, and chemists.

Bioengineers have entered technology industries in a wide variety of fields. They are often classified as biomedical engineers. Examples of occupations they

Bioengineering and Ethics 31

enter may be found at https://www.bls.gov/ooh/architecture-and-engineering/biomedical-engineers.htm. Actual job offerings reveal more details about the kinds of jobs available and may be found at https://jobs.sciencecareers.org/jobs/bioengineering/.

1.15 BIOENGINEERING AND EPIDEMIOLOGY

Because BEs tend to combine the truth professions medicine and engineering with biology their careers usually involve some aspect of engineering treatments or enhancements for humans. Opportunities for capital gain from development of products via such engineering lead to establishment of companies and employment for the so-inclined BE. Competition between companies stimulates constant improvement in products. In order to convince customers of the quality of their products, companies must demonstrate:

1. The product performs its task at least as well as its competitors (safety and efficacy)
2. If a problem develops with the product, it is not serious (minimizing liability)

The first requirement is met under the guidance of the FDA. It has the advantage of being supported by scientific laboratory experiments that were performed before the product came in contact with its human host. The second requirement will also involve the FDA, but the main concern of the company is a court case that may result in severe financial penalty and may even threaten company viability.

The causes of a product's failure in a given patient are not always clear. If it has failed in all its hosts, there can be little doubt that the product is faulty (although there is a possibility that the method for administering it—for example, poor instructions—is the actual fault). What usually happens is that some percentage of the population suffers a health disorder, and the suffering varies from patient to patient. Given the genetic variability of any human population and a prohibition against performing the relevant scientific lab experiments on humans (the test group would have to be isolated and controlled for long periods), it is difficult to scientifically demonstrate that the observed health disorder was caused by the product. As we shall see in our analysis of the Dow silicon breast implant case, this difficulty is sometimes ignored in actual court cases.

ENRICHMENT

1. The philosophy of science that deals with how we know what we know is explored in a lecture series on CD and DVD, produced by The Teaching Company. The title of this series is "Science Wars: What Scientists Know and How They Know It". The lecturer is Steven L.

Goldman, Ph.D. (Goldman 2006). Any causalist would gain significant insights from this series.

2. This chapter has referred to conflicts between science and certain religious beliefs. While the conflicts remain with fundamentalist forms of religion, other forms have accommodated science. If the reader is a serious member of a religion, he/she may have a moral vision already in place that will guide them in their professional life regardless of the moral theories discussed in this book. It may help them to be aware of the accommodations if they have concerns about potential conflict. The essay "Rocks of Ages: Science and Religion in the Fullness of Life" (Gould) by Stephen J. Gould, Ph.D. has been praised by religious leaders and some scientists as a major contribution to both magisteria. But skeptical atheists do not accept the magisteria model. Write a one-page essay summarizing your position.

3. Epidemiologists and immunologists are becoming more and more important in evaluating the biocompatibility of a medical product. They are often final arbiters in an FDA decision to approve a product. Some products approved by the FDA or its partner that focuses on products for plants and nonhuman animals, the Department of Agriculture have become controversial because of a perceived toxicity by nonexperts. Genetically modified plants/animals, vaccines, and synthetic foods are examples of such products. Use Google Scholar to compile a list of recently controversial products. Draw up a table with headings Product, Application, Proposed toxic effect, and Current status in the scientific literature.

4. Humanism has changed since the 13th century. Go to https://americanhumanist.org/ to find out what humanism is like today.

5. Go to the following websites and determine if your training has prepared you for the kind of work described in the occupations listed: https://www.bls.gov/ooh/architecture-and-engineering/biomedical-engineers.htm. and https://jobs.sciencecareers.org/jobs/bioengineering/

2 Ethics Biology: Are There Ethical Genomes?

2.1 SOME DEFINITIONS

This chapter explores the question of whether humans are hard-wired to behave in an ethical/moral fashion. Ethics is the study of how we ought to behave. If we have a predisposition to behave the way we "should", then we would be expected to be receptive to being educated with the details of that behavior. The hard wire would be our genetic code that is contained within our genes. Our genome is the physical structure that contains our total genetic code.

2.2 THE UNETHICAL EXPERIMENT

Consider the following experiment: 100 babies from a wide variety of cultures are taken from their mothers at birth. They are randomly split into two populations of 50 babies each and sent to two isolated islands A and B. There they are raised by programmed androids who act as "parents". These parents are programmed to nurture according to a consensus program developed by psychologists, with all necessary resources including teaching, feeding, and maintaining health, with one exception. Children on island A are taught no moral/ethical concepts. Children on island B are uniformly taught a specific set of moral/ethical concepts. At planned intervals during their upbringing, the children on both islands are presented with identical tests for altruistic behavior. The falsifiable hypothesis tested in this experiment is that the children on island A will display no altruistic behavior. If the hypothesis is disproved, there would be corroboration for the hypothesis that moral/ethical behavior is inborn, that is, is coded into human genomes.

This experiment could not legally be performed because it would violate the Helsinki Declaration of 1964, as we shall see in Chapter 11. Must we conclude, then, that we shall never be able to test our hypothesis? Not necessarily. There are two indirect approaches that have shed light on our quest for a moral/ethical genome. The first is medical and the second biological. There are clinical cases of patients who have been injured so as to lose function of certain areas of the brain, in particular involving the anterior cingulate cortex (ACC; Kennerly et al. 2006). As a result they were unable to exhibit moral/ethical behavior present before the injury. Where the loss was specific enough to have no apparent effect on non-normative behavior, there was evidence that the ACC played a crucial role in the moral/ethical behavior in question. The DNA sequences responsible for the ACC would then be part of the moral/ethical genome.

It may be stated that a sufficient number (referred to as *power*) of patients who share similar DNA will also express similar behavior. Therefore, DNA may be

DOI: 10.1201/9781003197218-2

34   Ethics for Bioengineering Scientists

analyzed to localize the specific site(s) of the malfunction. It may be possible either
to confirm a specific function of the gene set of interest by damaging target ACC
sites and observing resultant behavior or by knocking out the relevant DNA sequences in zygotes and observing resultant behavior as the child grows up. Both of
these experiments would violate the Helsinki Declaration.

2.3 CAN WE INFER A GENETIC BASIS FOR ALTRUISTIC BEHAVIOR FROM PSYCHOLOGY?

Psychologists and neurophysiologists have set themselves a difficult goal of seeking to
understand what causes humans to behave as they do. It has been evident since Plato
asserted a connection in 347 B.C. that the brain controls behavior. Brain neurons were
discovered in the mid-19th century. It was experimentally established in the first half of
the 20th century that these neurons function to form the thoughts we call "decisions"
that result in behavior. Since Freud, traditional experimental psychologists have focused on the mechanism—drives—underlying these decisions. Darwinian theory provided the link that convinced early behavioral scientists to look to nonhuman animals
for clues about neurophysiological mechanisms causing fundamental drives.

Hull (1943) proposed that hunger, thirst, sex, and escape from pain were the four
drives common to all animals. The implication of such a commonality is that drives
are a phenotype determined by specific genes. Of course, human society that developed as the species became civilized cultivated these primitive impulses (i.e.
drives) into what Reiss calls "motives" or "desires" (Reiss 2004). These are summarized in Table 2.1, adapted from his article. To what degree can science demonstrate causal links between the genes determining basic drives and Reiss's
desires? Stay tuned. As you read through the table, try to link each desire to at least
one basic drive. In this manner, you will be able to appreciate the challenge experienced by anyone faced with choosing a moral behavior that conflicts with one of
the other basic desires (e.g. fulfilling both desires #8 and #6).

TABLE 2.1
Reiss's 16 Basic Desires

Motive/Desire	Alternative Name	Animal Behavior (That Satisfies Drive)	Human Feeling
1. To influence (including leadership; related to mastery)		Dominant animal eats more food	Efficacy
2. For knowledge	Curiosity	Animal learns to find food more efficiently and learns to avoid prey	Wonder
3. To be autonomous	Independence	Motivates animal to leave nest, searching for food over larger area	Freedom
4. For social standing (including being noticed)	Status	Attention in nest leads to better feelings	Self-importance

Ethics Biology: Are There Ethical Genomes? 35

TABLE 2.1 *(Continued)*
Reiss's 16 Basic Desires

Motive/Desire	Alternative Name	Animal Behavior (That Satisfies Drive)	Human Feeling
5. For peer companionship (to play)	Social contact	Safety in numbers for animals in wild	Fun
6. To get "even" (to win)	Vengeance	Animal fights when threatened	Vindication
7. To obey a traditional moral code		Animal runs back to herd when stared at by prey	Loyalty
8. To improve society (including altruism, justice)	Idealism	Unclear: Do animals show true altruism?	Compassion
9. To exercise muscles	Physical exercise	Strong animals eat more and are less vulnerable to prey	Vitality
10. For sex (including courting)	Romance	Reproduction essential for species survival	Lust
11. To raise own children	Family	Protection of young facilitates survival	Love
12. To organize		Cleanliness rituals promise health	Stability
13. To eat		Nutrition essential for survival	Satiation (avoidance of hunger)
14. For approval	Acceptance	Unclear: animal self-concept?	Self-confidence
15. To avoid anxiety, fear	Tranquility	Animal runs away from danger	Safe, relaxed
16. To collect, value of frugality	Saving	Animal hoards food and other materials	Ownership

The question Reiss poses in the Animal Behavior column of desire #8 is fundamental to our understanding of the genetic basis for moral behavior. As we shall see in the next section, the illegality of performing certain experiments on humans has led to development of an alternative source of data about the genetic basis for altruism.

2.4 A PARTIAL SUBSTITUTE FOR THE HUMAN EXPERIMENT: EVOLUTIONARY PSYCHOLOGY

The second indirect approach to determining the existence of a moral/ethical genetic code is to take advantage of a relatively new field in biology, evolutionary psychology. Let us review the evolution of hominoids to establish the relationship of humans to other animals (some of which are employed in lab animal research). Since this is not a physical anthropology class, the account will be short: About 65 million years ago, an asteroid (or two), about a kilometer in diameter, slammed into what is now the Gulf of Mexico. The tectonic (recent evidence suggests volcanic eruptions contributed most of the effect) and meteorological events initiated by this catastrophe led to the extinction of nearly all dominant dinosaur species. Contemporary mammals were dominated by dinosaurs before the collision, and tended to reside in well-sheltered habitats. They not only survived, but with the disappearance of their tormentors, they experienced an explosion of population and evolution. About 50–35 (the number is hotly disputed in paleontology) million years ago, the first primate-like mammals appeared. These eventually produced a subgroup that resembled humans enough to gain the descriptor "hominids". About 5–6 million years ago the hominids (Figure 2.1) produced two main lines of descendants, one that eventually produced chimpanzees and bonobos and other that produced the more bipedal australopithecines ("Lucy" is a famous member of this group) (Diamond 1999), as shown in Figure 2.1. From the latter group, about 2–3 million years ago, there appeared the first member of the genus *Homo*, *Homo erectus*, who, as the name suggests, was fully capable of walking on its hind legs. A hominid like *Homo erectus*, who evolved in Africa, may have given rise to a number of species of the genus *Homo*. Some of them appeared on the European continent as early as 500,000 years ago (Diamond 1999). Two of them, *H. neanderthalis* and *H. sapiens*, have left the major number of fossils. *H. neanderthalis* migrated northwest and occupied what is now western Europe. Climate changes and resultant food shortages over the years forced a number of migrations of the descendants of *H. sapiens* and by 10,000 years ago, they had spread to all continents, except Antarctica (Diamond 1999). Anthropologists have designated descendants at about 50,000 years ago (Diamond 1999) (some recent discoveries have suggested earlier) as a subspecies, *H. sapiens sapiens*. The discovery of evidence for

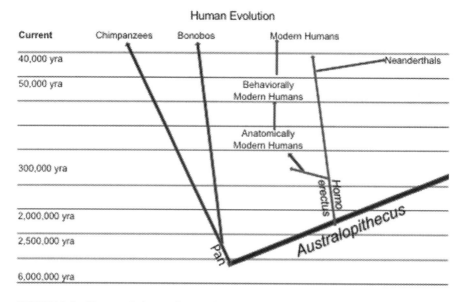

FIGURE 2.1 Human phylogenetic tree featuring main primate groups and how long ago they appeared.

Ethics Biology: Are There Ethical Genomes?

communication and the use of somewhat sophisticated tools have led to this designation. About 13,000 years ago after the last Pleistocene ice age species members in the "fertile crescent", a southern region of the Eurasian continent with a combination of climate, animals and plants relatively easy to domesticate, began to form social groups (tribes, etc.) that eventually became civilized (Diamond, 1999).

The common ancestry of humans and other primates provides a source of subjects on which experiments may be performed without violating any social codes such as the Helsinki Declaration. Since the genome of chimpanzees is the closest to that of humans and is only 4% different (DNA sequences are only 1.24% different; Marquès-Bonet et al. 2009), this species is the most likely to share conserved genes present in the ancestor that was common to both species.

Given this basis for expecting to shed light on human moral/ethical behavior with observations on primates, we need to define a specific moral/ethical behavior that chimpanzees and humans share. The most studied of this type of behavior is altruism, which is defined by the *Oxford Dictionary of Philosophy* as "Disinterested concern for the welfare of another, as an end in itself" (Blackburn 1994). It must be stressed that the structure of this "concern" and its similarity to what you feel when someone close to you gets hurt is not known. Unfortunately, the nonhuman subject cannot describe it.

When Charles Darwin formulated his theory of natural selection as the mechanism driving evolution, he assumed that all individuals act selfishly. When he tried to explain the behavior of social animals such as ants and bees, he could not fit them into his model. He never solved this paradox. E.O Wilson, the father of sociobiology (he specializes in ants), took up the problem without apparent success until a paper was published in 1964 by William Hamilton. Hamilton developed a mathematical model explaining the existence of altruism in social animals. His model is known as "Hamilton's rule" and its core equation as the "Altruism equation" (Hamilton 1964a, 1964b). It predicts that individuals will help others as a function of their genetic connection to them, that is, the likelihood of help is greatest when the genetic connection is close. This approach certainly explains tribal behavior where the members of a tribe are related.

Hamilton's rule and other cooperative behavior models have been incorporated into models of more complex behavior, using algorithms we call "game theory" (Axelrod and Dion 1988). The traditional starting point for game theory models is the prisoner's dilemma game:

> A crime has been committed. Two suspects have been arrested. Police are interrogating them in separate rooms, assuring they have no contact with each other. Besides, "I'm innocent", the suspects have two choices for answers that do not accept full burden for the crime: 1) "Defect", say the other suspect is the only guilty one. 2) "Cooperate", say nothing. If both suspects cooperate (say nothing) the police have sufficient circumstantial evidence to jail each for a year. If both defect, they go to jail for three years. Finally, if only one suspect defects, but his partner remains silent, the defector walks away a free man, but his partner goes to jail for five years.

If you were one of the prisoners/suspects, which path would you choose? At first glance, the prisoner's dilemma does not qualify as a moral/ethical problem. There is

38   Ethics for Bioengineering Scientists

no option allowed in the boundary conditions to simply take the blame alone (this might make sense if they were "blood" brothers, in accordance with Hamilton's rule) or share the blame. But there is a choice to be made according to some "criminal" code of ethics (e.g. "honor among thieves", an artificial substitution for Hamilton's rule). In this case, the altruistic choice between blaming the other and saying nothing would be to protect the other prisoner by saying nothing. Assuming that both are guilty, the altruistic choice turns out to be a dishonest choice.

In the 1990s, sociobiologists, anthropologists, primatologists, psychologists, etc., came together to form the field of evolutionary psychology to cooperate in detecting patterns indicating the evolution of altruism and other moral/ethical behavior. Of primary interest was evidence from animals closest to humans that were studied by primatologists such as Jane Goodall and Frans de Waal. Goodall performed her studies primarily in the natural habitat of her chimpanzees while de Waal performed more controlled studies in primate research centers. The next section presents an example of a Goodall-type observation.

2.5   ETHICAL/MORAL BEHAVIOR IN NONHUMAN PRIMATES (FROM DE WAAL 1997)

Mozu was a female macaque that lived in Jigokudani Park in Japan. She had neither hands nor feet due to a congenital malformation, but managed to keep up with her troop through the snow of winter and challenges of other seasons. She was sufficiently competent to have raised five offspring. She survived, unattacked by other members of her troop that could easily have killed her, until one spring when the troop reached a population level that triggers splitting ("fissioning") in this species.

Macaque society is matriarchal, being ruled by a cadre of alpha females. Fissioning is a society split that results in a dominant group, containing all the alpha matriarchs and a submissive group led by subordinate matriarchs. Mozu's family was pushed into the subordinates who were forced away from the park's feeding center by the dominants, and faced near-starvation conditions. At some point, Mozu decided to make overtures to members of the dominant group, violating her instinctual ties with her own family. She targeted peer females, those she had been familiar with during her nine years prior to fissioning. She endured attacks from dominant matriarchs while lurking at the periphery of their territory, and attempting to groom them. Grooming is a universal bonding behavior in primates. Gradually, the peer females allowed her to groom with her fingerless hands, accepting the poor quality of the effort. Finally, the peer females returned grooming behavior and offered protection, completing the social bond that marked her integration into the dominant group.

Mozu was able to elicit acceptance by her fellow monkeys by providing them with grooming of obviously poor quality. The fact that poor grooming quality did not prevent acceptance by the hosts creates an enticing basis for interpreting host behavior in human terms. However, we interpret it, there is an acceptance process taking place that needs explaining. Each interaction in this example is a step in the formation of some kind of bond. Mozu's behavior, over time, exceeds some reward threshold for the dominant females and as a result of their feedback to Mozu, a form of cooperation develops between the participants. It includes no apparent

Ethics Biology: Are There Ethical Genomes? 39

expectation on the part of the recipient for immediate repayment, or in the case of Mozu, mercy. In other words, one individual gives benefits to another—on a given occasion—without immediate reciprocal payback from the benefactor. This behavior is called "reciprocal altruism" and has the following characteristics:

1. The exchanged acts, while beneficial to the recipient, are costly to the performer.
2. There is a time lag between giving and receiving.
3. Giving is contingent on receiving, even if the gift is not of high quality (de Waal 1997).

The cooperation works because some characteristic of the performer seems to "expect" reciprocation. The term "expect" is in quotes, as should be the case for all behavioral terms in this chapter, because there is a danger the observer/casual reader will interpret the behavior anthropomorphically, that is, as having motive equivalent to that of humans (a misunderstanding common in pet owners).

2.6   THE KEY TO ETHICAL MOTIVATION IS THAT WHICH IS VALUED

What was the form of motive that drove Mozu's peers to accept her as a member in spite of the minimal value she appeared to contribute to the troop? The key word here for evolutionary psychologists is "value". Being careful to avoid equating the thought processes associated with the response, we can venture to say that, like a human group, a macaque troop would accept Mozu because she provides something of value. A human may accept another handicapped human because it makes him/her "feel humane", a valued emotion. Acceptance many be at a "lower" level as well. As an example of providing value, Mozu might have developed a greater sensitivity to sound because her handicap required that she react sooner to predators. She could help the troop by sounding an alarm before the others were aware of any danger. It is logical to assume that value at this lower level of acceptance appeared in primates before higher level motivators. Certainly, humaneness would be classified as a moral/ethical motivator. But we have no evidence for a human-level quality of motivation for nonhuman primate behavior that mimics our humaneness. Accordingly, the moral behavior they exhibit is called *proto-morality*.

The key evolutionary question for us is at what point during the past six million years did such proto-morality appear? Was it "punctuated" (some evolution occurred in jumps) or gradual? If gradual, what were its intermediate forms? Since we have no direct way of answering these questions, evolutionary psychologists have set up conditions for the development of morality. These may be considered necessary initial conditions regardless of species.

1. "**Group value**: Dependence on the group for finding food or defense against enemies and predators
2. **Mutual aid**: Cooperation and reciprocal exchange within the group
3. **Internal conflict**: Individual members have disparate interests" (de Waal 1997).

Once these conditions are established there is "environmental pressure" on all members of the social population for conflict resolution. Since natural selection determines which genes successfully respond to environmental pressure, it drives the evolution of the subject social species. Resolution occurs at two levels:

1. "**Dyadic level**: One-on-one interaction between individuals, such as direct reciprocation of aid and reconciliation following fights
2. **Higher levels**: Community concern, or care about good relationships between others, expressed in 1) mediated reconciliation, 2) peaceful arbitration of disputes, 3) appreciation of altruistic behavior on a group wide basis (indirect reciprocity), and 4) encouragement of contributions to the quality of the social environment (The last two may be limited to human moral systems; the first two are more widespread.)" (de Waal 1997).

2.7 THE BIOLOGICAL STRUCTURE OF MORAL/ETHICAL BEHAVIOR

Evolution has produced the requisites for morality: a tendency to develop social norms and enforce them, the capacities of empathy and sympathy, mutual aid and a sense of fairness, the mechanisms of conflict resolution, and so on. Evolution also has produced the unalterable needs and desires of our species: the need of the young for care, a desire for high status, the need to belong to a group, and so forth. How all of these factors are put together to form a moral framework is poorly understood, and current theories of moral evolution are no doubt only parts of the answer. (de Waal 1997)

What do we look for in primates that would indicate proto-morality? de Waal has specified certain minimum tendencies. But the scientific reader needs to be alert to his flirtation with anthropomorphism, such as de Waal's use of the term "empathy".

"Normative-Related Characteristics
1. Prescriptive social rules
2. Internalization of rules and anticipation of punishment*

Reciprocity
1. A concept of giving, trading, and revenge
2. Moralistic aggression against violators of reciprocity rules

Sympathy-Related Traits
1. Attachment, succorance, and emotional contagion
2. Learned adjustment to and special treatment of the disabled and injured
3. Ability to trade places mentally with others: cognitive empathy*

Getting Along
1. Peacemaking and avoidance of conflict
2. Community concern and maintenance of good relationships*
3. Accommodation of conflicting interests through negotiation"

Ethics Biology: Are There Ethical Genomes?

*It is particularly in these areas...that humans seem to have gone considerably further than most other animals. (de Waal 1997)

de Waal sets up bases for comparison with established human social categories that go well beyond the behavior of other social animals, but may be thought of as ultimate endpoints to which they might evolve. (There is no evidence that evolution is progressive; therefore, we may not assume these endpoints would ever be achieved.) These bases/endpoints are 1) culture (traditions such as tool use and communication handed down from one generation to the next), 2) language (reports of abilities in some primates to exhibit this sophisticated form of communication have become controversial and are now generally considered premature), and 3) politics (alliances, tit-for-tat deals between leaders and supporters, etc.).

As a result of the interaction of culture, language, and politics, each human has a complex concept of his/her relationship with the rest of the living world. de Waal summarizes this concept in the form of altruism. The degree to which each human feels altruistic (i.e. perceives the strength of his relationship to another human) may be represented, for de Waal, by an altruism pyramid, which is summarized in Figure 2.2. The pyramid represents a hierarchy of priorities arranged according to who deserves the most altruistic treatment. The pyramid is an answer to the question "To whom/what am I morally/ethically responsible?" The pyramid is consistent with the altruism equation of William Hamilton (Hamilton 1964a, 1964b).

It is tempting to view all social behavior in nonhuman animals (and pre-civilization humans) as products of natural selection. To do so is to claim that one can find the environmental pressures that drove each behavior's evolution. Darwin would agree with this approach, which has come to be called "adaptationism". Our understanding of genes has complicated his simple model. In addition to natural selection, mutation, recombination, and genetic drift are mechanisms of evolution. There is currently a polemic in biology between adaptationists (mostly evolutionary psychologists) and geneticists. The latter note that any gene may survive without being adaptive as long as it does not debilitate its host (Gould and Lewontin 1979; Gould 1997).

FIGURE 2.2 The expanding circle of human morality represented as a floating pyramid of disks. Altruism decreases (the disk shade gets lighter) as one moves farther away from our immediate family or clan. Its existence depends on whether resources (and affordability) are sufficiently abundant to lift the disk above the altruism boundary. In other words, the moral inclusion of more expansive populations is constrained by obligations to more closely related ones, but aided by increased resources (de Waal 1997).

2.8 CLASSICAL CASE SUPPORTING A BIOLOGICAL BASIS FOR MORALITY/ETHICAL BEHAVIOR

On September 13 of 1848 twenty-five-year-old railroad foreman Phineas Gage (Figure 2.3), while leveling terrain for a railroad track in New England, triggered a blast while leaning over a hole filled with explosive powder. The pointed tamping iron that slipped from his hands was hurled like rocket straight through his left eye, brain and skull. Incredibly, Gage was only briefly stunned. He instantly gained consciousness and was able to walk and talk immediately afterward. The meter-long iron lay in the sand meters away.

Gage recovered completely, retained all elementary mental functions, and remained able-bodied for the rest of his life. His speech was normal, he absorbed new information as before, and he showed no lapses of memory. However, his personality changed. From a pleasant and reliable fellow, popular among his peers, he turned into someone who could not hold a job because he had lost all respect for social conventions. He would lie and curse uncontrollably. Perhaps the greatest change was that his sense of responsibility vanished: he could not be trusted to honor commitments.

FIGURE 2.3 Phineas Gage with the track nail that shot through his brain, exiting his left eye. Image by GL Archive/Stock Photo, courtesy of ALAMY.

Ethics Biology: Are There Ethical Genomes?

According to his physician, the equilibrium between intellectual faculties and lower impulses had been disturbed by the accident.

The neurologist Hanna Damasio and her coworkers recently reported on an inspection of Gage's skull and the tamping iron—both preserved in a museum at Harvard University. They made computer models of the brain damage. Apparently, the transformation from an upright citizen into a man with serious character flaws had been brought about by lesions in the ventromedial frontal region of his brain. This pattern fits that of a dozen other brain-damaged patients known to science who have intact logical and memory functions but compromised abilities to manage personal and social affairs. (de Waal 1997)

There is a close relationship between the ventromedial frontal region, which is limbic and the ACC (Yücel et al. 2007).

2.9 EVOLUTIONARY PSYCHOLOGY AND SOCIAL DARWINISM

What does our new understanding that there exists some proto-morality in other primates teach us about how to solve moral/ethical problems? Not much, beyond some confidence that there is or may be some natural basis for moral/ethical behavior.

It also disproves a hypothesis—not really scientific at all—that led to public confusion about Darwin's theory of natural selection for almost a century. Herbert Spencer, a philosopher contemporary of Darwin in 1859, concluded that societies function more efficiently if governments practice a laissez-faire approach to their economies. After *The Origin of Species* was published, he claimed that those who succeeded in industry, commerce, and social position did so because they were more evolutionarily fit. His mantra "survival of the fittest" became the cornerstone of social Darwinism, a movement embraced by many capitalists, including the so-called "robber barons" who ruled industry and commerce for much of the late 19th and early 20th centuries.

According to Spencer, humans were akin to other animals and should be allowed to compete naturally—within the constraints of civilized behavior—to determine who is most fit. Evolutionary psychologists' discovery of evidence for a naturally inherited moral/ethical tendency raises the expectation that all humans will express the genotype. A geneticist would challenge this assumption as adaptationism. A modern laissez-faire advocate would claim this evidence makes regulation of industry and business unnatural. As we shall see later, Social Darwinism has not disappeared (Hofstadter 1944).

ENRICHMENT

1. To get a sense of how ethical thinking enters daily life problems, view the PBS episode of Ethics in America titled "Do Unto Others". It may be found at https://www.learner.org/vod/vod_window.html?pid=191.

2. Do biological drives play a role in financial decisions? Predictive modeling has won economists a number of Nobel prizes. Two competing approaches to human behavior have dominated the models. One, developed by Adam Smith (1723–1790), the so-called father of capitalism, predicts that people will behave reasonably based on consideration of what is in their own self interests. So, financial activity should be minimally regulated. The other, attributable to Maynard Keynes (1883–1946), asserts that people can be caught up in the emotion of the moment and behave irrationally. So, financial activity should be highly regulated. Present an argument for the approach you favor.

3. Are people basically "good"? A political view, prominent in the enlightenment and at the core of liberal parties is that based on Jean-Jacques Rousseau (1712–1778). He maintained that humans were naturally good, and if presented with the appropriate environment, they would develop into fully cooperative, constructive, and nonviolent individuals. He proposed that a democracy would be optimal for nurturing such development. John Marsh (1947–), citing analysis of the experimental psychology literature by psychologist Steven Pinker (1954–), maintains that humans cannot escape their evolutionary links and, regardless of their upbringing, they will act primitively in appropriate circumstances. Present an argument for the approach you favor.

3 Philosophical Basis for Moral Analysis

3.1 THE EUGENICS MOVEMENT, A GENERAL CASE STUDY ILLUSTRATING THE NEED FOR ETHICAL ANALYSIS

Social Darwinism was not the only social movement inspired by Darwin's evolutionary theory of natural selection. Darwin's cousin Francis Galton proposed, in the late 1800s, that society had created an artificial protection for *Homo sapiens* such that individuals who were otherwise "unfit" could multiply without natural controls and thereby dilute the "germ plasm" of Great Britain. To prevent this from happening, society had to conduct some form of artificial selection ruled by criteria deemed selective for its "improvement". The proposed social engineering movement was called "eugenics" and it spread from the United Kingdom to Europe; and the U.S. Eugenicists, in contradistinction from Social Darwinists, favored intellectuals and professionals over industrialists. It was also anti-aristocratic to the extent that the aristocrats in question did not achieve their status by intellectual pursuits.

Eugenics took two main forms—positive and negative. Positive eugenics focused on policies that would encourage carriers of desirable traits to reproduce more. Negative eugenics focused on policies that would discourage carriers of undesirable traits from reproducing at all. The movement was rather popular prior to WWII and resulted in the passage in the United States of legislation at the federal level to reduce immigration of "undesirables" and at the state level to restrict their reproduction. In some 15 states, this included nonvoluntary sterilization (Cohen 2017). One of the conditions targeted as undesirable in all legislation was "feeblemindedness" (the range of definitions for this condition was so wide that it included genetic, infectious, and traumatic causes). Since the "gene" was not defined by science in general until after 1900, it was difficult for early eugenicists to differentiate genetic from environmental causes of a given condition.

In the United States, the movement penetrated many universities. A number of research papers were published applying statistics to population genetics—a form of epidemiology—in order to predict the risk of certain traits appearing. In addition to feeblemindedness, a host of other conditions linked to race, ethnicity, and even religion were considered genetically determined and undesirable. The prototype for desirability was the Nordic (usually Christian) individual. Among the undesirable ethnic groups were eastern and southern Europeans. Among the undesirable races were Blacks and Asians.

After WWII, the movement lost steam, following disclosure at the Nuremberg trials of the Nazi eugenics program and how it was carried out. Nevertheless, the idea in some form is still favored by many and serves as a lively debate subject. Indeed, bioengineers have provided genetic engineering tools that make social

DOI: 10.1201/9781003197218-3

46   Ethics for Bioengineering Scientists

engineering advocated by the eugenics movement more feasible. The ethical questions "who?" and "how much?" human genetic engineering is desirable still remain. But now advocates of each position have far more facts to choose from when they argue their cases. The question to be addressed in an ethics course is: If one assumes that a eugenics program is of value to society, how should it be ethically implemented?

3.2   MACROETHICS VS. MICROETHICS (HERKERT 2005)

Whatever your answer is to the question just posed, you will have to face the fact that any solution you come up with will be beyond your ability as an individual to achieve. Society, government, or some targeted social group will have to agree to enact a policy that it has the power to enforce. Any ethical problem requiring this scale of commitment is part of macroethics. Solutions to macroethics problems are often political, and may involve legislation. Macroethical cases will be limited, in this text, to the ENRICHMENT sections.

The main text will be devoted to microethics, ethical challenges that depend for their solution on you, the reader. At any scale, one cannot face an ethical challenge without being armed with a definition of what it means to be ethical. Absent such fortification, we are in no position to judge in any logical way the degree to which we are following our chosen moral laws. "Moral law" is used here as a philosophical commandment to act in a certain way. The set of moral laws each of us choose to follow constitutes our "moral vision". Most younger readers of this book do not have a fully developed moral vision. They simply have not been tested enough to feel compelled to develop one. This will change. It is safe to predict that they will face at least one life-changing moral crisis at some time in the next ten years. Those with a developed moral vision will tend to decide, with more confidence, how to resolve the crisis.

A primary goal of this book is for readers to gain tools with which to arrive at moral decisions by applying the moral theories presented. Arriving at a moral decision means choosing an appropriate course of action. Those who have a developed moral vision derived from their religion or ethnic group will find the moral theories presented no more than an intellectual exercise they must endure in order to complete the text. Their moral vision is classified as "descriptive" because it is a set of rules— commandments—they follow without philosophical analysis. Moral visions developed from philosophical moral theories presented in this book are "prescriptive". They have to be reasoned out each time they are applied, and the reasoning will lead to a prescribed action. You have to decide: "Is the course of action being considered consistent with the moral theory?" In this instance, the word "consistent" may be replaced with "justified by". It often turns out that the most valuable quality of a moral theory appropriately applied is that it provides *justification* for your decision to apply it.

3.3   THE CONCEPT OF MORAL THEORY

The most developed form of reason is logic. Nearly everyone is rational. Most people are reasonable most of the time. But few of us are logical on a regular basis.

Philosophical Basis for Moral Analysis 47

One has only to consider our ancestry to come up with a cause for this behavior hierarchy. The source of a formal logic is a philosophical system of thought. It should not be surprising that the Greeks were the original authors of European-based philosophies. As described in Chapter 1, it is from Greek philosophies that we derive a typical structure for a formal philosophy:

1. Ontology, that answers the questions "What is reality?" and "How did it come about?"
2. Epistemology, that answers the question: "How do we know what we know?" and
3. Axiology, that answers the question: "What should we value based upon what we know/understand?"

Ethics is that part of axiology that stresses how we should behave based on what we value. Traditionally, "morality" has been used in place of ethics only when ethics is theology-based. However, the two terms have been interchanged so often we shall not make a distinction. Accordingly, the ethical criteria on which a course of action is based will be called a "Moral theory". A scientist must be careful when using "theory" as defined by philosophers. Philosophical theories are subjective justifications for courses of action. They are not based upon scientific hypotheses, nor are they supported by scientific data. Those ignorant of science will often dismiss a scientific theory as "just a theory". They are confusing science with philosophy. A moral theory denotes a well-reasoned normative proposal. From the many moral theories, we shall study five. So that you will become comfortable in seeing the points of view they represent, we shall practice applying them in as many case studies as feasible.

3.4 MOTIVATION FOR APPLYING MORAL THEORIES

If Hamilton's altruism equation is valid, then evolution has provided humans with few genetic determinants that make us act morally toward those to whom we are distantly related. Yet, you will sit in a classroom and not harm your fellow students. This behavior is predictable partly because you are aware that security officials would remove anyone causing such harm. But you are also aware that your ability to function socially in a civilized population is determined by the degree to which you fulfill a social contract you "signed" at birth. This contract did not contain instructions detailing how to act in every social situation; your parents were supposed to teach you that. Nor did it ensure that you would always obey the laws of your society. You can decide to take a moral position contrary to a given law. Such a position would, however, be risky and require justification to avoid prosecution (assuming you wish to do so).

In this book, we explore nondescriptive tools you may use to make moral decisions that you can philosophically justify to yourself and others. The tools you develop will be constructed as you practice application of moral theories. Intrinsically, a moral theory *stipulates* the following components of behavior

48   Ethics for Bioengineering Scientists

1. How one must behave
2. How one may behave
3. How one must not behave

It also universalizes behavior, that is, proposes that everyone should act the same way in a similar situation. All moral theories have been modified to be more practical by later philosophers. Their more modern versions recognize human limitations and do not expect behavior to be taken to its logical extreme regardless of extenuating circumstances (e.g. one could cause great difficulties by always telling everyone exactly what you think of them).

3.5 OVERVIEW OF MORAL THEORIES USED IN THIS BOOK

Moral theories are generally divided into two camps:

1. Consequentialist
2. Nonconsequentialist

A simple way to think of them is (1) the camp of good and (2) the camp of right. In this case, "good" is best thought of as beneficial. A consequentialist values what is of benefit to the individuals affected by the action being considered. In contrast, a nonconsequentialist values what is right, with little—in some cases, no—regard for how the individuals affected by the moral action will benefit. The assumption for a nonconsequentialist is that if one does what is right everyone will benefit in the long run. A sampling of moral theories is presented in Table 3.1.

Most practitioners of moral analysis are nondogmatic and not strict ideologues about applying moral theories. The five we shall use are:

1. Utilitarian
2. Deontological
3. Contractarian
4. Virtue
5. Feminist

3.6 CONSEQUENTIALISM—GENERAL AND SPECIFIC-TYPE UTILITARIANISM

Consequentialist moral theories evaluate actions in terms of their consequences. As long as a consequence can be shown to be an effect of the action, it will be a valid subject for moral evaluation. The effects that are most appropriate targets for evaluators are nontangibles such as health, enlightenment, happiness, pleasure, or welfare. If the action proposed or committed will lead to or led to the desired effect, it was a *good* choice. "The ends justify the means" would be a consequentialist aphorism. In philosophical terms, an individual who focuses on "ends" is a teleologist ("teleos" is Greek for end/goal). Goodness of an action is determined by how well it achieved the teleologist's end.

Philosophical Basis for Moral Analysis

TABLE 3.1

A Sampling of Moral Theories

Theory	Source of Obligation	Verification Procedure: How to Know What to Do and When It Is Done
	Consequential Theories	
EGOISM	One's own needs are paramount	Act so that consequences will enhance one's personal needs. This is the most natural theory.
NATIONALISM	The nation's needs are paramount	Act so that consequences will enhance the needs of the nation.
UTILITARIANISM	What is good in conduct is not the agent's own happiness, but that of all concerned	Act so as to generate optimal happiness for the most people.
EPISTEMISM	Increase of knowledge is paramount	Act so that understanding of the universe is enhanced by one's actions. Could this be "scientism?" What about artistic "truth"?
	Nonconsequential Theories	
THEOLOGICAL	Supernatural	Act in accordance with religious commandments.
DEONTOLOGICAL	Nature of morality itself; moral principles which are *prima facie* binding on all agents	Act so that the reason for your act is generalizable to all moral agents (as dictated by categorical imperatives).
CONTRACTARIAN	The inalienable rights that persons have by nature, that others must respect	Act in accordance with the rule that each person deserves rights and acquires obligations under contract with others.
VIRTUE	What it means to be a person who makes the right moral choices	Act so as to emulate what has generally been agreed is a moral person.
FEMINIST	Unique needs of females are of equal priority with those of males	Act so as to be inclusive of the needs of females.

The theories in bold are those applied in this book.

Consequentialism has many forms. But the one most used in moral theory applications is Utilitarianism, as developed by Jeremy Bentham (1748–1832) and refined by John Stuart Mill (1806–1873) (Figure 3.1). In Bentham's view, an action's positive effect is its "utility". So, the more the utility produced, the more the good being done. The primary categories of concern for Bentham were "pleasure" and "pain". An effect had major utility if it produced the former and minor utility if it produced the latter. Maximum utility is achieved when all people gain it and minimum if they are denied, that is, are subject to pain. This is a moral requirement.

Starting with Mill, a number of refinements to Bentham's theory have been proposed. Mill wanted the moral individual to be active in his desire to maximize utility for all. In his words, "The happiness which forms the utilitarian standard of what is correct in conduct is not the agent's own happiness but that of all concerned. As between his own happiness and that of others, utilitarianism requires him to be as strictly impartial as a disinterested and benevolent spectator" (Cohen 2004). Other measures of utility have been proposed, including satisfaction of preferences and "desires" (Cohen 2004).

FIGURE 3.1 John Stuart Mill. English philosopher who refined Bentham's act utilitarianism to a form more like its modern version. Image by Everett Collection, courtesy of Shutterstock.

There does not appear to be a consensus on a valid measure of utility among utilitarians. One may apply a cost–benefit analysis to utilitarian moral decision-making. But any quantification depends on the value placed on the utility,

Philosophical Basis for Moral Analysis

which must in practice be arbitrary. How does one measure "goodness" of a consequence?

In actual practice, Bentham quantified the decision-making process in a way that would appeal to engineers. If "maximization of happiness" is the target of the process, one may apply numerical values to all alternative actions and come up with a final sum that reflects maximization. Consider the following example:

> A cousin your age is visiting. Your family expects you to take her out on the town and would be satisfied with a single couple date. Her father is someone you would like to someday use as a reference, so you would like to please him. She would like to get acquainted with your friends, but she is kind of nerdy and they would tease you about her when she is gone. If you didn't introduce her to your friends she would be very disappointed. The morally correct action is the one producing the most overall happiness. The following happiness table summarizes these various effects, listing happiness scores for the main participants as perceived by the individual who must decide the action, you.

TABLE 3.2
Happiness Score Calculation

	Single Couple Date	Date with Friends
YOU	10	-7
COUSIN	-2	10
TOTAL	8	3

In this example, the estimated magnitude of the happiness of the participants determines the goodness of the action. Happiness here is measured on a scale of -10 to +10 units. In other examples, the happiness measure may be based on benefit without regard for the feelings of the participants. The table is reduced to just two participants. It could well be extended to include your family, the cousin's father, and your friends. To simplify decision-making, we reduce the participants to the one being directly acted upon, your cousin, and the actor, you. The others are represented by what you believe would be their pain or pleasure for each choice. These considerations, and any impact your cousin's feelings have on you, factor into your happiness score.

Bentham's utilitarianism is also termed "act utilitarianism". There is another version termed "rule utilitarianism". Rule utilitarianism considers the long-term effects of a moral decision and proposes that rules be developed to guide those making the decision to add to the long-term good. No happiness table can be generated because the people present at the start of an event may not be alive at an end far in the future. A common example of this theory is consideration of the long-term effects on a profession if it stands behind a certain standard. If the medical profession allowed the selling of organs for transplantation, the immediate result may be a greater availability of donors. The long-term effect may be unscrupulous entrepreneurs taking advantage of poor people by treating them as organ/tissue factories.

Other forms of consequentialism define goodness in terms more restrictive than utilitarianism. Here are some examples:

1. Nationalism—The measure of goodness of an action according to Nationalistic Moral Theory is the degree to which it benefits the nation. Thus, the universality of inclusion in the sphere of those one should seek to help ends at the border. According to this view, an act is bad if it harms the nation. Quantification of the morality of the action in question depends on some measure of the degree to which it benefits the nation.
2. Epistemism—From "epistemology", meaning "theory of knowledge". Epistemic moral theory considers the measure of goodness of an action as the degree to which it advances general knowledge. Acts that contribute, on balance, to increase ignorance are considered immoral. Epistemists are not always clear about whether they would restrict knowledge to "under-standing", as in comprehending how things work, as opposed to being able to recite an endless list of facts. Quantification of the morality of the action in question here would possibly be based on some sort of evaluation of those accumulating knowledge, that is, exams.
3. Egoism—Egoistic moral theory measures the goodness of an act by the degree to which it benefits the individual performing it. At first glance, this view appears to be a complete opposite of utilitarianism. It is more limited in scope than nationalism to the extent that it seems to be simply selfishness. It also appears to violate the philosophical requirement of being universally applicable, and, as a consequence, cannot be a moral theory at all. It is ethically stillborn. The argument against this criticism appears to be that an egoist takes care of herself so that she will be in prime condition to help others, which she will do because she recognizes that helping others will contribute to a society that all can benefit from (Cohen 2004).

3.7 NONCONSEQUENTIALISM—DEONTOLOGY

Consequentialism identifies the moral worth of conduct in terms of how well that conduct produces some effect. In this respect, consequentialist reasons are "forward looking". They look to the future in order to determine what a person ought to do. In contrast to this, a nonconsequential moral outlook is "backward-looking" or "present-looking". According to a nonconsequential outlook, an act is right or wrong due to something other than its consequences.

Philosophical Basis for Moral Analysis   53

The purest form of nonconsequentialism is "deontology" from the Greek etymological root, "deon" meaning "duty". Someone who holds this position is called a "deontologist". One needs to be careful about how one interprets duty as it applies to deontology and teleology. It is not true that the difference between teleology and deontology is that teleology sees only consequences as the morally relevant feature of actions, whereas deontology sees only duty as the morally relevant feature. Teleological positions can, in fact, talk about duties. But for a teleological position, the rationale for any duty is itself a matter of an action's consequences. For example, a teleologist might say "You have a duty to keep your promises, because otherwise people won't ever believe what you say." It is the purported *basis* of the duty that marks the distinction between deontology and teleology: according to a teleologist, the basis of duties is the matter of consequences, or effects; according to a deontologist, the basis of duties is the value we must place upon each other.

The reasons for keeping a promise differ between the various deontological moral theories that require it. For example, in Kantian deontology, a promise is kept because the making of a promise creates an obligation and you have a moral duty to fulfill an obligation. In Aristotelian deontology, a promise is kept because keeping it is consistent with the kind of model person you wish to emulate.

Perhaps the rightness of some act depends on the fact that the other party is a relative of yours (present-looking and predicted by the altruism equation). For example: "You owe him special concern, because he's your brother." The important feature to notice is that, unlike the consequentialist outlook, "rightness", the thing to do because it is right replaces "goodness", the thing to do because it will result in good consequences. Nonconsequential views are sometimes expressed in terms of intrinsic value; for example, you should look after a person because of their worth as a person, not because of anything resulting from looking after them. Or, you should look after that person out of respect, rather than concern for anything that might result from looking after them.

3.8 KANTIAN DEONTOLOGY

The most famous deontologist is Immanuel Kant (1724–1804) (Figure 3.2), who argued that morality is a matter of doing one's duty, regardless of consequences, and that duty itself is determined not by reference to consequences but by reference to consistency and the requirements of rationality. Kant also argued that if you are performing an action because of regard for the consequences, then, even if it is the same action as one that could be performed out of duty, the act in your case has no moral worth at all. For example, you should not keep your promise to help your friend paint his home, because you want to make him happy, but because you have a duty to keep your promise. In other words, according to Kant, even though the action you performed—keeping your promise—is what is morally required, your performance of it has no moral worth if your motive for performing it was not that of performing your duty, but rather, of making your friend happy. (By the way, could you ascribe this "motive" to a chimpanzee?)

FIGURE 3.2 Emmanuel Kant. German philosopher who wrote *Critique of Pure Reason* and developed the classical form of Deontological Moral Theory. Image by Science Museum Library, courtesy of Science Museum Library.

At the foundation of Kant's concept of moral law is his "categorical imperative". A categorical imperative is a requirement that is necessary for society to function. Thus, it applies to everyone regardless of their inclination. There are two arms of categorical imperative, "universal maxims" and "persons as ends". The universal maxims establish the basis for imperatives applying to everyone. They are arrived at by postulating behaviors that you would have everyone adhere to—including yourself—because their practice would always be consistent with a moral society. An example of this would be "never lie". The "persons as ends" categorical imperative arm protects individuals from being taken advantage of. It postulates behavior that is consistent with treating all people as ends rather than as means to an end. In the example of Table 3.2, you would take your cousin on a date with your friends because that is what you do with a visiting cousin, not because you will gain points with other relatives for the act.

Philosophical Basis for Moral Analysis 55

3.9 ROSSIAN DEONTOLOGY

In the 1930s and 1940s, W.D. Ross (1877–1971) concluded that Kantian categorical imperatives were often too rigid to be practical. He proposed that doing the morally right thing is basically about doing your duty. At any time, however, there may be a number of *prima facie* duties that impinge on us. A *prima facie* duty is a moral consideration that is a legitimate call on us. Unlike Kant, Ross saw that some of his *prima facie* duties conflict with one another; and aside from that, we simply cannot do everything that would be right. Faced with the competing moral claims on what we should do, we determine our "actual duty" by an intellectual weighing of relevant *prima facie* duties. Ross believes that one of the *prima facie* duties that impinge on everyone is the duty to benefit human kind; the duty of beneficence. (Note that this is an extension of the altruism equation that may be of benefit to the species but is certainly well beyond the more natural clan.) That is, Ross, in effect, characterizes utilitarianism *writ large* as one duty that people should pay attention to—and weigh—in determining what the right course of action is. It is ironic that in explaining the merits of his view, Ross argues against act utilitarianism as being basically counter-intuitive, in that it requires so much calculating that it simply cannot be what people, in fact, do when they are considering a moral matter. He offers, instead, an approach involving balancing *prima facie* duties; and he trumpets its simplicity, relative to that of a consequentialist ethic, particularly act utilitarianism, which if taken seriously, Ross argues, requires an incredible amount of calculation for each choice in order to decide how to behave. But how is one to decide degree of beneficence without some sort of calculation? Moreover, how is complexity being reduced when this beneficence is being applied to each of the *prima facie* duties?

Ross provides a professedly incomplete list of seven *prima facie* duties divided into six categories:

1. Duties resting on one's previous acts:
   fidelity—resting on an explicit or implicit promise
   reparation—resting on a previous wrongful act
2. Duties resting on others' previous acts: gratitude
3. Duties resting on the possible inappropriate distribution of pleasure or happiness: justice—duty to upset or prevent such distribution
4. Duties resting on the possibility of our being able to improve people's conditions with respect to virtue or intelligence or pleasure: directed beneficence
5. Duties resting on the possibility of our being able to improve our own condition with respect to virtue or intelligence: self-improvement
6. Duties resting on the recognition that there is a distinction between helping and not harming: nonmaleficence—duty not to harm others; a duty which is distinct from and more stringent than the duty of beneficence

According to Ross, these duties can impinge on us in any situation. They impinge on us as *prima facie*. At any particular time, there may be more than one *prima facie* duty impinging on us from any of these (and possibly other) categories. At any particular time, there can be a lot of moral "stuff"—and different kinds of moral "stuff"—impinging on us. The resolution of them, in any particular situation, is our *actual* duty. We determine our actual duty by weighing the *prima facie* duties that are applicable on the particular occasion. The result of the weighing—as best we can—is what we then recognize as our actual duty. For Ross, the weighing that we have to do is quite clearly not the one-dimensional quantitative calculation that utilitarianism would urge. (How many "utiles" would be produced by this action, as opposed to that one?) The weighing that Ross has in mind is much more multidimensional.

An individual's responsibility to perform *prima facie* duties is central to their ability to act morally. It is non-negotiable in the moral context. Accordingly, Kant refers to this responsibility as a "categorical imperative". Other members of society as part of performing their duties must give each individual the freedom to do the same. This allowance of others to be free to act in accordance with their own notion of ethical behavior is called "autonomy". Respect for autonomy is a core theme of Kantian deontology and will be invoked in many contexts in this book. Patient autonomy, client autonomy, citizen autonomy, etc., are fundamental concepts in each profession's code of ethics.

3.10 CONTRACTARIANISM

Contractarianism differs from the other moral theories we shall study in that it does not prescribe individual behavior. Instead, it sets up guidelines for societies drawing up rules that prescribe individual behavior. By society, we mean any organized group of individuals, from clubs to legislatures. For the contractarian, the moral values represented by these rules are a function of what all society members would agree to if they were constructing the ruling document. The document is a contract. But it is not signed by all members of the society, and the role of those constructing it is to anticipate what a document that all would sign should contain. Contractarianism is nonconsequential because it assumes that if the contract is drawn up correctly, the actions it prescribes will be the right ones. In contractarianism, what creates the legitimate authority of a state over individuals is their consent to be subject to the state's authority. It is a formalization of the social contract. A philosophical question that arises from this approach to ethical behavior is, "What do we mean by 'consent'?" In a small society, the consent can be direct by vote of all the members. For a state, this approach would be impractical (although it may become possible with total computerization). Such questions are beyond the scope of this text. But one can see how they would come up in any discussion of rules for behavior by members of an organization such as scientific or truth profession societies. Note that we are not referring here to the rules of operation of the society. We are referring to rules guiding personal judgment about right and wrong. Such professional society rules are called "Codes of Conduct" or "Codes of Ethics".

To show how the contract is more than just an instruction manual, we provide some examples. Suppose that a group consents to the obligation to educate all citizens about solar energy. A mere instruction manual would describe how to go about fulfilling this obligation. But an obligation, being a moral contract, answers the question "Must it be done?' In stating the obligation, the group may include a reason for carrying it out. One might be tempted to interpret such reasoning as a form of

Philosophical Basis for Moral Analysis

consequentialism. But if the reason is: "It is morally right to implement such education, *because* that is what the governed have agreed to as a moral value" then the moral theory retains its nonconsequential identity. The group should decide on a particular set of rules for its members *because these rules are what a reasonable group would agree to*. By repeatedly referring to what an imaginary group would do, contractarianism might, it may be argued, form a consequential–nonconsequential hybrid; stating as a consequence what a group would do, but not specifying what the consequence of not taking on the obligation would be.

In spite of all the implication that contractarianism is addressed to groups drawing up "contracts", it is possible for an individual to do the same thing. Individuals can construct contracts that lead the participants to expect certain actions from one another. These needn't be written. The reader has certainly constructed a few. They are still called "obligations". If you agreed to donate blood every three months or drive your elderly aunt to her monthly cardiologist checkups, you have made a verbal contract to do so. The blood bank and your aunt expect you to keep the contract because you freely chose to obligate yourself, and wouldn't do so without meaning it. When I signed on the dotted line, agreeing to pay for a car, I obligated myself to pay.

FIGURE 3.3 John Rawls. American philosopher who modernized Contractarian Moral Theory, introducing concept of "Veil of Ignorance". Image by www.mundiario.com, courtesy of SCRIBD.

58   Ethics for Bioengineering Scientists

Ethicists often distinguish between "duty" and "obligation". The content of an obligation might itself have no moral flavor to it at all. On its own, the content would be morally insignificant. What makes the performance of these actions morally significant at all—and refusing to perform them morally wrong—is the fact that one had an obligation to do them. The obligation promise is a contract. The situation is different for duties whose moral force does not result from special relationships. The duty to help someone in distress does not rest on any special relationship or any contract made between the parties. (It is not part of the social contract.)

A contractarian way of conceiving of moral value and what makes actions right or wrong has to do with how the contract is set up. In a contractarian relationship, there are actually two sets of requirements: (1) the overall requirement to follow certain rules in setting up the contract and (2) the rules of the contract itself. But we do not refer to these rules as duties in the same sense that Kant or Ross does. To avoid confusion, we shall avoid the word "duties" in discussions of contractarianism. The two main rules for #1 are (a) to include two forms of justice and (b) to formulate the rules under a veil of ignorance.

Philosophers associated with contractarianism include names most citizens of the United States know quite well. Locke and Rousseau are famous for their influence on framers of the Declaration of Independence and Constitution. The latter is, of course, a contract between the government and its citizens. It establishes individual rights and the system that assures them, which we call justice. Contractarianism defines two kinds of justice—distributive and retributive. Distributive justice lays down "rules specifying the just distribution of benefits and burdens: the outcome in which everyone receives their due" (Blackburn 1994). Retributive justice seeks to "balance an injustice by rectifying the situation, or by regaining an equality that the injustice overturned" (Blackburn 1994). Legislatures are charged with developing the laws that implement these two forms of justice. The executive branch enforces the laws and the judicial branch decides if enforcement is just ("just" means "agrees with the Constitution". It has nothing to do with "fairness"). These concepts are discussed more fully in Chapter 13.

A critical foundation for formulating these laws is a concept articulated by John Rawls (1921–2002) (Figure 3.3) termed "veil of ignorance". Rawls described a mindset that any legislator must have if he/she is to propose a truly just law. The legislator must act as if he/she is ignorant of the existence of different races, ethnic groups, nationalities, genders, etc., so the resulting law will be totally unbiased. The law must be written as being best for all *humans*. Application of this concept is not limited to legislation. For a contractarian, any contract involving client and professional should be drawn up under a veil of ignorance.

3.11 VIRTUE ETHICS

Since the 1970s, there has been a revival of "virtue ethics", a conception of ethics that dates back to Aristotle. Virtue ethics stresses qualities of an individual that put her in a position to act morally, whether after weighty deliberation or quick reaction. This view of ethics focuses on the character of the person performing the action, and rejects the idea of dealing with moral problems by applying the correct

Philosophical Basis for Moral Analysis

theory, at least in any mechanical or algorithmic way. Rather, a person will make the right moral decision because they are a *moral person*; that is, one with the requisite character. It should be obvious to anyone who has followed political campaigns that this measure of a candidate has become popular. Rather than "What should I do?" the central question for a virtue ethics approach is "What kind of person should I be?" Moral behavior, for a virtue ethicist is not a conscious and conscientious application of moral theory to practical situations. It is what a model moral person would do. By making a person who has a known moral vision one's reference, one avoids the time-consuming process of reasoning out how a moral theory applies to a given situation. In a situation where there is too little time to use a moral theory to decide how to behave (a pedestrian runs in front of your speeding car. Should you hit him or smash into a parked car?), it isn't practical to stop and reason. Virtue ethics disputes those who think that all ethical responsibility is removed if one hasn't time to make calculations of a utilitarian kind? Virtue ethics is not just about speed, however. And virtue ethics is not a view according to which moral decision-making becomes automatic or easy. More importantly it is about where the guiding moral principles or bases for decision-making come from, and what their authority is.

According to the moral theories discussed thus far, the authority, or basis, of decision-making rests with the appropriate principle: If you are a utilitarian, then the principle of utility is the basis on which moral decisions are to be made. The theory is applied to a situation in a way that is "outside-in"; that is, it comes from the "outside". If you are a deontologist, duties are imposed outside-in from universal maxims. If you are a contractarian, rules for creating a contract are imposed outside-in from constraints like "veil of ignorance".

A virtue ethicist tends to view authority differently. Here, the process of moral decision making is more "inside-out". Moral behavior should be the result of, and flow from, a person's character. This is not to say that moral behavior is only automatic or spontaneous. It can indeed involve difficult and perplexing thinking and deliberation. But, in virtue ethics, a person's character (the kind of person they are) is integral to the way that person will perceive ethical situations and the way that person will think about ethical matters. Cultivation of an ethical person, then, is very largely a matter of developing the right character. Here, ethics is not just a matter of what people *do*, or even, to a large extent, of *why* people do what they do (i.e. what their motives are); it is, rather, a matter of what people *are*.

Traditional virtue ethics is only in a limited sense an "alternative" or "in opposition" to consequentialism and deontology. Consequentialism and deontology are both views about what makes moral acts good or right. For the most part, virtue ethics is a view about how to go about achieving whatever it is that gives something moral worth, whether it is the production of desired consequences or adherence to a high priority deontological feature of the situation. A virtue ethics approach is one that focuses on the qualities of the virtuous characteristic that is the target for development. These qualities, which contribute to the character of the individual, will lead that individual to morally correct behavior. In other words, virtues are virtues for some reason, and depending on a person's moral outlook, that reason will be understood to be consequential, deontological, or some combination of the two.

60   Ethics for Bioengineering Scientists

Virtues are useful aids toward doing that which is morally desirable on other grounds. According to the interpretation used here, virtue ethics does not place any significant value on the distinction between what people do (or why they do it) and what people are. There is nothing special about the value of virtues, except as instruments for guiding people to act in a morally desirable way.

As an example, suppose that, on utilitarian grounds, it is a good thing if a person gives up their seat on a bus to someone who is elderly, say a university professor. The requisite utilitarian calculation will reveal that more utility is produced by younger people relinquishing their seats to older people. If one decides that they should habitually give up their seats to an elderly person because the virtue "politeness" is a moral characteristic of a cultured person, then they have developed a virtuous *habit*. It would also be a habit that one would want to instill in one's children.

How does one resolve a situation in which two virtues vie for primacy? Aristotle's *doctrine of the mean* decrees that any virtue taken to its logical extreme destroys the value of the virtue. Bravery is virtuous, but foolhardiness is too extreme to be virtuous. It should be evident that the *doctrine of the mean* serves the same function in virtue ethics as "weighing" serves in Rossian deontology.

3.12   FEMINIST ETHICS—THE ETHICS OF CARE

It is estimated that sex, actually haploid evolution, appeared about 1.5 billion years ago (Stearns 1987). With the evolution of haploid cells from different organisms, sexual reproduction was established as a mechanism for reconstructing the diploid state. This recombination process enhanced gene mixing and speeded up the formation of new species by creating a greater variety of organisms. It is doubtful that beings as complex as mammals would have evolved without sexual reproduction. As organisms became multicellular, sexual dimorphism evolved, establishing a norm of two sexes, male and female. Multicellular organisms produced haploid cells in specialized organs and evolved an action, coitus, that brought the male and female haploids close enough to fuse. Coitus does not enhance survival of an individual. In fact, it places animals in danger because they are distracted and subject to surprise by predators. The sex drive is the only basic drive with this contradiction. Natural selection produced sex drives that overcame normal fears from the other drives sufficiently to ensure that coitus occurred. In males, the libido, an adaptation driven by the hormone testosterone, evolved. A behavior pattern of competing with other males for access to females became part of this adaptation. In higher females, a number of hormones associated with being receptive to males, maintaining pregnancy and nurturing offspring, evolved. A parallel behavior pattern with tactics geared toward keeping the male committed to the relationship after coitus also evolved. This adaptation was naturally selected by environmental pressures that made sharing offspring care crucial for species survival, especially, as is the case in humans, when newborns are vulnerable for an extended period. They could more easily be defended by two than by one parent. This was the state of human sex-related evolution before civilization. To date, no genetic changes

Philosophical Basis for Moral Analysis

consistent with further evolution of sexual relationships in humans appear to have been confirmed.

To understand the arguments for feminist ethics, we need to take a closer look at the varied role of females in primate and civilized societies. Aside from behavior associated with the fact that females bear young and nurse them, the historic role of females in primate social structures is not constant. Chimpanzees, the species genetically closest to *Homo sapiens*, are patriarchal. Bonobos, the next closest, are matriarchal (de Waal 1997). There are a number of human matriarchal societies, like the Hopi and Iroquois tribes of our own country, as well as groups in South America, Asia, and the Pacific Islands (Goettner-Abendroth 2012). Observations of behavioral differences between Chimpanzees and Bonobos would lead a casual observer to expect that human matriarchal and patriarchal societies have different moral visions. Feminist Ethics arose in traditionally patriarchal western society because the feminists asserted that this expectation was true, and it put women at an unfair disadvantage (Gilligan 1982).

As seen by feminist ethicists, the society created by American independence appears to have exacerbated the disadvantage. The American Revolution introduced a form of government that redefined society. Before the Declaration of Independence, emperors, caliphs, kings, dictators, and pharaohs ruled people that related with one another within various classes in a very personal way. The U.S. constitution set up a society in which laws passed by a free people were administered by a dispassionate elected government that did not interact in any personal way with the governed (Ingold 1998). In a personal society, women, even though they had no suffrage, could influence their treatment through personal interaction. In a constitutional society, they had to be treated as the law dictated. Until suffrage, this usually resulted, ironically, in women having less control of their lives than they had before "independence". Feminist ethicists view the "egalitarian" contractarian society that grew out of the constitution as having ignored—through its veil of ignorance—the particular needs of women.

Accordingly, some feminist philosophers such as Carol Gilligan (1936–) (Figure 3.4) have proposed that there is a need for a re-conceptualizing of the nature of ethics. In particular, ideas of universalization and impartiality, which, as stated earlier, are formal requirements for a moral opinion being valid, are considered by feminist ethicists as being too limited. They should be replaced by "relationships", "conversations", and "voice". This viewpoint certainly deviates from the popular notion, if one can judge from media coverage, that feminism, and therefore feminist ethics, is about specific social issues, such as abortion, sexual harassment, employment, and advancement discrimination in professions and the workplace; rather than general moral theory. The tradition-minded might think such women's issues would perhaps be addressed by Contractarianism, particularly by laws dealing with gender discrimination. To the contrary, such laws are seen as merely scratching the surface of the real need, which is to recognize the psychological and, consequently, social characteristics unique to women (Gilligan 1982).

FIGURE 3.4 Carol Gilligan. American psychologist who developed the "Ethics of Care" Feminist Moral Theory. Image by Neil Turner, courtesy of ALAMY.

Relationships and caring are seen by some feminist ethicists, as very important and at the core of ethics. If this is so, universalization and impartiality as requirements of an ethical opinion are problematic. The requirements of universalization and impartiality seem to insist on even-handedness (i.e. treating everyone the same and no one is special), detachment, and judging from an appropriate arm's length. More traditional views of ethics, which stress these aspects, have been characterized as an ethics of strangers, in contrast to a feminist perspective, according to which, an ethics should be about nurturing, preserving, and having appropriate regard for relationships. Since personal relationships vary, given Hamilton's rule, some people must be regarded as special from a feminist ethics point of view.

Feminist ethicists see traditional notions of an "ethical theory" and then "argument" from theory as failing to appreciate the total environment of thinking about ethics, ethical discussion, and ethical interaction. Rather, conversation is considered to be a richer way to conceive of these things and should be our way of engaging each other about ethical matters. Carol Gilligan introduced the idea of "moral voice", in contrast to the idea of moral theory (Gilligan 1982). People talk, that is, they have conversations, which have hues, nuances, and alternative perspectives. People tell stories. This is the way that they provide accounts. Personal communication is the way that most people convey their viewpoints and communicate their perspective, or their take on an ethical situation. The notion of a philosophical "argument", consisting of a series of premises, and a conclusion that "follows" from

Philosophical Basis for Moral Analysis

those premises, where "therefore" is the appropriate signifier of the right inference one should draw, is seen to be an inadequate way to conceive of our ethical interaction with each other.

In Gilligan's view, moral theories from Western (European primarily) philosophies generate duties and rules that do not allow for differences between men and women that stem from biology, and, ultimately, psychology. Customarily, women who bear and nurture children are not free to spend as much time at work as men do. They are also impelled by nurturing—if not naturally—to be less self-centered than their male partners. Physiological differences lead to unique illnesses, both physiological and psychological—many linked to reproductive function—foreign to men. For women not taking chemical contraceptives, menstrual cycle effects, pregnancy, and breast feeding will severely impact work commitment, and, thereby, advancement.

Post-partum life brings on the challenge of child rearing that has traditionally been relegated to mothers. While some fathers, in a number of Western countries, have taken on more responsibility for child rearing, in a number of cases because the mother is the only one employed, the impact of such arrangements remains minor. If the incidence of male participation in child rearing grows, Gilligan's proposals may attract more male supporters. Specific work-related changes that may result from such support would include length of sick leave or time off post-partum, and health plan coverage.

3.13 CRITIQUES OF THE FIVE MORAL THEORIES

Anyone who fully investigates each of the moral theories presented will find significant criticisms that show clearly how difficult it would be to base their behavior on a single system. The reader is encouraged to take the plunge. Our challenge in this book is to perform moral analyses from the point of view of each one.

The ultimate criticism of these moral theories is that they and any other moral theories we may conjure up are unnecessary. The idea is that universal standards for ethical behavior are unnatural and would never be agreed to by all peoples. Therefore, everyone should be left to make up their own ethics based on what they value. This is *subjective relativism*.

It is difficult to philosophically argue against subjective relativism because it isn't really a structured philosophy. Rather it is a practical assertion. Newton (2004) points out the difficulty of a philosophical defense. Since the theory denies the existence of a philosophy that can be agreed to by all parties, it disqualifies any "universally applicable" philosophical defense (e.g. deductive logic). Another flaw of the theory is exposed when it is put into practice. How can two individuals, to say nothing of a group, interact with trust if their moral visions are so different that their behaviors are unpredictable and potentially in conflict? Unless one overpowers the other—and by extension the whole group—the projected consequence of applying this would produce chaos or a dictatorship.

64   Ethics for Bioengineering Scientists

ENRICHMENT

Thought Problem

1. At this point, it would be instructive to apply your understanding of consequentialist and nonconsequentialist thinking. Compose two arguments, one on each side answering the question: "Is the Golden Rule consequentialist or deontological?

Eugenics Debates

2. The general goal of any eugenics program is to alter the natural direction of genomes of a specie's population so that it tends to drift in a desired direction. Toward this end, over the past 13,000 years, wolves have been bred into tamable dogs, wild animals into productive farm animals, and wild plants into crops. Two eugenics categories are currently subjects of great debate: (a) human eugenics and (b) nonhuman eugenics.

   a. Human eugenics: The negative eugenics programs that led to involuntary sterilizations are no longer legal in the U.S. Abortion, contraception, and elimination of defective embryos from in-vitro fertilization are current remnants of negative eugenics, although their application is not sufficiently organized to be called a program. Positive eugenics programs have taken such forms as collecting desirable ova or sperm for artificial insemination, surrogate implantation, or in vitro fertilization; or altering the genes of individuals from zygotes to children. With the advent of epigenetics and the Clustered Regularly Interspaced Short Palindromic Repeats(CRISPR)-Cas9 gene editing scheme, it is now possible to engineer nucleotides in target cells to alter genes in chosen directions. Some parents would like to design their idea of a "perfect child" by genetically engineering their progeny. Arguments in favor tend to focus on respect for individual liberty or improvement of society. Arguments against tend to focus on diversion of health resources or unintended consequences or impact of "super humans" or liability.

   Proposition: *CRISPR-Cas9-type genetic engineering of genes not connected with a life-threatening genetic disease should be legal and sanctioned by the medical profession.*

   b. Nonhuman eugenics: Organisms genetically modified by humans have existed since plants and animals were hybridized by the first civilizations. Modern genetically modified organisms (GMOs) are produced by more sophisticated techniques, including editing with CRISPR-Cas9. A debate

Philosophical Basis for Moral Analysis

65

about all GMOs would be too unfocused to understand because there are too many animal, bacterial, and plant species to discuss; and some are more controversial than others. GM food plants are sufficiently in the news to provide material for a lively debate. Arguments in favor tend to focus on increased yields alleviating world hunger or more nutritious plants improving world health or a lack of evidence for the plants harming humans or the ecosystem. Arguments against tend to focus on lack of evidence that (1) the plants have no deleterious health effects, (2) the new genes won't escape into the environment and be incorporated by other organisms, and (3) making the plants resistant to infection will not lead to highly resistant pathogens.

Proposition: *GM food plants, having passed FDA testing for safety to humans, should be accepted in agriculture and supermarkets without restriction.*

Suggested format for a team debate may be found in Appendix A.

3. In student newspapers at highly academically rated colleges, fertility clinics have advertised for ova donors (they also exist for sperm donors, but rarely). Suppose one of your classmates became a donor and signed a waiver, but afterward had second thoughts about surrendering any right to have contact with the resulting child. If she pleaded her case with you, what would you advise her to do? What if she confessed she lied on her questionnaire about having a close relative with a serious hereditary disease; and you knew the recipient mother. What would you do? Evaluate your choice using each of the five moral theories.

4 Moral Analysis: Deriving a Moral Decision

Once you decide, according to your moral vision, which moral theory is the best one to follow in making an ethical decision, you need to apply the theory. The process of applying the theory is called a "moral analysis". The appropriate behavior is dictated by results of the analysis. This chapter examines the process of applying the theory.

4.1 RECOGNIZING THAT AN ETHICAL PROBLEM EXISTS

Unless it is a simple reflex, any action you take is preceded by a decision. If your action consists of following directions of a GPS in order to reach a destination, you have few mental conflicts, and the success of the venture depends on your skills. If your action will affect the lives of others, and you care about them, you are faced with a "moral challenge" and will wish to weigh the decision in terms of its consequences and/or its consistency with your moral vision values. This chapter is about the act of "weighing the decision".

Moral decisions are made challenging to the degree that they must resolve a conflict between our values. What we value may range from esoteric beliefs such as "sanctity of life" to concrete needs like financial security. Few of us have written out a list of what we value in order of priority. (Why not try it now? File the list and make another one in ten years. How much do you think they will differ?) Even if you have no hard copy of such a list, you use it throughout the day: "Should I be reading this chapter or playing basketball with my buddies?", "I want to get this essay assignment in on time. Should I plan it out so I can allow time to check and attribute references or should I include as many unattributed quotations as I can to impress the grader?" Most of the time your choice has no lasting impact on your future. But the more you accept responsibility as you move into your career, the more your decisions will have lasting impact on your life and those to whom and for whom you are responsible.

More to the point, there will come a time when you will have to make a choice between fulfilling two competing needs, and the one you value most, under the circumstances, will determine your decision. The bioengineering ethics course that led to this text exists because bioengineers, physicians, and engineers have made professional decisions that negatively impacted the lives of others (e.g. approved faulty products, fudged data, or prescribed a medicine because of a financial interest in it) and it was discovered. It is assumed that you are reading the book because you are the kind of person who wants to make reasoned moral decisions of sufficient quality to be defensible in a neutral court of inquiry.

DOI: 10.1201/9781003197218-4

68   Ethics for Bioengineering Scientists

In the previous chapter, we provided five moral theories that may compete for the basis of your reasoning. "May" is the operative term here because you may be guided by a moral theory not included in this text. Otherwise, the procedure you use to weigh your moral decision will be based on one of these five moral theories.

4.2 KINDS OF MORAL CHALLENGES

As noted in the previous chapter, we can classify moral challenges in two scales—macroethics and microethics. Macroethics is usually highly political. It includes subjects such as genetic engineering and organ selling. Debates are a particularly effective medium for moral analysis of macroethics cases, because the alternatives tend to be controversial. They may focus on a specific example, such as allowing an athlete with prosthetic limbs (e.g. Oscar Pistorius) to compete in the regular Olympics. Or they may be general, such as allowing use of human embryos for research.

A debate format is often not practical for microethics, because each individual case may have its own idiosyncrasies that demand the personal attention of the analyzer—you. Microethics case studies often contain situational facts with which the reader can identify and imagine as happening to him/her. We define two kinds of microethics case studies: (1) judgments and (2) personal challenges.

1. Judgments are usually about justice and the law. They state what is just (not "right" or "good"), that is, in agreement with the law. If existing law does not cover the issue being adjudicated, a judge (or group of judges at the state or federal level) must decide what behavior would be consistent with the intent of the most relevant law(s). Here, a defendant may claim that he broke no law because there was no law to break. Once the decision is handed down, it becomes a baseline or *precedent* for future judgments. In effect, a precedent establishes a new law. The adjudication process will be discussed more fully in Chapter 13. The moral theory being applied in the decision is not always clear. We shall try to match decisions with each theory to assess the best fit. An example from feminist moral theory would fit this kind of case study: Before there were laws allowing women to take a paid leave of absence after giving birth, most women used up their "sick leave" for this purpose. Technically, pregnancy is not an illness, so they were violating their employment contract.
2. Personal ethical challenges are situations that call for action that must be decided by a principle participant, the moral agent. In any tutorial on professional ethics, the only ethical challenges of interest are those that have major impact on the well-being of others. Like an observer of a play, the reader would benefit most if he were to imagine himself as the moral agent. We look at four ethical challenge formats:
    a. A format may be completely made up just to show how a conflict may arise (e.g. Ludlum example, below)
    b. A format may be partially made up using a current situation that has not yet resulted in an actual case but has potential in that direction (e.g.

Moral Analysis: Deriving a Moral Decision

Oregon has passed a law allowing assisted suicide with the help of a physician. Some have challenged physician impartiality. An enterprising bioengineer should be able to build a machine that a patient could activate easily, thereby overcoming the challenge, perhaps)

c. A format might be an example of a challenge that you might face some day (e.g. being pressured by your supervisor at a technology company to delete data from one of your experiments)

d. A format might be a study of a convicted perpetrator in an attempt to understand how his reasoning—or lack thereof—pushed him to become a lawbreaker (e.g. the Endovascular Technologies sales representative who, during a surgery that was failing, unlawfully advised a surgeon how to bypass a safety feature of his device to complete the procedure without expanding the surgery.). We often refer to the motivation for "d" as a "rationalization" that drives some individuals to commit crimes (e.g. the "Robin Hood" syndrome)

4.3 COMMITMENT TO IMPLEMENTING A SOLUTION

When one considers the possibility that any given action in response to an ethical challenge may have to be defended in some venue (e.g. a government agency hearing, a court trial, or an academic senate inquiry), it would be sensible to be able to show a reasonable basis for the decision to take the action. A moral analysis would provide just such a basis. Cohen (Cohen 2004) has provided a guide for evaluating the defensibility of an opinion—a moral decision—resulting from applying moral analysis:

A. Impartiality: The decision must apply regardless of the condition of the individual (e.g. being in a state of "depression" is not an excuse).
B. Universality: The decision applies to every human being in the same circumstances. "Same" should not be construed to mean exact. The decision not to cheat on a Bioengineering 10 exam is presumed to carry the same weight for any school exam.
C. Justifiability: The decision can be defended using some moral theory (to show it has a basis in logic, not to show the opinion holder is "right").
D. Overridingness: In the decision-formulating process, moral reasons take precedence over nonmoral reasons; and one moral reason can be shown to take precedence over the others.
E. Non-negotiability: The moral decision must be totally committed to. There can be no waffling.

4.4 BASIC STRATEGY FOR MORAL/ETHICAL ANALYSIS

Deciding a course of action reasonably means developing a strategy for solving the problem. The development process is called an *ethical analysis strategy*. The strategy we suggest is as follows:

70   Ethics for Bioengineering Scientists

A. WHO: Who is/was the person making the decision to be analyzed (name, age, and position)?
B. WHAT: What is/was the decision that has/had to be made (one sentence stating the exact action being contemplated)? This would apply to a policy analysis.
C. HOW, WHEN, and WHERE: Facts only.
   1. How did the dilemma arise?
   2. When did the various events contributing to the problem occur, and when must a decision be reached (or when was the decision reached in a judgment)?
   3. Where did the events contributing to the problem occur?

D. Extenuating circumstances. Facts considered important factors in some moral theories but not in others. This is often referenced to feminist moral theory because its orientation is dramatically different from the others.
E. WHY: According to each moral theory, why should/was an action (be) contemplated or was the action taken? This will apply to a policy analysis.
   1. For a personal challenge, why should/was the considered action be taken?
   2. For a judgment, what was the moral basis for the trial decision?
   3. For a policy, what is the moral basis for taking the chosen path?

4.5 EXAMPLE CASE (ADAPTED FROM ROWAN AND ZINAICH 2003)

Robert Ludlum is a 32-year-old engineer. He has a wife and one pre-school child. He designs tires for Tires R Us, Inc. One day he comes across one of his colleague's designs and notices an important flaw, one that might have life-threatening effects. The colleague now works for a competitor. Because the design of the tires is intended for sports recreational vehicles (SRVs), the problem is aggravated by their higher-than-usual center of gravity. A blowout may cause the SRVs to flip over. He checks his calculations and conclusions with an older engineer in his department who confirms them but refuses to get involved in the case and advises Ludlum to forget the problem because it will cause dissention in the company. Ludlum seeks advice from his supervisor. But she is not convinced his conclusions are right and attempts to set Ludlum's fears at ease. Official company policy allows him to go over his supervisor's head. He has never done this before. Ludlum is convinced his analysis is correct and takes his conclusions, following company procedures, to the director of research under whom the supervisor works and receives the same answer. He sends a memo to the company CEO and has gotten no response for six months. The tire is approaching production. The situation is also complicated because the design of the tires employs a trade secret. Ludlum knows that if he has to go public with this information, he may be required to defend his decision, which can be done only by revealing the trade secret. When he was hired, he had to sign a contract prohibiting him from revealing the company's trade secrets. He fears that even if he convinces the proper authorities that he is correct, he may lose his job.

Moral Analysis: Deriving a Moral Decision

But a lawyer friend tells him of a federal law that protects him and other whistleblowers from retribution.

MORAL ANALYSIS

A. WHO: Robert Ludlum is a 32-year-old engineer newly employed by Tires R Us.

B. WHAT: Should a potentially fatal flaw in a tire about to be marketed by Tires R Us be publically exposed?

C. HOW, WHEN, and WHERE:
1. Ludlum is employed by and is therefore under contract to Tires R Us.
2. Ludlum has analyzed the design of a new tire where he has found a structural flaw that is of high risk for failure.
3. He has advised his supervisor of the flaw.
4. The supervisor considers it a minor problem.
5. Official company policy allows him to go over his supervisor's head.
6. Ludlum has advised the company head of the flaw.
7. The head has not responded for six months.
8. Design of the tires involves a trade secret.

D. EXTENUATING CIRCUMSTANCES:
1. Ludlum has a wife and young child.
2. If Ludlum whistleblows, he may have to reveal a trade secret.
3. Federal law provides some protection from retribution to whistleblowers.

E. WHY: Why should Robert go public. Or should he?

---

1 Utilitarian Moral Theory

For an act utilitarian analysis, Ludlum's decision has consequences for the happiness of **six interested parties**. Put yourself in Ludlum's place and propose happiness scores you would choose.

> a. ***For Robert Ludlum****: He has told the company and they may stop production of the tire. He may be rewarded for his moral judgment or penalized for causing the loss of time and money already spent on the project.*
> [Point value for: reward____, vs. penalty____.]
> If the company ignores Robert's concern and he whistle blows, he would have to violate his contractual responsibility to keep trade secrets.

[Point value for: whistleblowing_____ vs. protecting trade secret_____.]

b. *For the engineering profession: If all the engineers in this situation act according to the profession's code of ethics, its standing in the community will be enhanced. If not, it will be damaged, assuming an account of the results is released.*
[Point value for: enhancement_____ vs. damage_____.]

c. *For the colleague who made the error: His/her reputation will be tarnished if the story is publicized.*
[Point value for: tarnishing_____.vs. non-tarnishing_____.]

d. *For Robert's supervisor: who underestimated an error she should have seen. There may be consequences for her reputation.*
[Point value for: going to higher-ups_____ vs. not going to higher ups_____.]

e. *For the company: Tires R Us, including its stockholders. It is necessary to know what the company values most. If the company accepts Robert's conclusions and the flaw was in the design, the project would have to be halted at least long enough to correct the design. If the company dismisses Roberts's conclusions, he has committed to going public. The company would risk having its trade secret revealed if Robert were asked to testify. A court case could result either if they are sued as a result of an injury or if the regulatory agency becomes involved when Robert whistleblows. In either circumstance, the regulatory agency may impose a penalty.*
[Point value for: time and money lost if company interrupts project _____ vs. insurance/reputation/penalty cost if tires are released and customers are injured _____.]
[Point value for: money lost if trade secret is revealed_____ vs. gain for maintaining high quality product_____.]

f. *For the customers: who would buy faulty tires not knowing of choices.*

[Point value for: possibility of injury_____ vs. money saved due to low cost of tire_____.]

If rule utilitarianism were used for this analysis, the numerical values would be replaced by opposing, more universal rules. For example, would it be good for society in the long run if the trade secret contract were not broken by Robert remaining silent or if the risk of injury was reduced by breaking this agreement? The existence of conflicting duties certainly exists in a teleological analysis.

2 Deontology

The response being analyzed deontologically in this case is carried out by one agent, Robert Ludlum. Accordingly, it is his duties that must be determined as a basis for deciding a course of action. The action in question is "Should he

Moral Analysis: Deriving a Moral Decision

be a whistleblower?" It is convenient to start with "keeping promises" (note the universality) because this duty was a major focus of Kantian ethics. Has Robert made promises that he must keep? If he is a licensed engineer, he has promised to follow all state laws pertaining to engineering. If he is a member of an engineering society, he has promised to follow its code of ethics, which includes (a) respect for clients (Who are his clients?) and (b) avoiding engineering of structures that would harm fellow citizens. As an employee, who has signed a contract he has promised to work for the interests of his company. These interests include the duty of keeping his company's trade secrets.

If we apply the Rossian iteration of deontology, we need to set up the list of Robert's *prima facae* duties that are his categorical imperative:

1. We have alluded to his duties resting on previous acts by citing the contract he signed when hired and any licensing earned from the state. Robert's *prima facae* duties include fidelity to his company. This would mean that he shows loyalty by protecting Tires R Us from an image as a producer of unsafe tires, or it could mean protecting it from competition by keeping its secrets.
2. Does Robert have duties resting on others' previous acts? The engineering code of ethics was set up by the fellow professionals on whose "shoulders" Robert stands. Within the company there may be standards not articulated in the narrative. Perhaps he has some duty with respect to the colleague who confirmed his diagnosis.
3. Duties with respect to inappropriate distribution of pleasure may be in play. If the company sells faulty tires, it will profit as long as they cause no injuries. Perhaps justice was served when Robert went over his supervisor's head.
4. Duties with respect to directed beneficence often imply one individual giving something directly to another, as in the example of making a date for your cousin. Robert does not appear to be involved in such an act. Perhaps the reader considers the company loyalty he would exhibit by not rocking the boat as an example of this kind of duty. Perhaps he would be giving his supervisor respect by not going over her head. This seems somewhat hollow given that he is convinced that she is wrong.
5. Robert's duty to improve himself may be fulfilled by taking the course of action that would most likely make him grow as an engineer. Is that course of action respecting his duty to not reveal company secrets or is it keeping the company responsible to its customers?
6. It is hard to argue against the duty of nonmaleficence when allowing a faulty tire to be sold would risk injuring customers. The Tires R Us stockholders may, however, object to the loss of income resulting from failure of a potentially great-selling tire to be marketed.

74 Ethics for Bioengineering Scientists

3 Contractarianism

If you are planning a career in law, this is your section. Unfortunately, you do not have sufficient training to be able to perform a contractarian analysis using the tools and knowledge of specific statutes available to a state-licensed lawyer. What you do have is an understanding of the social contract and the U.S. constitution (including its Bill of Rights), as well as an awareness of a federal law that protects whistleblowers (discussed in Chapter 6). Robert Ludlum is also required to know the law as it pertains to any engineering license he has earned. As a member of the engineering profession, Robert may be expected to conform to its code of ethics, but he is not contracted to do so. And there is no contractarian categorical imperative requiring such conformation. Robert has signed a legal contract as part of his employment in which he agreed not to reveal Tires R Us trade secrets. If he commits to whistleblowing about the faulty tire design as a result of an unsuccessful appeal to his supervisor's' superiors, he should expect to be faced with having to reveal these trade secrets as part of court testimony. He would then be violating a contract that, if lawful, is based on contractarian ethics.

On the other hand, he has a social contract with his fellow citizens that would be violated—albeit indirectly—by allowing a potentially hazardous device to be sold to them. The specific contractarian rule being violated in this case would be the veil of ignorance requirement that all citizens be equally treated so as to have the same advantages that he—Robert—has in knowing the tires are faulty. Such knowledge would allow them to decide if they wished to take the risk of riding on them.

Another contract that may appear to be in play is state, and possibly federal, law with respect to product safety. The U.S. Federal Trade Commission Bureau of Consumer Protection (FTC-BCP) and Product Safety Commission, and their state equivalents, may prosecute Tires R Us for violation of their regulations. But these regulations operate at the company level and Robert is not in a position of responsibility that can be prosecuted as a result of company officials' decisions. However, these are the agencies to which Robert would whistleblow.

Can you think of other contractarian arguments either way? Which would you follow?

4 Virtue Ethics

The virtue ethics analysis of this case seeks an answer to the question "What kind of a man is Robert Ludlum?" We know some facts about his identity. (1) He is an engineer and therefore a professional; (2) he is an employee of Tires R Us who are his clients at one level; and (3) the tires he designs are for customers who are his clients at another level. If you have been following these analyses and imagining yourself in his place, you would as a virtue ethicist be asking a similar question of yourself. If and when you become the bioengineer you hope to be, what will your character be? If you have "strength of character", you will exhibit the virtues you value. If what

Moral Analysis: Deriving a Moral Decision   75

you value most high is being a man/woman of your word, then you may very well conclude that Robert should not break his contractual promise to keep trade secrets. Perhaps another way can be found to scuttle the faulty tire project, but you will not go over your company president's head to start a process that may very well require you to break your promise. If what you value most high is nonmaleficence you may well conclude that you could not work for a company that did not maintain the highest safety standards. After all, your job is an extension of you. Accordingly, you would have no choice but demand that the faulty design be scuttled or you will resign.

The downside of having strength of character is that it may be so strong others will interpret your behavior as rigidity to the point of irrationality. Indeed, two rigidly virtuous individuals with different priorities are often doomed to be unable to get along with one another. It is not only possible to be virtuous without being rigid but required by the moral theory. Aristotle has addressed the problem of extreme behavior by invoking his *doctrine of the mean*. Those who are able to implement such balance are often called "statesmen". You may wish to bring other virtues into this analysis. At the end, you must decide on a course of action in the present case based on the virtues you value most. What would you do if you were a Robert Ludlum with the virtues you value most?

5   Feminist Ethics

A feminist ethics analysis of this case seeks to answer the question "Which course of action is most consistent with maintaining healthy relationships with the people most important to me?". In Ludlum's case, it is usually safe to assume that his nuclear family is priority one. Since his family is young with children not old enough to take care of themselves, his wife may not be in a position to earn a living should he give up his job, instead of whistleblowing. "And if he whistleblows?" He also has to consider his relationship with his supervisor who will be criticized for not heeding his warnings, should his accusations be confirmed. The CEO who ignored him will suffer a similar criticism. On the other hand, his relationship with peer supporters of his profession's code of ethics will improve as they will consider him a hero for standing his ground.

4.6   ACTUAL CASE EXAMPLE, *JOHN MOORE V. REGENTS*, UNIVERSITY OF CALIFORNIA ET AL. (SUPREME COURT OF CALIFORNIA NO. S006987)

For judgment cases that set a legal precedent, it is moral reasoning of the judges that requires analysis. Since the law is not clear in these cases, the defendant may be behaving in a manner considered normal by her peers. So, there is little concern that

76 Ethics for Bioengineering Scientists

an unethical act is being performed: "Everybody does it this way" is the norm. The Moore case set a precedent and so qualifies as a representative judgment.

The Case of John Moore
Adapted from "John Moore v. The REAGENTS OF THE UNIVERSITY OF CALIF-
ORNIA et al". Supreme Court of California No. S006987
On October 5, 1976, John Moore made his first visit to UCLA Medical Center for treatment of his newly diagnosed condition of hairy-cell leukemia. Upon arrival from his home state of Washington, John Moore met his treating physician, Dr. David Golde. After multiple tests in which significant amounts of bodily substances were extracted from Moore, Dr. Golde verified that Moore had hairy-cell leukemia and had him hospitalized. Little did Golde know that upon observance he would find a rare type of T-lymphocyte that produced an abnormally large amount of immune system regulating proteins called lymphokine proteins in Moore's blood.
On October 8, 1976 Dr. Golde strongly suggested that Moore undergo a splenectomy in order to remove his oversized diseased spleen to slow the progression of the cancer. John Moore signed a consent form permitting the operation. Golde then proceeded to take the formal steps to receive portions of Moore's spleen for further research purposes. Golde did not, however, inform Moore that he intended to use portions of his spleen for further research nor did Golde request Moore's permission for such research. On October 20, 1976, Moore's spleen was removed at UCLA Medical Center.
Following Moore's surgery, Dr. Golde required that Moore return to the UCLA Medical Center for follow-up care and treatments. These treatments included further extractions of bodily substances from Moore. Unbeknownst to Moore, these bodily substances were being used for Dr. Golde's research purposes rather than for medical tests pertaining to Moore's health. Moore made multiple visits to the UCLA Medical Center from his home in Seattle from 1976 until 1983. Dr. Golde also directed Moore to go exclusively to the UCLA Medical Center for treatment because his follow-up treatments could only take place there and under his care.
In 1979, Dr. Golde and Shirley Quan, a researcher employed by the University of California, developed a cell line, a culture of cells that reproduce perpetually, from Moore's T-lymphocytes, now called the MO cell line, without Moore's knowledge. This cell line was commercially important because it could biologically produce lymphokine proteins at a lower cost than the synthetically manufactured lymphokine proteins. Study of the cloned cells over a 7 year period eventually led to the development of 9 patentable pharmaceuticals. Dr. Golde and Quan applied for a patent of the cell line in order to establish and protect their invention of the MO cell line. Early in 1983 Golde had Moore sign a second consent form allowing Golde to use Moore's tissue for scientific research. During the waiting period for the patent, Genetics Institute approached Dr. Golde and the Reagents in order to gain the privileged and exclusive access to the MO cell line in exchange for thousands of shares of its common stocks, high paying salaries and fringe benefits. The transaction took place and Dr. Golde began to receive payment for his invention.
John Moore became suspicious of Dr. Golde's treatment regimen and began to question him about purposes of his visits to UCLA Medical Center. Moore even asked whether Dr. Golde was specifically using his bodily substances for any commercial endeavors. Dr. Golde denied Moore's allegations and discouraged further questions about possible research results. Moore's suspicion reached a climax when in

Moral Analysis: Deriving a Moral Decision

September of 1983 he was asked to sign a consent form that relinquished all of his and his heirs' rights to a cell line or any other type of product that may be developed from his blood samples. Although pressured to sign this form, Moore indicated that he would not give up his rights and proceeded to gain the advice of a lawyer. Golde and Quan were awarded their patent on March 20, 1984 with the Regents of the University of California named as the assignee of the patent. Moore's lawyer discovered the patent and determined it was based on a cell line developed from Moore's blood samples. Moore then took Dr. Golde, Quan, the Regents of the University of California, Genetics Institute, Inc. and Sandoz Pharmaceuticals Corporation to court on thirteen different causes of action including conversion liability, lack of informed consent and breach of fiduciary duty. On 9 July, 1990 the Supreme Court of the State of California ruled that a. Moore had no property interest in disposition of his tissues and b. Golde violated Moore's autonomy by not disclosing his reason for taking Moore's tissues.

MORAL ANALYSIS

A. WHO is the person making the decision to be analyzed?

This is a case that has already been adjudicated. We could try to analyze the ethical thinking of the perpetrator, Golde. If he broke the law we would be analyzing why he took the drastic step of becoming a criminal. But this book is not training you about ways to approach criminal level activity decisions. We assume you do not intend to break the law. It is about ethics that is independent of law. Law is about what is just (however, contractarian moral theory addresses making laws that are just because they are developed in an ethical manner.). Ethics is about what is good or right. The Moore case is important for us to analyze because it took place at a time when there were no laws covering Golde's actions. The judges in this case MADE LAW. That is, they set a precedent. It was their job to decide what verdict was consistent with the laws they had sworn to uphold. But judges have leeway in setting precedent. In that leeway they have room for moral analysis and an opportunity to do what is good or right.

At this point we can learn far more by understanding why Golde was judged as he was by his more ethically learned judges. Then you would have a better idea of what you would face if you were a defendant for an action not clearly covered by law. Accordingly, the "who" is the judges of the California Supreme Court. This judgment occurred in a courtroom so it had to be consistent with existing laws. If it had occurred in a faculty committee, it would have to have been consistent with existing academic standards. The challenge for the judges is to make a moral decision consistent with existing laws that at the same time extended them.

B. WHAT: What is/was the decision that has/had to be made (One sentence stating the exact action being contemplated)?

Was it just for David Golde to use John Moore's cells to establish a profitable cell line without Moore's consent and without compensation?

C. HOW, WHEN and WHERE: Facts only.

1. HOW did the dilemma arise?

a. Moore was a leukemia patient of Golde starting in 1976.

b. M. spleen was removed as part of his treatment.

c. M. signed a consent form in 1976 that designated his tissues be cremated.

d. In 1979 G. developed and cloned a cell line with useful properties from M.'s tissue.

e. In early 1983 G. had M. sign a consent allowing use of his tissue for scientific research.

f. In late 1983 M. refused to sign a consent waiving his rights to clones and products from his tissue.

g. G. and his partners eventually developed nine pharmaceuticals from the cell line.

2. WHEN did the various events contributing to the problem occur, and when must a decision be reached (or when was the decision reached in judgment)?

The relevant events occurred between October 6, 1976 and late 1983. The judgment was reached July 9, 1990.

3. WHERE did the events contributing to the problem occur?

The relevant events occurred at the UCLA Medical Center.

D. WHAT was the judgment?

1. *Moore had no property interest in disposition of his tissues.*

2. *Golde violated Moore's autonomy by not telling him how tissues were used.*

E. Extenuating circumstances

Facts considered important factors in some moral theories but not in others.

1. Moore's family did not benefit financially from his own cells. Thus, their financial burden of caring for him was not relieved.

2. This was a precedent-setting verdict. It gave future scientists greater freedom to use cells collected from patients to perform research and it gave biomedical product companies a financial incentive to develop treatments based on such research.

F. WHY:

According to each moral theory, why should or was the action taken?

For a personal challenge, why should the considered action be taken?

For a judgment, what was the basis for the trial decision?

For a policy, why should a chosen path be taken?

Moral Analysis: Deriving a Moral Decision

1 Utilitarian Ethics

The cost of research would increase if patients had access to profits gained from use of their tissue. Act utilitarians would consider the decision to not grant patients a property interest in this case of greater positive value because it would benefit society. Moore's unhappiness would have a lesser negative value. For the goal of maintaining patient autonomy, the score would favor the decision against Golde. Rule utilitarians would favor the property decision's long-term benefit for society over Moore's loss of profits. It would also favor the long-term effect of recognizing Moore's suffered injustice of not being informed about his tissue's use before signing the second consent form. Maintenance of patient autonomy is of general benefit to society.

2 Deontological Ethics

Golde was using Moore as a means to an end by violating his autonomy and not telling him what the tissue was being used for. By not requiring that Golde make Moore a business partner, the court was rewarding both Golde's duty of fidelity to his scientific profession and his duty of beneficence for other patients.

3 Contractarian Ethics

The informed consent is a contract. However, it does not involve financial claims. Therefore, it does not bind the clinician to surrender information or products resulting from treatment. Golde's behavior was not, therefore, a violation of a contract on this score. He did, however, fail to fulfill the "informed" component of the first consent form with respect to use of tissue.

4 Virtue Ethics

Golde was not honest with Moore. He should have informed him of the financial potential of the tissue. The court decided, however, that Golde was not required to be generous to Moore with profits from tissue products because the greater good was using the profits for more research to benefit society.

5 Feminist Ethics

The results of this case set a precedent that makes tissues and the fruits of their use for research more available for curing patients. The families of these future patients will be comforted in knowing their afflicted relative will have a chance to benefit from these fruits. On the negative side, Moore's family was denied the benefits of sharing in his royalties.

80 Ethics for Bioengineering Scientists

The Supreme Court of California's Decision

The Supreme Court of California concluded that Moore did not have a cause of action for conversion. The court found that Moore could not claim that his donated cells were still his property because he had consented to allow Dr. Golde to perform research on samples of his spleen following surgery. The court also stated that no court had ever "imposed conversion liability for the use of human cells in medical research".

The Supreme Court of California further determined that it would be too great of a burden upon research physicians to require that they know that each tissue sample had been obtained via extensive informed consent procedures before initiating research. If researchers had to obtain this specific information each time that they collected a tissue sample, their progress would be significantly reduced.

The court did find that Moore had not been sufficiently informed of Dr. Golde's financial interests, which may have affected his treatment of Moore. Therefore, Dr. Golde would have to compensate Moore for withholding pertinent information. The four other defendants were not indicted for "breach of fiduciary duty" because they were not physicians and did not owe this special obligation to Moore. The rest of Moore's causes of actions were demurred.

In 1991. Golde moved to the Memorial Sloan-Kettering Cancer Center in New York where he became Chief Physician. In August of 2004. Golde committed suicide. He had been suffering from a terminal form of leukemia.

4.7 A WORD ABOUT APPLICATIONS OF MORAL ANALYSIS IN THIS CHAPTER

Engineers are comfortable with formulas and clear procedures for solving problems. The step-by-step moral analyses just presented feeds into this. But the reader should not forget that *moral analysis is neither engineering nor science*. Its subjectivity dictates that there is more than one "correct" analysis. If you are a student, you will be evaluated on your understanding of the five moral theories as demonstrated by the way you use them in your analysis. Using social relationships to defend a proposed contractarian decision would be incorrect because such relationships are a feminist ethics concern. Using "duty" to defend a proposed act utilitarian decision would be mixing up this moral theory with deontology.

There was no mention of treating data as clients in this chapter. There are two reasons for this omission. First, the chapter was focused on practice in conducting a moral analysis in a way that would make the reader comfortable with applying each moral theory—uncluttered. Second, while applying virtue ethics to the scientist profession would be an obvious moral analysis approach, we believe that the treatment-of-data-as-clients issue should be addressed separately because it deals with the very meaning of "scientist". In other words, the relationship of a scientist to

Moral Analysis: Deriving a Moral Decision

data goes beyond the subjectivity of ethics, to the etymology of "scientist", and therefore carries the weight of being as inseparable as "breathe" and "air".

4.8 HOW WILL YOU APPLY A MORAL ANALYSIS?

As the reader may suspect, there is no perfect way to apply a moral analysis. One can easily substitute the processes described in Cohen's (2004) little handbook. We have chosen a more structured approach as it seemed more "engineer-like". The important goal for the reader is to practice the process enough to become more comfortable with the feeling of using reason to examine a subject so emotional as making a moral decision.

ENRICHMENT

1. The PBS series "Ethics in America" presents a panel format for analyzing an ethical challenge. The host, a lawyer, presents an imaginary case to a panel of experts who weigh in with their opinions of actions to be taken. The first episode, titled "Do Unto Others" explores the role of ethics in society. A number of general cases are examined; reporting cheating on exams, giving money to a beggar, allowing a homeless person to camp out in the alley behind your apartment building, etc. The episodes may be found on the web at http://www.learner.org/resources/series81.html#, and this specific episode at http://www.learner.org/vod/vod_window.html?pid=191. Watch, particularly, Reverend Hehir who often expresses himself in moral analysis terms. Make a list of each of the ethical challenges and take a side, in a short paragraph, naming the moral theory you used for this decision.

2. You are preparing to participate in a protest march. One of the members of your organization, the Trans-Neanderthal Freedom Party, was seriously injured by police at a demonstration in Daytona Beach, Florida, and you are committed to showing your displeasure. Unfortunately, there is a Covid-19 epidemic, and your city has passed a law requiring that you be masked and socially distanced from fellow demonstrators. You are aware that if you obey this law, your voice will be muffled. You have to weigh the consequence obeying the law versus the consequence of spreading influenza, being arrested, isolated, and fined. Assume that you have decided to break the law and use each of the five moral theories to defend your decision.

---

5 Separating Professional from Lay Ethics

We have been examining ethical behavior toward mainly the sources of data for bioengineering scientists (or physicians, or engineers). In this chapter, we examine ethical behavior toward coworkers and clients as persons. While the subject explored is not data, the people addressed are crucial for making the workplace function. If they are rendered ineffectual by the professional reading this text, data integrity may eventually suffer. Moreover, there are laws that protect how these people are treated. Violation of a law usually makes moral analysis moot.

5.1 ETHICS AND PROFESSIONAL RESPONSIBILITY

The ethics one learns as a child guides one's behavior in the direction of "fitting in" to the family. Gradually the fitting in extends to the tribal or ethnic group level. During adolescence, the child begins to experiment with self-guidance and fitting in to peer groups composed mostly of other adolescents. How long this period lasts depends on the individual. At the end of it, some kind of moral vision is achieved. It is rare that the average person's moral vision conforms to any of the five moral theories in detail. While they are simplified to focus on how one individual behaves toward another, they are so broad that it may be too difficult to see how they can be implemented in every situation. How does one define "happiness"? Are there really no circumstances when a "small" lie might be required? Ross saw this problem with Kantian moral theory and made useful adjustments. But real-life situations may include "extenuating circumstances" that confound the average person committed to ethical behavior. We call the circumstances surrounding an ethical situation "context". Two important components of context are (1) the specific situation and (2) the roles that each participant is expected to play by society. Take, for example, a taxi driver and his/her customer. The driver's role is to pick up customers and deliver them safely to their destination, while obeying traffic laws and business laws (such as not overcharging). He/she may be a company employee or be the owner of the taxi company with employees such as secretaries and dispatchers. The customer's roles are to give a reasonably clear direction to the destination, avoid dangerous distraction of the driver, and to pay the fare.

The role of a taxi driver in society is defined by the law and "common sense". Taxi drivers are not thought of as "professionals" because their "intellectual" component is not sufficiently scholarly (see later), nor do they conform to the criteria proposed by Davis (2009). The role of a professional in society is also defined by his/her profession. While a bioengineer, like the taxi driver, may also be an employee or an employer, he/she would operate under a professional code, unlike the taxi driver. The definition of a profession is not set in stone and has been

84   Ethics for Bioengineering Scientists

the subject of polemics. According to Bayles (2003) to count as a profession, an occupation must

1. require extensive training
2. have an intellectual component
3. provide an important service to society.

It would appear that any bioengineering graduate would easily fulfill the first two requirements. Qualification based on the final requirement would depend on the application of his/her training. Working for a software company that produces games is not generally considered to be providing as important a service to society as does working for Medtronics and designing heart pacemakers. (Of course, making an unsafe game would make the software company "important" to concerned parents.) It is the potential risk to the people served by a bioengineer that causes society to be concerned about his/her ethics. And since most bioengineers enter health fields—developing devices/chemicals/procedures for or directly treating patients (a significant fraction of bioengineers enter medicine)—and may be involved in research that receives federal funding, the National Institutes of Health (NIH) have required that ethics courses be part of their training.

If you are a bioengineering student, your training will be so extensive; there is a good chance you will advance beyond the initial levels of employment and become a supervisor. Of course, if you start your own company, you will be an employer. In either case, you will have to address ethical problems associated with the context of playing the role of supervisor. Thus, before investigating the ethical challenges of interacting with clients of your chosen profession per se, we shall consider the nuts and bolts issues of (1) interacting with peers and (2) interacting with those you supervise at a fundamental pre-professional level. It may be noted that business ethics, which includes the financial aspects of a profession and usually applies to owners and CEOs, is not considered here. This decision is not based on any conclusion that it is not important. Business ethics includes economic matters beyond the scope of most bioengineering science concerns.

5.2   LAY ETHICS OF EMPLOYEE–EMPLOYEE AND SUPERVISOR–EMPLOYEE INTERACTIONS

The workplace and the cave as primary sites for human interaction outside family are removed by over 10,000 years. But the basic animal drives, cited earlier, that ensure that members of a species survive and sustain the species have not changed. Also, the employer–employee and supervisor–employee relationships have no counterpart in pre-civilization human behavior because reward for the work done is now deferred. (Cooperation during stone-age tribal hunts resulted in shared food immediately after the hunt.)

The following case illustrates one of the ethical consequences of male and female employees working together under circumstances that wouldn't have existed in the stone age:

Separating Professional from Lay Ethics?

> Sue, Dave, Mary, and John work under the same supervisor at Bioengineering-R-Us. Sue and Dave have been neighbors since kindergarten and have established a close friendship. Both were brought up in homes with relaxed attitudes toward sexual roles. They joke around with each other and sometimes get each other's attention with a playful slap on the butt. Dave is newly married. Sue is not married. Mary and John did not know each other before they were hired. Both were brought up in homes where religion was strong and fundamentalist. They have moral visions consistent with their upbringing and consider physical contact of a sexual nature in a workplace as sinful. One day the supervisor calls Dave into his office and warns him that other employees have complained about his sexual joking, considering it sexual harassment. If it does not stop immediately, Dave will be charged, under federal law, and fired for sexual harassment.

The critical point for a future employee to note here is that two peers involved directly in the behavior being called "unethical" do not consider it so. But the workplace is a community and other workers have appealed to the official in charge to bring Dave and Sue to community standards. The supervisor is constrained to respond to this appeal by a federal (and in some cases state) law known as Title VII. Here is its link: https://www.eeoc.gov/statutes/title-vii-civil-rights-act-1964. Colleges have student and employee Codes of Conduct based on Federal Title VII. They are most certainly online for reference, and the reader who is a college student would be well-advised to become familiar with them, particularly if they have a relevant issue in need of resolution.

An employee is required to unnaturally trust in compensation for services rendered and to not be harmed while rendering these services. Establishing and maintaining this trust is the basis for *fiduciary* behavior by supervisors. Since workers are peers, they ideally have no basis to fear any retribution if the appeal of an employee-vs.-employee disagreement or complaint is decided in their favor. The supervisor, in contrast is in a far different position. He/she is the local government of the workplace community and has fiduciary duties toward his/her "constituents", as summarized in Table 5.1 from Newton (Newton 2004).

There are a number of familiar concepts connected with nonconsequential ethics in the table. Reference to the constitution, legislation, and equality connects with contractarianism. Autonomy is a central concept of deontological ethics. Integrity is a component of virtue ethics. Here is a study case of a common employer–employee situation that may be seen as an ethical problem:

> Helen Whip is the CEO of Bioengineering-R-Us. She has a type A personality and works very hard, expecting her employees to do the same. A much-anticipated order for robotic hands for disabled veterans has come in late with a very quick due date. Helen knows the due date will not be met unless her employees work until midnight. She orders them to do so. Convinced that this job is a test, that if passed will generate a large military contract, she threatens to fire employees not staying to completion of the job.

You should attempt a moral analysis of this case. As you prepare your outline, consider the duties outlined in Table 5.1 and track their origins in the five moral

86   Ethics for Bioengineering Scientists

TABLE 5.1

Fiduciary Duties of Managers/Supervisors

Duty	Examples of Implementation	Grounds, Legal, Moral, and Practical
A. Respect for Rights		
Nondiscrimination in hiring	Affirmative action program	*Legal*: Broadly, the Constitution.
Reward for performance	Scrupulous adherence to contract, fair. and thorough personal records, incentives	Civil rights legislation and court decisions, labor laws, Equal Employment Opportunity
Privacy	Personnel inquiries strictly job-related, no polygraphs	Commission rules for federal contracts. *Moral:* Respect for
Participation in community, exercise of rights of citizens	Noninterference in noncompany related political activity	autonomy, equality, individual dignity. *Practical:* Attitude of respect is essential to foster integrity, initiative, and moral behavior in employees
B. Concern for Welfare		
Safety	Concern for safety: education, regulations, enforcement	*Legal:* Labor laws, OSHA, workmen's compensation,
Health	Maintenance of medical and exercise facilities	income security, and maintenance programs. *Moral:*
Economic security	Job stability, retirement benefits	Altruism, responsibility for those in your care. *Practical:*
Personal and Professional growth	Reimbursement for education, in-service training	Employees increase productivity, reduce
Community participation and recreation	Contribution to recreational and other community activities of employees	absenteeism, and are less error prone when they perceive a pattern of general concern by supervisors.

theories. Keep in mind that technically no crime is being committed in the case as described.

5.3   PROFESSIONALS AS EMPLOYEES AND SUPERVISORS

The topic of employee rights is important in professional ethics for at least two reasons. First, professionals are often employees themselves. Teachers and professors are accountable as employees. Bioengineers as employees, particularly if they are engaged in product development, may be confronted with ethical challenges of national impact. Physicians are increasingly serving as employees, not only of the hospitals or clinics for which they work, but also of the health care companies like HMOs. Second, professionals have employees reporting to them (Rowan 2003).

Separating Professional from Lay Ethics?

"Understanding the nature of and moral justification for employee rights is important if managers of professional organizations are to make ethically sound decisions. These decisions may involve apparent conflicts of rights between different employees, between the rights of the employee and those of the organization, or between the employee and those in other stakeholder groups" (Rowan 2003; e.g. customers and stock holders).

Professionals who are employees and supervisors wear two hats. The employee is like the soldier who is following orders, but must be aware of limits to following orders that may be in violation of the Geneva Conventions of 1949. The supervisor owes subordinate employees a fiduciary obligation. An employee cannot know the thoughts of his/her supervisor and must trust that the latter will not misuse his/her power. Fiduciary obligations are not the same as professional codes of ethics. The former assure subordinates that they will be treated justly by the supervisor. The latter apply to professional activities alone and include clients as well as other professionals.

5.4 PROFESSIONALS AND CLIENTS

In a client–professional relationship, expectations are not like those of an employee–supervisor relationship. Here, trust is being bestowed on someone who is supposed to help the client; and the client is often paying for the relationship. The kind of help provided may range from something as invasive as surgery to the noncontact extreme of financial advice. The relationship may be as direct as physician-to-patient or as indirect as bridge-design engineer-to-driver who motors to work across the bridge. In the latter case, the government agency that hires the design engineer is acting on behalf of the driver, who will probably never meet either the engineer or the bureaucrat (most likely another engineer) most responsible for monitoring bridge construction.

A scientist has a client as well. Many scientists work for companies to investigate problems related to product development, the products are used by clients/customers who trust in their safety and efficacy. But neither the company nor the customers are a scientist's *professional* clients. They may be professional clients of the company's engineers and physicians. (Recall the case of the engineer Robert Ludlum.) At another level, they are the company's clients. In contrast, a scientist's clients are data. As has already been asserted, a scientist's highest priority is data integrity. If data leading to conclusions about product safety and efficacy are invalid, application of the conclusions could be disastrous. (A favorite example of this problem is the conclusion by certain NASA supervisors that low temperature does not significantly affect the mechanical properties of rubber O rings. Failure to correct this erroneous conclusion resulted in the Challenger space shuttle disaster; Feynman 1999.)

In succeeding chapters, moral theory will be applied to specific problems in Engineering, Medicine, and Scientific Research. For the remainder of this chapter, we will explore three components of client–professional relationship common to all three professions.

88   Ethics for Bioengineering Scientists

a. Individual goals that should be accomplished
b. Level of participation in decision making and implementation
c. Responsibilities of the ethical professional

5.5 INDIVIDUAL GOALS THAT SHOULD BE ACCOMPLISHED (ADAPTED FROM FABER 2003)

Part of the reason one goes to a professional is to have the professional probe the problem more thoroughly than the client can do by himself. Does the client need help articulating his problem, listing his needs, seeing the depth and cause of his problem, and seeing a path to reaching his goals? If any of these questions remain, the first object of the professional is to *analyze* the client's requirements.

Often, there are alternative ways of solving the problem available. A person with shoulder pain may be helped by exercise, cortisone injection, or rotator cuff surgery to ease the pain. A professional is familiar with or knows how to research alternative approaches to the problem. Some alternatives solve the client's problem better than others. The patient may find that shoulder exercises takes more time and energy than does a cortisone injection, but has fewer pharmacological side effects. Usually, benefits and harm of each alternative treatment must be considered. Because the professional has expert knowledge, she has some basis for offering the lay person client some advice about these alternatives, too. In any case, the professional owes her client comprehensive *consideration of alternative responses* to the client's need.

Consideration may be an interesting intellectual exercise, but it won't lead to action. At some point, the patient or physician must decide to use exercise or drugs. The client or engineer must decide how hi-tech a planned robot should be. Or, maybe all the alternatives, after much debate, turn out to be unappealing. The third goal of the client–professional relationship is the decision, that is, the *deciding* of which from among the alternatives will be pursued.

Once a decision is made, someone will have to act on that decision. The physician may write a prescription, and the patient may take the drug. The engineer may start working on the design. This fourth goal of the relationship might be termed *implementation* of the decision.

For a client to consider alternatives, and make decisions from among them, he must understand them. Implementing a decision may also require some special understanding, particularly if use of an instrument is involved. Understanding can come from one's own experience of trial-and-error (i.e. an empirical approach), or it can come from independent (library?) research. But one of the most efficient ways to become educated about the subject at hand is to have someone who already has the understanding impart the necessary knowledge to the client, or lead the client to the knowledge. One of the criteria upon which the client selected a particular professional was the latter's depth of knowledge on the subject at hand. Sometimes the professional may not know the answer immediately, but she is expected to know how it can be found. Accordingly, a fifth goal of the client–professional relationship is **education**—typically education of the client, but possibly that of the professional as well (e.g. a patient may present with a previously unreported disease).

Separating Professional from Lay Ethics? 89

5.6 LEVEL/FORM OF PARTICIPATION IN DECISION-MAKING AND IMPLEMENTATION (ADAPTED FROM FABER 2003)

We can discern at least five forms of involvement in the client–professional association that specify level of participation by each party. The form of choice should be the one appropriate for a given set of circumstances. Before we list the forms, let us identify the critical characteristics that make them different:

a. who has to do what
b. why the client should trust the professional.

As shown in Section 5.5, there are five things the client–professional "team" should accomplish. Ideally, at the outset, the team decides who should be responsible for each. One way in which some of the relationships differ is whether analyzing the problem, for example, or deciding among alternatives, is the responsibility of the client or the professional. If the professional has significant responsibilities, her actions will have a powerful effect on the client's welfare. For a particular client and a particular professional, one of these forms will be more *appropriate* than the others.

But how does one determine appropriateness? We shall answer this question in two parts. First, a client goes to a professional to get a problem solved, to have a need fulfilled. So, a client–professional relationship that does the best job reaching this goal would seem the most appropriate. But more than mere problem solving may be involved in a relationship. A quick solution may conflict with moral values of the client or professional. Among the highest of moral values is the autonomous feature *personal freedom*, the opportunity for a person to do as he/she rationally wishes. Moral values cannot always be 100% achieved. Sometimes a choice must be made between two highly valued solutions. So, for example, a parent will limit a small child's freedom in order to protect the child from injury. Clients value having their problem solved. But what if the cost of the solution is the client's freedom to decide a course of action? In general, members of most professional societies advocate client–professional relationships that maximize freedom of the client while meeting the client's need (Faber 2003). Thus, professionals tend to judge appropriateness of a relationship by the degree to which it meets the needs of the client and at the same time respects his/her freedom as much as possible.

With a little better understanding of what distinguishes one form of participation from another and a little better understanding of what we mean by one form being more appropriate than another, we can decide which form fits each circumstance.

5.6.1 THE AGENCY FORM

When you go to a hardware store and ask a sales clerk to bring a plywood board down from a high shelf, because you are unsteady on a ladder, you are entering an agency form of participation in a relationship. The sales clerk does not ask what you will use the board for. You do not ask him. He is acting as your agent to help you, his client, fulfill a specific request. The sales clerk contributes nothing to the transaction beyond his labor. No expertise is required. You have no expectations of the clerk beyond one helpful act. You have expectations of the hardware store. The board must be plywood and not infested with beetle larvae. The cart you place it on must be safe to handle. The forklift drivers who stock the shelves with boards will drive safely. But these expectations are based on state/city business laws and Occupation, Safety and Health Administration (OSHA) standards.

In an agency model, obligation to analyze the problem, consider alternative solutions, choosing a solution, and becoming educated about the process remains with the client. The professional, not literally a professional in the case of the store clerk, has one responsibility, which is to perform the requested task.

A professional may become a client, of sorts, in an agency relationship. He may have the expertise to fulfill his own needs or solve his own problem, but he lacks some other resource—time, perhaps, or physical skill to perform the solution. An architect may wish to build a playroom. She is perfectly capable of drawing up the design, planning the details of construction, and hiring the skilled labor. But she hasn't the time to hassle with the city agencies for licenses and inspection, nor is she physically capable of the labor. So, she hires a contractor and directs him to follow her plans, which she monitors throughout construction. Obviously, this approach maximizes the client's freedom and, if all goes well, fulfills her needs. If all does not go well, however, she has little foundation for finding fault with a contractor who has followed her orders.

With recent increased emphasis on personal freedom more individuals are pressing for agency relationships with professionals. For example, pharmaceutical manufacturers in recent years have begun advertising prescription drugs and implants in lay magazines, on television and over the Internet. The very idea of a prescription drug—a drug you can obtain only with permission of a legally certified professional of a certain sort—is seen as a denial of personal freedom. To overcome this, barrier patients are told they should get their physician to prescribe the drug for them. Physicians who do not provide the requested drug or surgery might be sued for malpractice. Indeed, a number of such suits have been brought, and been successful in enough cases to scare some physicians into providing the demanded treatment. If it becomes sufficiently common for physicians to just give a patient what he wants, the patient–physician relationship will have become an agency relationship.

5.6.2 The Paternalism Form

At the other extreme is a form wherein the client performs no tasks beyond following orders. The paternalistic form of client–professional Interaction shifts the maximum responsibility for client welfare onto the professional. Implicit in such a shift is the client's trust that the professional is committed to his needs and the client's belief that the professional has the expertise and skill to fulfill the client's needs.

Parents of an eight-year old child will send him off to summer camp because they assume camp counselors have the training and experience to teach him how to swim and camp safely and effectively. They assume that counselors will actually

Separating Professional from Lay Ethics? 91

use their abilities for the benefit of their charges. The parents trust the counselors have abilities the parents lack.

Paternalistic forms of relationships seriously limit a client's freedom. At one time, the patient–physician relationship was typically paternalistic. An educated modern patient may wonder at such a statement. The key may be what is known as "bedside manner". A modern physician will offer a semblance of freedom by respecting her client's input, up to a point. The patient will (a) not be pressured to follow instructions, (b) be informed—or be given reasonable access to needed information—about alternative treatments and the likelihood of their success, and (c) be monitored for feedback to see if instructions are understood.

Paternalistic client–professional tasks usually occur in the context of guidance by the profession to which the professional belongs. Professionals often consult with each other. The programs that trained the professional result from studies of how to best carry out the tasks in question. But sometimes implementation of the chosen task requires a team. Surgeries frequently require teams that include anesthesiologists and surgical nurses. But whether a professional works alone or in cooperation with other members of her profession, the defining feature of the paternalistic relationship remains the same. It occurs when the responsibility for analyzing, considering, and deciding falls to the professional or professionals in the situation.

5.6.3 THE CONTRACTUAL FORM

A contract is a voluntary agreement between two or more parties, that may be written, oral, or "understood" from a less formal context. Its most unassailable form is written, so that no participant need rely on the fallible memories of individuals. It specifies the rights and prerogatives of the contracting parties.

One of the contractual items might be the tasks, for which, each party is responsible. Suppose one wishes to custom-build a yacht. He might get together with his ship designer and builder, and figure out just who is going to do what. So, perhaps he will design the cabin plan of his yacht, while the designer will consider alternative ways of placing the plumbing and electrical systems, and then just decide upon the most appropriate one herself. The owner may decide that it is his job to learn about solar-assisted heating systems, consider alternative ways of incorporating them into the design, and decide upon a particular alternative. His builder may be given the responsibility of designing the dock (since that is too humble for the architect to consider). Then his coordinator may be charged with coordinating his decisions with those of the designer and builder. If this sort of division of responsibilities is spelled out in a formal agreement, the relationship between the three parties is a *contractual* form relationship.

The connection between such a relationship and contractarianism is evident. However, the structure of contractarian ethical theory is not sufficiently delineated to instruct parties to a contractual form relationship in the details of how to construct a task contract. There is no single division of responsibilities that is inherently more valid than its alternatives. In the earlier example client, designer, and builder might divide up the responsibilities quite differently, and the result would be just as ethical, as long as they all agreed. The context of the situation determines if a task contract has moral components. Veil of ignorance-related ethical concerns might arise if characteristics of participants that have nothing to do with their competence to perform their task (e.g. race, grooming, religion) were written into the contract.

Since a contract is a legal entity, it is enforceable by the courts. Thus, trust in the professionals to perform their responsibilities as best they can is not absolutely necessary, as long as the conditions of the contract to do so are clear. Problems arise, however, when the contract is not designed to match the ability of its participants to understand. If the client has no awareness of boat hydrodynamics, he may end up with a vessel that looks great, but is slow and inefficient. The client would do well to know (1) what the problem is and (2) just what has to be done to solve it.

Consider a typical patient–physician relationship, say the case of a high school-educated gastritis sufferer seeking relief from a gastroenterologist. The patient may be perfectly capable of following instructions for taking medication and changing his diet. But this client cannot set up a contract specifying who will do what because he hasn't the background to understand the details of the physician's part. The client might be taken advantage of because he cannot critically evaluate the contract. Here, is a case where lack the ability to understand on the part of the client would hinder the client's ability carry out the task at hand. A contractual form relationship does not fulfill the veil-of-ignorance requirement of contractarian moral theory. The contractual form of client–professional relationship, then, has the potential to wander into areas of ethical concern that trigger contractarian analysis. Thus, in its simplest form as a legal document, a contractual form of participation will be ethically—not necessarily legally—neutral.

5.6.4 THE AFFINITY FORM

When there is an affinity between client and professional, they can establish another path to dividing responsibilities and trusting the professional. This affinity-form relationship is similar to a contractual form relationship but the basis for trust is completely different.

The affinity relationship, like the contractual relationship, is at a level between the extremes of the agency and paternal relationships in terms of its division of responsibilities and tasks. As in a contractual relationship, this division is not set according to any formula. But, unlike a contractual relationship, the responsibilities and tasks are not set up at the outset. In an affinity relationship, they may be altered as conditions dictate, without negotiation. These conditions result from the depth of trust that stem from the client having a close affinity to the professional. Affinity, in this case, refers to a connection that gives the client confidence in the professional independent of the traditional client-professional relationship.

Affinities arise among friends, family—an expression of Hamilton's altruism equation—religious groups, ethnic/racial groups, or even alumni. Students of a particular ethnic group may tend to seek advice from a professor they know is of the same ethnicity. There are theological and even mostly secular religion-founded colleges. Students may attend the more religious ones because they trust they will be advised by pillars of their religious community. Such trust may run afoul of the reality that some faculty of a number of religion-sponsored colleges may not be of

Separating Professional from Lay Ethics? 93

the sponsoring religion at all—particularly if the institution is funded by a federal agency. Schools funded by the government are prohibited by law to discriminate on the basis of race, gender, religion, etc., in hiring. Notre Dame University is a good example of this circumstance. It is endowed as a Catholic university, but has faculty from many faiths.

It is not uncommon for students belonging to minority groups at a university to seek out certain members of the faculty for advice and support because of their ethnic affinity. This behavior is known in sociobiology as positive ethnocentrism. Conversely, a student may avoid contact with a faculty member of a particular religion or ethnic group because the student's religion or ethnic group has a long-standing conflict with that of the faculty member. This behavior is known in sociobiology as negative ethnocentrism. *However, it must be emphasized that any faculty member who acted as an agent of such a conflict in dealing with students, would be in violation of both university and professional codes of conduct.*

To someone who has never entered one, an affinity form of client–professional relationship may seem unprofessional or un-businesslike. As with all forms of client–professional relationship, trust may be infringed in an infinity relationship. But, unlike other relationships, trust in this case is based substantially on an intangible that may have no relation to the problem being confronted. To a zoologist, however, this need is an expression of tribal urges that are an extension of the altruism equation. If affinity is anything, it is tribal; making this form of relationship the most primitive. If the tribal bond is strong enough, the client will be convinced that the professional is diligently seeking the client's welfare. An affinity relationship is considered successful by professionals, if it is likely to meet the needs of the client and, at the same time, maintain as high a level of client freedom as possible. If a client trusts the professional, then the client is more likely to agree freely to the evolving arrangements with the professional. If the professional is actually good at solving the client's problem, then both participants will profit from the relationship.

One caveat is crucial to consider before entering into or initiating an affinity client–professional relationship. If (1) the professional is a family member, (2) the consequences of the problem not being solved would be catastrophic to the family, and (3) the professional could be at fault for the catastrophic result, the relationship may be inappropriate. A common example, leading to this caveat, is the physician who treats a member of her own family. At an extreme, it is the surgeon operating on a member of his own family, and the surgery is fatal. This example brings to mind an old medical proverb: "A physician who treats a member of his own family has a fool for a patient and the patient has a fool for a physician".

5.6.5 THE PROFESSIONAL FIDUCIARY FORM

A typical client looks to a professional's professional society as a watchdog for assuring that the professional is trustworthy, and has the expertise to solve the problem at hand. Of course, the client wishes to maintain enough control over the relationship to preserve her own freedom to question any decisions. The financial commitment of a fiduciary relationship gives clients the desired control. There is no contract, so there exists no pressure to spell out the details of the relationship; another advantage to client freedom, because the professional is always bound by

94   Ethics for Bioengineering Scientists

his professional code of conduct. The client has less freedom here than in an agency relationship because there is a financial commitment. She also has less freedom than in an affinity relationship because there is less limit on the size of the affinity group. If an affinity relationship does not go smoothly, the affinity group (particularly if composed of family members) may not be pleased with the client, if she is seen as the cause.

The professional, in a fiduciary relationship, is depended on to fulfill his client's needs by (1) consulting with the client to determine the nature of her problem, (2) performing an analysis of the problem, that may include testing, that leads to a selection of solutions to the problem, (3) advising her about the advantages and disadvantages of the alternative solutions, (4) educating the client so that she understands the problem and its solutions, and (5) where possible, implementing those solutions that fall within his expertise.

Most client–professional relationships involve some element of trust on the part of the willing client. In a fiduciary relationship, trust is "up front". In fact the Oxford dictionary meaning of "fiduciary" is trust. In essence, a client trusts an expert, and backs up that trust by willing to pay him for his services. Professional codes of conduct often include rules that address the expectation of payment for services rendered. It is difficult to imagine a nonfiduciary professional relationship in the United States. Lawyers, dentists, physicians, college professors, engineers, and architects are just some examples of professions that employ them. Public school teachers are not paid by their students, but they are employed by boards of education who are their fiduciary clients.

5.7 PRIMA FACIE OBLIGATIONS OF ALL PROFESSIONALS: CONFIDENTIALITY, CLIENT AUTONOMY

What are the obligations that all professionals are required to fill? There are two that stand out, and both relate to client's rights and personal freedom. These are confidentiality and client autonomy. Before exploring these, let us examine the initial obligation of commitment to the client. A professional asked to serve a particular client, who has no alternative help, has the freedom of declining, but if she did she might be considered unethical by her peers on grounds that she would be violating her client's rights. For example, a defense lawyer cannot ethically refuse to defend a client because she believes he is guilty. A physician may not ethically decline treating an airplane passenger with chest pains because the physician is on vacation. Nor—in either case—may a refusal be based on the fact that the client is of an ethnic group or religion with which the professional's ethnic group or religion is in conflict.

5.7.1 CLIENT AUTONOMY

Autonomy is a Kantian concept. It is integral component of his deontology. Kant defined an autonomous individual as one who governs himself free from any outside influence. The autonomous professional acts in accordance with a free will; that is, as one unfettered by "desires" that developed during his upbringing. An individual who succumbs to these desires is "heteronomous". The autonomous

Separating Professional from Lay Ethics?

professional is subject to a sense of duty that arises out of his free will. According to Kant, an autonomous professional would resent being thought of as only a "means to an end" and would therefore never take such an attitude toward his client. This professional would give his client every opportunity to take part in making the decisions about solving her problem. In the case of the defense lawyer cited earlier, the professional would take care to apprise the defendant of all she has to do to help her case. Similarly, the physician of an organ transplant donor would not remove the donated organ until it was safe for the donor, or, if the donor was dying, until death had been firmly established. These statements are not judgments about what must be done in all situations; they are merely illustrations of the meaning of client autonomy. Client trust in the professional includes a faith that the professional will use his expertise to serve the ends—assuming they are legal—of the client. An exception to the latter statement may exist in the mind of some professionals. There have been instances when a professional has performed an illegal act believing it was beneficial to the client. For example, a physician might perform an abortion on a patient whose health he judged to be in danger in a jurisdiction where the procedure was against the law under any circumstances. Such situations are severe tests of a professional's ethical standards.

5.7.2 CONFIDENTIALITY (ADAPTED FROM ARMSTRONG 2003)

Confidentiality, or the keeping of a confidence, has a foundation in both deontological and utilitarian moral theories. In deontology, confidentiality is based on notions of privacy, autonomy, promise-keeping, and loyalty. Its *prima facie* justification follows from the premises:

1. Each client has autonomy over his own personal information.
2. Intimate information about a client's relationships must be respected.
3. Any pledge of silence creates the obligation to be silent.
4. Both clients and society as a whole are better served by silence about certain matters.

The utilitarian basis for justification of confidentiality is that society benefits when professionals can be trusted to keep confidences.

In all professions, some provision is made for circumstances whereby the *prima facie* (a genuine obligation with the implication that it competes with some that are less genuine) status of a confidence may be infringed upon. Usually, four conditions must be met for infringement:

1. There must be a reasonable expectation of achieving the ethical goal of the infringement.
2. There is no ethically defensible alternative to infringement under the circumstances.
3. The infringement level must not exceed a value that would violate conditions "1" or "2".
4. The consequences of the infringement for the client must be abated by the professional.

96   Ethics for Bioengineering Scientists

The move from strict confidentiality to infringement should not be made lightly if professional ethics are to be maintained. In deontological terms, one has to balance a negative versus a positive duty. The negative duty is keeping the confidence and the positive duty is the infringement. A negative duty is negative because it is against changing from the default position (keeping confidentiality). Professionals within their societies try to anticipate situations in which infringement must be considered. Society as a whole may develop policies that guide professionals. A consensus that has evolved to help professionals is the following:

1. Negative is stronger than positive, assuming that the magnitude of potential harm to society of keeping a confidence is less than or equal to the magnitude of harm to the client.
2. In deciding the magnitude of potential harm to society, the profession should consider:
   a. The degree to which silence is not an obligation (varies with profession). This measure is referred to as relentlessness.
   b. One's uncertainty of the outcome of revealing the information. (If it would be catastrophic to the client, is there a way to avoid or ameliorate the expected consequence?)
   c. Who is involved in the consequences? Carrying out a negative duty may cause one person or group to respond to the decision one way, and another to respond differently. The same could be said for carrying out a positive duty.
   d. How much will those affected react? To the differences between individuals or groups reacting, may be added the magnitude of the reactions.

A classic example of a confidentiality infringement case, *Tarasoff v. Regents, U. Calif.,* is one in which the courts found that a positive duty should have been performed:

> On October 27, 1969 Prosenjit Poddar stabbed Tatiana Tarasoff to death with a knife. The plaintiffs, Tatiana's parents, alleged that two months earlier Poddar confided his intention to kill Tatiana to Dr. Lawrence Moore, a psychologist employed by Cowell Memorial Hospital at the University of California, Berkeley. They alleged that on Moore's request, the campus police briefly detained Poddar, but released him when he appeared rational. They further claimed that Dr. Harvey Powelson, Moore's superior, then directed that no further action be taken to detain Poddar. No one warned the plaintiffs of Tatiana's peril. The specific complaints of the plaintiffs were "Failure to detain a dangerous patient" and "Failure to warn of a dangerous patient". The defendants contended that imposition of a duty to exercise reasonable care to protect third persons (Tatiana), is unworkable because 1) it would violate patient confidentiality, and 2) therapists cannot accurately predict whether or not a patient will resort to violence. Thus, the courts should not render rulings that base the liability of therapists upon the validity of such predictions. The majority of judges of this California Supreme Court case ruled for the plaintiffs that there is a public interest in supporting effective treatment of mental illness, and in protecting the rights of patients to privacy, and the consequent public importance of safeguarding the confidential

Separating Professional from Lay Ethics? 97

character of psychotherapeutic communication. Against this interest, however, must be weighed the public interest in safety from violent assault. The one dissenting judge stated that "Overwhelming policy considerations, weigh against imposing a duty on psychotherapists to warn a potential victim against harm. While offering virtually no benefit to society, such a duty will frustrate psychiatric treatment, invade fundamental patient rights and increase violence". He further stated that without assurance of confidentiality, patients would 1) avoid treatment due to fear they would be exposed and suffer society stigmatization, 2) have so little trust in the therapist that full disclosure of potentially shocking revelations would be avoided, and 3) as part of the patient's lack of trust he may balk at treatment which makes him uncomfortable.

5.8 WHEN OBLIGATIONS CONFLICT: CONFLICT OF INTEREST

When a professional's client's rights are at risk, a simple formula for choosing good over bad does not apply. When a professional has multiple commitments, and cannot devote herself to any one of them sufficiently to fulfill its obligations, she has a conflict of interest. The limit on her ability to devote herself to the obligation in question may be lack of time. But it may also be that the goals of the obligations are in conflict. An engineer who consults for two companies that make the same kind product has a conflict of interest. A physician who prescribes drugs and owns stock in a drug company has a conflict of interest. A mortician–physician has a conflict of interest. There are more specific examples of conflict of interest in later chapters.

5.9 COWORKERS AND CLIENTS

This chapter has delved into the most subjective elements of ethics, personal relations of people who work together or consult, and have a controlled, neutral, or controlling connection. Taken as a whole, what has been described is essentially a blueprint for ethically based civilized behavior. In each case, we have tried to present alternative ethical modes of behavior. Where evident, they have been related to the moral theories. This chapter ends the moral theory section of the text. We now move on to profession-specific ethics.

ENRICHMENT

1. Perform a moral analysis on *Tarasoff v. Regents, U. Calif.*
2. How does Bayles (2003) definition of a professional differ from that of Davis (2009) presented in Chapter 1? How do they agree?
3. Case: Endovascular Technologies. Lay person assuming professional functions. See case at http://news.findlaw.com/hdocs/docs/ guidant/endo61203plea.pdf and http://www.usdoj.gov/usao/can/ press/html/2003_06_12_endovascular.html

EndoVascular Technologies of Menlo Park, California was a division of Guidant Corp. of Indianapolis. The company had developed the Ancure Endograft System a medical device that offered a less invasive way to surgically correct an abdominal aortic aneurysm. The $10,000 device was supposed to allow correction of the vessel bulges with minimal hospitalization and a shortened recuperation time.

From September 30, 1999 to March 15, 2001 there were malfunctions of 2,628 of the 7,000 devices sold; 57 patients had to undergo emergency reoperations and 12 patients died. The company was charged and convicted—including a $92.4 M settlement—by the U.S. Justice Dept. of nine counts of introducing a "misbranded medical device with the intent to defraud or mislead" and one count of lying to the FDA about the extent of the problems. A number of suits followed. A more detailed description of the case follows, in which "defendant" refers to EndoVascular Technologies. Pay particular attention to the bolded sections.

The Ancure Device sold by defendant has two primary parts. One part is a delivery catheter used to place the vascular endograft into the aorta. The delivery catheter is inserted into a blood vessel through an incision made in the patient's leg. The second part of the Ancure Device is a vascular endograft that is placed in the patient's aorta using a delivery system to prevent an aneurysm from rupturing. The vascular endograft consists of a woven fabric graft with an attachment system that includes hooks. The vascular endograft is designed to remain in the patient's aorta permanently after being implanted. The delivery catheter is designed to be removed from the patient after the vascular endograft is implanted. Defendant developed and marketed the Ancure Device as an alternative to the traditional and more invasive treatment for abdominal aortic aneurysms: surgery in which the patient's abdomen is cut open to enable the physician to reach the aorta. The use of the Ancure Device was indicated at the time of its approval for commercial marketing by the U.S.F.D.A. ("FDA") for the endovascular treatment of infrarenal abdominal or aorto-iliac aneurysms in patients having (i) adequate iliac/femoral access; (ii) infrarenal non- aneurysmal neck length of at least 15 millimeters and a diameter of no greater than 26 millimeters; (iii) distal segment lengths of at least 20 millimeters and diameters no greater than 13.4 millimeters; and (iv) morphology suitable for endovascular repair.

FDA first approved the Ancure Device for commercial sale in the United States on September 30, 1999. On the same day, FDA also approved a competing product for commercial sale in the United States. The competing product approved by FDA also was designed to treat abdominal aortic aneurysms by the insertion of an endograft into the aorta. From the first day the Ancure Device was approved for commercial sale in the United States, defendant faced competition for market share.

Before FDA approved the Ancure Device for commercial sale, defendant learned from physicians during clinical trials that the delivery system of the Ancure Device was perceived as more difficult to use than the competing product. Certain of defendant's employees viewed the complexity of the

Separating Professional from Lay Ethics?

delivery system of the Ancure Device as the company's primary marketing challenge. Certain officials of defendant believed that if the Ancure Device could not be successfully deployed in a significant number of cases, it had the potential to harm marketing efforts and discourage physician customers from choosing the Ancure Device.

After defendant began selling the Ancure Device in the United States, the company became aware of various malfunctions that occurred in the delivery system of the Ancure Device. In some instances, physicians were unable to implant the Ancure Device due to a problem in using the delivery system of the Ancure Device. In other instances, physicians were able to implant the Ancure Device but could not do so in a way that was consistent with the approved instructions for use. Some of the malfunctions resulted in the delivery system of the Ancure Device becoming improperly lodged in the body. In these latter cases, some of the patients had to undergo traditional open surgical repair to remove the delivery system of the Ancure Device and correct the aneurysm. The malfunctions leading to resulting penalty relate only to the delivery system of the Ancure Device, and do not relate to the Ancure Device after it has been implanted. Some sales representatives of defendant provided information to doctors regarding a procedure that involved breaking or cutting the handle of the Ancure Device when the delivery system became lodged in a patient and could not be removed without resorting to traditional open surgical repair ("Handle Breaking Technique"). The Handle Breaking Technique was devised in part by a sales representative of defendant. The Handle Breaking Technique involved breaking or cutting the handle of the delivery system and removing the catheters housed within the delivery system of the Ancure Device individually from the patient's body.

At the time defendant first provided information to doctors regarding the Handle Breaking Technique through its sales representatives, the technique had not been tested; doctors had not been trained on its use; sales representatives who described the technique to doctors during surgery had not been trained by the company on its use; the instructions for use had not been altered to include the Handle Breaking Technique; and defendant had failed to seek prior approval of FDA concerning the use of the Handle Breaking Technique. On or about January 26, 2000, in an unnamed hospital, the Handle Breaking Technique was utilized in an operation unsuccessfully. The patient in that operation ultimately died. This incident caused a group of defendant's employees to conclude that the safety of the Handle Breaking Technique was uncertain; that the Handle Breaking Technique required testing and validation; and, if it were to be used, that the Handle Breaking Technique should be submitted to FDA. Defendant became aware that physicians continued to use the Handle Breaking Technique and that its sales representatives continued to provide information to doctors regarding the Handle Breaking Technique during surgical procedures where it was believed necessary to avoid standard open surgical repair. During the times relevant to the Information filed in this case, the Handle Breaking Technique was not submitted to FDA for its review and approval and was not included in the instructions for use.

After FDA approved the Ancure Device for commercial sale in the United States, defendant received information about the number and type of malfunctions (as defined in the relevant regulations) through complaints by physicians, reports from the company's own sales representatives, and from other company employees. The incidences of recurring malfunctions were repeatedly tabulated, distributed to certain officials in the company, and discussed internally. Defendant received information that some of these malfunctions (i) may have caused or contributed to patients' deaths and serious injuries or (ii) would be likely to cause a death or serious injury if the malfunction were to recur. Defendant did not provide information to FDA of these malfunctions by filing MDRs, or otherwise, and did not seek FDA approval to modify its instructions for use to reflect this information.

In or about July 2000, FDA conducted an inspection of defendant's headquarters in Menlo Park, California. During the inspection, the inspector requested a list of all complaints regarding difficulties of the catheter's jacket to retract properly during surgical use of the delivery system of the Ancure Device. Defendant provided the FDA inspector with a list of 55 complaints. In fact, as defendant well knew, there were more than 200 incidents that constituted complaints (as defined in the relevant regulations) concerning this malfunction that had occurred between October 1999 and April 2000 alone. Defendant knowingly and intentionally misled FDA about the frequency with which the delivery system of the Ancure Device malfunctioned in this manner.

In or about October 2000, seven anonymous employees sent a letter to FDA and to an official of defendant's parent corporation describing ethical, legal and safety concerns with the Ancure Device. Among other such concerns, the letter stated:

a. defendant had conducted incomplete testing and analysis on currently recommended procedures;
b. defendant had recommended the use of the device in a manner that was outside the directions for use approved by FDA;
c. The jacket retraction failure mode, which involved the failure of the sheath of the Ancure Device to retract as intended, had a corresponding complaint rate of approximately 20%;
d. defendant had failed to report to FDA product changes that affected safety and efficacy as legally required; and
e. defendant failed to submit MDRs to FDA as legally required.

The letter listed numerous circumstances that were not reported and specifically named two surgeries during which the Ancure Device malfunctioned that had resulted in death.

4. The Hamilton Equation implies that tribal tendencies are naturally strongest where there is a genetic link. A logical prediction from this theory is that humans are naturally complexes of positive and negative racism. If we were to admit to such a burden, and committed to a goal of reducing its expression in the work environment, what kind of rules would have to be imposed to fulfill relevant fiduciary responsibilities?

Following the receipt of this letter, an investigation authorized by the defendant concluded that, at certain times relevant to the Information, defendant had serious quality system regulation violations, incomplete and untimely complaint handling and documentation, incomplete MDR reporting, inadequate corrective and preventative action activities, incomplete record keeping and poor traceability practices, and was significantly out of compliance with FDA regulations and its own internal policies. Between September 30, 1999 and March 16, 2001, defendant filed 172 MDRs for the delivery system of the Ancure Device. On or about March 23, 2001, defendant disclosed to FDA the existence of approximately 2,628 additional MDRs concerning the delivery system of the Ancure Device that had not been previously reported to FDA, as required by law. Among those 2,628 MDRs that had not been timely filed were 12 deaths and 57 conversions to traditional open surgical repair. Defendant suspended commercial sale of the Ancure Device as of March 16, 2001.

A summary of this case may be found at: https://www.justice.gov/sites/default/files/pages/attachments/2016/10/05/endopress.pdf

Perform a moral analysis of this case from the point of view of the sales representative who advised the surgeons.

6 Engineering Ethics

There are over 2 million engineers in the United States, according to the Bureau of Labor Statistics. American engineering's traditions are rooted primarily in British and French traditions (Reynolds 1991a). Engineering in the United States, before 1800 was dominated by foreign-born engineers. The first major U.S.-native engineered project, the Erie Canal, was completed in 1825. Its engineers were "practically trained" on the job (Reynolds 1991a). First, civil engineering, then mechanical engineering developed this way, using British traditions, for the most part. Between 1820 and 1860, French methodology was applied at the U.S. Military Academy at West Point, to train army engineers. A four-year curriculum was followed. It wasn't until 1874 that the Naval Academy at Annapolis followed West Point with a four-year engineering curriculum. Engineer program development at civilian colleges in the 19th century was spotty. Norwich College, then Rensselaer Polytechnic Institute, developed three-year civil engineering programs in 1834 and 1850, respectively. The Morrill Act establishing grants to colleges for engineering programs stimulated growth of civilian programs to 85 in number by 1880.

The American Society of Civil Engineering was established nationally in 1865. Other societies followed, as did the kind of communication that led members to convince each other that they had to develop an American style of engineering different from both the British and French traditions. The new style placed more emphasis on reducing labor costs, promoting economy of construction, and emphasizing strength, endurance, attractiveness, and safety (Reynolds 1991a).

As noted in Chapter 1, the industrial revolution transformed a nation of small commercial enterprises of the early 19th century into large, capital-intensive corporations that institutionalized the inventive process with research laboratories that operated on an industrial scale (Reynolds 1991b). Entrepreneurs like Thomas Edison and Henry Ford interacting with engineers like William Stanley and Nicolas Tesla created national companies that employed engineers. These engineers did not at first directly apply natural science to technology. Instead, they "borrowed the methods of science—systematic, quantitative experimentation and mathematical theory—to build their own unique 'engineering' sciences that were based on existing craft practice rather than the study of natural phenomena" (Reynolds 1991b). Corporations grew, with the help of a transformation of independent consultant and proprietor engineers, into company leadership positions, and of an influx of mid-level engineer managers, who were experts in technology.

The government, from the local to the federal level, also employed engineers. At the local level, in growing urban centers, engineers, who were thought to be "unbiased" often replaced politicians (Reynolds 1991b). At the federal level, the growth of "big" government, initially to help regulate the impact of corporations, was eventually enhanced by government projects, developed to offset unemployment

DOI: 10.1201/9781003197218-6

104   Ethics for Bioengineering Scientists

during the 1930s Depression. An example of such projects was the Tennessee Valley Authority, which was a major employer of engineers. When WWII started, engineer employment in the defense sector rose. The Cold War and its products, agencies like the Atomic Energy Commission and NASA, helped bring the total federal employment to about 15% of all engineers by the late 1980s (Reynolds 1991b).

After the 1950s, there was increasing incidence of engineers and scientists working together, if not thinking alike (Reynolds 1991b). The Manhattan Project where Big Science was launched helped win WWII. NASA's exploration of space has produced much scientific data as well as useful technology. Bioengineering, an academic major almost exclusively in schools of engineering, because of the efforts of engineering societies (Requena-Carrión and Leder 2009), has combined engineering and medicine with science, to produce data that help us understand life processes, and help us to obtain cures for diseases and agricultural problems. The three professions have coordinated, even when they abjured learning each other's specialty, as illustrated by the work of NASA. According to Reynolds (Reynolds 1991b), by the end of the 20th century, "American engineers had sharply increased the emphasis placed on basic science, on mathematics, and on theory in engineering training".

The conversion of engineers from individuals in small enterprises to "bureaucratic employ[ees]" in corporations and government, has resulted in a profession that, unlike the case for the medical profession, is not dominated by one society. Therefore, it has no single source for a code of ethics. The National Society of Professional Engineers comes closest to filling this role, but can claim only a 5% membership. Reynolds summarizes the history of U.S. engineering: "Although it cost the American engineering profession the independence and individualistic values that it had prized in the 19th century, association with management preserved for the profession at least some of the autonomy and much of the status it had so feared losing at the beginning of the 20th century" (Reynolds 1991b). For the remainder of this chapter, we shall examine engineers as ethical individuals.

6.1   THE ENGINEER'S CLIENT

Given the evolution of U.S. engineering, it is not surprising that the U.S. engineer tends to view her clients through an organizational filter. Typically, in truth professions, the professional has one or a few clients for each problem that needs solving. A marriage counselor has one client or family. An accountant has one client or firm or department. A lawyer has a single client or a group. A teacher has a student or a class. A physician has a patient. The clients in these encounters exit from them, hopefully, with a solved problem. Cars, bridges, x-ray machines, space suits, airplanes, computers, and toasters have to be engineered. This means that not only the structure, but the methods and materials used to construct it require engineering.

And since these structures are used by millions of humans with whom the engineers will never interact, these problem solvers may never face their ultimate clients. Therefore, the quality of their work has to be built into their solutions. And to assess how well quality is built in, the engineer has to assess his product long

Engineering Ethics 105

before it reaches his ultimate client. The assessment is a prediction of how well it will do its job. The job has two components that occupy the highest priority level in any such assessment: (1) safety and (2) efficacy. When cost becomes a concern, either because funds are limited (e.g. a government project) or a profit is expected, cost containment becomes a high-priority concern.

When an engineer designs a project, she must consider its impact on its human users. Some assessment must be made about the chances the structure will fail and the harm it may cause. The assessment is based on previous experiences with similar structures and any enhancements in the new structure. The numerical form of this assessment is statistical in nature and called "risk". From its origins, as purely a safety measure, risk assessment has morphed into complicated models that include efficacy, safety, and cost. These cannot be calculated from physics first principles because of the large number of confounding variables (including weather, human error, earth movements, shifts in the earth's magnetic field, and even sun spots). Thus, engineering is still empirical to a large degree, but it is helped along by data accumulated from extensive experience. Just as tendencies for spread of disease can be estimated from field accumulation of geographical distribution of cases, tendencies for safety, efficacy, and cost of an engineered product can be estimated from experience with similar products. Both engineers and public health statisticians use forms of epidemiology to estimate risk.

A classic example of the application of risk assessment with modern parameters is the Ford Pinto case.

6.2 THE CLASSIC ENGINEERING ETHICS CASE—MONETARY VALUE OF A HUMAN LIFE

Ford Pinto Case

[Adapted from caselaw.findlaw.com/ca-court-of-appeal/1835119.html]

1 The Accident

On May 28, 1972, Mrs. Lily Gray was driving 13-year-old Richard Grimshaw to Barstow, CA on Interstate 15 in a six-month-old Ford Pinto that had about 3,000 miles on its odometer. She had just filled the gas tank and was driving 60–65 miles per hour (mph) in lane one, but as she approached the Route 30 exit, she switched lanes to lane two of the three-lane road. Suddenly the car stalled and coasted to a halt. Investigators later concluded that the carburetor float had become sufficiently saturated with gasoline to suddenly sink, creating an opening in the float chamber that allowed the engine to flood and stall. The second of two cars traveling behind the Pinto, a 1962 Ford Galaxie moving at 50–55 mph, could not avoid the stalled car and was braked down to 28–37 mph before the rear-end collision. At the collision, the Pinto interior

---

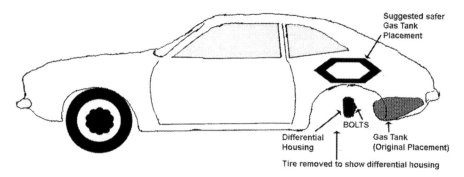

FIGURE 6.1 Diagram of the 1972 Ford Pinto, showing placement of the gas tank, differential housing, and safer placement of the gas tank.

compartment burst into flames. The expert testifying for the subsequent plaintiffs maintained that the impact of the Galaxie had driven the Pinto's gas tank forward sufficiently for it to be punctured by bolts projecting from the housing of the car's differential (see Figure 6.1). As a result, fuel spraying out of the tank entered the interior compartment through gaps in the floor. The gaps were created by collision-caused separation of rear wheel well sections from the floor pan. Sparks from scraping metal ignited the gas and both occupants were engulfed in flames by the time their car came to rest. Grimshaw, who suffered burns over 90% of his skin, survived, but only after nearly 70 surgical procedures, including skin grafts on his hands and face, over a 10-year period. Mrs. Gray's burns led to congestive heart failure and she died less than a week later.

2 Liability

The victims' families sued Ford for negligence. Finally, in 1978, after a six-month trial the jury awarded the Gray family $560,000 and Grimshaw $2.5 million in compensatory damages. An additional award of $125 million in punitive damages was reduced to $3.5 on appeal in 1981.

This accident and subsequent others similar to it sparked a controversy about the safety of the placement of the Ford Pinto's fuel tank. It was located behind the rear axle, instead of above it, as shown in Figure 6.1. This was initially done in an effort to create more trunk space. The problem with this design, which later became evident, was that it made the Pinto more vulnerable to a rear-end collision. This vulnerability was enhanced by other features of the car. The gas tank and the rear axle were separated by only nine inches. Positioning of the bolts that punctured the gas tank was also an issue. Finally, the fuel filler pipe design resulted in a higher probability that it would disconnect from the tank in the event of an accident, causing gas spillage that could lead to dangerous fires. A summary—with illustration—of the defects may be found in Figure 6.1 and at the website: engineering.com/Library/ArticlesPage/tabid/85/ArticleID/166/Ford-Pinto.aspx.

Engineering Ethics

TABLE 6.1

Calculation of Collision Price *Grimshaw v. Ford Motor Co., 1981*

Component	1971 Rates
Future productivity losses	
Direct	$132,000
Indirect	41,000
Medical costs	
Hospital	700
Other	425
Property damage	1,500
Insurance administration	4,700
Legal and court	3,000
Employer losses	1,000
Victim's pain and suffering	10,000
Funeral	900
Assets (lost consumption)	5,000
Miscellaneous	200
Total	**$200,725**

		Cost-benefit Analysis		
Cost	Number	Price Per	Total	
Cars	11,000,000	$11	$121,000,000	
Trucks	1,500,000	$11	16,500,000	
	TOTAL		137,500,000	
Benefit				
Burn deaths	180	$200,725	36,130,500	
Burn injuries	180	$67,000	12,060,000	
Burned vehicles	2,100	$700	1,470,000	
		TOTAL	49,660,500	
	Difference		**$87,839,500**	

These design problems were first brought to the public's attention by Mark Dowie in a September 1977 article in *Mother Jones* magazine, which cited not only the Grimshaw mishap (the case was still being litigated) but other fatal "exploding" Pinto cases. The article condemned the Ford Motor Company and the author was later given a Pulitzer Prize. It instigated a public debate over the risk/benefit analysis used by the Ford Motor Company in their determination as to whether or not the design of the Pinto fuel tank be altered to reduce the risk of fire as the result of a collision.

The focus of the public debate was Ford's decision to abstain from making improvements to the gas tank of the Pinto after completion of the risk/benefit analysis (that Ford claimed occurred in 1972). Internal Ford documents revealed Ford had developed the technology to make improvements to the design of the Pinto that would dramatically decrease the chance of a Pinto "igniting" after a rear-end collision. This technology would have greatly reduced the chances of burn injuries and deaths after a collision. Ford estimated the cost to make this production adjustment to the Pinto would have been $11 per vehicle. Public reaction to the notion that Ford determined an $11 cost per automobile too high to make the production change to the Pinto model was generally negative.

3 Risk/Benefit Analysis

The Ford Motor Company defended itself by contending that it used a risk/benefit analysis in determining whether or not to make the production change. Ford stated that its reason for using a risk/benefit analysis was that the National Highway Traffic Safety Administration (NHTSA) required them to do so. A risk/benefit approach excuses a defendant if the monetary costs of making a production change are greater than the "societal benefit" of that change. One can see in these numbers application of act utilitarianism that appeals to the calculation sensibilities of an engineer.

Ford's approach conforms to the same line of reasoning as does the negligence standard developed by Judge Learned Hand in *United States vs. Carroll Towing* in 1947. The philosophy behind risk/benefit analysis promotes the goal of allocative efficiency (resources are allocated efficiently if the ratios of benefit to cost are optimized).

Ford contended that by strictly following a standard approach to risk/benefit analysis, they were justified in abstaining from the suggested production change to the Pinto model. Ford estimated the cost for the change at $11 per vehicle. If applied to 11 million cars and 1.5 million trucks, the total cost to the company would have been $137 million.

For the "benefit" component of the equation, Ford estimated that making the change would result in a total of 180 fewer burn deaths, 180 fewer serious burn injuries, and 2,100 less-burned vehicles. These estimates were multiplied by the unit cost presumed by the NHTSA as $200,725 per death, $67,000 per injury, and $700 per vehicle equating to the total "societal benefit" of $49.5 million. The $200,725 estimate is shown in the "Collision Price" table (Table 6.1) and represented what an average worker would earn in a lifetime adjusted for the average age of an accident victim (future productivity losses). Ford employees obtained earnings numbers from the 1970 census. (The current (2016) collision price is $9.6 million, according to the U.S. Department of Transportation).

Since the benefit of $49.5 million was much less than the cost of $137 million, Ford felt justified in its decision not to alter the product design. The

Engineering Ethics

109

> risk/benefit results indicate that it is acceptable for 180 people to die and 180 people to burn if it costs as much as $11 per vehicle to prevent such casualty rates. If one's frame of reference is local (the individual driver) death becomes the issue and most people would condemn Ford's decision. If one's frame of reference is global (the entire population of Pinto drivers) there may be a rule utilitarianism-based case made for Ford's behavior in terms of long-term risk/benefit analysis logic.

An engineering-intensive corporation may have a number of projects vying for company resources at any moment. Managers have to decide which project will gain a profit, with minimum taxing of financial resources. The cost-benefit analysis, shown in the table, is one form of risk analysis. For commercial ventures, like auto manufacturing companies, its goal is to maximize profits. For government ventures, its goal is to minimize cost to the taxpayer, while serving as many of them as possible. For both there is the parallel goal of maximizing safety. But safety can be expensive, even to the point of eliminating profits. Consequently, safety has to be included in the risk analysis. The engineers at Ford knew that placement of Pinto gas tank affected safety of the vehicle. They could not make a calculation without quantifying safety. For a car that could be threatened by collisions, the chief safety concerns were death and injury. The costs associated with them were hospitalization from burns, funerals, and loss of income to the family from death of a provider. The latter cost had to be estimated by projecting what the provider would have earned had they lived an average life span. Life expectancy and earnings are obtainable from government agencies like the Department of Labor Statistics. This accident cost had to be weighed against the cost of labor involved in reconfiguring the Pinto design and lengthening the labor time involved in executing the new plan. The differences shown in the table appear to be a clear indication for decision making by Lee Iacocca, the president of Ford and his managers. Such was the conclusion of Mark Dowie (Dowie 1977). His conclusions have been challenged, however (Lee and Ermann 1999).

6.3 ENGINEERING CODES OF ETHICS

For a profession as established as engineering, one might expect that there existed a single society, to which a majority belong, and from which there is a representative code of ethics. There is no such organization. There are dozens of engineering societies which together claim over a quarter of the profession's 2 million members. In 1912, a Code of Ethics of American Institute of Electrical Engineers was published. In that code, an engineer was told that he (there were almost no female engineers then) should consider *the protection of a client's or employer's interests his first professional obligation* (Peterson and Farell 1986). In 1947, the Engineers' Council for Professional Development (ECPD), a model for many engineers' codes in current engineering societies, called for the engineer to *discharge his duties with fidelity to the public, his employers and clients, and with fairness and impartiality to*

110   Ethics for Bioengineering Scientists

all. It is his duty to interest himself in public welfare and to be ready to apply his special knowledge for the benefit of mankind (Peterson and Farell 1986).

The 1974 revision of the ECPD Canons of Ethics stated that *Engineers shall hold paramount the safety, health, and welfare of the public in the performance of their professional duties* (Peterson and Farell 1986). Thus, in 62 years the engineers' thinking on the issues had evolved from a primary duty to clients and employers to simultaneous (and presumably equal, and sometimes conflicting) duties to clients, employers, and the public, and finally, to a primary duty to the general public. Currently, the American Society of Civil Engineers, the America Society of Mechanical Engineers, the Institute of Industrial Engineers, and Tau Beta Phi have adopted language similar to the 1974 ECPD Canons. The American Association of Engineering Societies (AAES), an umbrella organization comprised of 22 engineering societies, uses even stronger language: *Engineers perceiving a consequence of their professional duties to adversely affect the present or future public health and safety shall formally advise their employers or clients and, if warranted, consider further disclosure* (Gorlin 1990).

In 1989, the AAES issued *Public Policy Perspectives: Ethical Standards,* which stated the following policy, intended to aid engineers who feel they have no choice but to blow the whistle (Gorlin 1990)

Engineers, in their contributions to technological endeavors, must continually balance creativity and the end effects of their work upon the public welfare. Their contributions may be affected by management and financial decisions which are in conflict with their own ethical standards.

AAES urges that these conflicts be disclosed and resolved with appropriate mechanisms to protect the public safety, and adequate protection for the engineer who jeopardizes his or her career, reputation, and well-being by making such disclosures in the public interest. To this end, AAES is cooperating with various organizations in examining these points and developing measures to enhance ethical approaches wherever technology is present. Action agenda:

1. *Encourage disclosure necessary to protect the public safety*
2. *Establish active society support of individuals who make disclosures*

6.4   THE BART CASE—UNPROTECTED WHISTLEBLOWING BY ENGINEERS

The BART case is a good example of engineering *society support of individuals who make disclosures.* The following is based on two publications Anderson (1980) and Peterson (1986), and two web sites www.cs.umd.edu/~gasarch/ethics/Case-BART.doc and https://courses.cit.cornell.edu/engrwords/memos/Jain_A_memo_issue_3.pdf.

The Bay Area Rapid Transit (BART) system connects cities around the San Francisco Bay. During its 25-year development, it employed a large number of engineering consultants. Early in 1971, three of its engineers Max Blankenzee, Robert Bruder, and Holger Hjortsvang, became concerned about the reliability of the automatic train

Engineering Ethics

control system (ATC) that regulates train speed. Rather than operating in "fail-safe" mode whereby the trains would come to a stop if there was a failure in the system, the ATC would shift to a backup mode, which the engineers felt, was inadequate. Their concern was heightened by the lack of documentation provided by Westinghouse, the ATC designer and builder. They wrote a number of memos to their supervisor expressing their concerns. When these produced no action, they wrote to their general manager. Again, all three received no significant response. The manager had a policy of restricting contact between the engineers and board members. This policy may have been based on the fact that board members were political appointees and not engineers. Toward the end of 1971 the three engineers decided that the threat to public safety was serious enough, and the day the system would go on line close enough, to warrant taking their concerns to Dan Helix, a member of the BART Board of Directors. Helix took the engineers' memos to the Board. He also released them to the *Contra Costa Times,* which published them. The Board was upset and skeptical of the engineers' concerns. Helix did not tell the Board who gave him the published memos. After an investigation, the engineers confessed, after initially denying, to authoring the published memos. The engineers maintained they had never pursued press coverage. Nevertheless, they were dismissed from their jobs on the grounds of lying to their superiors (about the memos being theirs), failing to follow organizational procedures, and insubordination(Peterson and Farell; Anderson 1980).

All three engineers suffered unemployment and emotional problems after their dismissal and finally sued BART for $875,000. The fact that they had initially lied about the memo release weakened their case and they settled for $25,000 each. During the trial, the Institute of Electrical and Electronic Engineers (IEEE) tried to help the three plaintiffs by filing an *amicus curiae* ("friend of the court") document that asserted the three acted in accordance with the their code of ethics that requires they "notify the proper authority of any observed conditions which endanger public safety and health". They were implementing their professional duty.

One of the engineers later enlisted the support of the California Society of Professional Engineers (CSPE), which began a study of the situation. The study brought to light many engineering and management problems which confirmed the claims of the three engineers. Actual malfunctions, such as an October 1972 incident where the system gave a command to a train to speed up when it should have slowed down (causing the train to jump the tracks and injure several people), also confirmed the engineers' complaints. Thus, with the help of the CSPE, the three engineers were publicly vindicated, but were still out of work and experiencing difficulty getting hired by *any* company. (Armstrong 2003)

"A comparison of the AAES guidelines with those of the AMA (see chapter 7) reveals an interesting difference: The engineers appear more willing to break professional confidences in the absence of laws requiring them to do so. Indeed, the engineers are in the process of providing structures to encourage necessary disclosures among their ranks and to protect their members from resulting repercussions...." (Faber 2003).

In grappling with the confidentiality problem, engineers, like the BART case whistleblowers, have apparently concluded that the duty to the public's safety, health, and welfare is a higher duty than conflicting *prima facie* duties.

The BART case, and others involving whistleblowers who suffered for their exposures, generated passage of the Levin-Grassley Act of 1989. Levin-Grassley

112   Ethics for Bioengineering Scientists

offered limited protection from retribution, and covered federal agencies only. It wasn't until 2002 that protection was extended by the Sarbanes-Oxley Act to include penalties for retribution and substantially increased rewards for the whistle-blowers. This act also applies to federal employees, but it extends to nonfederal employees if they are working for a federally funded company (BART was built with federal funding).

6.5   THE CHALLENGER CASE—FAILURE TO BLOW THE WHISTLE*

On January 28, 1986 (note this is before Levin-Grassley Act), the space shuttle *Challenger* exploded a few minutes after its launch, killing six NASA astronauts and an elementary school teacher. Repeated broadcast of the disaster stimulated public outcry and William P. Rogers, Secretary of State responded by organizing a commission to investigate its cause, and recommend measures to prevent its reoccurrence. The commission was composed of politicians, astronauts, military men and one scientist, Richard Feynman, a physics Nobel laureate. The published report assigned no clear blame. Feynman, after conducting an investigation on his own, disagreed with the commission's conclusions. The scientist had travelled to NASA facilities, manufacturers, and universities all over the country to interview engineers who were involved in construction and maintenance of the shuttle. The results of his investigation were so embarrassing to NASA that the commission relegated them to a minority report in the Appendix. Feynman's report would have remained an obscure footnote in history had a press conference to announce results of the commission's investigation not been held. Remaining silent until he was asked directly, Feynman demonstrated with a rubber O-ring and a glass of ice water how the ambient temperature at launch time was so low that shuttle rubber gasket O-rings could not expand to seal fuel leaks that led to ignition of the fuel tank.

The embarrassing conclusion that Feynman arrived at was, that NASA engineers knew the shuttle's fuel tank gaskets would fail in cold weather. Some of them even recommended aborting the flight. None of them whistleblew, not even after the disaster. Why did they remain silent? Feynman interviewed both working engineers and management to find answers to this question. He found that management insisted that the risk of failure leading to loss of the vehicle was 100,000 to 1. The working engineers pegged the odds at 100 to 1, three orders of magnitude greater. Feynman found that this pattern persisted with engineers who dealt with the solid fuel rockets or the liquid fuel engine. Moreover, management had maintained an atmosphere of "don't rock the boat" that became entrenched because of a series of successes in previous flights and a need to "assure the government of NASA perfection". Their confidence was so great and their commitment to keep within budget so strong that each time a part had to be replaced its replacement was not tested separately. Only the entire engine or rocket was tested. In 250,000 seconds of operation, serious failure of the engines occurred "perhaps 16 times". As a result of

---

* (This Account Is Based on the Minority Report Described in a Book Edited by J. Robbins. Quotes are from Chapter 7)

Engineering Ethics 113

this record, and the felt need to maintain a high public image, the working engineers were pressured by management to keep any concerns they might have to themselves. Many of these suppressed concerns had to do with material fractures, particularly in second stage turbine blades. Failure to address such defects is in violation of the FAA (Federal Aviation Administration) convention for all airplanes.

Feynman ends his report with the admonition "For a successful technology, reality must take precedence over public relations, for nature cannot be fooled".

6.6 BASIC ENGINEERING BUSINESS ETHICS

As biotechnology and e-commerce have grown, engineers have become keys to product development, marketing, and maintenance. The bioengineer is uniquely trained to understand interactions between a product and its user because she speaks both "biologese" and "engineerese" languages. Consequently, business managers, biologists, and engineers who do not usually cross-communicate well have come to depend on bioengineers for guidance in optimizing how a product's biology and engineering work together. The result has been improvement in product safety and effectiveness.

Bioengineers in industry work in a world of conflicting goals. Business managers work to maximize earnings of owners and stockholders. Engineers work to optimize product design for its stated function while minimizing cost based on traditional engineering practices. Clinical biologists work to optimize the interface between product and user based upon a scientific understanding of the biological function being enhanced. Both engineer and scientist work to maximize safety. But the engineer views safety in terms of epidemiological risk assessment. The scientist views safety in terms of how much the product alters normal physiological function.

Industry watchdogs have come to realize that the traditional profit motive that drives business managers and their companies may direct them away from a course that leads them to work for a "reasonably" safe product. Resulting public concerns have led to growth of two kinds of establishments: (1) government regulatory agencies that work with enforcement agencies (e.g. the FDA with the Department of Justice) and (2) tort lawyers. In extreme cases where public safety (e.g. by pollution) or life is threatened, prosecution attorneys working with police departments may become involved. In such cases a misdemeanor crime may escalate to a felony that requires criminal proceedings and potential for incarceration.

Implantable product liability will be discussed in Chapter 13. There is liability if a product does not perform as intended or advertised. If the product is unfit for its intended use the seller has violated a contract and is automatically liable under "contractual theory" of the law. If the seller deliberately deceives he has committed fraud and is criminally liable.

6.7 CULTURAL VARIATION IN BUSINESS ETHICS

Engineers working in the United States who have come from foreign countries, and integrated U.S. citizen engineers who work in foreign countries, may face conflicting concepts of what is considered ethical business practice. A lack of

114   Ethics for Bioengineering Scientists

awareness of these differences could well lead to disruption of any business venture. The main behaviors that are considered acceptable in some cultures but not in others are: kickbacks, cronyism, nepotism, bribes, and discrimination (racial, sexual, religious, etc.).

BRIBES: Bribes are secret payments to induce people to do business that they otherwise would not do. The U.S. Foreign Corrupt Policies Act forbids U.S. company representatives from bribing foreign officials. Yet, bribes are common in many cultures to the extent that business cannot be conducted without them. Some consider kickbacks bribes; others consider them commissions.

KICKBACKS: A kickback is an unrecorded payment, similar to a commission, to a person who has facilitated a transaction. While generally in violation of all state laws (it is not a federal crime unless federal agencies are involved), kickbacks in other countries (e.g. Egypt) are part of long-term business relationships. In these cases, they serve as assurance that the seller will not disappear if there is a problem with the product.

CRONYISM: Cronyism is the practice of directing one's business to one's friends rather than choosing the best product or service. Cronyism is based on having more trust in people one knows personally. While this practice is not illegal for companies without government contracts in the United States, it may be the basis for a stockholder claim of financial malfeasance. Cronyism is common in a number of cultures. In China, it is associated with the concept "guanxi".

NEPOTISM: Nepotism is the practice of hiring one's relative rather than choosing the most qualified candidate for the job. This practice is common in many cultures and may be traced to Hamilton's rule. If the practice can be shown in a court of law to have harmed a company, it may be the subject of a stockholder suit.

DISCRIMINATION: Discrimination is the avoidance of hiring or doing business with members of a given, ethnic, cultural, or racial group. This behavior is traceable to Hamilton's rule. In the United States, it is against the law for race, religion, gender, and national origin, among others, to be discriminated against by any company that sells to the government (state or federal).

6.8   INTELLECTUAL PROPERTY

Much of what an engineer creates is design. Indeed, as indicated in Chapter 1, architecture was the dominant function of early engineers. A design is a form of intellectual property (IP). There are three kinds of IP: patented inventions, trade secrets, and copyrights. Software may be copyrighted, so engineers may be involved with any of the three. The engineer who works independently will often own his own IP. If the IP was developed while the engineer was employed, and was connected to the job, the employer may own its copyright or patent

6.9   THE KEY LESSONS

The structures of civilization are the consequences of engineering. The corporations, government agencies, and private institutions that employ engineers shoulder the responsibility for safety and efficacy of these structures. If they fail, the

Engineering Ethics

engineer's employer becomes a legal target. Engineers at the managerial level may become targets, as was the case in the Challenger incident, if they can be shown to have had the authority to make final decisions. But the engineers who perform the work most immediate to production of the structure will not be liable, unless they make a construction error. In addition to recognizing that society is the chief client of engineering, there are two other lessons to carry forth from this chapter: (1) Engineering decisions, even the moral analysis kind, tend to involve risk analysis. (2) Engineers usually are not scientists (except for academics working in "Engineering Science"). But they use scientific discoveries and the methodology of science to solve problems.

ENRICHMENT

1. Perform a moral analysis on the Pinto Case, using Lee Iacocca, the then-president of Ford, as a defendant. The article by Lee and Ermann may be found at https://www.coursehero.com/file/p1j8n26/Read-Lee-Matthew-T-and-M-David-Ermann-1999-Pinto-Madness-as-a-Flawed-Landmark/. Does your analysis change as a result of reading this article? Why?
2. Perform a moral analysis on the Challenger Case, using the "working engineers" who disagreed with their managers, as defendants.

7 Medical Ethics

According to the U.S. government census there are about 131 million people employed in health care in the United States, as of 2017–2018. This is the largest employment sector in the country. As of 2019, there were about 752,000 physicians, as of 2020 about 326,000 medical technologists and about 3 million registered nurses, all according to the Bureau of Labor Statistics. If the reader has not been a health-care client, they are a rare person.

In Chapter 1, we followed the medical profession, the source of the physicians who are most responsible for patient care, up to the end of WWI. The Depression and WWII that followed saw increased involvement of government in health care as victims of the economic downturn could not afford care and the military had to be attended to in many world venues. Chapter 1 described the growth of government-sponsored clinical research, establishment of the NIH, and development of other sources of encouragement for science to play a role in medicine, after WWII. A document that helped set the stage for these advances, was the 1945 report to the president, by Vannevar Bush, director of the Office of Scientific Research and Development, titled "Science, the endless frontier" (Bush 1945). When the United States entered the 1950s, it was involved in a Cold War with the U.S.S.R. By the end of the decade, the Soviets had launched Sputnik, the first satellite, starting the "race for space". Fear of losing this race, and fear of not being able to defend itself against Soviet missiles, motivated a push to upgrade U.S. science and engineering education. As indicated in Chapter 1, it was in this atmosphere of having to "catch-up" in science, that science and medicine began to cooperate seriously (with one of the consequences being the development of bioengineering in the late 1960s).

Certain changes began to appear in medicine that reflected a scientific influence. In the 1970s, the initiative "translational clinical science" appeared, stressing the proposals of Vannevar Bush to translate scientific discoveries into clinical applications (Juengst et al. 2016). This was followed in the 1980s by an "evidence-based medicine" initiative, which proposed that medical decisions be in agreement with the latest scientific evidence (Juengst et al. 2016). Medicine was now officially focused on data; not so much for their accuracy, as for their role as evidence. The next major initiative appears to have awaited completion of the Human Genome Project in 2003 (Juengst et al. 2016). This landmark event led to an expectation that a new medicine based on genome sequencing would create a paradigm shift in patient treatment. One of the first terms used in 2012 to describe this initiative, was "personalized medicine" (Juengst et al. 2016). It targeted the diagnosis function of medical management. The data to be gathered were the DNA codes for every function and its diseased states. The resulting genomic library would become a reference to be matched with each patient's genome to identify that individual's unique program. Critiques of this initiative attacked the presumed assumption that

DOI: 10.1201/9781003197218-7

118   Ethics for Bioengineering Scientists

its supporters claimed that they had found the key to "individually tailored" medicine in genes. This meant that environmental factors, uncovered during doctor-patient interviews, could be ignored, thereby negating the true meaning of "personal" (Juengst et al. 2016). An apparent death blow to the initiative was delivered by President Obama in his 2015 State of the Union address when he announced a "precision medicine initiative" (actually coined in 2009; (Juengst et al. 2016)), since formalized by the NIH and a variety of programs and institutes throughout the country (Juengst et al. 2016). The "precision" referred to in this case is precise classification of diseases in terms of "specific molecular causal factors". These factors are data. The scientific question they beg is "are they causal or associative"?

These developments overlay the daily occupation of and ethical challenges for health professionals. For the remainder of the chapter we shall explore these core ethical concerns, particularly as they affect the patient–physician relationship.

7.1 THE PHYSICIAN'S CLIENT

The clients of physicians are patients. Physicians' ethical concerns are of the same kind as the concerns of other health professionals. However, physicians, veterinarians, and dentists may overrule decisions of all other professionals in their field. Practitioners of veterinary medicine and dentistry are usually not required to make human life and death decisions, so it is understood that any references to emergency situations carry a different weight for them. Nurses carry a different weight as well. They sometimes are left to make life and death decisions in spite of the fact that officially they are not allowed to do so.

7.2 THE STANDARD OF CARE

Since medicine is a truth profession, the focus of medical schools is training of individuals who can solve patients' medical problems. As a profession with a long history, medicine has developed standard approaches to solving medical problems that consistently yield satisfactory solutions. Physical examination and diagnosis procedures are core constituents of traditional medical school curricula. During internship and residency the student learns to use these procedures to arrive at a diagnosis and also learns to choose an appropriate specific course of treatment. For cases where the condition is too complex to resolve with basic training knowledge, the student is taught how to determine the appropriate specialist for a referral. With this training behind her, the newly minted physician is launched into a career of service. For some, specialization may be attractive. Pediatrics, gynecology, oncology, pathology, anesthesiology, and hematology are just a few of the possibilities. These require residencies that may add another four years or more to training. Even further training with a fellowship would be required for subspecialties such as pediatric oncology or sports medicine.

Certain elements of medical training are consistent from school to school. A physician must display proficiency in these elements to gain a state license to practice medicine. Each state determines the level of proficiency sufficient for its needs. Collectively these elements are termed "Standard of Care". As long as a physician

Medical Ethics   **119**

applies the standard of care proficiently in treating all her patients, the state medical board will be satisfied. A licensed physician may perform any medical procedure. However, if a chosen procedure is not part of the standard of care for the diagnosed condition, and if it is not successful, the physician is liable for malpractice prosecution.

Standard of care actually operates at two levels. At the general practice level, it includes procedures all physicians should know (e.g. How to open a blocked air passage). At the specialty level, it includes procedures learned during a residency (e.g. general orthopedic procedures) and, possibly, a subsequent fellowship (e.g. advanced shoulder surgery procedures). In medical specialties, the standard of care may change, from year to year because new techniques, instrumentation, drugs or implants may be introduced that have been shown to be safer and/or more effective than current ones. Every company that produces a medical product dreams that their product will become a standard of care.

7.3   AUTONOMY AS IT RELATES TO THE HEALTH PROFESSIONS

In Chapter 3, we presented autonomy as the right of a client in a professional–client relationship that is specified by most professional codes of ethics. We also noted its derivation from deontological ethics. Kant starts with logic and the meanings of the words rather than the notion of human nature, but comes to the same conclusion. In brief, he shows that if we place value on anything at all, if we take value choices seriously, then we must place the highest value on autonomy—the ability to make moral choices in the first place. One can also find provision for it in virtue ethics. Aristotle takes very seriously the problem of ascertaining the *voluntariness* or freedom of acts and consents. Respect for autonomy and respect for rationality and the freedom and rational choice they make possible, are fundamental concepts in many European-based philosophies. Its codification in the U.S. constitution provides a connection to contractarian moral theory.

In the physician–patient relationship, autonomy assumes a life and death dimension. A patient invoking this right may be choosing death voluntarily or inadvertently. If the reader is a bioengineering undergraduate, they may be a (1) pre-meds who will face the bioethical challenges of patient care or (2) potential designer of devices (or drugs) that will automate patient care, possibly to the point of allowing them to program their own death. In this era of precision medicine, the individuality of each patient will complicate treatment for both physicians and bioengineers. The need to determine the unique condition of each patient requires an invasion of their privacy that could overwhelm their autonomy. Consider a situation in which there is a conflict between a patient's concept of their condition and/or its treatment gained from television or search engines and the diagnosis of his physician. Accordingly, we need to understand what autonomy is in order to determine when it is in danger.

7.4   EXAMPLE OF AUTONOMY IN ACTION

A patient announces to his urologist that he has just heard an infomercial touting the miraculous relief a drug will give for patients suffering from urethritis. The claim is that drug's effectiveness has been "proven" in clinical tests. A traditional paternalistic physician would have chuckled and lectured the upstart patient about the physician-to-patient gap in knowledge.

This scenario is less likely today because of the acceptance of patient autonomy. The physician is aware that his patient's condition may worsen and require surgery. The urologist will have to obtain an informed consent before such surgery may be performed. A patient aware of their autonomy will not easily give consent unless she trusts her physician.

7.5   THE COMPONENTS OF AUTONOMY

"Autonomy" is philosophically understood as a union of two components. The first is *rationality* (variously defined, but always including the ability to evaluate situations and choose a coping tactic directed at each challenge). Note that "rationality" not "reasonableness" was the choice here. A patient may make a rational choice that is not reasonable. For example, he may refuse a necessary surgery because the surgeon belongs to an ethnic group his ethnic group fears. He would be in a vulnerable position during surgery and there is a small but real chance the surgeon will ignore her "do no harm" professional vow in a stressful moment that awakens a vengeful urge. The second component is *freedom* or *noncontrol* (meaning the right and ability to do what you choose to do or at least to act without coercion or restraint).

In general, an action is *autonomous* if it is (1) intended (by the actor), (2) understood in its details and consequences, and (3) freely chosen. Consent to medical treatment is autonomous if (1) it is deliberately or intentionally given, (2) the treatment and its alternatives, estimated risks and benefits, are understood (i.e. the patient is "informed"), and (3) the patient is not pressured into giving it. When a patient formally agrees to a treatment under these conditions, he/she has delivered an *informed consent*. In general, a signed informed consent is required before a physician may begin a course of treatment. Exceptions occur if the patient is unable to sign or no responsible agent for the patient is available. The components of autonomy are evident in the informed-consent process. Information is essential to rationality. We have to understand the situation before we can decide what we ought to do about it. Consent presupposes freedom. But unless it is truly devoid of pressure, it cannot be free. An example patient consent form for a research procedure is provided in Appendix B.

The requirement to respect an informed and competent patient's refusal of treatment was written into federal law in 1990 as the Patient Self Determination Act (PSDA). The law applies only to medicine controlled by the federal government, that is, Medicare. But it affects all hospitals and physicians treating Medicare patients. So, to avoid confusion that would arise by trying to separate patients into "covered" and "not-covered" categories, the law tends to be applied universally. This is not to say that there is clear guidance about how to apply the law. There are two crucial issues it does not address: (1) What is the order of priority of between "rationality" and "freedom", which are logically independent of each other, and have no obvious order of priority. (2) What levels of rationality and freedom (in

Medical Ethics **121**

terms of the law, information and competence) are sufficient to achieve the goals of the law? Rationality may vary from complete ignorance or derangement to a complete understanding of all that is entailed in a choice. Freedom may vary from complete coercion (the gun at your head, or better yet, the head of your child) through infinite degrees of pressure and manipulation to some ideal absolutely free choice (Can such an ideal really be achieved? What does "absolutely" mean here anyway?).

7.6 TWO INTERPRETATIONS OF AUTONOMY

There appears to be some consensus that there are two philosophical models of autonomy, Libertarian and Rationalist.

In the Libertarian model, freedom is paramount. The individual's impulse reflects her autonomy, even if that impulse may seem deleterious. The individual is entitled to information and advice needed to make a rational decision, but she alone makes the decision. If there are doubts that the individual knows what she is getting into, that is, doubts that the decision was fully informed, the outcome typically is resolved by respecting the individual's wishes. A patient refusing a life-saving blood transfusion or surgical procedure is making an autonomous decision which must be respected. The libertarian viewpoint is characteristic of Anglo-American ethical tradition and was espoused by J.S. Mill and J. Bentham who, it may be recalled, also espoused act utilitarianism.

In the Rationalist model, rationality is paramount. The individual's choice has to reflect his real rational interests, regardless of his impulse. If his impulse leads him in another direction, he is being deceived by himself or others, his freedom is an illusion. Paternalism may thus be justified. The forces compelling an individual to make an irrational choice may come from the person's personal or family or societal background. Karl Marx points out that society may promulgate deceptions useful to the ruling class, and thus the person may not have a true disinterested choice. A patient refusing a life-saving medical procedure would be viewed as being deceived and would be overruled. The rational viewpoint is characteristic of European ethical tradition and was espoused by Kant and Rousseau who, it may be recalled, also espoused non-consequential moral theories, and by Karl Marx.

The duty to respect autonomy, then, can be fulfilled by two different routes, depending on whether we assign higher priority to the patient's expressed desire or to the patient's real interests. Once the choice is made, how is it implemented in real life settings? What measure do we apply to gauge the degree to which both components of autonomy have been optimized? At present, unfortunately(?), we have no standardized criteria for determining the presence or absence of autonomy in any human on either the libertarian or rationalist interpretations. We have no sure knowledge that autonomy is even a possible condition for humans. After all, if we allow for self-deception and incomplete understanding of information, we may have to conclude that no-one can ever be completely *rational*, so rationality may have practical limits as a component of the autonomous individual. And if we consider emotional stresses, felt constraints, or strong desires to be coercive, no one can ever be totally *free*. So, we could argue that *autonomy* expresses an ideal that may help guide human moral theory but can never be an absolute reality in human life. Notwithstanding such caveats, in order to treat a patient with respect for her autonomy we have to decide whether or not she is *competent* enough to make decisions for herself and protect her own interests; if not, professional ethics require that we protect those interests for her. And there are times when we have to know if a person is sufficiently rational to participate in medical decisions to start, continue, or end treatment. If we set our standards of information and liberty too high, we will be unable to establish any practical basis for making a decision of how to act.

7.7 DECIDING IF THE PATIENT HAS TRUE AUTONOMY

In medical settings, questions about autonomy come from three different directions: (1) physiological, (2) philosophical, and (3) psychological. They all, however, are concerned with determining the degree of autonomy (How free and informed is the patient?) and deciding whether freedom or rationality is more important (Newton 2004).

1. **Is the physiological state of the patient at a level that would allow autonomy?** Illness itself typically compromises a person's ability to think clearly. In addition, a sick person may be sedated by medication and depressed by the fact of being ill. Can his decisions be taken seriously?
2. **Does the patient's reason for his choice address the actual problem?** If a patient would rather die than have a leg amputated because it would spoil his appearance, the life-and-death problem is not being addressed. In the Libertarian model, however, the answer to the philosophical question would be yes. If the patient denies there is anything wrong with the leg, it would be no. If the patient insists the leg will get better because it did for one of his ancestors, the philosophical question would be more difficult to answer.
3. **Is the psychological state of the patient at the time of the decision a true reflection of who he is?** This question penetrates deeply into medical practice. If a Jehovah's Witness refuses a blood transfusion repeatedly, and all next of kin and friends concur in the decision, should we honor that refusal? The weight of law and tradition says that we must. Now, close to death, the same Witness suddenly cries *Save me! Save my life!* has the patient just changed his mind (in which case we must give the transfusion), or is this just a cry of fear, expressing no authentic desire of the patient's in these circumstances? In which case what should we do? If a pregnant woman agrees ahead of time that no painkillers should be used during her labor, but starts crying out for drugs during the very last contractions of normal delivery, that request is routinely ignored. If a patient dying of cancer has agreed ahead of time that no intubation to assist breathing should be introduced during the ebbing of his life, and then, in extreme discomfort, cries out for help in breathing, should we intubate him, or routinely just sedate him to reduce the discomfort?

Up to now, we have considered the effect of a patient's autonomy on the patient only. The document called the *informed consent* that gives permission to the

Medical Ethics

physician to perform the procedure in question does not mention effects of the decision on any others. *Are* there circumstances that dictate widening this circle? Are there individuals who are so affected by the patient's decision that their autonomy must be factored into any decision? These questions arise when the decision involves withholding life-sustaining treatment, which often significantly affects the interest of others. In such cases, it is generally accepted that those others must have a hearing before the decision is carried out. But what counts as *significantly affected*? Patient's spouses will always be affected by patient's decisions; they should certainly have the right to say something. But should they have a veto? A mother of a minor's decision to withhold treatment that would save her life might be overruled (Newton 2004). What if the "minor" is a fetus? May we remove the quotes in that sentence? A pregnant patient who is close to delivery usually may not abort unless her life is in danger. The unborn child is considered a minor. At what point is the fetus just part of the mother's body? Or as some women going through a difficult pregnancy have said, a parasite. Since the unborn cannot speak for themselves, their autonomous interests must be assumed by others. Whose interest should be primary?

Suppose the decision affects only some policy or practice? Consider the practice of removing feeding tubes from a dying person. One nurse has been quoted as saying: "You know there are lots of places in this world where a person can starve to death. My hospital should not be one of them." Traditionally, medicine has not *given up* on a patient until everything has been tried to improve her condition. Suppose a patient refuses further treatment before that point has been reached. Is the traditional medical standard *of care* an appropriate limit on autonomy? Or should autonomy be taken most seriously precisely at that point where some set of professional standards, developed by professionals (for the greater happiness of professionals), imposes unwanted invasions on the patient? (Newton 2004).

Example of overruling autonomy: *The case of United States v. Sell, 2003*

A dentist named Charles Sell was committed to a mental hospital because he had homicidal delusions. He believed that God told him he could save a soul every time he murdered an FBI agent. Sell was released later and submitted insurance claims that the company claimed were fraudulent. Allowed bail while awaiting trial for this offense, he was soon arrested by an FBI agent on charges of attempted murder of two agents, the one making the arrest and the one investigating Sell's fraud indictment.

At the trial, it was determined that Sell was not mentally competent and needed to be committed again for further evaluation. The psychiatric staff of the hospital concluded that he should be prescribed anti-psychotic medication so he could stand trial. Sell refused to take the medication and the hospital took their case to court claiming Sell was so dangerous he should be forced to take the drugs. The lower court agreed with the hospital, but their decision

124 Ethics for Bioengineering Scientists

> was reversed by the Supreme Court. The higher court reasoned that the lower court had not considered the argument that the kind of drugs needed to suppress psychosis would so debilitate Sell that he could not take an active part in his own defense.

The Supreme court has ruled that there are conditions under which forcible medication is allowed. It must be administered in a controlled environment like a prison or it has to be ordered by a court. An ethical dilemma is created when the defendant would commit self-incrimination be agreeing to accept treatment (e.g. the crime may be a common symptom of people with the alleged condition). The right to autonomy covers the right to refuse self-incrimination. The higher court has held that autonomy may be violated under four circumstances: (1) the issues affected by the crime are critical to the state, (2) the defendant's ability to understand and take an active part in the proceedings is not impaired, (3) the medication chosen is optimal for the condition, i.e. it is the most effective and least invasive of all the alternatives, and (4) the mode of administration is consistent with standard of care (Budinger and Budinger 2006).

7.8 PHYSICIAN ROLE IN AUTONOMY

How is autonomy recognition practiced in the modern physician–patient relationship? Prior to the 1960s, the role of the physician was more paternalistic, and a patient's involvement in his or her own medical care was relatively minimal. A series of malpractice court cases in the 1960s (see section 10.7) exposed an array of violations (see section 10.7) that led to establishment of a requirement for informed consent in many states as part of "patient's rights" (Rodwin 1994). Now a dialogue exists between patient and physician, wherein it is the physician's responsibility to describe treatment options, to outline what adverse events might occur, and to work with the patient to find the best possible solution for a particular situation. Ideally it is a fiduciary form of relationship.

In addition, informed consent is now required before a treatment regimen begins. This means that the physician must decide what to tell a patient about an illness and provide sufficient information for the patient to make an informed decision regarding treatment. How should one balance informed consent versus telling the patient everything? For example, when a nervous patient who tends to magnify what should be minor pain is diagnosed with what is rarely a painful disease, should he/she be told that pain is a possibility? Aristotle's doctrine of the mean would have the physician find the appropriate balance between giving every detail of the truth and giving no information except the treatment the physician is recommending (Budinger and Budinger 2006). In other words it is most virtuous to give the patient sufficient information for decision making but not enough to confuse or unduly worry him/her. In the author's experience, consent forms are becoming longer and more informative because hospital legal counsels advise their clients to cover all issues that might be targets in a lawsuit.

Medical Ethics 125

> ### Example autonomy case (fictional): Monitoring patient compliance in an epidemic
>
> There are a number of group challenges in an epidemic/pandemic. (1) Epidemiologists need to know how many people are infected so they can estimate R_0 the average distance between people at which the germ is infective. This number becomes part of models predicting graphs of the daily rate of infection. It can only be confirmed by frequent testing. (2) People need to be encouraged to wear masks to reduce the aerosol spread of infection. (3) People need to reduce social contact to reduce the chance of disease spread by surface contact.
>
> Consider the following scenario: COVID-19 has returned. A physician watching the news on television notices that a set of her patients show up at political rallies without face masks. Another set has not been tested at her testing facility, nor have they requested and returned a free kit. The city has passed an ordinance that will cause anyone not volunteering for testing, and anyone caught without a mask to be fined for each incidence. They will have their driving license suspended after five incidents. Physicians are requested to aid in locating any of their patients not conforming to the epidemic laws. Does patient autonomy override a physician's health responsibility in an epidemic?

7.9 PHYSICIAN ROLE IN CONFIDENTIALITY

Patient autonomy includes protection from revealing medical records. How are the guidelines for keeping a confidence followed? By law a patient has the right to control or keep private his medical information unless he has given specific permission to the physician to act otherwise. The underlying motives for this protection are to maintain privacy and to avoid revealing information that might compromise the patient at work, financially, or socially. A breach in confidentiality can lead to revocation of a physician's license.

The duty to "do the right thing" is deontological and extends to respect for patient rights. Thus, control of information about one's self would be violated if any patient's personal information is publicized or even divulged to a fellow physician unless such sharing is part of the treatment. To ensure that not only physicians, but all health care workers would abide by this restriction, congress passed a Uniform Health-Care Information Act (UHCIA) in 1988 that:

1. prohibited any health giver from releasing any information pertaining to a patient without the patient's written consent
2. restricted the power of a subpoena to acquire confidential information, and protected the patient as well as the custodian from being required to release private information summoned on a subpoena.
3. gave the patient access to his or her medical records, something that had never before been allowed.

In the 1990s, more safeguards were added to cover patient data stored electronically on multiple databases that could no longer be controlled by the treating physician. These data were being provided to or accessed by a wide variety of agencies not involved in patient care. Such violations of individual privacy had widespread consequences, including bias in eligibility for employment, financial aid, and insurance. Accordingly, the UHCIA was updated and expanded in 1996 to form the Health Information Portability and Accountability Act (HIPAA), the first comprehensive federal law pertaining to privacy of electronically accessible patient information. The Health and Human Services department added its own *Standards for Privacy of Individually Identifiable Health Information* in 2002 and both sets of regulations took effect in 2003. They covered such items as health plans, health care clearinghouses and health care providers who electronically transmit any health information in connection with financial transactions.

In those cases, where a health care provider is also a scientist performing human research, these laws apply in so far as the research utilizes patient information. Even email exchanges between health-care provider and patient are covered. The standards were enacted not only to protect patient confidentiality, but also to improve efficiency of utilization of patient information by encouraging the widespread use of electronic data in health care.

7.10 PHYSICIAN GUIDELINES WHEN PATIENT INFORMATION MUST BE SHARED

In addition to federal laws, there are state laws regulating patient confidentiality. However, there are legal limits to this duty; some of them imposed as a result of Judge Clark's dissenting opinion in the *Tarasoff v. University of California Regents* (presented in Chapter 5). A physician must divulge a patient's medical problem, in some cases only after so ordered by a court, if:

1. the safety of other individuals is at risk (e.g. as was the case in Tarasoff)
2. the patient is suicidal
3. the benefit to society outweighs the autonomy of the patient (e.g. the patient has a highly contagious fatal disease)
4. the medical problem has resulted from a crime (e.g. rape or other physical abuse)
5. the patient is so mentally incompetent his judgment about his own treatment is not rational (This circumstance requires a court order.)
6. the patient is a minor with no ability to understand the danger he is in and the parent or guardian refuses to sign an informed consent (This circumstance requires a court order).

7.11 PHYSICIAN'S CODE OF ETHICS

To instill confidence in patients' trust of their physicians, a code of conduct for physicians has been developed by the American Medical Association. This Code of Medical Ethics first appeared in 1847. Currently there is an AMA Standards Group with activities divided into three programs: Council on Ethical and Judicial Affairs;

Medical Ethics

Ethics Resource Center, and the Institute for Ethics, which researches emerging issues (Budinger and Budinger 2006).

A physician is guided by three standards for behavior that may at times conflict: (1) the personal code of if ethics that shaped him/her as a person, (2) the medical profession's code of ethics (ostensibly based on the Hippocratic oath), and (3) the law. The latter is based on the constitution of the state, and thereby connected with contractarian ethics, but it is enforced by the justice system.

7.12 CONFLICT OF INTEREST IN THE HEALTH PROFESSION

The most frequent circumstance that leads to a reduction in patient trust of or confidence in a health-care provider is perceived conflict between the various providers' interests. Whether actual or suspected the existence of a conflict of interest undermines autonomy. There are at least three circumstances presenting a conflict of interest:

1. The physician may gain financially beyond patient fees for work performed by the physician. The physician may own or be a partner in a laboratory performing tests he has prescribed. He may be a stockholder of a drug company that produces medications he has prescribed. He may split fees with an expensive specialist to whom the patient is referred. He may be paid for recruiting patients for a research study.
2. Physicians gain prestige, and thereby attract more patients, when they publish reports of cases, particularly unusual ones, in highly regarded medical journals. Medical school clinical faculty enhance their chances for tenure and promotion with similar publications. Advancement is greatly enhanced if the physician is part of a research study that includes other universities. As a result, a physician may bias his selection of patients, preferring "interesting" cases or those with conditions attracting a lot of research.
3. If a physician is an employee of a large health care organization such as an Health Maintenance Organization (HMO), he may be under pressure to reduce costs or increase profit. Pressure is greatest in for-profit organizations where profits may be increased by reducing patient time-per-visit, thereby increasing patient load. Cost reduction can occur by choosing cheaper drugs that may be generics or less effective alternatives that still meet standard of care (Budinger and Budinger 2006).

In each of these circumstances, the patient's interests may be relegated to a lower priority if they interfere with a physician's competing self-interest.

Conflict-of-Interest Case study: *Fraud by Tenet Healthcare*
Based on web site: www.uow.edu.au/~bmartin/dissent/documents/ health/tenet_reddingupdate.html

Mark Colombo and 768 other heart patients (or their estates) sued Tenet Healthcare Corp. in 2004 for fraud, battery, negligence and elder abuse (most were over 60 years of age and on Social Security, with Medicare); 51 of the patients had died and were represented by their estates, which added the accusation of "wrongful death"(White 2003). They were joined by the U.S. Department of Justice (for Medicare fraud), the State of California (for Medical fraud and malpractice), and TRICARE medical insurance (for fraudulent claims).

For Colombo, the torment began when he visited the Redding (CA) Medical Center in 2002. He was diagnosed with coronary disease and told he needed double bypass surgery. He asked for a second opinion at the time of his diagnosis, but was told he had to be hospitalized at once because his condition was too serious to delay the surgery. Months later his cardiologist in Sacramento disputed the need for any surgery, prompting Colombo to retain an attorney. "I was shocked. You have such trust in your physician" said Colombo (Budinger and Budinger 2006). Another patient, Rev. John Corapi, was told that he should have cardiac catheterization in spite of having passed his stress test. He opted to have the procedure done in Las Vegas where his cardiologist found no evidence of pathology. Several other patient plaintiffs suffered strokes, brain damage or amputations after questionable cardiac surgeries. Most patients had less severe side effects, such as short-term memory loss (Budinger and Budinger 2006).

Corapi and a Redding physician, Patrick Campbell, filed complaints against Tenet with the U.S. Justice Department under the False Claims Act (1986 version—It was originally enacted in 1863). This made them eligible for whistleblower financial rewards. The federal government had jurisdiction in this case because most of the surgeries were reimbursed by Medicare. In 2002, FBI agents raided the hospital and obtained medical records and billings.

At least four law firms represented the patient plaintiffs who waived their HIPPA confidentiality rights to the extent needed for prosecution. They were awarded $395 million dollars for having been subjected to unwarranted heart surgeries. The surgeries were conducted between 1992 and 2002. In addition to the Tenet fine, four of the surgeons were sued for malpractice and settled for over $32 million. Two of them, Chae Hyun Moon, chief cardiologist and Fidel Realvasquez, top cardiac surgeon, were fined an additional $1.4 million each and had to agree to never perform any cardiac procedures on Medicare, Medical or TRICARE patients. Dr. Moon is no longer practicing medicine (Martin 2007). Federal funds recovered from the defendants amounted to $64.55 million, 15% of which was divided by three whistleblowers as a FCA award. In 2004 Tenet, beset by numerous convictions for fraud that drained their funds, sold the hospital to Hospital Partners of America for $60 million (Martin 2007).

The False Claims Act covers all financial dealings of the federal government. It has been amended a number of times, most recently with adjustments for rewarding and protecting whistleblowers.

Medical Ethics

7.13 THE IMPACT OF SCIENCE ON THE PHYSICIAN–PATIENT RELATIONSHIP

The Mesmer case, described in Chapter 1, was one of the early examples of science impacting the physician–patient relationship; not because Mesmer used scientific understanding in his treatment, but because he used the idea of science as a sales gimmick. He had a serious conflict of interest. Even Jenner's use of cowpox vaccine to cure smallpox was not a true application of science. The germ theory of disease had not yet been established in 1796. He demonstrated the value of well-reasoned empiricism after (1) noticing that milkmaids do not contract smallpox and (2) receiving news from Asia of successful inoculations for smallpox. Without knowing anything about immunology or the germ theory of disease, he artfully mused that something entered their bodies through the hand abrasions caused by milking that rendered them resistant to the disease. He rubbed the cow secretion into a nick created in an eight-year-old's arm and a few days later did the same with fluid from a smallpox pustule. Thousands of lives were saved by the resultant smallpox vaccine. Today Jenner's experiment would be unlawful.

An understanding of physiology and pathophysiology grew in the 19th century as laboratory science became laboratory medicine. With the establishment of the germ theory of contagion by Pasteur (1822–1895) and Koch (1843–1910), Lister (1827–1912) was able to show a scientific basis for sterilization. Although progress was uneven in the various medical specialties, laboratory science, utilizing animal experimentation, and field science, utilizing epidemiology, began to seriously influence patient care by the mid-19th century (Worboys 2011).

Full integration of science into medicine is indicated by the term "biomedicine". Edward Jenner is considered the "father" of this field. The "biomedicalization" process was not a dominant trend until after WWII (Löwy 2011). Between the mid-19th century and 1950s; clinicians for the most part utilized the fruits of scientific research without comprehending how they worked. There were physician scientists like Cannon (1871–1945) who could "connect-the-dots". But these were academicians and, consequently, small in number. Biomedicine has become an academic, clinical and industrial giant since then, generating a large fraction of research and GNP in the United States.

Clinicians have become an integral part of biomedicine. Through their patients they provide data for field (=clinical) science, that is, epidemiological research on humans. By deciding which drug to prescribe or which device to implant they influence popularity of the product, thereby impacting the data that accumulates. Product manufacturers have a strong financial interest in convincing physicians to make the "right" product choice. Many physicians become involved with products before they are made generally available by the FDA. FDA approval is based on successful human testing in clinical trials. Epidemiological analysis of results from these trials requires sample sizes sufficient to achieve high statistical levels of confidence (The smaller the difference between control and experimental data, the larger the sample needs to be.). Accordingly, physicians become patient recruiters and principal investigator physicians become physician recruiters. To encourage all, the product manufacturer will often offer incentives.

True conflict-of-interest for physicians between medicine and science arises when patients become involved in scientific studies. *Moore v. University of*

130   Ethics for Bioengineering Scientists

California, an example of such conflict, was presented in Chapter 4. In addition, the need to attract patients for studies puts physicians in a position where they cannot afford to be paternalistic. (If a patient senses he has been coerced to enter a study, a lawsuit may result.) Also, the explosion of media advertising of drugs and devices, including claims that the effectiveness of the product has been "clinically proven", has convinced many patients, aware of their autonomy, that they know enough to want a say in their treatment. Attempts at paternalism do not fare well with such patients.

7.14   THE HOSPITAL IRB AS THE PATIENT'S LOCAL WATCHDOG

A significant indicator of a physician's competency is membership on a hospital staff. The privilege comes with a responsibility to adhere to hospital standards for patient care. One of these standards is respect for patient autonomy that is monitored by its Institutional Review Board (IRB) and contracted to the patient via an actual hardcopy document—the human informed consent form (HCF). There are in general two kinds of HCF:

1. The standard permission form to treat the patient for a specific medical condition. If an invasive procedure such as surgery is required this form may be more complicated than the one used for an in-hospital non-invasive treatment.
2. A permission form for an experimental treatment that is part of a study. This form is usually composed by the group of individuals conducting the study. An example of this form is presented in Appendix B.

The IRB is responsible for approving the HCF. Every hospital in the United States is required by federal law to have an IRB that reports to the state government on a regular basis. Requirements for makeup of the IRB vary from state to state, but generally include at least one lay member who serves as a watchdog for the community. Where human experimentation is conducted reports must be sent to the federal government as well. The makeup of an IRB in an institution that performs such experiments must conform to standards set by Title 45, Part 46 of the U.S. Department of Health and Human Services Code of Federal Regulations. This will be discussed in the chapter on human experimentation.

7.15   THE ADVANCED HEALTH-CARE DIRECTIVE

The last autonomous act of a patient is his being subjected to his instructions for treatment while dying. He also has some legal power over the conduct of the health professionals caring for him during this process. He may direct them on the limits they are to extend themselves to delay his death. The legal document specifying these limits is called an *Advanced Health Care Directive*. In a sense, it is the final bookend on a medical care process for which the Informed Consent is the initial bookend. An example of an AHCD is presented in Appendix C.

Medical Ethics

7.16 ETHICAL ISSUES ASSOCIATED WITH TREATMENT

The initiatives discussed at the start of this chapter dealt with diagnosis. The act of curing the patient is encompassed in treatment. Treatment for a disease is the most traditional function of a physician, after assisting with birth. The success of clinical science has allowed medicine to extend beyond life-saving to include treatments that improve the so-called "quality of life". There are ethical challenges for all treatment modalities. There are also ethical challenges associated with the patient-physician relationship that relate to: patient autonomy, patient confidentiality and physician conflict of interest. A sampling is presented in Table 7.1, which is adapted from Newton (Newton 2004). The "life and death" issues have a strong bioengineering component because they all rely on some kind of technology. Accordingly, they and others such as human gene therapy, human genetic engineering, reproductive cloning, contraception and superhumans with prosthetic devices are suitable subjects for debates. Possible moral theory approaches in the debates are suggested in the table.

TABLE 7.1
Health Professional Ethics Issues

Issue	Consequentialist Debate Approach	Nonconsequentialist Debate Approach
LIFE AND DEATH		
Artificially assisted reproduction	Desire of couple to have a child vs. possibility of exploitive commercialization	Value of life, right to form a contract vs. separation of marriage and reproduction
Surrogate motherhood	", + advantage to surrogate vs. possibility of fostering callousness in contracting parents	". + possible injustice, unnatural use of reproductive capacity
Abortion	Prevents birth of unwanted or defective children vs. expedient view of life	Right of woman to control own body vs. right of fetus to live
Refusal of vigorous treatment for imperiled newborns	End suffering of infant and parents, avoids low-quality of life, suffering, burdensome treatments vs. ends lives, misses opportunity to develop and test medical technology	Right of family to refuse treatment on behalf of the infant when interests so indicate vs. right of infants to whatever level of care they need
Allowing competent patient to die on request	Minimizes suffering and expense for patient and family vs. may lead to death under pressure, eliminates possibility of any recovery	Right of any conscious, competent patient to refuse unwanted treatment vs. requirements of law and medical ethics to preserve life

(Continued)

TABLE 7.1 (Continued)
Health Professional Ethics Issues

Issue	Consequentialist Debate Approach	Nonconsequentialist Debate Approach
Deciding to terminate life support for irreversibly comatose	Minimizes expense, futile use of scarce resources, shortens suffering of family vs. if hastily done, may kill recovering patient, may make euthanasia a standard	Right of next of kin or guardian to exercise substituted judgment for incompetent vs. duty to sustain life

PROFESSIONAL RESPONSIBILITY (Issues other than research)

Shaping client-professional relationship	Need to get patient well vs. keep patient calm and compliant with treatment	Respect for patient autonomy; vs. provider's integrity
Avoiding malpractice suits	Need to practice good medicine and document treatment vs. avoid costly defensive medicine	Patient's right to compensation for injury, right to use of courts vs. "good medicine is good law"
Harvesting organs from the dead	Need to have organs available for transplants to improve chances of survival vs. quality of life for very sick patients	Respect for feelings of family vs. religious community objections
Developing allogeneic and xenogeneic implants as well as artificial organs	Need to supplement living donations. vs. Investigation of tissue implants may divert resources from cure research	Respect for patient's and family's privacy. vs. Some issues with rights when patient is an experiment subject
Developing rationing schemes to cut costs of healthcare	Cost of technology may reduce funds available to other areas of health care. vs. technology saves lives	Right of every patient to health care vs. duty of physician to provide best health care

7.17 THE PHYSICIAN, A LIFE OF DIAGNOSIS AND TREATMENT

This chapter has dealt with a number of issues surrounding diagnosis and treatment. Just 100 years ago these were relatively straightforward activities for a paternalistic physician. Today, the entrance of data into medical thinking and technology into everyday practice, has produced an information overload that challenges a physician's decision-making ability at every level. Notwithstanding this change, the patient-physician relationship soldiers on, and with a vengeance, of sorts. The information overload is more terrifying than ever for the patient, who does not even know how to figure out which source of information is the most trustworthy. The physician has to develop trust that opens the mind of the patient to becoming a constructive participant in his own medical care, and receptive to being educated. Recognition of patient autonomy and reduction of the physician's own conflicts of interest would go a long way toward developing that trust.

Medical Ethics

133

ENRICHMENT

1. Ethical questions stimulated by the PBS Ethics in America episode "Does Doctor Know Best?"Go to website: https://www.learner.org/series/ethics-in-america/does-doctor-know-best/ The episode contents are arranged as follows: (1) The alarming test results, (2) Who chooses the treatment? (3) The mother or the child?, (4) The crisis, (5) Coma, (6) The endgame.

Personal questions to ponder as you listen (from Newton 2004)

a. If you were in trouble like Betty Bright, who would you turn to, other than a professional, help you sort out the best course of action?
b. Would you be comfortable if your friends and family were calling each other trying to protect your welfare without your knowledge?
c. If you were about to be a parent and learned that the mother had a disease that could be easily treated to save her life—but only at the cost of the child's life—what would be the desirable course of action? (Of course, the answer might well differ if you were the mother or the father.)

Ethical questions to discuss (from Newton 2004):

a. Are you the only one to whom your life belongs?
b. The question of the point at which the medical community may intervene for the medical welfare of the individual is central to any care regimen. Intervention is suggested at several points in the episode: phoning the husband to get the wife in for an appointment, manipulating the patient to accept an unwanted therapy that the physician believes is best, surgical intervention to separate a baby from its dying mother. The question is a subset of the larger question of when a community should intervene for the welfare of any given individual. Which of the following background circumstances should be considered on ethical grounds when deciding when to intervene?
Age of the individual
Apparent composure of the individual
Apparent intelligence of the individual
Apparent wealth of the individual
Whether or not the individual has sought any kind of medical help before
How the individual got into this situation
Threats of lawsuits
c. Betty isn't alone in that hospital. What is the role of her primary nurse in her last illness? Can he serve as her advocate? How? What is the role of her mother? Are there other potential advocates?

134   Ethics for Bioengineering Scientists

   d. At what point may, or must, the physician begin to consider the embryo, fetus or unborn child as a separate patient, whose interests may, or must, be balanced with the mother's?

   e. How would the rationalist and libertarian answers to question 4 differ?

  2. Debate: Euthanasia

Improvement in post-operative management of cystic fibrosis patients receiving lung transplants has improved so much—due to machines developed by bioengineers that monitor recovery—that one recipient has actually completed a triathlon. A young cystic fibrosis patient is lying near death awaiting a transplant. All physicians on the case do not expected him to last the week. In a hospital, a short helicopter ride away, is a teenage victim of an automobile accident who is comatose—not quite brain dead—being kept alive by instrumentation, and not expected by her physicians to survive the week, even with life support. Her parents had signed a waiver to allow donation of her organs, but cannot bring themselves to give the final word approving withdrawal of life support. A nurse attending the accident victim can interrupt life support long enough to terminate her without being detected. He had known her all her life and is convinced she would have wanted him to save the cystic fibrosis patient.

   Resolved (assertion to be debated): *The nurse should interrupt life support to save the cystic fibrosis patient and honor the memory of his friend*

  3. Debate: CRISPR

Before land animals existed, single and multicellular organisms battled with viruses for their existence. When the parasite developed a new tactic, its unwilling host would respond or become extinct, through natural selection. Bacteria vs. bacteriophages is one of the oldest wars. In 1987, a strain of *E. coli* was found to have at least one "locator" gene with an attached CRISPR cluster composed of a series of repeated palindromic codes separated by spacers, and a nuclease with its genes (Cas + Cas genes). The palindromic codes are remnants of phage that have attacked the bacterium and have now become blueprints for adaptive immunity against the parasite (Why didn't the phage evolve to not leave behind any living bacteria who could develop a defense? Evolution is random. Such terminally virulent phage probably did evolve. But having killed all the host they could reach, they went extinct.). During the adaptive immunity process each palindromic code is transcribed to form a pre CRISPR RNA (in a minority of cases, a DNA) which is then processed with the Cas nuclease to form a mature CRISPR RNA-Cas complex. The complex will match up with phage RNA (or DNA) strands during replication and the Cas nuclease will digest (i.e. cleave) the nucleic acid at a specific site (Sontheimer and Barrangou 2015).

   The targeting ability of one of the Cas nucleases, Cas9 (from *Streptococcus pyogenes*) attached to a synthetic RNA complex (crRNA + tracrRNA), often

Medical Ethics

referred to as a "guide RNA", is crucial to the editing process. The Cas9 can cleave almost any DNA site preceding a chemical signature called a PAM (protospacer-adjacent motif) has made this nuclease a prime tool for the first step in genome editing (Salsman and Dellaire 2016). The CRISPR-Cas9 system has been used by a number of laboratories for mammalian cell genome editing since appearance of the "seminal" (Salsman and Dellaire 2016) publication of its success with DNA in 2012 (Jinek et al. 2012). Any gene-based disease is a potential target, and there are more than 50 companies pursuing applications that would eliminate unwanted genes, add wanted genes, reduce the activity of overactive genes or increase the activity of underactive genes. Unwanted side effects include off-target effects due to guide RNA matching with untargeted domains and promiscuous action of Cas9 that cleaves untargeted domains.

Resolved: *The potential for CRISPR-Cas9 application is so great that its therapeutic application should be thoroughly explored and applied where feasible.*

4. Perform a moral analysis to answer the "Monitoring patient compliance in an epidemic" case question.

8 Bioengineering Scientist Ethics

8.1 BIOENGINEERS AS SCIENTISTS

Bioengineers may be technicians, engineers, or scientists. It is as a scientist that the bioengineer has a special link with data. Technicians and engineers are obligated to others before they are obligated to the data they gather. Bioengineering scientists are defined as scientists by the integrity of the data they gather. All scientists have a unique relationship with the data they generate, whether it is meant for problem-solving (empirical/clinical science) or scholarly understanding of the natural world (causal science). This chapter examines this relationship.

8.2 BIOENGINEERING SCIENTISTS CANNOT BE TRUTH PROFESSIONALS

Anyone can "do" science. But it is not a natural activity. Typically, humans are satisfied to extract from their experiences, solutions sufficient to get them through the day; alive, uninjured, and neither hungry nor thirsty. By accumulating these experiences, and seeing patterns in the series of events that characterize them in time and space, humans can reason out schemes to predict the best ways to avoid death, injury, thirst, and hunger. In the context of civilization, humans have learned to share their experiences and the patterns they have detected. Over centuries they have built a compendium of empirical knowledge that has resulted in the truth professions, technological inventiveness, and craft vocations that solve problems to make society function effectively. To review, a truth professional is a highly trained and educated individual who investigates problems in the natural world, with the goal of achieving truth. They take on cases, like a detective, and solve them. Solutions are the "truths" that mark the end of the problem they have solved for their human clients. Once the truth is achieved they go on to serve the next human client. Any scientist can solve a problem. That would mark the completion of the empirical component of her work. But the solution is local. It becomes global when its data are connected with the great body of science, adding to our understanding of the natural world. The strength of that connection is a function of the integrity of data. Loss of data integrity corrupts any understanding we reach from its analysis. Fleming solved the problem of finding an antibiotic, penicillin, effective against *Staphylococcus aureus*. But scientists had to research bacterial physiology to uncover the mechanism of its action, in order to give direction to the process of developing other antibiotics, when bacterial resistance to penicillin evolved. Scientific research is geared for the "long haul". It is never ending because we will never understand all.

DOI: 10.1201/9781003197218-8

138   Ethics for Bioengineering Scientists

Ideally, to do science one has to have a desire to understand, not just association patterns (e.g. a disease is more common in a certain ethnicity), but what causes them (e.g. disease may be associated with incidence of a parasite common in the region that people of certain ethnicity come from). When cause and effect are logically connected, that is, when the hypothesized causal pattern is corroborated by a pre-ponderance of evidence, our understanding of the underlying process (e.g. Is it climate or the parasite that causes the disease?) has been advanced. For an empirical scientist, the ideal of understanding is limited by a more immediate need to solve a problem. Accordingly, causal understanding (e.g. a sufficient comprehension of the disease's pathophysiology to predict potential contributors to it) is not practical for an empirical scientist. Nevertheless, all scientists require minds that can handle logic.

If the requirements for a scientist ended with a logical mind, the occupation would be a journey of never-ending ego inflation. Nature is not generous enough to allow that. It constrains a scientist to a life of consistent uncertainty and frequent failure. The reasons for the uncertainty, explored in Chapter 1, are revealed in the musings of the philosopher Emmanuel Kant and the evidence of physicist Werner Heisenberg. Failure, a direct result of our ignorance, is our teacher.

When a scientist generates data to test a hypothesis, probability takes the place of certainty. Probability has a value, P. But P is not the probability that our data match the truth (i.e. the value predicted by our hypothesis). It is the likelihood that the antithesis of our prediction is false. The value of P is calculated by the statistical method we choose to evaluate our data. For bioengineering scientists, the data are usually measures of some varying process presented in graphs, with curves that indicate dose-response or time-response relationships. The shape of the curve tells a story. Wound healing rate, blood drug concentration over time, infection incidence over time, and length of life as a function of daily Vitamin C dose, are examples of data curves. Curves, as graphic representations of mathematical functions, are ex-amples of modeling. In curve modeling, the P value is a measure of hypothetical curve-fit to the data. Common systems for calculating P are Pearson's chi-square, Fisher's ANOVA (ANalysis Of VAriance), and Student's t test (from a table). A certain value of P (< 0.05 by convention, not statistical principle) is accepted ty-pically by scientific journals as being sufficiently significant to reject the antithesis of the proposed hypothesis.

We can define precision as the reproducibility of measurements. Acknowledging uncertainty is the equivalent of expecting less-than-perfect precision. The visible result of fulfillment of this expectation, is data scatter, that is, variance. One would expect that a good scientist would take care to reduce scatter. The best way to insure precision, is to jealously guard the efficiency and exactness of the measuring pro-cess, and its reporting. This is another way of saying "insuring data integrity". The moment another priority exceeds a bioengineering scientist's commitment to in-suring data integrity, she stops being a scientist; by definition.

Science is a societal function. Engineers and physicians can ply their trade in the relative isolation of small groups. Practitioners of truth professions seek empirical goals that mark the end of a successful job performance. As a profession with the goal of increasing humankind's understanding of the natural world, science depends

Bioengineering Scientist Ethics

139

on social interactions in which new discoveries are shared, debated, analyzed and incorporated into the current body of understanding, thereby raising its level. Paradigms may be uprooted and the body of understanding may take a new direction, but it continues to grow.

8.3 THE SCIENTIFIC INVESTIGATION

Suppose a scientist wishes to understand why a certain biomaterial failed after being implanted. There are at least two frames of reference by which the failure may be understood

1. A challenge (the implant's affects) has exceeded the physiological limits of the body. It is important to understand what these limits are and how they are set in the presence of this biomaterial—the causal approach
2. The failure must be overcome. The biomaterial or its deployment must be changed to prevent failure from taking place—a truth-seeking approach (truth= solution to the problem).

Greater understanding can be achieved in either frame of reference, by performing laboratory experiments. The experimental approach in very general terms would look something like the following:

1. Make a prediction (hypothesis) of the next logical step in the path to understanding the phenomenon of interest, based on a careful analysis of what is understood, so far. *This is a deductive reasoning process. It differs from the approach of Francis Bacon that was inductive. There is a current fashion to jettison the hypothesis. It appears to be based on the assumption that its derivation is inductive* (Firestein 2012). *Since a modern hypothesis is based on previous understanding, this assumption is intrinsically incorrect.*
2. Design an experiment to test the prediction that includes clearly defined control and experimental cohorts, and uses repeatable techniques.
   a. Decide on the most appropriate statistical method for hypothesis testing to apply to the kind of data that will be generated (most likely one based on Fisher's ANOVA rather than Pearson's Chi Square).
   b. Run a power calculation to determine sample/cohort sizes necessary to achieve statistical significance at the level desired (if this is a lab animal experiment, be aware of NIH monitoring to minimize use of nonhuman animals—One of the reasons not to use the Pearson system).
3. Run the experiment so carefully that all results may be duplicated by a scientist sufficiently trained to apply the techniques correctly.
4. Analyze the resulting data—including all that relate to the hypothesis—and present them so clearly that anyone who understands the techniques would draw the same conclusions as the scientist performing the experiment. *This is an inductive reasoning process.*

140 Ethics for Bioengineering Scientists

    a. Determine the specific statistical test to apply to the kind of data generated (e.g. Mann-Whitney, Tukey).

    b. Investigate outliers to determine their probable cause.

The most unequivocal experimental test of a hypothesis compares a control cohort (a group of individuals as alike as possible that is untreated), with an experimental cohort (a group of individuals that cannot be distinguished from the control cohort except that it is treated). A laboratory environment ensures that there are no environmental factors that affect the experimental subjects unevenly. If data collection requires days to complete, and the subjects must depart the measuring site in-between, the experiment cannot be considered laboratory-based. However, experiments with certain animals kept in zoos or nature-simulating facilities like primate centers, approach laboratory experiments in the purity of their data. Group factors, such as animal interaction (e.g. a fight that causes wounds), introduce extra data that are difficult to include in the baseline we call "normal". In sum, causal science is difficult to conduct outside a laboratory, particularly if it involves animals. Empirical science often does not require a laboratory. In fact, for the problem solver who wishes to test the efficacy of an implant under "real" conditions, a laboratory experiment might yield irrelevant results (people don't live in laboratories). To be sure, testing a cure for a disease in an animal model in a lab or a human in a hospital research ward would yield more reproducible data, but the data would be more relevant for predicting success of the cure if it were tested under conditions of its actual use. These considerations are crucial for understanding the role of science in biomedical product development. They will be discussed more in Chapters 12 and 13.

Consider the common model for forensics, a murder case. The victim is discovered and soon police swarm all over the scene of the crime. At the center is a team of empirical (often "clinical" in the case of bioengineers) scientists; crime-scene investigators. CSIs are limited in their ability to perform controlled laboratory experiments that would test each hypothesis about how the murder was committed. While the science of performing each form of killing on groups of volunteers in sufficient numbers to be statistically valid might be methodologically sound, volunteers for such experiments would be hard to come by, and such an experiment would itself be illegal. The CSIs can model scenarios to test hypotheses—if the murder was committed with a knife they might stab synthetic skin to see if the stab marks are similar to those in the victim's wound, in an attempt to reconstruct the stabbing angle. Reconstruction is a lot of what astronomers and physical anthropologists do. Reconstruction is also what bioengineering scientists do when they retrieve an implant that has been in a patient for years and try to determine how biocompatible it was so they can answer the question "How come it failed?" or "How come it succeeded?".

Whether causal or empirical, scientific investigations of host-medical product interaction require background knowledge of what is understood about both. This knowledge becomes the basis for choosing a subject to investigate and predicting, by deduction, what the result of that investigation will be. A scientist must have knowledge of the methods and materials required to carry out an investigation, to

Bioengineering Scientist Ethics

formulate a research design. After analysis of the generated data, conclusions about whether the hypothesis is disproven or supported, can be drawn.

8.4 DATA, THE SCIENTISTS' CLIENTS

The products of a scientist's work are research data; these are also his/her clients, whose integrity he/she must preserve. Because of this special relationship, an individual fits the definition of a scientist to the degree that these data have integrity. According to the Singapore Statement on Research Integrity (2010) "Research findings have integrity if they can be trusted by researchers who will learn from and build on those findings; by practitioners who will base decisions on them; and by funders, institutions and publishers whose credibility is linked with the results they support and promote" (Anderson et al. 2013).

Until 1986, when research fraud was targeted by the National Institutes of Health, scientists in the United States were, as a group, self-regulated. They were assumed by society to:

1. be devoted to scholarly inquisitiveness
2. be committed to achieving an objective understanding of the natural world
3. be obligated to following scientific procedures to achieve this understanding
4. always display the following attributes
   a. freely share their discoveries
   b. avoid conflicts of interest
   c. maintain connections with the rest of the scientific community
   d. maintain a formal skepticism
5. have sufficient background and experience in their field to be able to conduct meaningful investigations, with experiments where needed, that generate valid data
6. publish their results consistently in peer-reviewed journals
7. describe their methods sufficiently to allow replication of their work by peers
8. be completely honest about errors committed and demanding of peers to be just as honest (Anderson et al. 2013)

Attempts to codify these assumptions in a professional code of ethics have met with limited success. There is no licensing body that can enforce such a code. Because it lacks the traditional formal structure of a truth profession, science has no traditional formal code of ethics. It has no one society that all scientists must join.

8.5 SCIENCE PROFESSION CODE OF ETHICS

Sigma Xi, The Scientific Research Society, was formed in 1886 and had a presence in most U.S. universities until the 1970s. It was the closest thing to a formal society for all scientists. But it had no enforcement powers and membership dwindled as new Ph.Ds. opted to join societies in their specialties. A code proposed by Woodward and Goodstein and published in the Sigma Xi journal *American Scientist* is presented as follows.

142   Ethics for Bioengineering Scientists

SCIENTISTS' CODE OF ETHICS (Woodward and Goodstein 1996)

1. Scientists should always be disinterested, impartial and totally objective when gathering data.
2. A scientist should never be motivated to do science for personal gain, advancement or other rewards.
3. Every observation or experiment must be designed to falsify a hypothesis.
4. When an experiment or an observation gives a result contrary to the prediction of a certain theory, all ethical scientists must abandon that theory.
5. Scientists must never believe dogmatically in an idea nor use rhetorical exaggeration in promoting it.
6. Scientists must "lean over backwards" (in the words of the late physicist Richard Feynman) to point out evidence that is contrary to their own hypotheses or that might weaken acceptance of their experimental results.
7. Conduct that seriously departs from that commonly accepted in the scientific community is unethical.
8. Scientists must report what they have done so fully that any other scientist can reproduce the experiment or calculation. Science must be an open book, not an acquired skill.
9. Scientists should never permit their judgments to be affected by authority. For example, the reputation of a scientist making a given claim is irrelevant to the validity of the claim.
10. Each author of a multiple-author paper is fully responsible for every part of the paper.
11. The choice and order of authors on a multiple-author publication must strictly reflect the contributions of the authors to the work in question.
12. Financial support for doing science and access to scientific facilities should be shared democratically, not concentrated in the hands of a favored few.
13. There can never be too many scientists in the world.
14. No misleading or deceptive statement should ever appear in a scientific paper.
15. Decisions about the distribution of resources and publication of results must be guided by the judgment of scientific peers who are protected by anonymity.

8.6 FUNDING AND GOVERNMENT REGULATION OF SCIENTIFIC ETHICS

Modern science, unlike pre-29th-century science, is not funded by rich patrons who sponsor individuals in small private laboratories, or on exploratory field trips such as Darwin's voyage on the H.M.S. Beagle. Instead, laboratories are part of

Bioengineering Scientist Ethics

institutions such as universities, companies (e.g. General Electric), or the government (e.g. Walter Reed Army Institute of Research). Additionally, field trips are funded by museums, foundations or government agencies. Materials used for conducting research (e.g. instruments, chemicals, lab animals) or field trips are expensive and require funding levels beyond the income of individual scientists.

As scientific research has grown, funding has not kept pace, leading to competition between scientists to secure adequate support. Big Science (see Chapter 1) has sapped much of the funding, giving preference to large research groups investigating popular diseases. Nowadays, the scientific community shows strains caused by new pressures of the competitive research system that has evolved. To quote The National Academy of Sciences:

> *The research system exerts many pressures on beginning and experienced researchers alike. Principal investigators need to raise funds and attract students. Faculty members must balance the time spent on research with the time spent teaching undergraduates. Industrial sponsorship of research introduces the possibility of conflicts of interest. All parts of the research system have a responsibility to recognize and respond to these pressures. Institutions must review their own policies, foster awareness of research ethics, and ensure that researchers are aware of the policies that are in place. And researchers should constantly be aware of the extent to which ethically based decisions will influence their success as scientists (NAS 2009).*

In 1985, partly as a result of a 1982 publication exposing the Darsee case (see below), which led to passing of the Health Research Extension Act by Congress, the Secretary of Health and Human Services (HHS) directed all institutions receiving HHS funding to develop programs for reporting research fraud. In 1986 the NIH redefined "research fraud" as "scientific misconduct", and by 1989 it set up what became the Office of Research Integrity (ORI). The NSF followed quickly by assigning its Inspector General to the same function.

Certain limits need to be made clear at this point. First, this chapter deals only with research integrity. Human research ethics will be dealt with in Chapter 10. Second, the authority of NIH and NSF does not apply to the military or industry, unless the project in question is funded by either agency.

8.7 SCIENTIFIC MISCONDUCT

Scientific Misconduct as defined by the NIH Committee on Scientific Conduct and Ethics is: Fabrication, falsification, or plagiarism in proposing, performing or reviewing research, or in reporting research results.

1. **Fabrication** is making up data or results and recording or reporting them.
2. **Falsification** is manipulating research materials, equipment, or processes, or changing or omitting data or results such that the research is not accurately represented in the research record.
3. **Plagiarism** is the appropriation of another person's ideas, processes, or results without giving appropriate credit.

144   Ethics for Bioengineering Scientists

Scientific misconduct does not include honest error or difference of opinion.

8.8 GOVERNMENT DECREED SCIENTIFIC ETHICS

Research ethics courses at universities exist, because in December of 2000 the National Institutes of Health implemented a policy that required all institutions receiving NIH funding for scientific research to train their graduates in scientific ethics. Misconduct by scientists in the form of data falsification in publications of research supported by the federal government had moved the U.S. Congress to demand action by all government agencies. It should be evident to the reader from section 8.4 that data falsification is not bad science; it is not science at all because it is outside the definition of science. An anonymous questionnaire sent to 8,000 grantees of government funding was responded to by 3,247 of them and the percentages of types of misconduct admitted to is shown in Table 8.1:

It should be pointed out that less than half of the grantees responded to the questionnaire. Notwithstanding such reluctance, it is interesting that those that did respond were willing to admit to at least questionable scientific practices.

TABLE 8.1

Violations of Accepted Practices in Scientific Publications (Martinson et al. 2005)

Faking research data	00.3%
Plagiarism	01.4%
Removing data	06.0%
Multiple publication of the same data	04.7%
Inappropriate inclusion of authors	10.0%
Changed a study design without reporting	15.0%
Inadequate record keeping	27.5%

8.9 EVIDENTIARY REQUIREMENTS FOR FINDINGS OF RESEARCH MISCONDUCT

In order to ensure that anyone accused of research misconduct is treated justly by the investigating body, most universities have had their lawyers craft a set of requirements for conducting and adjudicating each case. An example of such a document, UCLA Policy 993 (Appendix D), may be summarized as follows:

A finding of *research misconduct* requires that:

1. *there be a significant departure from accepted practices of the relevant Research community*
2. *the misconduct be committed intentionally, knowingly, or recklessly*
3. *the allegation is corroborated (lawyers often use the word "proven" here) by a preponderance of the evidence.*

Bioengineering Scientist Ethics

Evidence of research misconduct may include showing, by a preponderance of the evidence, that the Respondent had Research Records and intentionally, knowingly or recklessly destroyed them, had the opportunity to maintain them but did not do so, or maintained them and failed to produce them to the Vice Chancellor for Research (VCR), or the equivalent official at the institution involved in a timely manner. Such actions constitute a significant departure from accepted practices of the relevant Research community.

The Respondent has the burden of going forward with and proving by a preponderance of the evidence: any and all affirmative defenses raised, proof of honest error or difference of opinion; and any mitigating factors relevant to a decision to impose administrative sanctions following a Research Misconduct Proceeding. Preponderance of the evidence means proof by information that, compared with information opposing it, leads to the conclusion that the fact at issue is more probably true than not.

There are circumstances in which these rules are insufficient to define an act of misconduct. Consider the degree of plagiarism. If information is conveyed and its author is not cited, is the means of conveying an attempt by the writer/speaker to claim credit for the information or is it an oversight? Presentation of published ideas, problems, or teaching materials without attribution is often part of university teaching. The phrase "there be a significant departure from accepted practices of the relevant research community" is subject to interpretation because a new technique may by definition be a significant departure from accepted practices. Further, what is the standard for "accepted practices"? The prohibited experiment described in Chapter 2 could be made to conform to the definition of science. But it is prohibited by laws that have nothing to do with science. Science is, after all, a social activity and scientists as members of society are legally constrained to limit the scope of their experiments. When legality changes, the scientist ignorant of the new law may find herself accused of scientific misconduct.

8.10 POPULATIONS WHERE SCIENTIFIC MISCONDUCT OCCURS

8.10.1 RESEARCHERS

Accusations of research dishonesty may result in ruined careers and lifelong scars. If an allegation is disproved, hours of time and effort must be spent in the investigation. Thus, there is some basis for care in avoiding misconduct and in being sure misconduct has occurred before making an accusation. As UCLA Policy 993 (see Appendix D) indicates, most misconduct is handled locally through peer review, administrative procedures and within the laboratory itself when the researcher is not a principle investigator. If the accusations deal with published results or documents submitted to public funding agencies, they cannot stay local. In the extreme, individuals outside the scientific community immediately concerned with the research may be harmed; as when a medical treatment is developed based on falsified data.

Common scientific misconduct by laboratory researchers is listed in Table 8.2.

As indicated in Policy 993, anyone may accuse a researcher of scientific misconduct. However, no formal charges are permitted until the appropriate

146 Ethics for Bioengineering Scientists

TABLE 8.2

Most Usual Forms of Scientific Misconduct by Researchers (Budinger and Budinger 2006)

1	Cover-up of errors
2	Misuse of funds
3	Fabrication of data
4	Deletion of data without justification
5	Falsification of data
6	Major deviations from protocol
7	Unjustified manipulation of data during analysis
8	Use of inappropriate statistical analysis in place of a well-known appropriate method
9	Performance of or knowingly participating in unauthorized human experiments
10	Performance of or knowingly participating in unauthorized lab animal experiments
11	Failing to report scientific misconduct sufficiently obvious to have been seen
12	Misrepresentation or purposeful exclusion of relevant historical data
13	Plagiarism of ideas for the research

investigation by officials qualified to understand the field of research has been completed. When adjudication is finally pursued the accused has the right to due process, including review of evidence gathered during the investigation, and cross-examination of witnesses.

In cases where "the cat is out of the bag", that is, the data have been submitted outside the institution and the institution is a recipient of NIH grants, the NIH Office for Research Integrity (ORI) becomes involved. The institution is required to file a report to the ORI when the investigator has been found guilty. The ORI will then decide what sanctions are to be imposed on the researcher and, in some cases, the institution. The sanctions are published in the NIH Bulletin, which is sent to all NIH-funded laboratories, with full identification of the guilty researcher.

8.10.2 AUTHORS

The reporting of research results is the fundamental act that makes science societal. For most professional scientists, peer-reviewed publication is the main measure of their contribution to science. The quality of these publications will, to a great extent, determine one's ability to advance in their place of employment and to obtain funding for their work. Obtaining patents may also be considered a form of authorship in that it requires publication of conclusions resulting from scientific research. Writing in a manner that is difficult for other scientists in the field to understand is not unethical. It is incompetent science, because societal science cannot operate without communication. But it is not unethical. The grounding of professional conduct by authors in moral theory is evident in a number of ways (adapted from Budinger and Budinger 2006) (see Table 8.3):

Bioengineering Scientist Ethics

1. The *duty* of communication is based both on its necessity for scientific function and, where the work has been funded, to fulfill the contract that provides the funding.
2. There is also *justice* in publication because co-authorship acknowledges the contribution of those who contributed directly to the work. By citing previous work that established the foundations for ideas used in the study, the author(s) is providing them justice as well. Adding an author who did not contribute to the work is not just because it is false credit, and, since all listed authors must now defend the work the gratuitously added author, who will likely be unfamiliar with its details and will probably provide a faulty defense. New ideas are difficult enough to promote without employing an incompetent promoter.
3. The commitment to *truthfulness* is beyond the social interactions of the "doctrine of the mean". One does not lie in a scientific publication to save a colleague who may suffer pain from exposure of invalid data resulting from his faulty technique. If the new results to be published were obtained with data extracted by a valid application of the technique, they are needed, lest someone be harmed by a treatment based on the faulty data.
4. The principal author has the responsibility of respecting the *autonomy* of all co-authors and previous authors whose works provided the background on which the tested hypothesis was based. Thus, the order of authorship should include and reflect the actual scientific contribution of each individual; and references should be as complete as possible.
5. Care in gathering the data and completeness in reporting it are the best safeguards against generating faulty data and allowing it to contaminate the pool of scientifically valid results. Avoidance of such harm is an example of *nonmalfeasance*.

TABLE 8.3

Misconduct by Authors (adapted from Budinger and Budinger 2006)

Citable misconduct

Describing data or artifacts that do not exist

Describing documents or objects that have been forged

Misrepresenting real data or deliberately distorting evidence or data

Presenting another's ideas, text or work without attribution, including deliberate violation of copyright

Presenting statistical analysis in which required conditions are not met or discussed

Omitting negative results from corollary experiments

Misrepresenting authorship by omitting an author

Misrepresenting authorship by including an author who did not make a significant scientific contribution

Misrepresenting publication status

Citing work irrelevant or unsupportive to a point being made in the text

Citing work as confirming a point that it does not

Omitting citing the work of competitors whose work has been represented

Failure to mention equally likely interpretations or hypotheses not tested or testable

Citing literature without verifying the legitimate source of the citation

148   Ethics for Bioengineering Scientists

8.10.3 Processors of Submitted Work

There are at least five kinds of reviewers of scientific work. They all tend to be more senior members of the scientific community because the agencies seeking a review assume that experience breeds the wisdom needed for judging a work's quality.

1. Advanced degree committees, usually judging masters and Ph.D. theses
2. Peer reviewers of journals or societies, who evaluate submitted manuscripts or meeting abstracts
3. Application reviewers of grant awarding agencies, who evaluate proposed research projects and other requests for funding
4. Supervisory reviewers and senior peers who are scientists and/or scholars engaged by the institution to evaluate the work of scientists and employees seeking promotion and/or tenure.
5. Honor agency/society reviewers working for prestigious institutions that award membership or prizes.

8.10.3.1 Advanced Degree Committees

Members of an advanced degree committee are usually chosen by a graduate student in consultation with his/her mentor. These faculty are charged with evaluating the research of the scientist-in-training through the thesis submitted as partial fulfillment for the degree. The expectation is that the completed work will be published in peer-reviewed scientific journals. Since it will probably be the first full article of the new scientist, committee members in recognition of the autonomous rights of the student owe him/her their best counsel. By the same token, they must maintain confidentiality of the thesis work lest a competing scientist "steal" the project idea. As part of their contract with the institution engaging them, committee members must require that the work done be scientifically valid. Only then can the degree awarded be valid. As chair of the committee, the mentor has the responsibility to make sure committee members are performing their roles appropriately. In a real sense, the graduate student is a client of his/her mentor.

8.10.3.2 Journal/Abstract Reviewers

The journal article is the fundamental communication medium in science. Manuscript reviewers are charged with their honest opinion of the validity and value of the work reported. One of the greatest challenges for reviewers is conflict-of-interest. An editor will choose a reviewer who is an authority in the field of the work being reported. There is a high probability that the reported work and the work of the reviewer overlap. Thus, the two parties may be in competition for the next great breakthrough. Because of the danger of retaliation—scientists are human after all—and the general reluctance of many to be publicly critical, reviewer names are kept confidential. (It is the bias of this author that confidentiality be waived for

Bioengineering Scientist Ethics

reviewers who wish it. An honest review is itself good science and may lead to constructive dialogue. A scientist consistent with the goals of science is not insulted by constructive criticism. Of course basic human drives do conflict with such consistency.) Another dimension of reviewer conflict-of-interest is the danger that by rejecting the manuscript, the reviewer may use the rewrite interval to steal its ideas—or to submit for publication a manuscript on the same subject that he/she is in the process of writing; because it is more prestigious to be first to publish. Journal editors have tried to protect against such behavior by listing the date submitted in the published article. If the scientific advance being described is flashy enough, so much acclaim will be garnered by the first published report that subsequent articles by other authors will be ignored.

Since abstracts for a scientific meeting often describe incomplete studies, they are rarely citable, so the impact of reviewer misconduct is small. Many such abstracts are written by graduate students. The main conflict-of-interest occurs when students in different laboratories have done the same work. A mentor of one of them may not be the ideal person to review the competing students' submissions. But neither is the student's own mentor. Since both mentors are usually the most qualified to evaluate the work, there is an ethical dilemma for the meeting organizers who choose reviewers. Another source of review misconduct is the editorial staff. Editors of scientific journals are usually scientists in the journal's specialty field. As such they have access to confidential manuscripts just as do the reviewers. Conflict-of-interest may lead to their misconduct as well. Budinger (Budinger and Budinger 2006) has suggested some major misconduct by reviewers and journal officials (Table 8.4).

TABLE 8.4

Misconduct by Reviewers (adapted from Budinger and Budinger 2006)

Reviewer misconduct

Misrepresenting facts or lying in communications with authors or editors

Unreasonably delaying review in order to achieve personal gain

Stealing ideas or text from a manuscript under review

Allowing conflicts of interest to bias recommendations for publication

Editor/Staff misconduct

Forging or fabricating a reviewer's report

Lying to the author about the review process

Stealing ideas or text from a manuscript under review

Allowing conflicts of interest to bias acceptability of a manuscript

---

8.10.3.3   Application Reviewers

Competition for grant awards has increased greatly since clinical science has grown to claim an increasing share of limited funding. A typical grant application to an NIH institute will claim that the project being proposed will uncover a key

150   Ethics for Bioengineering Scientists

discovery in the quest to cure at least one dreaded disease. Reviewer decisions will determine the professional lives of many scientists—particularly at academic institutions. The same conflict-of-interest challenges exist in this arena as in the journal reviewing arena. The impact on the scientist being reviewed, however, is much greater. Also, greater are the potential benefits to a reviewer who succumbs to conflict-of-interest-based temptations. A reviewer working on the same problem as the applicant may be progressing slowly in some area of his/her research because a certain precise measuring technique is missing. An applicant who has developed the technique describes it fully in order to convince reviewers he/she has solved the problem. Should the application fail, the applicant may lose his/her job for failure to be funded, and the technique may not get published as a consequence. It is not difficult to imagine that the reviewer may be tempted to help the applicant fail, and then take up the technique as his/her own. Some protection against this scenario is provided by federal laws forbidding any reviewer on a federal scientific grant evaluation committee to reveal any aspect of the review process.

Misconduct may occur in the review of industry grants. Companies often fund investigation of one of their products. Obviously, the company has a conflict-of-interest in preferring that the results of any scientific investigation show that the product fulfills all marketing claims. The misconduct would occur if the company selected an applicant who they know favors the product. R.J. Reynolds, a company that manufactures cigarettes, funds research on the physiological effects of nicotine. They send out inquiries on a regular basis for established scientists to act as reviewers for their grant applicants. Misconduct would occur if the reviewer let it be known that he/she would favor applicants who could show that nicotine was not addictive. The author can cite an instance in which his funding was cut off by a company following his reporting of experimental results not supporting its claims. Industry funding of extramural (outside the company) research on one of their products that is used in or on humans is usually motivated by the testing requirements of the Food and Drug Administration (FDA). This requirement will be discussed in Chapter 12.

8.10.3.4 Supervisory Reviewers

A university graduate who joins the scientific work force after earning a bachelor's degree would probably join a company, government agency or university as a lab technician. He/she would be supervised by a more experienced supervisor or the head of the lab, who would probably be a Ph.D. Technicians are usually not involved in the decision process associated with designing and drawing conclusions about research results, nor writing up research for publication in peer reviewed journals. They are not expected to understand how the results of their work relate to current knowledge in their specialty. They are employees who carry out assigned work. Accordingly, they are not usually included as authors of published articles. Their relationship to their boss is as employee to supervisor, with one important exception. To the extent that they take a serious interest in the scientific meaning of their work, they are scientists, and they occupy the same position of responsibility as an engineer in a similar

Bioengineering Scientist Ethics

151

relationship. They may have to become whistleblowers. Their supervisors, in turn, may have to process whistleblowing reports. If the supervisor has a connection with the accused in a whistleblowing report such that he/she is biased in favor of the accused, there may be a conflict-of-interest that would be detrimental to the whistleblower.

In a university setting there are often both technicians and graduate students working on the same project. They are all under the supervision of a faculty member but operate in different spheres of responsibility. While the technician is exclusively an employee, the graduate student is both a client of his/her mentor and, to the extent he/she is paid for work related to the mentor's research (e.g. a research assistantship), also an employee.

A faculty member—in particular one on tenure-track but not yet tenured—is in turn not supervised but judged by senior faculty members in his/her quest for promotion and tenure. Universities make varying commitments to assure that this process is objective and fair. But, as a former speaker of the house of representatives, Thomas (Tip) O'Neill, said, "All politics is local". The specific ethical challenges for those involved in the process include judgments about the "impact" of the work done by the faculty member being evaluated. "Impact" should mean the degree to which this scientist's work has advanced understanding of the part of the natural world addressed by his/her specialty. Reference letters from highly respected external fellow specialists are critical for this judgment, since members of tenure and promotion committees are mostly from other specialties—including nonscience fields—and are not qualified to make the evaluation. In many cases, however, impact has come to mean a combination of grant money attracted and number of publications. In response to the numbers pressure, some faculty have committed misconduct in authoring and applying for grants. In other cases, powerful faculty (often department chairs) have threatened to take their grants and accept a job offer at another university if their protégée is denied tenure or promotion.

8.10.3.5 Honor Agency Reviewers

Every institution from universities to research institutes (e.g. Bell Laboratories) will brag about the Nobel laureates they have in residence. The movie "The Prize" suggested a substantial amount of politics and intrigue surrounding the choice for this award. There are other prizes that bring almost as much prestige and each has attracted its own story of politics and intrigue from cynics. There are also prestigious societies, membership in which guarantees respect, advancement and reward. It is of interest to note, in this context, the opinion of these awards by one highly respected scientist. The physicist Richard Feynman was a Nobel laureate. He was awarded and accepted the prize that recognized his work in quantum electrodynamics. As is the case for every U.S. scientist recipient of this prize, he was made a member of the National Academy of Sciences, the U.S. equivalent of the British Royal Society. He responded to this inclusion with a letter requesting that his membership be rescinded. The flabbergasted officers of the society could not understand Feynman's decision to reject this honor. Nor could they understand the reason he gave (and spent over a year trying to change his mind). He said the society was merely a collection of individuals on an ego trip who joined together to congratulate one another for their brilliance. It differed from an honor like the Nobel Prize in that the latter was recognition for a specific accomplishment and was based solely on the value of the accomplishment to science as judged by specialists in the field who had won respect from their peers by achieving similar advances. *What do you think of Feynman's comment?*

8.10.3.6 Predatory Publishers

In 2008 the gold Open Access movement was initiated on the web. Two of its goals were to make publishing of scientific articles easier, and enhance access to them. A side effect was that it attracted individuals with a profit motive. Jeffrey Beall, a librarian at the University of Colorado, Denver, noticed a rapid increase in the number of online scientific journals, and decided to study their credentials. By 2013 he had collected a list of some 225 that had preyed on, apparently unsuspecting, scientists by such actions as requiring exorbitant publishing fees for articles they sometimes did not publish, having no editorial boards, conducting no peer review, and/or not monitoring submissions for scientific misconduct. When an author submits her bibliography as part of CV evaluation for a job or promotion application, her publications are evaluated, and the impact factor of the journals they are published in is an important indicator of her qualifications. Predatory publications have low impact factors. For an update on the current status of predatory publishing, the reader is referred to Beall's website: https://scholarlyoa.com/?s=predatory+publishing (Beall 2013). Predatory publishers email heavily. From the author's experience, they seem to have success with post-doctoral fellows. A similar industry, predatory conferencing, has also grown on the web. One of the easiest ways to identify one of these predators, is the case that the title of the conference has no practical relationship to the specialty of the target scientist.

8.11 SCIENTIFIC MISCONDUCT CASES

8.11.1 The Classic Scientific Ethics Course Case: The Piltdown Man

In 1908 fragments of an unusual skull were found in a gravel pit near Piltdown, England. Near it was an unusual jawbone with ape-like characteristics that had up to that time never been associated with humans. Over the next few years more bone fragments were uncovered in the same pit. The stratum at which the find was located indicated the fossil was much less than a million years old. If the combination of bones were from the same skeleton it would have meant that a kind of "missing link" between humans and other primates existed much more recently—the estimate was the Pleistocene period—than any paleontologist had imagined. Some questioned the authenticity of the combination, but the weight of scientific and public opinion won the day. Some years later, when carbon dating had been developed, an analysis of the bones found that whereas the main skull was about 50,000 years old, the jawbone and other nonhuman fragments were less than 50 years old. It was concluded that the perpetrator of the hoax was the original discoverer who had been exposed for faking other antiquities.

Bioengineering Scientist Ethics

8.11.2 Scientific Misconduct in Cloning, Woo-suk Hwang Case (see https://embryo.asu.edu/pages/hwang-woo-suks-use-human-eggs-research-2002-2005)

Woo-suk Hwang, Ph.D. (in theriogenology: the study of animal reproduction), PI of a research group at Seoul National University, published a report in the August 2005 *Nature*, claiming that his group had cloned a dog. The same team had reported, in *Science* in 2004 and 2005, creation of a stem cell line from cloned human blastocysts. Both achievements were firsts, and therefore, breakthroughs in their fields. But the dog cloning was thought by many to be not yet possible, so there was skepticism of the results and attempts were made to duplicate them. The number and source of oocytes for each experiment were also concerns of most skeptics. In response to the outcry, the university investigated data validity. It reported in January 2006 that all three papers were fraudulent to such a degree they had to be withdrawn completely. Also, human oocytes for the *Science* paper were obtained from Hwang's female lab technicians in violation of Korean law. Dr. Hwang was prosecuted for misuse of research funds and, after appeal was sentenced to 18 months suspended prison time.

In *Science*, an editorial retraction was published, stating: "Because the final report of the SNU investigation indicated that a significant amount of the data presented in both papers is fabricated, the editors of *Science* feel that an immediate and unconditional retraction of both papers is needed. We therefore retract these two papers and advise the scientific community that the results reported in them are deemed to be invalid." The *Science* editorial also pointed out: "*Science* regrets the time that the peer reviewers and others spent evaluating these papers as well as the time and resources that the scientific community may have spent trying to replicate these results."(Kennedy 2006). Scientists trying to replicate Dr. Hwang's results or conduct new investigations based on them lost the equivalent of several year's work. His conduct had a negative effect on public perception of stem cell research, adding fuel to arguments against it. *Science* initiated an independent review of its editorial procedures, leading it to impose new rules to ensure the authenticity of images, stipulation of the specific contribution of each author, undertaking a "risk assessment" of papers likely to be prone to fraud(NAS 2009).

8.11.3 Data Malfeasance: The John Darsee Case (see https://www.nytimes.com/1983/06/14/science/notorious-darsee-case-shakes-assumptions-about-science.html)

John Darsee, M.D., was a NIH cardiology fellow working in the research group of a well-established cardiology scientist at Brigham and Women's Hospital of the Harvard Medical School. He had a larger than usual number of publications in peer-reviewed journals for someone so early in his career. He also had an offer of a faculty position at Harvard. His accomplishments came under scrutiny in 1981 when other members in his laboratory became suspicious of an abstract he was composing for presentation at a scientific meeting. It contained a description of experiments they knew he had not performed. They approached the chief director of the laboratory with their concerns. They told him that when he was asked for unprocessed data from the dogs he was measuring, he made recordings from a single dog and multiplied the resulting data so that they appeared to come from several experiments (events that lab personnel witnessed directly). When confronted by the chief he admitted to falsifying these data but denied any other scientific misconduct. His fellowship and faculty appointment were revoked, but he continued to work in the lab, and publish.

Darsee's supervisor and chief reviewed his records. The dean of the School of Medicine also reviewed his records and absolved him of any other misconduct. Several months later the NIH, which had funded a multicenter study under which Darsee's research was financed, notified Darsee's lab that data reported by them varied significantly from that reported by the other centers. An NIH investigation ensued that reached all the way back to Darsee's undergraduate laboratory research work. It was found that he had performed multiple acts of manipulation or fabrication of data at both Harvard and Emory universities that became part of 8 published articles and 21 abstracts. Coauthors were added to the abstracts without their knowledge (this may have influenced acceptance of the abstracts.). The Harvard misconduct resulted in retraction of nine papers and 21 abstracts. Darsee was barred from NIH funding and from sitting on advisory boards for ten years.

8.11.4   DATA FABRICATION. THE WILLIAM SUMMERLIN CASE

William Summerlin, M.D., a dermatologist, was a tissue transplantation immunologist at the Sloan-Kettering Cancer Center in New York. His research was in xenogeneic transplants (i.e. grafting tissue between different species). Genetically unmatched tissue implants typically generate immunological responses in the host that often result in rejection of donor tissue. Xenogeneic transplants always do. Summerlin published an article with established scientists around 1973 reporting successful xenogeneic transplantation of skin between two species of mice with different colored skin. The article was considered a breakthrough at the time and attracted considerable publicity. Summerlin's results could not be replicated, however, and other scientists at the center challenged their veracity. His superior threatened to publish a retraction of their article unless Summerlin could verify his results. He brought some of his reputed transplanted mice to the superior's office to demonstrate their existence. After he returned to the laboratory with them, however, a lab technician discovered that the transplanted "patches" could be removed with alcohol. They had in fact been painted with a black marker pen. Summerlin rationalized that he was forced to paint the patches by the great pressure he was under to succeed.

This is considered a classic case in data falsification because the reported data was physically created by the perpetrator. How much pressure would you have to be under to duplicate Summerlin's behavior?

8.11.5   THREATENING HUMAN LIFE. THE ANDREW WAKEFIELD CASE (ADAPTED FROM ANDERSON ET AL. 2013 AND GROSS 2015)

Andrew Wakefield, M.D., was a gastroenterologist at the Royal Free Hospital and Medical School in London, England. He was an investigator in a study of possible correlation between vaccines for measles, mumps and rubella (MMR) and the incidence of autism and bowel disease. John Walker-Smith, M.D. was the principal

Bioengineering Scientist Ethics

investigator of this epidemiological study. The project was at a preliminary stage of evaluating a cohort of 12 children when, in 1998, Wakefield submitted an "early report" to *Lancet* that showed, to its editors' satisfaction, that the hypothesized correlation was supported by the data. As a result of this "preliminary report" MMR vaccination rates dropped in the United Kingdom, United States, Germany, and a number of other countries. Measles incidence increased and was declared endemic in England and Wales in 2008.

In 2004 Brian Deer, a journalist for the *London Times*, investigating a lawsuit filed by Wakefield against the manufacturers of MMR vaccines, found discrepancies between data made available by the lawsuit and data published in the *Lancet* article. He reported his suspicion that Wakefield was possibly guilty of research fraud, unethical treatment of children and conflict of interest with the lawsuit's potential rewards. The UK General Medical Council acting on Deer's suspicions launched an examination that resulted in public disclosure of children's medical records. Deer could now compare the *Lancet* article with data from the records and in 2011 he published a series of articles presenting evidence that Wakefield falsified data from all 12 subjects to make them match his assertions. In addition, Wakefield had been paid $600,000 by attorneys trying to prove that vaccines were unsafe(McCoy 2015)

None of the other 11 authors of the *Lancet* article were aware of Wakefield's alterations, they testified. Of this group, only Walker-Smith, as head of the laboratory, was found guilty of scientific misconduct and lost his medical license. (He was reinstated on appeal two years later.) The *Lancet* article was retracted. Wakefield's medical license was invalidated in 2011, as a result. He moved to the United States and became director of an autism research center in Florida; never admitting to any wrongdoing, and insisting that his conclusions were valid. None of the epidemiological studies attempting to confirm Wakefield's results have been successful.

8.12 THE BIOENGINEERING SCIENTIST AS A PROFESSIONAL

This chapter completes our preliminary examination of the three professions and their ethics. After an examination of the role of nonhuman animals in scientific research, we shall return to the arena where the three professions and their laboratory animals interact, medical product research.

ENRICHMENT

1. In the Piltdown case, what would you surmise was the motivation of the hoaxer?
   What harm, if any, was caused by this hoax?
2. Before the Hwang fraud was discovered, there were undoubtedly some graduate students attempting to achieve the goal reported by Hwang

with another technique. What effect do you think the fraud and its consequences had on these students?

3. How can one explain the ignorance of the other authors added to the article by Wakefield (Note that *Lancet* is the most prestigious medical journal in the United Kingdom—just as *The New England Journal of Medicine* is in the United States)?

4. John Darsee's research was in the clinically relevant field of cardiology. His reported results may have inspired a drug company to invest in a line of research to discover a drug that would enhance or block the process his conclusions supported. If the drug produced was discovered to be more harmful than helpful in a lab animal model, the drug would have been abandoned and not used on humans. Would it be fair to conclude "No harm no foul" in this case? Explain your answer incorporating a moral analysis.

5. How would you evaluate Summerlin's behavior and Wakefield's behavior in terms of feminist ethics?

6. Go online to Pub Med or Google Scholar, and check to see if Woo-suk Hwang's *Nature* and *Science* articles can still be found in unretracted form.

9 Ethics of Research with Non-Human Animals

9.1 HISTORY OF ANIMAL USE BY HUMANS

On this planet, humans are just one species among many, and until recently their impact on the environment was negligible. Even allowing for the magnitude of anthropogenic environmental changes, the sudden disappearance of humans would have little effect on the ability of the planet to return to a balanced pre-human state. There is little doubt that the artificial urban and rural ecosystems created and maintained by *Homo sapiens sapiens* would also collapse to this natural state soon after human disappearance. The History Channel television series "Life After People" presents scenarios for such a collapse and its aftermath.

It is not unusual for animal species within a given ecosystem to use one another for survival. Predator-prey relationships are, of course, non-cooperative at the individual level. Being devoured is of no benefit to the meal (unless the meal is a parasite and the host is part of its life cycle). But at the ecosystem level, predators keep herbivores from over-reproducing and devouring so many plants that there are none left to eat. Parasites that weaken prey also help keep down their numbers. If a parasite is too virulent, however, it kills all its hosts and dooms itself. Cooperative relationships such as symbiosis, where both species benefit, and commensalism, where one benefits and the other doesn't but is not harmed, have also contributed to species survival for millions of years. A number of ant species use aphids like cows, milking them for sap that only the aphids can extract from trees. Remora fish attach themselves to sharks for a free ride to their host's feeding leftovers.

Humans interact with, and depend on, many plant and animal species. Non-human species have used humans throughout their existence. Sabre-toothed tigers found them nourishing. Protozoa, tapeworms, and a variety of roundworms, parasitize humans, particularly in third world countries. Ticks, leeches, and mosquitos suck our blood. Skin lice that have lived on all humans for many thousands of years munch on our cornified epithelium.

Human use of non-human animals has a long history. The first animal domesticated by humans appears to be the dog. Bones of at least five different varieties of *Canis familiaris* have been found in campsites more than 16,000 (Perri 2016) years old. There were no wound marks indicating these animals were slain as prey, although they could have served as food when too old to help their domesticators. Other evidence suggests they were used in hunting. Sheep were probably the next to be domesticated and probably were so while the Neolithic tribes were still nomadic. One can see remnants of their way of life in contemporary nomadic tribes of the Middle East. An explosion in domestication occurred in the Fertile Crescent area (a roughly crescent-shaped region which runs from Europe to East Asia through India)

DOI: 10.1201/9781003197218-9

158   Ethics for Bioengineering Scientists

and eventually ended nomadic existence for most of its human occupants. Animals were used for food, shelter, clothing, tools, transportation, and farming. The latter use took advantage not only of their superior strength and compliance but of their droppings as a source of fertilizer. A model for the events during this transition to civilization is presented by Diamond (1999). The most important conclusion of his book, for our purposes, is that civilization would have been impossible without domestication of plants and non-human animals.

Over 10,000 or so years that civilization has developed, many humans have been concentrated in urban settings far removed from caves. Today, interaction with non-human animals of any kind tends to be limited to pets and visits to public zoos (including Sea World and aquaria) and camera safaris. One subset of humans that utilizes other animals in an urban environment in a manner not unlike the cave dwellers includes those who use pets as partners (e.g. K-9 police), protectors (guard dog owners), or as guides (e.g. for the blind). One subset that utilizes such animals in a manner similar to farmers and ranchers is the scientist who acquires specially bred animals for laboratory research. One might argue that the breeders of race horses, show dogs, and so forth qualify as urban versions of traditional farmers and ranchers.

9.2   CHANGES IN HUMAN LINK WITH DOMESTIC ANIMALS

In urban environments, the relationship between domesticated animals and humans has changed. The two groups no longer share a mutual struggle for existence because they are isolated, first, from the threat of predators that would themselves be in danger given citizen police protection that is now part of civilization's social contract, and second, from the need to hunt for prey, which can be purchased at a grocery store. Some remnants of the shared struggle exist in rural environments such as farms that are threatened by crop failure or natural disasters (flood, fire, tornado, infection, etc.). Ranchers with large herds have similar challenges but are less linked to individual animals. Also, in some western states, there are familiar remnants of primitive struggles with predators such as coyotes, wolves, and hawks. Aborigines and nomadic tribes come closest to facing these primitive challenges.

For their part, city dwellers grow up identifying with their domestic animals in an almost parent–child (or child-doll) relationship referred to as a pet owner–pet linkage. Much as a parent derives emotional satisfaction from a child's affection, so the pet owner may feel some fulfillment from his/her animal and develop an attachment that has in some cases exceeded that felt toward fellow humans. Such attachments often include a strong need to protect the pet and may even extend to a need to protect all pets. For some, this need encompasses all non-human animals. To the farmer, the rancher, the nomad and the aborigine who utilize other animals to survive, as well as many non-Western cultures (e.g. those that consume dogs), this need makes no sense. When advocates of animal protection act politically or physically against those that use NHAs, a conflict is inevitable.

Another major change in the link between humans and domestic animals was their employment in the quest to understand human physiology. Aristotle and some of his contemporaries made observations on some species that could only have been

Ethics of Research with Non-Human Animals | **159**

gained from dissection (Adams and Larson 2007). One of his students, Erasistratus, demonstrated one way flow in heart valves (Mcpherson and Mattingly 1999). But systematic invasive examination of living specimens that became known as vivisection was apparently first performed by Galen the Physician (126–216 A.D.). He utilized mammals such as apes and pigs but not humans (because their dissection was forbidden by Roman law) (Adams and Larson 2007). His conclusions formed the basis for Western medical practice until the 16th century (Mcpherson and Mattingly 1999) when Vesalius at the beginning of the Enlightenment was allowed to publish *De Humani Corporis Fabrica* that exposed a number of Galen's errors (Dyer and Thorndike 2000). The church placed restrictions on vivisection for research between the eras of Galen and Vesalius and his contemporaries (New 1993).

From the beginning of The Enlightenment until the 19th century, experiments on laboratory animals were on a small scale. One subject might be placed in a chamber and subjected to a stimulus, and its reaction would be written down in a notebook. Little attention was paid to care for the animals. When experiments began to include statistics which demanded cohorts as was the case in France with Claude Bernard's (1813–1883) experiments utilizing many mammals, and Louis Pasteur's (1822–1895) 1880s dog experiments testing treatments for rabies, more attention was paid to ensuring that all the cohorts started as healthy animals. With the advent of ether and sterilization during their lifetimes, aware 19th century scientists were able to reduce infections and stress in their lab animals. It is worth noting that these scientists implemented their care practices in the absence of any laws requiring them (Adams and Larson 2007).

The political movement to treat domesticated animals humanely began formally in the United Kingdom in the 19th century. It was initiated by Victorian women who saw themselves as being treated like farm animals that were bred for sport or high meat quality, and were often mistreated. The women—this was before women suffrage—claimed they could identify with these animals because they themselves were mistreated, particularly by obstetricians, by being valued only for breeding. The product of this movement was the first Society for the Prevention of Cruelty to Animals (SPCA) in England in 1824. As a result of the efforts of this organization a number of laws were passed. Nearly all enterprise involving domesticated animals in the United Kingdom today requires some form of national government licensing. In the United States the American SPCA (ASPCA) was founded in 1866. Laws this organization was able to get passed were almost exclusively local in scope. It was not until the 1980s that federal laws for humane treatment of domesticated animals became a congressional priority as is described in section 9.5.

9.3 THE ANIMAL RIGHTS MOVEMENT

In 1975 the philosopher Peter Singer published *Animal Liberation*, an attack on humans who placed *Homo sapiens* above all other species. He called these individuals "speciesists", who had deprived other animal species of their "rights". The ultimate act that would return these lost rights was for every human to become a vegan (a person who consumed only plant products). Given the developing urbanite pet-owners' relationship with their pets, this conclusion from an urban Australian

160 Ethics for Bioengineering Scientists

non-scientist is not surprising. Zoologists, however, could make no sense of this point of view. As pointed out in the previous account of Hamilton's altruism equation, not only are humans—as are all other animals—clannish, but by extension they are "speciesists" naturally. Moreover, a human baby will grow into a sentient being that will understand what it means to have rights, so it is logical to attribute to a child, rights before he/she is able to claim them. At what age does a non-human animal reach a similar sentient state? Does the "parent" of a pet have the same standing as the parent of a human child in representing "rights" of his/her charge? Evolutionary psychology has provided no evidence for a yes answer to this question. Any debate over this issue would be merely academic if Singer's book had not spawned the Animal Rights movement. The movement at first targeted the meat industry, the clothing industry, zoos, and scientists who employ laboratory animals for research. The meat and clothing industries were targets because of their use of animal products. Zoos were targets because they "imprison" animals. Scientists that use laboratory animals in their research were looked upon as torturers and pet-nappers.

Initial demonstrations by animal rightists to spawn legislation against the clothing and meat industries were unsuccessful partly because these industries had powerful lobbies and produced products enjoyed by a majority of voters. There was some spurious success against zoos whose administrations were sensitive to public perception of the way animals in their care were treated. Demonstrations against laboratory scientists also had some legislative success; spawning the U.S. Animal Welfare Act in 1966, more than a century after the United Kingdom passed its first national animal welfare law.

It is likely that the movement would have remained peripheral if an incident had not taken place in the NIH-funded laboratory of Dr. Edward Taub where neurological research using primates was being conducted. The following summary of the case is adapted from Matfield (Matfield 2002).

Case A: The Taub Incident

In May 1981, Dr Edward Taub of the Institute of Behavioral Research at Silver Spring, Maryland, allowed a political science major at George Washington University, named Alex Pacheco, to work in his laboratory. Taub was studying the somatosensory apparatus, trying to determine whether primates, macaques in this case, could re-learn the use of deafferented limbs. Pacheco volunteered to work in Taub's laboratory, claiming to be interested in medical research. In fact, Pacheco was one of the founders of a tiny protest group called People for the Ethical Treatment of Animals (PETA), which had been organizing protests outside the National Institutes of Health (NIH) only weeks before. Pacheco's colleagues in PETA decided to send him to infiltrate Taub's laboratory and expose what they considered to be cruel and unnecessary experiments.

In September that year, Pacheco made a series of allegations that resulted in Taub's arrest on 119 charges. Of these charges, 113 were dismissed at the first court case, 5 more in the second case, and the last charge was overturned

Ethics of Research with Non-Human Animals

2 years later. With the string of court cases and media attention, the whole situation became a cause célèbre. The NIH started an investigation and suspended Taub's research funding. The macaques were seized by the police, were allegedly kidnapped by PETA, returned, handed back to Taub, then almost immediately remanded to the NIH Animal Centre in Poolesville. Their custody and fate became the subject of a series of court cases that lasted for more than a decade.

Later, it was discovered that the photographs and videos submitted to police as evidence of macaque mistreatment had been staged by Pacheco in such a way that they misrepresented the protocols used by Taub (MacArthur Clark 2008). Taub's experiments became the basis for a successful stroke-patient treatment known as "constraint-induced movement therapy" (Marchalik and Jurecic 2015).

This episode brought PETA to the public eye. The work of this organization has inspired violence against scientific laboratories and scientists performing laboratory animal research. PETA-inspired activists believe violence is warranted because they are protecting their "children". In contrast, scientists believe their research on animal models extends the domestication policy of using non-human species for the benefit of humans and other animals, including animal rights activists.

The debate spawned by the animal rights movement has revealed a range of attitudes about using non-human animals for research. Table 9.1 summarizes the degrees of polarization within this range.

TABLE 9.1
Attitudes toward Lab Animal Research

Conflicting Positions about Animal Research---Levels of Polarization

Pro Animal Research		Anti-Animal Research
Animals may be used as one wishes even to vent cruel tendencies	Most polarized positions	Animals have the same rights as humans
Animals may be used for any research but must be treated humanely	Difficult but has been the case in the United Kingdom for decades	Animals have no rights but vivisection is unethical
Pets should not, wild animals may, and Bred animals should be used for research; as humanely as feasible	Least polarized	Pets must never, wild animals rarely and bred animals may be used for research; humanely

9.4 THE SCIENTIFIC BASIS FOR HUMANE TREATMENT OF LABORATORY ANIMALS

A typical experimental design utilizing laboratory animals requires a control and at least one experimental or treatment cohort. The control cohort provides measurements which serve as a baseline to which all measurements from the treatment group are compared. Baselines are considered in statistics to be normal populations or "norms". It is the level of confidence that norm and treatment data are statistically significantly different that determines if the hypothesis being tested has been corroborated as a result of the falsifiable hypothesis being disproved.

In order for a comparison to be valid, variables not being measured must be kept as constant as possible. Animal stress is a confounding variable. How does one keep constant the amount of stress produced by threatening behavior toward the subject? How does one quantify the resulting strain? Suppose threatening behavior is sufficiently violent to cause injury. How does one subtract out the effects of such an injury on other measurements? If one of the side effects of a treatment on the treatment group is stress, how does one subtract out the amount of stress due to maltreatment of the subject?

One can only conclude from these considerations that data from maltreated laboratory animals is highly suspect. It follows that performing experiments in which such animals are mistreated, is a waste of time and resources because it is not science.

9.5 DEVELOPMENT OF ANIMAL RESEARCH REGULATIONS

One would expect that the 1824 formation of the British SPCA would lead to earlier appearance of regulations controlling animal research in the United Kingdom than in the United States, and they would be correct. Such regulations were part of the British "Cruelty to Animals Act" that was passed in 1876. Its counterpart did not appear in the United States until almost 90 years later (Adams and Larson 2007).

As noted in Chapter 1, there was little government support of academic research in the United States before World War II. Animal research at universities was on a small scale, with the exception of agricultural research (Lassman 2005), and causal rather than empirical. University animal colonies appeared first at Harvard and Johns Hopkins in 1880. Elsewhere, investigators had individual animal housing units, some located in their own homes (Mcpherson and Mattingly 1999). The first university to establish the position of animal laboratory veterinarian was the Mayo Clinic in 1915 (Mcpherson and Mattingly 1999). Some laboratory animal research was also carried out in military medical facilities. The Naval Medical Laboratory was established in 1853 and Walter Reed Army Institute of Medical Research evolved within the Army Medical School which was established in 1893. As early as 1898 overseas military laboratories were established to study tropical diseases *in situ* (Peake et al. 2011).

WWI, the distractions of the 1920s, and subsequent depression, relegated any public concerns about laboratory animal vivisection and research to a low priority status. With the onset of WWII, both the U.S. Army and Navy expanded their

Ethics of Research with Non-Human Animals

vivaria and ramped up experimentation on a variety of animals. Large programs were motivated by the realization that troops would be exposed to infectious diseases they had not previously encountered. Species as diverse as canaries, cats, dogs, ferrets, monkeys, rats, and rabbits were employed in the various projects (Cobert Jr 1949). Studies on wound healing, frostbite prevention, surgical techniques, high altitude, and deep-sea diving provided useful data for understanding the physiology underlying these conditions. Animal experimentation in studies of biological warfare agents were of low priority during the war but increased afterward. Because they were more valid models for humans, monkeys were often used to test the effectiveness of these weapons in delivery form (Sidell, Takafuji, and Franz 1997).

University faculty were employed for some of the military projects. Their laboratories were enhanced considerably with equipment and personnel. Those who employed animals often received funding to build or upgrade the university vivarium. The influx of military money and accompanying laboratory expansion gave university principal investigators considerable leverage for promotion and tenure, setting up a competition for government funding. Once this competition was set in motion it created political pressure for increases in government funding. As a result there was an increase in the use of animals for science after the war (Phillips and Sechzer 1989). It became evident that the growing populations of lab animals, particularly mammals, had to be cared for by experts to maintain their health. Vivaria hired veterinarians who developed laboratory animal care as a specialty and eventually organized to form an Animal Care Panel(ACP) in 1950. The ACP worked to upgrade and standardize laboratory animal care and the training of animal technicians, producing a number of publications. Meanwhile another group of academic veterinarians, working within the National Academy of Sciences, established the Institute for Laboratory Animal Resources (ILAR) that concentrated on animal care standards. It was agreed that to avoid overlap, the ACP would focus on accreditation of animal facilities and care while ILAR would focus on animal care standards. In 1967 the ACP became the American Association for Laboratory Animal Science (AALAS) (Mcpherson and Mattingly 1999).

Veterinarians were not the only ones campaigning for laboratory animal care improvement. In 1959 two British biologists, W.M.S. Russell and R.L. Burch published *The Principles of Humane Experimental Technique* in which they proposed that investigators exhaust alternatives to animal experimentation before committing to it. Their mantra of *replace* (seek *in vitro* substitutes), *reduce* (limit cohort sizes to the minimum allowed by statistical constraints), and *refine* (minimize stress on the animals utilized) (Russell and Burch 1959) has become a requirement for principal investigators funded by the federal government and is often referred to as "the 3 R's".

In 1962 in response to the concerns of ACP and ILAR, the NIH contracted with ILAR to develop a *Guide for Laboratory Animal Facilities and Care*. No federal laws regulating laboratory animal care were passed, however, until 1966. The two events that tipped the scales for passage dealt, not with care in the laboratory, but with handling, care, and transport of the animals before investigators saw them. The

November 29, 1965, issue of *Sports Illustrated* carried a story of a pet Dalmatian "Pepper" who somehow was transported from its owners back yard to the truck of a laboratory animal dealer. By the time Pepper's owner located it, it had been euthanized. The February 4 issue of Life Magazine carried a story titled "Concentration camp for dogs" that showed emaciated dogs at a Maryland dog dealer's farm. The public outcry driven by fears of petnapping descended on Congress with such force that it passed an Animal Welfare Act (AWA) that was signed into law in August. The AWA specified primates (non-human), cats, dogs, rabbits, hamsters and guinea pigs to be handled, sold, and transported exclusively by federally licensed dealers who had to document the legal status of each animal to prevent petnapping (Adams and Larson 2007).

The AWA of 1966 was "enforced" by the USDA. Quotes are needed because the law did not address regulation of lab animals in the lab. Therefore, the USDA had no jurisdiction over animal experiments. The following 20 years was marked by a growing animal rights movement, which was spurred to action by Singer's *Animal Liberation*. The AWA was amended in 1970 to include all warm-blooded species and to require use of anesthesia and analgesia on them when stress or pain was expected. Further amendment in 1976 upgraded animal care during transport (Adams and Larson 2007).

The 1981 Taub incident, and confirmed lab animal mistreatment incidents (see Case B below) convinced Congress that more direct regulation of lab animal care was necessary. The NIH had no enforcement component, so Congress strengthened the animal care regulatory link, giving enforcement power to the USDA, by 1) specifying that it monitor compliance with the new standards, and 2) attaching the new regulations to the Food Security Act (a farm bill that required funding) of 1985(Adams and Larson 2007). Important additions to the AWA, which applied to all federally funded institutions required the institution to:

1. Establish an Institutional Animal Care and Use Committee (IACUC). It must be composed of at least three members, one of which is a veterinarian and another someone unaffiliated with the institution. The members must be able to assess all use of lab animals by inspecting the animal use laboratories, vivaria, protocols and the animals themselves at least twice a year.
2. Provide for a healthy and minimal stress environment, particularly for dogs (that must be exercised) and primates (that must be housed in a psychologically healthy cage)
3. Limit use of each animal to one major recovery surgical experiment
4. Follow the 3 R's unless a clear case can be made for proposed animal use. Implementation of this approach will be aided by an information service housed in the National Agricultural Library in cooperation with the National Library of Medicine (A perspective on animal modeling may be found in a lecture at http://www.nyas.org/MediaPlayer.aspx?mid=820c2da3-f8ce-4c03 –99db-b4ab75c52a4b)
5. Train all personnel that handle lab animals in correct handling procedures

Ethics of Research with Non-Human Animals

> ## Case B: Baboon head injury experiments (adapted from Murphy, 2004)
>
> Thomas A. Gennarelli, M.D., a neurosurgeon and professor at the University of Pennsylvania in the early 1980s, sought an animal model in which to study the effects of head trauma in humans. He used baboons, which he sedated with phencyclidine hydrochloride (PCP) and partially anaesthetized with nitrous oxide (NO) in order to tolerate being strapped down and having their heads cemented into helmets. The NO treatment was stopped before (up to one hour) having their heads subjected to blunt trauma with a hydraulic piston that either shook or twisted them. NO was stopped so that the animal at the time of injury was not mentally compromised so as to alter physiological reactions. The animals were rendered comatose and paralyzed, and some died. Survivors were sacrificed after two months to study their brain tissue.
>
> In May (?) (exact date cannot be found in any search), 1984, members of the Animal Liberation Front (ALF) stole videotapes of the experiments from the laboratory. The tapes, which showed the injured animals, were edited to present them in a most inflammatory style. A public outcry ensued. Gennarelli was criticized for inadequacy of anesthesia used, and for general management of the baboons, as well as the validity of the scientific hypothesis his experiments were testing. An investigation by 18 veterinarians of the American College of Veterinary Medicine, commission by OPRR (Office for Protection from Research Risks), concluded: "Despite the fact that [the film from the edited tapes] grossly overstated the deficiencies in the Head Injury Clinic, OPRR found many extraordinarily serious violations of the *Guide for Care and Use of Laboratory Animals...*"

Case B raises a number of ethical questions. Of particular interest is the use of primates for invasive experiments. Baboons are members of the same suborder of primates to which humans belong (Anthropoidea). From Chapter 2 we can infer there is evidence they have some elements of altruistic behavior. Is there a line that should be drawn separating lab animals it is ethical to use for invasive research from those non-humans it would be unethical to use? One group particularly interested in this research is the Department of Defense. They are concerned with saving the lives of troops. Primates are compelling models for brain injury—including those caused by ordnance—investigations. Pigs have been used for burn injury investigations, because their skin models that of humans well.

The ALF followed this raid quickly with two others, stealing 13 animals from the University of Pennsylvania veterinary school. The FBI has classified the ALF and its recent partner the ELF (Environmental Liberation Front) as terrorist organizations (See https://archives.fbi.gov/archives/news/testimony/animal-rights-extremism-and-ecoterrorism). It reports that from 1996 to 2002 followers committed 600 criminal acts and caused $43 million in damages.

> ### Case C: Non-human animals as organ donors (adapted from Murphy, 2004)
>
> Thomas Starzl, M.D., Ph.D. performed the first human liver transplants, in the 1960s, at the University of Colorado. In 1992, at the University of Pittsburgh, he transplanted a baboon liver into a man in a coma whose own liver had been destroyed by hepatitis C, and who also had a HIV infection, and was not eligible for a human transplant. The patient experienced only mild treatable rejection of the implant. His recovery was considered comparable to that of an allogeneic (human-to-human) transplant recipient. Two months after the transplant, a diagnostic procedure led to sepsis and, in a few days, a fatal stroke. Although failure of the liver did not appear to be a direct cause of death, there was some suspicion that the immune system may have played a role.
>
> Starzl, predicted that liver xenografts would eventually be successful. Another of his later human recipients survived 70 days (Cooper 2017). Animal rights activists protested the use of baboons as a source of spare parts for humans.

Patients with terminal diseases are often allowed to participate in "last chance" procedures that are risky but are believed, from preliminary evidence, to have potential benefit. It should be possible to analyze both the xenogeneic donor organ and host to determine the cause of failure. If this were done at the time of the episode, some information may have been uncovered that increased our understanding of the pathophysiology of transplantation failure. To the extent that such an understanding contributed to advances in transplantation, the efforts of Starzi were considered by a number of people to be beneficial. Through the use of cloning and genetic engineering, animals have been grown that may be immunologically compatible with human hosts. From these donors, organs may be harvested at will. Some have suggested extending this idea to cloning humans. Actual cases of families having extra children to provide tissue for siblings, e.g. kidneys, have been reported (English et al. 2002). The situation leading to Case C is the shortage of living donor transplants. As a result, a number of patients have died waiting for kidneys, hearts, lungs, or livers. Cadaveric allogeneic tissue is relatively abundant and can be used for structural replacement (bones, ligaments, etc.).

> ## ENRICHMENT
>
> 1. Debate: Animal Rightist
>
> Peter Singer, the philosophical founder of the animal rights movement, claims that non-human animals are sufficiently aware of their existence to

Ethics of Research with Non-Human Animals

qualify for rights equivalent to those of humans. Biological scientists have worked with non-human animals for centuries to learn about the nature of life and how the body functions. With increasing use of intervention to cure diseases non-human animals have become testing instruments to detect the causes of disease and to test the safety of proposed cures. There is some evidence from evolutionary psychology that non-human primates exhibit rudimentary forms of moral behavior. If non-human animals have rights they are moral agents and it would be just as unethical to employ them for experiments without their permission as it would to use humans for the same purpose. A key to the success of this debate as a rich learning experience is clarification of the difference between "animal welfare" (that the debate **is not** about) and "animal rights" (that it **is** about).

Resolved (assertion to be debated): *Non-human animals are not moral agents. Although they should not be abused for the simple reason that stressed animals generate compromised data, laboratory animals are valid subjects for scientific experiments.*

2. Use the following links for a 1991 review and 2021 update of Edward Taub

https://www.washingtonpost.com/archive/lifestyle/magazine/1991/02/24/the-great-silver-spring-monkey-debate/25d3cc06–49ab-4a3c-afd9-d9eb35a862c3/ and https://lifeboat.com/ex/bios.edward.taub. Was the overall impact of his experiences as a scientist on science, constructive, or destructive? What lessons about performing lab animal research have you learned from them?

10 Health Professionals and Historic Human Research Ethics

10.1 THE TRADITION OF EXPERIMENTING ON HUMANS

Since the early days of "witch doctors" patients have been "guinea pigs". Any new substance or procedure suspected of or rumored as being effective for a given ailment was tried on an afflicted subject. The development of medical professions in Egyptian and Greek civilizations did not eliminate the need to test medicines and procedures empirically on ill patients. Of course, riskier treatments were probably not attempted on members of powerful classes such as the rich or well educated. As medicine became a profession, practitioners shared the results of their treatments with each other. This body of empirical knowledge accumulated and became the subject matter of medical training. With no understanding of cells, physiology or even how fertilization took place, medical reasoning was based on assumptions that had little to do with science until the 19th century. Consequently, medical practice was called an "art".

The trial-and-error testing of a medicine or procedure is empiricism. We refer to this method as "experimenting ON" a subject. Enlistment of a subject in a scientific study of a medicine or procedure is referred to as using that patient "FOR an experiment" (or for a scientific study which includes trials or experiments). A poorly designed study intended to be scientific is in danger of deteriorating into mere empiricism. The use of a human for a procedure setup as an experiment appears to have been formally attempted first in the 18th century, as indicated in Appendix E. Human consent forms did not exist for these experiments, which were not structured for statistical validity.

The science of physiology was developed during The Enlightenment with the help of physicians who moonlighted as scientists. William Harvey was an example of a physician-scientist. Harvey did not perform his observations on humans. Louis Pasteur, who was not a physician, did. He used non-human animals as a rule but was forced to include humans as experimental subjects when faced with a group of workers already infected with the test disease (rabies). Technically, these subjects were, in fact, experimented on. Luckily, his vaccine worked on both his experimental dogs and their human counterparts. No human consent forms were signed for these experiments either.

Paternalistic treatment of patients continued well into the 20th century until events took place that made patients demand more respect for their autonomy. Physicians like Andrew Ivy and Leo Alexander helped lead the resulting transformation of their profession. Humans were both experimented on and used for

DOI: 10.1201/9781003197218-10

169

170   Ethics for Bioengineering Scientists

experiments without their consent to such an extent that international laws were passed to prevent a repeat of the incidents. Much has been made of experiments with humans in Nazi concentration camps and Ping Fan in China, but they were not the first government-sanctioned episodes of the last century. The United States had its own smaller scale version that started well before WWII.

10.2   THE TUSKEGEE SYPHILIS STUDY

During the 17th and 18th centuries, an unplanned (for the most part) "cultural" exchange took place between the indigenous peoples of the Western hemisphere and invading Europeans. The natives received the virus *Variola* that causes smallpox, and the Europeans, the bacterial spirochete *Treponema pallidum,* that causes syphilis. The exchange had uneven effects. The natives suffered death rates estimated at well over 50% (Crosby 1976). The immigrants suffered mainly chronic debilitation and had much lower death rates. They also introduced the disease to Europe.

Vaccination, based on the vaccine popularized by Jenner, helped quell smallpox in 19th-century Europe. But its dissemination to the indigenous tribes was too late to alter their course of depopulation, which had been made inevitable by a number of factors, including wars and forced migrations that kept them contained. There was no vaccine for syphilis and it could not be produced in laboratory animals, so it had to be studied in human populations. Treatments had to be developed, as a result, without the controlled environment needed to evaluate their effectiveness. There was scant understanding of the newly discovered immune system. But scientists recognized it had a role in fighting disease, and there was concern about internalized substances that reduced its function.

Dermatologists C. Boeck and J.E. Bruusgaard of Norway hypothesized that heavy metals compromised immunity and studied hospital charts to test their hypothesis. In the early 1900s they discovered that 73% of patients with *T. pallidum* were asymptomatic (Pence 1995). This finding created great confusion in medical science and inhibited further studies. What was needed was a clear picture of the natural history of syphilis, so that physicians could relate symptoms to a particular stage of this chronic disease.

The philanthropic Julius Rosenwald Foundation of Philadelphia started a project early in 1929 to eradicate syphilis with the promising drug neosalvarsan (arsphenamine, a molecule containing two arsenic groups). Target patients were selected from six counties with syphilis rates above 20%. One of these, Macon County, Alabama had a rate of 36%, the highest in the United States. The county was 82% black (Pence 1995). The depression struck late in 1929 and the Rosenwald Foundation ran out of funding for their project. They hoped the U.S. Public Health Service (USPHS) would take it over. But federal funding also plummeted; from $1 million in 1929 to $60,000 by 1935 (Gamble 1999; Pence 1995), so the agency could not continue treatments.

While the USPHS could not afford to treat syphilis victims, they saw an opportunity to learn from them. They tested 4.400 black residents of Macon County and found 22% with the disease, 62% of whom had it congenitally. Of these, 399

Historic Human Research Ethics

had not been treated. The Surgeon General, H.S. Cumming, concluded that if this group was left untreated and studied long enough, USPHS physicians could learn how syphilis progressed naturally. The long-sought course of the disease would be revealed. USPHS physicians partnered with physicians of the Tuskegee Institute of Macon County to treat these patients as if they were animals in nature, i.e. the project was, more or less, an ecological study. In a 1936 *JAMA* (*Journal of the American Medical Association*) issue, Cumming called the project "an unusual opportunity to study the untreated syphilitic patient from the beginning of the disease to the death of the infected person" and pointed out that the patients "had never received treatment". A "control" group of 201 age-matched individuals without syphilis was included in the study (Gamble 1999; Pence 1995).

After Cumming retired in 1936, management of the project passed to one black nurse E. Rivers and a few Tuskegee physicians. No physician assumed supervision nor was there a protocol for Rivers to follow. Federal physicians visited "every few years" (Gamble 1999; Pence 1995) to evaluate the patients. Evaluations included spinal taps of 271 of the 399 patients with the disease. To keep the patients compliant the federal physicians told them they were being treated for "bad blood", and the spinal taps were part of their treatment. To reinforce compliance they were sent this letter:

Dear Sir:
Some time ago you were given a thorough examination and since that time we hope you have gotten a great deal of treatment for bad blood. You will now be given your last chance to get a second examination. This examination is a very special one and after it is finished you will be given a special treatment if it is believed you are in a condition to stand it.

During World War II (WWII) project patients were kept out of the draft by instructions to the local draft board, from the USPHS. Penicillin, an antibiotic effective against *T. pallidum,* was developed between 1941 and 1943. Because it was difficult to mass-produce, it remained available to the military only, during the war. Tuskegee study patients did not receive it during the project at any point after the war.

Peter Buxtun, B.A. a European History major, joined the Army in 1966 and served as a Psychiatric Social worker in San Francisco. He worked with sexually transmitted disease patients under the supervision of the Centers for Disease Control (CDC), which had replaced the USPHS disease investigation function. He was shocked to learn of a physician who had been reprimanded for inadvertently treating a patient, who was part of an "experiment", with penicillin. After further investigation Buxtun learned of the Tuskegee study and reacted by writing a critical report to the USPHS, comparing it to Nazi experimentation on prisoners during WWII. In response, the USPHS flew Buxtun to Atlanta to confer with the physicians managing the project. They reacted in anger to his accusations, but did not, to Buxtun's surprise, fire him. In 1967 Buxtun entered Hastings Law School and a year later sent USPHS another report challenging the project. In 1969, the CDC, in response to Buxtun's persistence, convened a panel of their physicians to evaluate

172   Ethics for Bioengineering Scientists

the study. They concluded that it should be continued. In 1970 W.J. Brown, a member of the panel, published a monograph describing treatment of late benign syphilis with benzathine penicillin G. None of the Tuskegee study patients (except for the one inadvertently treated) had received the antibiotic.

In 1972 Buxtun, having graduated law school, became a whistleblower. He mentioned the story to an Associated Press reporter, who passed it on to J. Heller of the *Washington Star*, who published it on July 26 (Heller 1972). The Director of Health and Human Services was "shocked", and Senator Edward Kennedy held hearings, calling Buxtun as a witness. J.D. Millar, CDC's head of Venereal Disease Control, defended the USPHS citing the publication of results in 15 articles, in peer-reviewed journals. In apparent contradiction to the reprimand of the penicillin-dispensing physician, Millar claimed that the subjects knew they could get treatment any time they chose to (Gamble 1999; Pence 1995). The Macon County Medical Society—to which the Tuskegee physicians belonged—reported they had never agreed to withhold treatment and had given remaining patients "appropriate therapy" (Gamble 1999; Pence 1995). The USPHS refuted their claim, offering as evidence the original signed agreement to withhold treatment.

The Secretary of Health, Education and Welfare (HEW, the replacement of USPHS), Casper Weinberger, officially terminated the Tuskegee study on November 16, 1972. At that time, CDC estimated that during the study 28 of the original syphilitic group had died of syphilis, 100 of related complications (Nix 2017), and 154 of unrelated heart disease (Heller 1972). About 43 had been lost to follow-up, leaving the 74 who were still alive. These subjects now received penicillin. In addition, 40 (assuming singular marriages) of the patients passed the disease on to their wives, who in turn passed it on to 19 children (Nix 2017).

A subgroup of the remaining 74 patients sued the federal government in 1973. The settlement gave $37,000 to each of them, $15,000 to each heir of those who had died, $16,000 to each living control, and $5,000 to each heir of controls who had died. An apology was delivered by President Clinton to the last syphilis survivor in a White House ceremony on 16 May, 1997.

10.3   NAZI USE OF HUMAN EXPERIMENTAL SUBJECTS

The subjects being experimented on by Nazi doctors during WWII were in different circumstances from the Tuskegee patients. The ethics of their physicians would qualify as nationalistic. The subjects were in concentration camps and under direct control of the experimenters. In a scientific context, their circumstances were comparable to that of laboratory animals. Had their treatment matched the requirements of the Animal Welfare Act described in Chapter 9, integrity of the resulting data would depend mainly on the integrity of the data obtained. The subjects were prisoners, however, and under considerable stress from physical abuse, exposure, malnutrition, and forced participation in the experiments. They often ended up mutilated, disabled, and/or dead. Up to 30 categories of these experiments were performed by Nazi doctors (Dyson 2000). They included:

Historic Human Research Ethics

1. *Simulation of high-altitude flight:* At Dachau during 1942, S. Rascher, M.D. and his coworkers subjected 200 prisoners to environmental conditions that would be faced by fighter pilots ejecting at high altitudes. Subjects were held in hypobaric chambers simulating pressure and temperatures found at 68,000 feet while their physiological responses were being measured. They ran each test until the subject fainted or died. It was alleged that some had their brains exposed while still alive to test the hypothesis that high-altitude sickness was caused by accumulation of air emboli in blood vessels. Eighty of the subjects died during the experiment and the rest were killed (Dyson 2000).
2. *Simulation of extremely cold weather:* Also at Dachau the same staff subjected an unknown number of prisoners to cold weather conditions that would be faced by soldiers fighting in Russia or bailing out in the North Atlantic. Subjects were either placed in icy water or tied down outdoors in winter either naked or dressed in flight suits. During as much as 5 hours of exposure their vital signs—heart rate, body temperature, reflexes, etc.—were measured. When their body temperature reached 79.7°F, subjects were warmed in hot sleeping bags or baths. An estimated 80–100 subjects died during the experiments (Dyson 2000).
3. *Simulation of wounds to test antibiotics like sulfanilamide:* At Ravensbrük prisoners were subjected to wounding and infection to test the effectiveness of antibiotics. Battle wounds left untreated are at high risk for infection from bacteria like *Clostridium perfringens* the bacillus that causes gas gangrene. To test the effectiveness of treating such wounds with synthetic drugs, physicians inflicted wounds in prisoners and infected them with the bacilli bacteria *C. perfringens* or *C. tetani* (cause of tetanus) or the coccus bacterium *Streptococcus sp.* To further simulate battlefield conditions, they shoved glass and wood particles into the wound, and ligated blood vessels feeding the wound area, to compromise healing (Dyson 2000).
4. *Chemical warfare poison testing at Buchenwald:* At Buchenwald medical staff injected prisoners with poisons like phenol or cyanide. Other chemicals were administered in food or loaded into bullets that were shot into the subject. If the administered chemical did not kill the subject, he was executed. All corpses were autopsied (Dyson 2000).
5. *Chemical warfare poison testing at Fort Ney:* At Fort Ney in France medical staff exposed prisoners to the toxic gas phosgene in order to test antidotes. They exposed 52 subjects to various concentrations of the gas, which was breathed in. According to German records the subjects were already weak and malnourished. Four died directly from the exposure (Dyson 2000). Phosgene was developed in 1917 by Fritz Haber Ph.D. and was used on the battlefield in WWI. Ironically, Haber won the Nobel prize for chemistry in 1918, having developed a process for manufacturing ammonia from atmospheric nitrogen in a form critical for making fertilizer (necessary for growing crops), and he was Jewish.
6. *Study of immune system response to tuberculosis:* At Neuengamme, Dr. Kurt Heissmeyer and his staff injected into the lungs of at least 200 prisoners the bacillus bacterium *Mycobacterium tuberculosis*, the primary cause of

174   Ethics for Bioengineering Scientists

tuberculosis. The first phase of the project was conducted to determine if natural immunity to the disease existed. Their second project's goal was development of a TB vaccine (Dyson 2000).

7. *Musculoskeletal transplantation experiments:* At Ravensbruk, medical staff transplanted limbs or parts of them from one prisoner to another, to determine if the implant would be compatible (Dyson 2000). Immune rejection was not known at this time, so there was no attempt to match the allogeneic implant to its host. Also not known, was the treatment necessary for implant survival if transplantation was not immediate. Consequently, transplantation usually failed, and the subject suffered permanent disability.

8. *Testing sterilization methods to enhance eugenics program:* At a number of camps, including Auschwitz and Ravensbrük, medical staff tested sterilization techniques on men and women prisoners. Radiation was applied to the male testes, which were then removed for pathology. To come up with an effective means of sterilizing millions of people with a minimum of time and effort, doctors at Auschwitz, Ravensbrük, and elsewhere conducted experiments on both men and women. They radiated the genitals of young men, and then castrated them, to study the resulting changes in their testes. Caustic substances were implanted in uteri or cervices. The women suffered pain, bleeding, and bursting spasms in the stomach (Dyson 2000).

9. *Engineering seawater to make it drinkable:* At Dachau, Dr. Hans Eppinger and others forced 90 prisoners on a strict diet of seawater. The subjects became sufficiently dehydrated to seek unusual sources (e.g. wet floors) of fresh water. The treatments produced pain and kidney injury (Dyson 2000).

Available evidence reveals no prisoner consent for any of the procedures described. At the Nuremberg "doctor's trial", which brought 23 German doctors to trial immediately after the war, the defense attorney used U.S. Surgeon General Cumming's (et al.) 1936 *JAMA* Tuskegee study article to claim that the Nazi experimenters were following a policy acceptable to the U.S. government and should not be prosecuted for it. Prosecutors found 15 defendants guilty of war crimes and crimes against humanity; seven were hung.

10.4 JAPANESE ARMY EXPERIMENTS USING CHINESE CIVILIANS IN PING FAN

A decade before the attack on Pearl Harbor, the Japanese army had concluded that their plan to conquer southeast Asia could not be achieved without resorting to nonconventional weapons. Chemical and biological warfare appeared to be the most qualified means for subduing their adversaries. But, in order to optimize the effectiveness of chemical and biological agent weapons, the army had to test the end products under battlefield conditions, that is, on human subjects. A network of 26 testing camps, distributed over southeast Asia, was built as the Japanese military gained footholds in the targeted countries (Working 2001). The headquarters for this setup—called "unit 731"—was in the Harbin, Manchuria suburb of Ping Fan. Its commanding officer was Lieutenant General Shiro Ishii, M.D. A workforce of

Historic Human Research Ethics

some 20,000, including botanists, microbiologists, physicians, veterinarians, and zoologists was employed (Harris 1994). About 15,000 prisoners were interned in the camps, but testing extended to tens of thousands of people living in the surrounding areas, which served as "battlefields".

An estimated 250,000 Chinese were killed in field tests using the bacteria *Bacillus anthracis* (Anthrax), *Rickettsia typhi* (Typhus), *Vibrio cholerae* (Cholera), and *Yersinia pesitis* (bubonic plague) (There were some other non-Japanese victims, such as Russians) (Working 2001). The tests consisted of distributing food tainted with the pathogens; mixing water wells, streams, and reservoirs with them, and creating epidemics by injecting them into the veins of unsuspecting peasants, who were told they were being inoculated against the disease. The Japanese air force sprayed or dropped various biological weapons on villages, towns, and cities from the air.

With the exception of 12 participants, who were brought before a show trial in Khabarovsk, Russia in 1949 by the Soviet authorities, most of the architects of Japan's biological warfare programs were never prosecuted for their crimes. None of those convicted received more than 5 years in prison (Working 2001). They were treated generously by the Allied occupation forces because American (and Soviet) military scientists wanted access to experimental data collected by the Japanese scientists. The carefully recorded data revealed how the human body reacted to the pathogens to which the mostly Chinese subjects has been exposed. It also detailed the weaponization processes developed for pathogen delivery.

Although the 1925 Geneva Protocols banned chemical and biological weapons, two major powers had not signed it by the 1940s, Japan and the United States. Additional protocols were added to the Geneva Conventions in 1977. They forbid "medical and scientific experiments" on humans, even when the subject consents. The 1972 Biological Weapons Convention forbids "developing microbial or biological agents or toxins and equipment" intended to deliver "such agents or toxins for hostile purposes or in an armed conflict" (Harris 1994).

Until the 1980s, the Japanese government denied that the crimes committed by its doctors and scientists had even taken place. When the accumulating evidence, particularly from the Khabarovsk trials, forced Japanese authorities to admit to its validity, they contended the program had been the work of renegade militarists. The Japanese government, at this writing, has neither apologized nor offered compensation to survivors of the germ warfare experiments, nor to the families and descendants of those killed by them (Harris 1994).

10.5 DEVELOPMENT OF FIRST CONVENTIONS REGULATING EXPERIMENTS USING HUMAN SUBJECTS

The full extent of human experimentation on the scale of the Tuskegee, Nazi concentration camp and Ping Fan projects was not publicized until well after WWII. Since the United States was not a signatory to the 1925 Geneva protocols for chemical and biological warfare, and its military was intent on learning what Japanese and Nazi experimenters had discovered, there was no official pressure to press for legislation protecting human subjects like the campaigns for animal

176 Ethics for Bioengineering Scientists

welfare laws in the 1980s. The U.S. Navy had developed rudimentary informed consent protocols in 1932 (Murphy 2004). But they were not further developed until after the war. Globally, research on human subjects continued much as it had in the early 20th century until 1947. In the United States, there were no significant changes in the relevant law until the 1970s. A table summarizing human experimentation is presented in Appendix E. The seminal event that led to international laws regulating human experimentation was the Nuremberg trials. The document that resulted from these trials was the Nuremberg Code.

10.6 THE NUREMBERG CODE

Preliminary to each of the 13 Nuremberg war crimes trials, conducted between 1945 and 1949, ethical standards had to be defined, against which the defendants' behavior could be evaluated. The movie "Judgment at Nuremberg" about the trial of judges gives one a sense of the difficulty of formulating relevant ethical standards. For the 1947 doctors' trial, the tribunal assigned U.S. physicians Andrew Ivy and Leo Alexander the task of defining ethical standards for research using humans. Upon learning the results of Ivy and Alexander's efforts in 1946, the American Medical Association (AMA) adopted formal ethical advisories for human research based on them. Defense lawyers at the trial challenged the notion of standardized ethics. In fact, there were no international standards that specified the difference between licit and illicit experiments with human beings. Dr. Ivy responded by admitting standards were not formally documented but "were understood only as a matter of common practice". To comments like this, defense lawyers threw up a challenge that said, essentially, "Who are doctors from the U.S. to claim they know ethical common practice when they were responsible for the Tuskegee syphilis project?" The challenges did not convince the judges, who found the defendants guilty. In its deliberations, the court used the standards to identify what it termed "permissible medical experiments". The resulting document has become known as the Nuremberg Code. Here it is:

"The great weight of the evidence before us is to the effect that certain types of medical experiments on human beings, when kept within reasonably well-defined bounds, conform to the ethics of the medical profession generally. The protagonists of the practice of human experimentation justify their views on the basis that such experiments yield results for the good of society that are unprocurable by other methods or means of study. All agree, however, that certain basic principles must be observed in order to satisfy moral, ethical and legal concepts:

1. The voluntary consent of the human subject is absolutely essential.
   This means that the person involved should have legal capacity to give consent; should be so situated as to be able to exercise free power of choice, without the intervention of any element of force, fraud, deceit, duress, overreaching, or other ulterior form of constraint or coercion, and should have sufficient knowledge and comprehension of the elements of the subject matter involved as to enable him to make an understanding and enlightened decision. This latter element requires that before the acceptance of an

Historic Human Research Ethics

affirmative decision by the experimental subject there should be made known to him the nature, duration, and purpose of the experiment; the method and means by which it is to be conducted; all inconveniences and hazards reasonably to be expected; and the effects upon his health or person which may possibly come from his participation in the experiment.

The duty and responsibility for ascertaining the quality of the consent rests upon each individual who initiates, directs, or engages in the experiment. It is a personal duty and responsibility which may not be delegated to another with impunity.

2. The experiment should be such as to yield fruitful results for the good of society, unprocurable by other methods or means of study, and not random or unnecessary in nature.
3. The experiment should be so designed and based on the results of animal experimentation and a knowledge of the natural history of the disease or other problems under study that the anticipated results will justify the performance of the experiment.
4. The experiment should be so conducted as to avoid all unnecessary physical and mental suffering and injury.
5. No experiment should be conducted where there is an a priori reason to believe that death or disabling injury will occur, except, perhaps, in those experiments where the experimental physicians also serve as subjects.
6. The degree of risk to be taken should never exceed that determined by the humanitarian importance of the problem to be solved by the experiment.
7. Proper preparations should be made and adequate facilities provided to protect the experimental subject against even remote possibilities of injury, disability, or death.
8. The experiment should be conducted only by scientifically qualified persons. The highest degree of skill and care should be required through all stages of the experiment of those who conduct or engage in the experiment.
9. During the course of the experiment the human subject should be at liberty to bring the experiment to an end if he has reached the physical or mental state where continuation of the experiment seems to him to be impossible.
10. During the course of the experiment the scientist in charge must be prepared to terminate the experiment at any stage if he has probable cause to believe, in the exercise of the good faith, superior skill, and careful judgment required of him that a continuation of the experiment is likely to result in injury, disability, or death to the experimental subject."

from *Trials of War Criminals Before the Nuremberg Military Tribunals Under Control Council Law No 10*, Vol. II. Nuremberg, Germany, October 1946 - April 1949.

The Nuremberg trials were military trials. Their records were the property of the U.S. military who chose the judges. The Department of Defense had the power to decide which details were available to the public, and which were classified as top secret. It chose to not release the Nuremberg Code except to carefully selected parties (Murphy 2004). Implementation of its standards within the military was slow. They were invoked in 1953 by the Secretary of Defense for projects that dealt with atomic radiation, biological, or chemical weapons. The post WWII military projects described in Appendix E were all classified.

10.7 THE HELSINKI DECLARATION AND OPRR

A series of scandals that included the spate of congenitally deformed babies, who were victims of the pregnancy sedative/morning sickness drug Thalidomide, in the early 1960s, moved the World Medical Association in 1964 to adopt a Helsinki Declaration that asserts for human experiments: "The interests of science and society should never take precedence over the well-being of the subject". This document was the first globally adopted declaration for ethical experimentation with humans (Murphy 2004). It is periodically modified to reflect advances in technology (e.g. DNA analysis). In the United States the medical community displayed signs of concern for human research subjects. Henry K. Beecher in a 1966 *New England Journal of Medicine* article cited 22 published clinical research projects that he considered unethical. In one project 26 newborn babies were exposed to X-rays to determine if they alter flow of urine in the urethra (Murphy 2004). That same year the NIH established their Office for Protection from Research Risks (OPRR) which was charged with overseeing NIH-funded human research.

It was the 1972 exposure of the Tuskegee syphilis project that served as a catalyst for federal legislation. The press sensationalization that same year of a reputable study involving deliberate infection with Hepatitis A virus of mentally disabled children at Willowbrook State School in New York, from 1955 to 1970, only provided impetus for the Tuskegee effect. Congress soon enjoined an ad hoc panel to assess the need for federal human research legislation. The panel's 1973 conclusion was "Society can no longer afford to leave the balancing of individual rights against scientific progress to the scientific community". Ironically, the Tuskegee study methodology would not have been acceptable for a peer-reviewed scientific journal in 1936.

10.8 THE NATIONAL RESEARCH ACT AND THE BELMONT REPORT

Congress passed the first version of the National Research Act (NRA) in 1974. It constituted the National Commission for the Protection of Human Subjects of Biomedical and Behavioral Research (NCPHSBBR), which would serve to advise it on development of relevant legislation. It directed the Department of Health, Education and Welfare (DHEW) to have all its funding agencies require each recipient institution to establish an Institutional Review Board (IRB) that would evaluate all clinical research activities, for adherence to medical ethics standards. Approval by the IRB would be necessary before any application for funding could be submitted to a federal agency. At the NIH the OPRR was assigned the task of

Historic Human Research Ethics

monitoring the IRBs. The NRA did not cover military, private nor state-sponsored research.

In 1975 the U.S. military declassified the Nuremberg Code (Murphy 2004). The NCPHSBBR now had access to a worked out set of standards and could include them in their report. It came out in 1978 as the *Belmont Report*. Rather than follow the Nuremberg Code formula, the *Belmont Report* set out three main criteria for ethically evaluating research using human subjects.

1. **Respect for persons**: This criterion comes from Kantian deontological ethics and is the basis for autonomy. Individuals may not be used as a means to an end. The end of most concern at this time was science, as exemplified in the eyes of congressmen by the Tuskegee and Willowbrook studies. As we shall see in Chapter 12, the target shifted to product development in the 1990s. To ensure autonomy, researchers are required to provide information about the experimental protocol that allows the subject to arrive at an educated decision about their consent.

2. **Beneficence**: This criterion has roots in utilitarian, deontology and virtue ethics. It requires the researcher to consider the impact of the protocol on the welfare of the subject (deontology), to weigh the risk (utilitarianism) of compromising that welfare against the benefit to society of the study (virtue ethics).

3. **Justice**: This criterion is obviously derived from contractarianism's Veil of Ignorance. While there are no laws specific to the way a research project is conducted, there is a protocol. The protocol acts as an analogy for law. The criterion requires that the protocol be formulated so as not to take advantage of any group, as was the case in the Tuskegee study.

Updating of the NRA will be discussed in the next chapter. But one aspect of the original that will not change is the responsibility of IRBs to implement these criteria as they are embodied in the latest federal regulations.

10.9 HUMANS BEING HUMANS

The three landmark episodes of violation of human autonomy presented in this chapter and the many others summarized in Appendix E were carried out by a variety of cultures. Given the role of natural selection in *Homo sapiens sapiens* evolution, the social psychologies that nurtured such behavior should not be surprising. One might reasonably predict that any human society given appropriate circumstances is capable of rationalizing violation of autonomy of any defined group (gypsies, Hindus, redheads, etc.), while at the same time self-righteously condemning the same behavior against members of their own group. Often, a country at war with another may violate the autonomy of their own citizens of common ancestry with their enemies, using the rationalization that anyone so closely related must be a "sympathizer". A prime example of this pattern is the U.S. government's official restriction and interment of its citizens of Japanese descent during WWII.

ENRICHMENT

1. Regarding the Tuskegee case:

If you had been in Peter Buxtun's place, would you have performed as he did? Analyze your response using the five moral theories. Can you defend the actions of the USPHS physicians using moral analysis? Try it. How might supporters of the Eugenics movement judge the actions of the USPHS physicians? Was the settlement of the class action suit both fair and just?

2. Moral superiority

Three regions of the world are not mentioned in the chapter or the Appendix E table; South America, Africa and the central fertile crescent (Middle East to India). Does this mean the people who live there are incapable of such behavior? Did it occur but was not reported? If it did not occur, how come? If your ancestry is from these regions, do you think your behavior would be different from those mentioned in the table?

3. Debate

While one can find scientific flaws in the methodology employed by the Nazi and Japanese human experimenters, the Japanese came close enough to a scientifically valid protocol in some laboratory projects to make their research results valuable to the U.S. and Russian military. It is conceivable that some military body is conducting or will conduct non-consensual experiments on prisoners that are scientifically valid. Some hold that data from these projects are off-limits ethically and should be destroyed. Others say data are data and provide useful information that may be of critical value.

Resolved: Data are data. While experimenters who violate internationally accepted standards for research by using non-volunteering prisoners should be punished severely and be prevented from profiting from them, their results should be made available to all scientists.

11 Health Professionals and Modern Human Research Ethics

This chapter explores the ethical consequences of physicians becoming part of the human research equation. The transition became significant after World War II (WWII). It changed the patient–physician relationship from mostly paternal to fiduciary. In cases where the patient was also a research subject, there was a potential conflict of interest. Clinical research became an arena for lawyers, government-regulating agencies, and industry, as partners and adversaries to a greater degree than ever before. The most scientifically important disclosure in the chapter is the contribution of epidemiologist Bradford Hill to clinical science. It established the relevancy of epidemiological data for application to public health policy. We begin by examining the stimuli for physician transition from health provider to member of a research team. Crucial seeds were actually planted by the development of the drug industry.

11.1 THE INDUSTRIAL REVOLUTION CREATES A DRUG INDUSTRY

In the first pharmaceutical epoch (1850–1945) (Malerba and Orsenigo 2001), industrialization of chemistry was just beginning, and new drug development was rare. Synthetic dye production preoccupied the blossoming chemical industries. What there was of a drug industry was 80% concentrated in Europe (Malerba and Orsenigo 2001). Understanding of human physiology was too rudimentary for targeted research, so the new drug companies in the United States and the United Kingdom focused on mimicking effective drugs that had been found in nature. Paul Ehrlich, the 1908 Nobel laureate, improved on this approach by targeting the agents of a variety of diseases with "magic bullets", introducing the concept of "chemotherapy". But his antibacterial drugs, like neosalvarsan (see Chapter 10), were often toxic (salvarsan contains arsenates) in high dos or used chronically. Some were even used for cancer treatment, with usually disastrous results (DeVita Jr and Chu 2008). Construction of the Panama Canal, where yellow fever was a threat (McCullough 1977), and World War I, added the Department of Defense (DOD) to the quest. It instituted studies of infectious diseases of potential threat to soldiers, mostly in the tropics (e.g. the Philippines that had been won from Spain in the Spanish-American war) (Peake et al. 2011). But the worst infectious disease, in terms of deaths, to afflict fighting soldiers in the early 1900s was the HIN1 virus-caused flu that they caught in Europe. Its epidemic caught the medical community

DOI: 10.1201/9781003197218-11

182   Ethics for Bioengineering Scientists

completely off guard (Morens et al. 2010). In fact, the epidemic ended with no medical intervention; that is, it just died out naturally.

A decade later penicillin was discovered. It was an antibiotic that targeted bacteria, instead of all cells, as did previous drugs. Advances in chemical manufacturing allowed its large-scale production in time to save many soldiers' lives during WWII, thereby setting the stage for post-war mass production of antibiotics and vaccines (like the Salk polio vaccine). But penicillin's discovery was an accident. The truly transforming model for disease-targeted research was the military-directed antimalarial drug development program organized by the Committee on Medical Research of the U.S. Office of Scientific Research and Development. Its success made it not only an organizational model, but also a source of talented scientists, who had been recruited for the project. These scientists spread knowledge of the techniques they had learned to the drug industry and academia. They helped transform the drug industry into a research and development (R&D)-intensive business (Malerba and Orsenigo 2001). At least 20 business enterprises and a fair number of universities were involved in the project. They served as a critical mass to start a pharmaceutical revolution.

11.2 SCIENCE, MEDICINE, AND TECHNOLOGY COME TOGETHER AFTER 1945

WWII marked a major turning point in the history of scientific research using human subjects in the United States. The panel that advised President Roosevelt's Director of the Office of Scientific Research and Development, Vannevar Bush, when he prepared his 1945 report to the president on the future role for government in support of science, contained a number of university presidents and prominent scientists. Bush had guided much of the research for the war effort that was funded by the government. He concluded from this experience, and the testimony of his advisors, that industry and university scientists and physicians could work together to improve the health of U.S. citizens through "targeted research" (Bush 1945). A number of Congress members, particularly in states with universities and/or industries that were potential recipients of the resultant government funding, were in favor of the prospect. For Bush, science was an "Endless Frontier" (Bush 1945). The potential role of industry in this effort was already becoming evident, as the pharmaceutical industry, driven by the promise of antibiotics that would succeed penicillin, was entering a new, what Malerba calls its "second", epoch of development (1945–1992) (Malerba and Orsenigo 2001). In addition, the medical implant industry was beginning to grow beyond materials placed on the body surface, driven, initially by intraocular lenses, first implanted in 1949. Enthusiasm was tempered, however, by revelations from the 1947 Nuremberg doctors' trials. A growing realization that new drugs, implants, and procedures would have to eventually be tested on humans raised concerns. But the FDA (Food and Drug Administration) remained relatively inactive as a premarket regulator, during the 1940s and early 1950s. It was the Department of Justice that protected victims of unsafe drugs and devices with "after the fact" regulation to have them removed

Modern Human Research Ethics

from the marketplace (Munsey 1995). The National Research Act that mandated a more active regulatory role for the FDA would not be passed until 1974.

The decade 1950–1960 has been called the "Heyday of Drug Development" (Lee 2003). The drugs that led to the title were predominantly antibiotics. Of the 33 antibiotics marketed by 1960, 29 were generated after 1950 (Lee 2003). More broadly, the period from 1945 to 1965 has been called the "Gilded Age of Research" because of all the clinical research that was conducted, mostly on drug development (Rothman 1991).

Implanted devices, like fracture plates, also started to become established in the 1950s. They were not feasible until the mid-19th century, when anesthesia and antisepsis were developed. From then until the mid-20th century they were limited by biocompatibility problems that resulted from long periods of contact with internal tissues. A chance discovery by Harold Ridley, M.D., that polymethylmethacrylate was well tolerated by the eyes of RAF pilots led to his implantation of the first intraocular lens in 1949 and launched targeted research in the medical implant industry, and its accompanying foundation, biomaterials science. External instruments like respirators steadily improved and increased in application along with technological advances described in Chapter 1.

11.3 MEDICAL RESEARCH IN UNIVERSITY AND PHARMACEUTICAL LABORATORIES

With the success of antibiotics, public support of medical research grew, as prospects for cures seemed genuine (Malerba and Orsenigo 2001). Pressure to develop new medicines provided opportunities for scientists entering universities and pharmaceutical companies from WWII projects subsidized by the military. Military grant aid followed, in particular funding from the Office of Naval Research, which became the organizational model for the NIH. Understanding of disease pathophysiology and its causative agents was still poor. Consequently, there was little foundation on which drugs could be "designed". So, the pharmaceutical companies developed a strategy of randomly screening chemicals for therapeutic activity. Tissue cultures were used to screen out immediately-toxic candidates. Those that passed would graduate to laboratory animals. This is how the second pharmaceutical epoch (Malerba and Orsenigo 2001) began. The upper time limit of 1992 is not sharply defined because genetic engineering, the marker for the beginning of the third epoch, was sprinkled through the industry as early as the 1980s (Malerba and Orsenigo 2001).

The first candidates for random screening were molecules with structures similar to those that had demonstrated some success. Biochemists poured out thousands of candidates and chemical engineers developed efficient procedures for their manufacture on a large scale. Eventually, the NIH was sufficiently funded by Congress to support both causal and disease-based empirical research. With help of basic discoveries, like Frederick Sanger's detection of the first protein structure, that of insulin, in 1951, and revelation of DNA's structure by Watson-Crick-Franklin in 1953, more complex drugs could be synthesized. Disease wasn't the only motivator for drug product development. Vitamins and other products for health maintenance were seen as profit generators by the pharmaceutical industry. Infertility and the desire to be infertile—at least temporarily—became foci as well. The desire to control fertility led to synthesis by Carl Djerassi et al., of 19-nor-17a-ethynyltestosterone, the active component of the contraceptive pill. It is difficult to imagine a synthetic pill that has had more influence on how U.S. men and women relate. Such drugs were made possible by advances in hormone research.

Research funded to unprecedented levels (Malerba and Orsenigo 2001) by NIH, NSF and emerging scientific institutes enabled scientists using animal models to uncover physiological mechanisms underlying functions compromised by disease. Advances in cell biology, enzymology and pharmacology provided understandings of the mechanism of action of existing drugs, and some basis for predicting potential effectiveness of variations in their chemical structure (Malerba and Orsenigo 2001). As a result, the random screening approach to drug development transformed to drug design. Molecular genetics and methodologies like recombinant DNA formed a foundation for advance to the third major epoch of the pharmaceutical industry, biotechnology. In 1976, a pattern began in which academic scientists partnered with venture capitalists to form medical product development companies. Herbert Boyer Ph.D. (a co-developer of recombinant DNA methodology at UCSF) and Robert Swanson formed the first new biotechnology company, Genentech.

11.4 SCIENCE AND TECHNOLOGY CREATE BIOMEDICAL PHYSICIANS

When Jenner in 1796 performed a "clinical trial" with his smallpox vaccine on an 8-year-old boy, he was practicing the empirical art of medicine with no understanding of the germ theory of disease or immunology. His version of biomedicine was primitive. In the 1950s the typical physician was still ruled by a standard of care dominated by the art of medicine. But the second pharmaceutical epoch forced these physicians to enter into the world of scientific research in significant numbers. In 1962 the FDA began requesting safety and efficacy data for drugs (safety only for cosmetics) and in 1976 for devices, before they could be marketed. These data could only be gathered by testing the product in humans, i.e. by clinical trials. For a Ph.D. to undertake a clinical trial would be equivalent of him practicing medicine without a license. If the dispensed product was considered life-threatening, this crime would be considered a felony in any state. Louis Pasteur, a Ph.D. chemist, would have been convicted of murder if the infected Russian peasants he vaccinated against rabies had died. Luckily, he had two populations of dogs in his laboratory on which the vaccine was being tested. He experimented on the peasants and performed an experiment with the dogs. A modern Ph.D. with similar success would not escape prosecution as did Pasteur.

As a result of these new circumstances, physicians were drawn more and more into research. Some were hired by pharmaceutical and other product companies to manage clinical trials. The ideal place to conduct such research under highly controlled conditions was a medical school hospital. Consequently, medical schools became centers for clinical trials. The laboratories of various departments within the medical school soon became, by their proximity, logical locations for conducting

Modern Human Research Ethics   **185**

pre-clinical research with laboratory animals. As noted earlier, a number of these laboratories had already been developed to aid research into infectious diseases for the Department of Defense. One of the academic developments that showcased the extra training of these individuals was the M.D.-Ph.D. degree programs that appeared in the late 1950s.

11.5 WHAT IS PRE-CLINICAL RESEARCH?

Pre-clinical research is all the biomedical laboratory research that does not target humans. In our context it is the research that precedes clinical research. Why is it necessary? Chapter 10 described pitfalls of performing an experiment using human subjects. It is seldom possible to sequester two groups of humans to form experimental and control groups that are so closely monitored that the experimenter can claim only one variable was tested. It is just as difficult to isolate humans to study their normal physiology in a manner that ensures that no stimuli appear that create a data bias.

Laboratory animals allow a scientist to control variables to the extent that he is reasonably sure that all significant differences between control and experimental groups are due to the variable being measured. Such pre-clinical research is the foundation of any scientific basis for concluding that a drug or device is safe and effective.

Investigators performing laboratory animal studies do not require licensing, although they do require approval of a licensed veterinarian. There were, of course, physicians who followed the path of William Harvey before the 1940s. Frederick Banting, M.D., and his medical student Charles H. Best of the University of Toronto in 1921 discovered insulin and confirmed its function. They worked with dogs, as did Pasteur.

If pre-clinical testing is to assess the potential for a product's effectiveness and eliminate as many sources of unsafe performance as possible, it must be scientific. The data must be so well characterized (there must be a complete accounting for it) that if the product fails there is a reasonable basis for confidence that we can find out the mechanism for that failure. Computer modeling has been suggested to replace human subjects and, indeed, it may narrow the number of variables. But we do not sufficiently understand normal or patho-physiology to jump directly to humans from computer models. The risk of a misfire is, at present, unacceptable. Animal models that most nearly simulate the human condition are required to obtain predictive test results. There are no guarantees of 100% predictiveness. Lab mammals are different species. But their physiology is mammalian, and so linked to us by evolution. Typically, these experiments are required before humans may be exposed to the product. Often one particular animal model is more predictive than others for modeling a particular organ or disease. Some example models are presented in Chapter 9.

11.6 WHAT IS CLINICAL RESEARCH?

Clinical research is any formal investigation that seeks data from human subjects. The investigation may be scientific (Can angiogenesis during wound healing take place in the absence of vascular endothelial growth factor?), engineering (What artificial joint materials show the least wear *in vivo*?), medical (How much do effective insulin doses vary in elderly diabetes II patients?), sociological (Do the health habits of subjects in a longitudinal study like the Framingham Heart Study improve as compared with the population at large?) or psychological (How can medical personnel determine the emotional stability of a patient considering euthanasia alternatives?). A bioengineering scientist would tend to be involved in the first three. However, all would have to be approved by the Institutional Review Board (IRB). In our context, clinical research is all the testing on humans associated with medical product development. This testing is for determination of the safety and efficacy of the product.

The question of how to interpret the "truth" of data from epidemiological studies that are such an important part of clinical science was defined for the medical profession by epidemiologist A. Bradford Hill in 1965. He sidestepped the issue of whether a statement connecting cause and effect, by association rather than by a direct mechanism, is equal to a strictly causal conclusion. Hill contended, instead, that such a conclusion could be considered "counterfactually causal" if sufficiently supported by the data. Hill identified nine criteria that had to be met to establish that the association had a causal component—the underline stresses the word "component" so that the reader keeps in mind Hill's assertion that the conclusion is only operationally (strongly supported by data, for purposes of public policy, but not scientifically determined to be completely) causal (Hill 1965).

Bradford Hill's Criteria for Assessing Causal Component Relationships

1. *A strong association is more likely to have a causal component than is a modest association.*
2. *A relationship is observed repeatedly.*
3. *A factor influences specifically a particular outcome or population.*
4. *The factor must precede the outcome it is assumed to affect.*
5. *The outcome increases monotonically with increasing dose of exposure or according to a function predicted by a substantive theory.*
6. *The observed association can be plausibly explained by matter (e.g. physiological) explanations.*
7. *A causal conclusion should not fundamentally contradict present substantive knowledge.*
8. *Causation is more likely if evidence is based on randomized experiments.*
9. *For analogous exposures and outcomes an effect has already been shown* (Hill 1965).

Modern Human Research Ethics 187

Hill is credited with having performed the first randomized controlled clinical study (Höfler 2005).

11.7 CASE STUDY: HYMAN V. JEWISH CHRONIC DISEASE HOSPITAL (JCDH) OF NEW YORK AND INFORMED CONSENT—VULNERABLE PATIENTS

This classic bioethics case is a window into the minds of its professional perpetrators that reveals their concept of what their clients are owed, in terms of informed consent. The testimony of Dr. Southam disclosed here shows how he factored in patient ignorance and vulnerability, in deciding what to tell them about what he was using them for.

Chester Southam, M.D., was head of a research team at the Jewish Chronic Disease Hospital, investigating the immune response to injected live allogeneic cervical cancer cells (HeLa cells) in a study designed to determine if these cells would live longer in debilitated non-cancer patients than in patients debilitated by cancer. In 1963 three of the physicians working for him injected 22 chronically ill and debilitated patients at two body sites. They analyzed blood samples weekly for six weeks without telling these patients that the injection contained cancer cells, because the physicians "did not wish to stir up any unnecessary anxieties in the patients" who had "phobia and ignorance" about cancer (Katz 1972). The physicians claimed each patient gave "oral consent"; no written consent forms were administered (Later evaluation in court concluded that many of the patients were not in a physical or mental condition to give valid consent; Katz, 1972). The research was funded by USPHS and the American Cancer Society. Hospital administration tried to cover up lack of consent, and some written consents were fraudulently obtained after the fact. Hyman Strauss, M.D., of the JCDH attending staff, when learning of the activities of Southam's group, wrote a letter of protest to the hospital medical board. William A. Hyman, one of its members, was convinced by Strauss' letter and follow-up discussion, and moved to have the board support him. When the majority refused, Hyman sued the hospital to terminate the project.

Southam's deposition for the trial reads in part:

> The procedure, as I explained, requires simply the hypodermic injection of a suspension of tissue-cultured cells at two sites on the anterior thigh or arm and observation of the sites at about weekly intervals for six weeks or until regression is complete. These cells are of two or more cancer cell lines. These cancer cell lines were chosen because they have the necessary growth capacity to produce a measurable reaction. It is, of course, inconsequential whether these are cancer cells or not, since they are foreign to the recipient and hence are rejected. The only drawback to the use of cancer cells is the phobia and ignorance that surrounds the word *cancer*. It would be possible to study the same process by experimental skin grafts, but this is less satisfactory for quantitation, is much more difficult technically, and is unacceptably annoying to your patients. Other than the two hypodermic injections and observations of the reaction, the only other procedure would be drawing serum for study of

188   Ethics for Bioengineering Scientists

antibody reactions to the transplanted cells at approximately two-week intervals during the observation period.

I have no hesitation in suggesting these studies since our experience to date includes over 300 healthy recipients and over 300 cancer patients, and for two years we have been doing the tests routinely on all postoperative patients on our gynecology service as a measure of immunologic status, with the collaboration of Dr. Alexander Brunschwig, chief of the gynecology service. You asked me if I obtained (written) permissions from our patients before doing these studies. We do not do so at Memorial or James Ewing hospital since we now regard it as a routine study, much less dramatic and hazardous than other routine procedures such as bone marrow aspiration and lumbar puncture. We do get signed permits from our volunteers at the Ohio State Penitentiary but this is because of the law-oriented personalities of these men, rather than for any medical reasons.(Katz 1972)

Three physicians at the Hospital resigned when the administration did not seriously consider their complaints about the experiment. The case was tried in the Supreme Court of the State of New York and won by the plaintiff. Since JCDH was part of the State University of New York system, there were also disciplinary actions imposed by its grievance board. The chief of medicine at JCDH and the principal investigator (Southam) were placed on probation for one year by the New York State medical licensing board, as a result of a unanimous guilty verdict on fraud/deceit and unprofessional conduct. Two years later, the American Cancer Society elected Chester Southam to be its Vice-President. The actions of the medical licensing board were evidently of low priority to Society members.

The patients at JCDH that Southam used as subjects may be characterized as combinations of elderly, intellectually challenged and terminally ill. The FDA now requires IRBs to take special care to protect these and other "vulnerable populations" before approving a clinical trial application. The vulnerable population list includes but is not limited to: children, minors, pregnant women, fetuses, human in vitro fertilization products, prisoners, employees, military persons and students in hierarchical organizations, terminally ill persons, comatose persons, physically and intellectually challenged individuals, institutionalized persons, elderly people, visually or hearing impaired individuals, ethnic minorities, refugees, individuals involved in an international project, economically and educationally disabled individuals, and disabled and healthy volunteers (Shivayogi 2013). Given that the human consent form must supply a patient with sufficient information to uncover all the risks and benefits, and some of the vulnerable subjects would be seriously challenged in their ability to mentally process the form, is there some ethical way researchers can deal with subjects like these so as to maintain the scientific structure of a study? Shivayogi makes suggestions in his article. A human research informed consent form example is presented in Appendix B.

11.8   CLINICAL RESEARCH AND THE PRACTICE OF MEDICINE

Clinical research is not just about product safety and efficacy. Its main purpose is to supply physicians with information that will help them solve clinical problems. When we say that a physician is constantly engaged in risk assessment we mean she

Modern Human Research Ethics

is estimating the chances that 1) her diagnosis is correct, 2) she has considered all reasonable courses of action to take in response to the diagnosis arrived at, and 3) the course of action selected has the greatest chance of solving the problem and achieving medical truth. Her medical training may have taught her how to make these assessments, but it couldn't provide the latest information in each of these areas. A new disease may have been discovered that has symptoms similar to the ones she was taught fit another condition. There may be new, presumably more reliable, diagnostic tools; or newly discovered faults with the old tools. There may be new products to treat the condition. How can she obtain all this information and a trustworthy evaluation of its relevance and/or effectiveness?

The clinical studies that provided new information to physicians during the second pharmacological epoch were reported in peer-reviewed journals, medical society meetings and continuing medical education courses. Nowadays, one has to add the internet as a source. As with any scientific research in biology, data in these studies tended to scatter. This is also the case in lab animal studies, but because the animal subjects are under constant control (being in cages when not undergoing procedures) the scatter tends to be less than it is for humans. The tendencies they indicate (e.g. that the falsifiable hypothesis is disproved) may be stated with more confidence using statistical analyses that resemble those used for physical science experiments. The less controlled human cohorts tend to produce highly scattered data that must be analyzed with statistics that take on the form of risk analysis we call "epidemiology" discussed previously. Epidemiology applied to clinical research predicts the probability that members of a population will 1) catch a disease, 2) die from a disease, 3) have a disease cured by drug X, 4) accept a new health diet, 5) tolerate a new implant, 6) have an immune response to a new vaccine, and so on. Because of data variation due to subject differences and unconfined activity, large cohorts were often required for detecting significant but small differences between experimentals and controls.

Since clinical research is primarily concerned with risk, any understanding of the condition being studied need only be at a level that would allow us to apply results to establishing a treatment most likely to be safe and effective. "Practice" of medicine refers to a class of activities designed solely to enhance the well-being of an individual patient or client. The purpose of practice is to diagnose and treat. Treatment according to the accepted standard of care is expected to be successful. Success is not certain, and sometimes treatments do not work as they are expected to work because patients vary. At this point a practicing physician may try a drug in a new application (so-called "off-label" use), or a combination of drugs that she has not used before—in short, she may "experiment on" her patient to see what, if anything, will help him.

11.9 IMPACT OF THE "HEYDAY OF DRUG DEVELOPMENT" ON MEDICAL PRACTICE

Research articles reporting results of clinical trials became a boon to the physician in the field. She now had actual data on which to base her treatment decisions. But the number of alternatives and the rate at which they were appearing threatened to overwhelm those practitioners who were not trained in science. Recognizing physicians' need for drug information, and realizing the advantages of presenting it in one publication, the pharmaceutical industry in 1946 began to publish an annual drug reference (now online) that summarizes all the information included in each drug package's insert. This *Physicians' Desk Reference* (PDR) carries the implied approval of the Food and Drug Administration (FDA) that must approve the insert's content. Drug effectiveness is represented by "indications", conclusions about what symptoms might prompt use of the drug in question. In this source the newly minted physician will find the drug she learned as the standard of care. The PDR may still list the drug, but it may no longer be the standard of care, because it may have been replaced, based on further epidemiological studies that have found a drug more effective, in the judgment of the specialists who use it. These specialists will report new study results in medical journals and at meetings of their societies. By going to these meetings physicians learn the latest details about new drugs, often before results are published.

Product effectiveness is only half the story. The other half of the story is "safety", which is not usually advertised. Unsafe use and effects of the drug are reported in the PDR as "contraindications" and "side effects/complications". There is no PDR for implanted device safety. Consequently, surgeons who implant devices depend on communication with other surgeons—such as that which takes place at medical meetings—news media for spectacular cases, and FDA reports to get their "heads-up" about implant failure. Once this information is published they can further discuss the device and any problems implanting it with colleagues who have tried it. This approach avoids the risks of an empirical one. As a truth professional, the surgeon cannot achieve her truth of a successful implant by performing surgeries on a patient empirically until one works. As obvious as this conclusion is, each surgeon must make some decision to alleviate pain when a patient is in pain from a failed implant. Analgesics may hold off the pain but a revision surgery (sometimes more than one) may be necessary to solve the problem.

The existence of many treatment alternatives is one of the consequences of the second pharmaceutical epoch. Patient pressure to improve treatment beyond standard of care has become a major challenge to a physician's practice. They want to be sure they are getting the "best" product—usually equated with latest and often driven by commercials. Matching treatment to specific needs of the patient may conflict with what the patient wants. But the alternatives are still quite numerous (google "headache medicine" for an insight).

Another challenge to the physician is presented by literature and visitations from marketers representing companies that sell medical drugs and devices. Competition for market share is intense and is reflected in the quest for physician consideration. Sometimes the company offers incentives to the physician, like free samples, to use their product. Attractiveness of the incentive constitutes a conflict of interest, although the Sunshine Act (see below) has reduced this inducement considerably.

Modern Human Research Ethics

11.10 CASE STUDY: POSSIBLE CONFLICT OF INTEREST IN RESEARCH USING HUMAN SUBJECTS

The Bayh-Dole Act of 1980 made it lawful for universities that developed products from government funded research to patent and profit from sale of the developed products. It was thought that the universities would be better at bringing a product to market than the U.S. government. In 1999 Novartis, a Swiss pharmaceutical corporation, announced an agreement that would provide the University of California, Berkeley, with $25 million to support scientific research in its Department of Plant and Microbial Biology. The university, in exchange, would sign over to the company licensing rights to some one-third of its patented research discoveries. Also, two Novartis representatives would become members of the department's research committee, a committee that decided if a proposed research project was sufficiently up to scientific standards to be allowed to proceed. Why is this story in a chapter on human research subjects? Because the development of pharmaceuticals requires FDA approval that in turn requires demonstration of their safety and efficacy via animal and clinical research. At least some of this clinical research would be conducted at the university medical school (in this case, most likely the University of California, San Francisco). Critics of this arrangement see too much conflict-of-interest potential. Having company representatives on a university research committee may bias the committee's decisions. Also, they are in a position to conduct espionage to detect research on drugs from a competing company.

11.11 NON-MEDICAL SCIENTIFIC RESEARCH USING HUMAN SUBJECTS

Purely physiological, sociological, and psychological research involving human subjects is performed with the goal of understanding human function. There is no immediate prospect of clinical application as the goal is understanding rather than problem solving. Nevertheless, a client–professional relationship exists between the researcher and the human subject. While the subject is not seeking counsel from the professional, he/she is in a vulnerable position that requires a fiduciary commitment. The law requires a signed human consent form and maintenance of subject autonomy. While there is no physical danger in a sociological study, it may produce information that must be kept confidential. If the information is to be published or made public in any way, subject identity must be anonymous unless a waiver was clearly included in the consent form. Psychological research does not usually include physical danger, but, if drugs are administered or measuring instruments attached, injury may result from drug side reactions or instrument malfunction. Physiological research poses the greatest threat for injury to subjects. Strenuous exercise or precarious positioning may lead to injury or worse, if the subject's health is already compromised when he/she enters the study. If invasive procedures such as indwelling catheters or implanted transmitters are used to gather data, the subject must be treated as a patient and monitored by a health professional. If the subject is compensated or is an employee of the institution in which the research is being conducted, the compensation must be fully justified when the project is

192   Ethics for Bioengineering Scientists

proposed. As with all research, the appropriate institutional committee must evaluate the scientific merit of the proposal. But since human subjects are involved, Institutional Review Board (IRB) approval will also be required.

Participation of bioengineers in sociological research is minimal. However, experimental psychology employs fairly sophisticated instrumentation for evaluating brain function and a bioengineer may be involved in a research project to assess instrument function. Beyond this he/she may be one of the investigators seeking to understand the neurophysiologic basis for behavior and/or pathophysiology of abnormal behavior. Most graduate work in bioengineering involving human subjects that is not targeted as a clinical application, is dedicated to uncovering physiological mechanisms. Undergraduates who continue to graduate school may engage in similar research. A bioengineer with a bachelor's degree may be hired by a laboratory in a medical school for a project focusing on understanding a physiological function. In this case he/she may well be dealing with subjects who are volunteers.

11.12 NAMING THE THIRD PHARMACEUTICAL EPOCH

The explosion of biomedical science that started during the second pharmaceutical epoch and resulted in a new kind of company, the biotechnology firm, created many opportunities for bioengineers. It also changed the traditional structure of universities and the medical products industries. At the end of the 1960s few bioengineers had been graduated, but research funding to universities was abundant. Thus, those with bachelor's degrees found jobs as lab technicians, as specialists in maintaining biomedical instruments or in industries manufacturing biomedical products, and those with a Ph.D. in bioengineering, still relatively rare, would be a prime candidate for supervisory positions in industry, such as running a research lab or in an academic position in a newly forming bioengineering (or "biomedical engineering") department.

By the end of the 1970s an economic downturn in the United States had resulted in a slowing of the expansion of the NIH and NSF. As a result the number of bioengineering Ph.Ds planning an academic career outstripped available positions. Many chose to continue in unsecure (non-tenure track) appointments, while others moved to medical products industries or government positions. The large pharmaceutical companies utilized these graduates in two main ways dictated by their drug development strategy. Companies that had transformed to a drug design strategy had difficulty absorbing the new skills and techniques that university graduates in bioengineering, chemical engineering and chemistry brought with them and so tended to utilize only the skills and techniques they could apply (Malerba and Orsenigo 2001). Companies that had persisted with a random screening approach to drug development were less specialized and, therefore, more flexible in adapting the relatively simple setups to biotechnology. But their undeveloped research technology prevented them from fully utilizing the new techniques. They resorted initially to using these techniques to continue the process of evaluating new drugs randomly.

Gradually, through the 1980s, the new techniques led to profitable new drugs. Pharmaceutical companies that had maintained a design strategy could not transform quickly enough to take advantage of biotechnology directly. Instead, they partnered with newly emerging smaller companies that followed the Genentech

Modern Human Research Ethics

model. These new technology firms were up-to-date and nimble. They started with a small stable of innovative drugs or procedures. If their products showed sufficient promise, the larger partner would buy them out and incorporate the new technology. A number of scientists and entrepreneurs started more than one company only to sell it off to a large pharmaceutical company at a substantial profit. To a lesser extent, this pattern occurred with innovative devices, implants, and instruments as well.

So how do we define Malerba and Orsenigo's (Malerba and Orsenigo 2001) third epoch? Since their article was published in 2001, they could not have known what followed completion of the Human Genome Project (HGP) in 2003. The HGP started in 1990, which is close enough to the end of their second epoch to offer "genomics" as a logical component of the new name. Taking into consideration of the current drive to implement the precision medicine initiative, and all the chemistry that will be brought to bear on DNA analysis and editing, we would offer "genomic technology epoch" as a reasonable name for the current era.

11.13 PHYSICIANS IN PRACTICE AND THE FDA IN THE THIRD PHARMACEUTICAL EPOCH

As we shall learn in Chapter 12, by 1962 the second pharmaceutical epoch had generated so many new drugs that the Department of Justice needed help from the FDA to detect safety and efficacy problems before product marketing. By 1969 medical device production had reached a similar critical mass causing the Department of Health Education and Welfare to appoint a committee to study the need for FDA scrutiny for their safety. The committee report led to congressional passage of the Medical Devices Amendments (MDAs) to the Federal Food, Drug and Cosmetic Act (of 1938). The MDAs distinguished between drugs and devices and expanded the FDA's duties as a regulating agency for all medical products. Now physicians could scan (this was before the web) FDA announcements for the latest safety information on both drugs and devices approved for marketing. As scientific discoveries and medical product development grew, so did the armamentarium for patient care. Clinical trials by the end of the 1980s had become so commonplace, it wasn't unusual for any given physician to have patients involved with them, particularly if the patient's disorder required a potentially profit-generating drug. Product developers in need of subjects for clinical trials would often recruit physicians for access to target patients. The recruitment might be enhanced with a "finder's fee" for the physician. Of course, the physicians running the trials—university/hospital faculty—had ultimate responsibility for determining which patients were acceptable for inclusion in a clinical trial cohort. The university/hospital IRB, in turn, had responsibility for allowing the institution to house the study.

By the early 1990s many diseases once thought incurable, like some forms of cancer, hemophilia, and AIDS were stimulating product development based on scientific discoveries of aspects of their pathophysiology susceptible to treatment. Methods for delivering drugs were improving. Tissue engineers were developing ways to deliver them at the site of localized disease so that their action would be

194   Ethics for Bioengineering Scientists

spatially targeted and kept local. Scaffolds composed of resorbable polymers like polylactic acid held the promise not only to deliver drugs at a programmed rate but also to dissolve away so they wouldn't have to be removed.

Completion of the HGP was an important step on the road to finding cures for genome-based incurable diseases. The discovery of a gene editing complex CRISPR (Clustered Regularly Interspaced Short Palindromic Repeats)-Cas9 brings within reach a tool for making the corrections that would create a cure. This is perhaps the most significant event so far in the genomic technology epoch, as indicated by its generation of a Nobel Prize. In 1987 a strain of *E. coli* was found to have at least one "locator" gene with an attached CRISPR cluster composed of a series of repeated palindromic codes separated by spacers, and a nuclease with its genes (Cas + Cas genes). The palindromic codes are remnants of phage that have attacked the bacterium and have now become blueprints for adaptive immunity against the parasite. During the adaptive immunity process, each palindromic code is transcribed to form a pre CRISPR RNA (in a minority of cases, a DNA) which is then processed with the Cas nuclease to form a mature CRISPR RNA-Cas complex. The complex will match up with phage RNA (or DNA) strands during replication, and the Cas nuclease will digest (i.e. cleave) the nucleic acid at a specific site (Sontheimer and Barrangou 2015).

The targeting ability of one of the Cas nucleases, Cas9 (from *Streptococcus pyogenes*) attached to a synthetic RNA complex (crRNA+tracrRNA), often referred to as a "guide RNA", is crucial to the editing process. The ability of Cas9 to cleave almost any DNA site preceding a chemical signature called a PAM (Protospacer-Adjacent Motif), has made this nuclease a prime tool for the first step in genome editing (Salsman and Dellaire 2016). The CRISPR-Cas9 system has been used by a number of laboratories for mammalian cell genome editing since appearance of the "seminal" (Salsman and Dellaire 2016) publication of its success with DNA in 2012 (Jinek et al. 2012).

Any gene-based disease is a potential target, and there are more than 50 companies pursuing applications that would eliminate unwanted genes, add wanted genes, reduce the activity of overactive genes or increase the activity of underactive genes. Unwanted side effects include off-target effects due to guide RNA matching with untargeted domains and promiscuous action of Cas9 that cleaves untargeted domains. As a potential eugenics tool, this technology presents ethical challenges that could complicate its regulation. It is not an office-based treatment. But if it becomes one, regulation will be difficult.

11.14 IMAGINARY CASE STUDY: FINANCIAL CONFLICT OF INTEREST

Anne Cole is a gynecologist in private practice with a large clientele of ovarian cancer patients. Toolies University Medical School, the major institution in her town, has been included in a multi-center project to conduct clinical trials of a new drug, Shrinkov that shrinks ovarian tumors. The Curemenow pharmaceutical company that produces Shrinkov has offered Dr. Cole $5,000 for each patient she can recruit to the trial. This money is considered a "capitation payment". Lotta

Modern Human Research Ethics

Sponge, one of Dr. Coles's patients has no medical insurance. She is a prime candidate for the trial but is apprehensive about joining it because Dr. Cole has told her she might be in the control rather than the experimental group. Lotta eventually agrees to join the trial because she trusts Dr. Cole and has been assured that all medical expenses related to the trial will be paid. Dr. Cole intends to use some of her capitation payment to pay for extra help related to the trial. She tells none of her patients about the capitation payment.

Is the author of this example implying that Dr. Cole's failure to reveal her capitation payment is unethical? Is it? Why or why not?

11.15   FINANCIAL CONFLICT OF INTEREST AND THE GRASSLEY-KOHL SUNSHINE ACT

The actions of the imaginary Curemenow pharmaceutical company presented in Section 11.14, are quite straightforward, in that money is paid to a physician for delivering much needed subjects for a clinical study. Physicians entering the 21st century had a variety of similar opportunities. They received from the pharmaceutical industry gifts, meals, payment for consulting, research grants, drug samples, payment for taking part in speakers' bureaus, travel to meetings, attending meetings, continuing medical education courses and free travel to any of these events. Some 314,000 events for physicians were sponsored by the industry. About 90% of its 21-billion dollar marketing budget was directed at physicians (Brennen et al. 2006). The target of these investments is quite reasonable. It is the physicians who decide the course of their patients' treatments. Early in 2001 a series of reports of myocardial infarctions associated with the Merck drug Vioxx led to an investigation by an FDA committee of discrepancies between emerging evidence and the evidence reported to physicians by Merck marketers at CME meetings (Waxman 2005). The Vioxx scandal will be discussed further in Chapter 12. The point to be made here is that industry support of physicians may include not only financial incentives but an opportunity to market the pharmaceutical according to rules controlled by the company.

The prime targets for industry marketing were physicians from academic medical centers. They are the prime publishers of results from clinical studies and their conclusions command respect from the medical community. Accordingly, taking the year 2000 as an example, journal editors reviewing submitted results expected the data presented by the authors to have absolute integrity. To allow the reader to assess potential conflict of interest, editors asked authors to list links and any benefits from the company producing the pharmaceutical. Bekelman et al. reviewed articles published in 2000 and found that "few" authors publishing in journals with stated disclosure policies, revealed connections with industry, and only 43% of 47 high impact medical journals had disclosure policies (Bekelman et al. 2003). Bekelman et al. suggested that favorable reports of clinical results for pharmaceuticals in which the authors had a financial interest must be suspected of bias because of an inherent conflict of interest.

From 2004 to 2009 financial rewards from pharmaceutical marketers to physicians who were not orthopaedic surgeons fell mainly into the categories of drug samples, gifts, and/or reimbursement payments for professional services. Of physicians sampled, 83% admitted to being recipients (Campbell et al. 2010). The average cash value of compensation received per physician was not reported publicly so numbers are not available. But it is generally agreed that the amount is far less than the mean values of $190,331 in 2007 and $401,951 in 2008 for a sample population of orthopaedic surgeons receiving payments from the top five orthopaedic device makers (Hockenberry et al. 2011). The difference in payments is partly due to these surgeons' frequent need to get special hands-on training in someone else's surgery for implantation of newly designed implants, or to learn a new way to implant established devices. Orthopaedic surgeons are involved in the design of the devices they implant to a much greater extent than other physicians are involved in drug design. Starting with the Charnley hip (pre-1950 orthopaedic hardware is not of interest here) it is common to find a surgeon's name associated with an orthopaedic implant.

Reports of the ubiquity of industry compensation to physicians and the magnitude of payments, particularly to orthopaedic surgeons, and the Vioxx scandal, moved Senator Charles Grassley to investigate the extent to which physicians received industry payments they failed to disclose to the proper authorities. His discoveries led him to accuse a number of prominent academic physicians of failure to disclose and to partner with Senator Herbert Kohl in 2009 to add a Sunshine Act to the Patient Protection and Affordable Care Act (Schoen et al. 2012). Among its provisions, the Sunshine Act required public reporting by medical product manufacturers of any annual payments to physicians totaling $100.

11.16 *HUMAN SUBJECT DISREGARD FOR SCIENCE* (BASED ON AN ACCOUNT FROM MURPHY 2004)

In the early 1980s a new and fatal infectious disease appeared, first affecting a youthful urban male population. AIDS is caused by the human Immunodeficiency virus (HIV) attacking CD4 T lymphocytes and thereby rendering the adaptive immune system powerless to fight infections. No vaccine was available to fight a disease that attacked the very system vaccines are supposed to activate. Many of the early anti-AIDS drugs were toxic to an extent reminiscent of early cancer chemotherapy treatments, and toxicity often could not be detected in preclinical trials because their target was the DNA of a primate-specific virus.

Paul Sergios developed symptoms and signs of AIDS in 1983 at the age of 23. No treatments were available so he tried a variety of chemicals rumored to be effective against the virus. By 1986 AZT, a pharmaceutical targeting the virus, was in clinical trials. Sergios applied for inclusion in a phase II trial and was tested for low activity of his CD4 T lymphocytes, weight loss or swollen lymph nodes, presence of a mucosal infection called "thrush" and non-reaction to a series of immunity skin tests performed on his forearm. If he showed all these symptoms he would have been eligible for the trial. Instead, he showed some reaction to antigen at the four skin test sites. To avoid being disqualified as a subject Sergios had a friend copy the skin test number markers on his other

Modern Human Research Ethics

forearm which he presented to a test nurse at the authorized test site. He was accepted in the trial.

As a test subject, Sergios was aware that the pills he had received had a 50:50 chance of being placebos. He took them to a chemist friend who had a reputation for working "around the law" to have them analyzed. The chemist was unsuccessful in his analysis but suggested that Sergios swap half his pills with another subject. While this tactic would be useless if both subjects had placebos, it did increase the odds in Sergio's favor. Sergio hesitated because such a move would violate his informed consent agreement. The chemist disagreed, he asked,

> What about their twisted morality in giving half of us a sugar pill for a year or two in order to see how fast we go to our deaths while others get a drug that could potentially save their lives? Not only that—this study prohibits us from taking certain drugs to prevent opportunistic infections. The odds are stacked against us (Murphy 2004).

Paul Sergios made the swap for the remainder of the trial.

11.17 THE FDA AS A REGULATOR OF RESEARCH WITH HUMAN SUBJECTS

The clinical research that establishes risk for a given product is not merely a convenience for the physician and/or the product manufacturer. It is required by federal law. The government agency responsible for regulating safety and effectiveness of products released for human use is the FDA. Product manufacturers must convince the FDA that their creation has a low risk for harm and meets a reasonable standard for effectiveness before they are allowed to market it. Demonstration of a product's fitness usually involves two levels of experiments: 1) Pre-clinical research: Studies on cells, tissues and animals usually performed by the manufacturer in-house to confirm safety and provide a physiological indication of effectiveness; 2) Clinical research: Three clinical phases, the first two may require participating physicians to recruit patients who will be study subjects. The cases in Sections 11.14 and 11.16 are examples of ethical challenges on both sides of the recruitment process.

A more complete description of the FDA approval process is provided in Chapter 12. It should be noted before leaving the subject that if sophisticated equipment or devices are involved in these studies, bioengineers may be required to maintain and/or use them. They may also be involved in product development to the extent that they will invent and, consequently, profit from patent royalties they generate. For example, biomechanicists have been involved in bioengineering orthopaedic implants at least from the 1950s. It follows that ethical issues facing bioengineers in development and testing of biomedical products are intensified when the prospect of royalties from patents creates a conflict between an interest in developing the safest and most effective products and a desire to earn as much as possible and as quickly as possible.

ENRICHMENT

1. Ethics in America episode "The Human Experiment" (https://www.learner.org/vod/vod_window.html?pid=199)

The physician's obligation is to care for the patient. That is a fiduciary responsibility, like the professional obligation that a lawyer has to the client. Is that compatible with a role as investigator for an experimental drug? Can the same person wear both hats? Would you trust a physician who you knew was doing research on you? Would your tendency to trust that physician change if you knew he stood to make a profit on his stock in the company that produced the experimental drug, if experimental data indicated was effective?

The dialogue is arranged as follows:

1. Getting on the protocol
2. The placebo possibility
3. Autonomy in the face of death
4. Research for profit
5. Treatment vs. research
6. Publish and perish

2. Debate: The question of whether a human blastocyst may be defined as "a human being" for the purpose of establishing its rights is important for bioengineers who will use them as a source of cells. The "pro" position in this debate would be that the blastocyst is not a human. This conclusion would lead to more involvement of the bioengineer in experiments with blastocysts. Abortion is not a valid subject in this discussion because it is not a bioengineering activity.

Resolved: *A human embryo is not a human being until it can live outside its mother without instrumentation. Thus, a blastocyst may be used for obtaining stem cells and certain experiments.*

12 Ethics of Medical Product Development

12.1 THE BIOENGINEER AS A PRODUCT DEVELOPER

In this chapter we look at the data produced as a result of bioengineering scientists seeking to improve the well-being of other living beings, primarily their own species. For the most part these scientists do not interact directly with their beneficiaries. They do interact with their data that are used to make products for these beneficiaries, who are clients of health providers, veterinarians, farmers, and so forth. Successful application of the products is almost certainly impossible if the data are corrupt, leading to production of what is essentially a "snake oil". The only specialists who can protect data from corruption, i.e. loss of integrity, are the scientists. Just as surely as a patient needs a health professional committed to protecting her client, data need a scientist committed to protecting his "client". The fact that data are records, not living things, does not reduce their need for professional security. When all is said and done, the integrity of scientist's data is the core measure of his value to society.

Bioengineers may be involved in food development (e.g. genetic engineering of crops and food animals), development of non-medical devices that nevertheless affect people's health, such as safety belts or safe baby pacifiers, or development of cosmetics. Bioengineers may be employed in development of products not sold to the general public, such as indwelling receptors that must function in a space station. A bioengineer would make the most ideal astronaut, combining the engineering skills needed to run and maintain a space vehicle, with an understanding of physiology that would allow critical assessment of the biological functions of its passengers. Medical products range from over-the-counter chemicals and devices that enhance human health to life-saving drugs and devices that require medical supervision to administer and/or implant. While as a scientist, the bioengineer's main clients are data, users of any product he helps produce or sell (bioengineers are widely employed in marketing), run a close second. Responsibility to these second clients is most compelling when they are patients.

12.2 BIOENGINEER, ENGINEER AND PHYSICIAN: THE MEDICAL PRODUCT DEVELOPMENT TEAM

In order to serve the patient, a medical product must be safe and effective. A company that cannot fulfill these two needs is in danger of extinction. The professional team responsible for constructing the product is composed of engineers, physicians and scientists. Physicians define the medical need as unambiguously as possible, to ensure that those that design the product stay on track. Scientists,

200   Ethics for Bioengineering Scientists

including physiologists and bioengineers, determine if current understanding of human physiology is sufficient to allow effective targeting of the proposed medical product. A time-release implant carrying an anti-calcification agent for a heart valve, will be ineffective if flow patterns in the heart are not sufficiently understood to design a tube layout that will direct the agent to its target. Bioengineering scientists design the device and perform experiments testing it. Engineers are usually chemical, mechanical, or electrical. They are responsible for determining how the device will be manufactured so as to ensure its structural validity. The safety and effectiveness of the device depends on the commitment to integrity of the engineers and scientists responsible for constructing and testing it.

12.3 THE PUBLIC AND THE GOVERNMENT PLACE LIMITS ON MEDICAL PRODUCTS

There are external pressures that challenge the success of a medical product. One challenge is the constant threat of liability lawsuits that may or may not have merit, but in any case, increase the cost of producing the product. Another challenge is the pressure to sell the product in the face of competition. This challenge may lead to overselling that will raise expectations of patients beyond the capabilities of the product. A human reaction to a product's failure to fulfill expectations is disappointment that may lead to what is essentially a "false advertising" lawsuit.

Attention to product quality has not always been a hallmark for medical product manufacturers and sellers. Snake-oil salesmen were real people in the 19th and early 20th centuries. There are some who classify most "infomercial" participants in this category. Nevertheless, as indicated in Chapter 11, a spirit of free enterprise dominated regulation of medical products in the United States until patients were harmed in sufficient numbers and to a sufficient degree to cause an outcry for stronger regulation.

The federal agency responsible for regulation of products used by patients is the Food and Drug Administration (FDA). As the name suggests food is a major concern of the FDA and it would be appropriate to examine the role of bioengineers in its development and manufacturing. But the planned length of this text is too short to cover them, except for case reports and debates. FDA regulation enforcement differs from that of the other clinical research monitor, the NIH. While the latter may penalize someone convicted of scientific misconduct by denying him access to NIH amenities, it cannot prosecute anyone in court. The FDA has no police unit beyond its inspectors, but it can turn a case over to the Department of Justice for prosecution that can lead to imprisonment in a federal prison.

Example of the Work of the FDA: The Vioxx Case

In May of 1999 Merck & Co. began marketing its drug rofecoxib, an inhibitor of cyclooxygenase-2 (COX-2) under the trade name Vioxx. COX-2 is an enzyme that catalyzes the Arachidonic Acid cascade down a pathway that leads to an inflammatory response. Vioxx's asserted advantage over other

Ethics of Medical Product Development

anti-inflammatories was a reduction in gastrointestinal complications. Merck financed two clinical studies of Vioxx. The first, published as the VIGOR trial in 2000, noted an increased risk of myocardial infarction that was four times that of Vioxx's main competitor, naproxen. Merck claimed the effect was due to a cardio-protective feature of naproxen. In 2001 the FDA's Drug Advisory Committee, after examining published results and data volunteered by Merck, voted to require Merck to notify physicians of VIGOR's cardiovascular complications. Following this decision Merck sent a bulletin to the 3,000 sales representatives marketing Vioxx, instructing them "Do not initiate discussions on the FDA Advisory Committee...or the results of the...VIGOR study"(Waxman 2005). If the physician brought up the VIGOR study the rep was directed to say "I cannot discuss the study with you" (Waxman 2005). In cases where the sales rep was asked directly if Vioxx caused myocardial infarction she was to show the physician a "Cardiovascular Card", which was a pamphlet that indicated that other inflammatory drugs were associated with eight times the mortality rate associated with Vioxx. Instead of including data from the VIGOR study, the pamphlet was based on pooled data from studies that did not evaluate cardiovascular effects and used short term and low doses of the drug. Vioxx was withdrawn from the market in September, 2004. Its cardiovascular risk was confirmed by three studies published in 2005.

Because their background helps them understand the physiology and pharmacology of drugs better than employees with no biological background, bioengineers are attractive candidates to be sales representatives for pharmaceuticals. It is relatively easy to imagine the bioengineer reading of this case being in a position similar to that of the 3,000 Merck sale representatives portrayed. The data at issue here are the incidences of cardiovascular complications. Their suppression is a direct attack on their integrity.

12.4 A HISTORY OF THE FDA

The history of the FDA is marked by a number of health scandals that occurred before it got its name. In 1902 Congress passed the first medical product law, the Biologics Control Act in response to patients suffering injury from tetanus-contaminated diphtheria vaccines. Four years later, in response to public outcry after publication of Upton Sinclair's *The Jungle* about the meat packing industry, and a series of magazine articles by Samuel H. Adams about quack medicines, Congress passed the Food and Drug Act that required manufacturers to identify the ingredients of their products. It was administered by the USDA's Bureau of Chemistry which prosecuted violations and finally formed the FDA in 1930. In 1938 Congress gave the FDA power to enforce their regulations—although only against products that crossed state lines—with the Food Drug and Cosmetic Act (FD&CA). It specified that drugs could not be misbranded or adulterated. It also specified devices as subject to regulation.

Because the market was flooded with new drugs and cosmetics in the 1940s after the second pharmaceutical epoch began, and the events described in Chapter 11 and section 12.3 caused increased public pressure on congress to regulate, the FDA responded by announcing regulation of over-the-counter drugs in 1961 and requesting safety and efficacy data on new drugs in 1962.

A book that amply demonstrates the ethical challenges of drug development, *The Emperor of all Maladies* by S. Mukherjee (Mukherjee 2011), is a history of cancer. Its chapters on chemotherapy from 1960 to 1990 explore a world of desperation, ignorance, unfettered trial-and-error and suffering that characterized the race to find "a cure" for what we now understand is many diseases (no two cancers are alike). There are enough ethics cases presented to fill a college course. FDA history for devices is different. In any case, any boundary between the two domains is now disappearing where nanotechnology is applied (Smith and Lodder 2013).

From this point we shall follow the FDA with a focus on devices because the ethical questions raised by device cases are more instructive and easier to understand than the pharmacological chemistry of drug cases. By 1969, the medical device industry, particularly in cardiology, had grown sufficiently to gain the attention of officials at the U.S. Department of Health, Education and Welfare (USDHEW, now the U.S. Department of Health and Human Services). They perceived that provisions of the FD&CA did not sufficiently cover device safety for the surgeons who implanted them or the recipient patients. A special committee, the Cooper Committee, was appointed to assess reports in the scientific literature concerning medical devices for indications of needed regulation. The committee concluded that there were about 1,000 injuries annually connected with medical devices, 7.3% of which were fatal. Cardiac and reproductive devices headed the list)(Fries 2005). Recommendations of the Cooper Committee led Congress to update the FD&CA in 1976 by adding the Medical Device Amendments, which were discussed in Chapter 11. The FDA now had the authority to "assure" devices were properly labeled, including directions for application, safe and "effective" (in quotes, because, as we shall see, assuring effectiveness has proven difficult). It could do this by regulating medical device development, testing, manufacturing and application. The immediate impact of this amendment was minor because it contained a "grandfather clause" limiting the FDA's authority to devices first marketed after 1976 or *substantially equivalent* to those already marketed. An accounting of the MDA's impact in 1981 found that less than 2% of the 17,000 devices submitted to the FDA since 1976 failed the substantially equivalent test, and so escaped inspection. As we shall see, the enigma surrounding determination of "substantially equivalent" results in serious problems for the FDA. It has not been solved as of this writing.

The MDAs were extended in 1978 to include regulations directed at device manufacturing. The new regulations called the Good Manufacturing Practices (GMP) program covered the manufacture, packaging, storage, distribution, and installation of medical devices. This program of quality assurance allowed the FDA to inspect a device manufacturer's operation and require correction of any regulation violations before the product could be shipped. It has been proposed that no program has had a greater effect on the industry than the GMP (Fries 2005).

Ethics of Medical Product Development

By the 1990s the FDA was able to convince Congress that the GMP needed a prevention component that would help manufacturers avoid penalization after having set up for fabrication of a medical device. In 1990 they passed the Safe MDA (SMDA) that gave the FDA power of "pre-production design validation controls". Now, obvious safety violations inherent in product design could be detected and corrected before the company committed to its manufacture.

It is quite expensive and time consuming to run a clinical trial for an implanted device meant to last a decade or more. The FDA recognizes this challenge and does not require trials to last longer than three years or so, particularly if the device is not life-saving, as is the case for orthopedic devices. Nevertheless, the agency is interested in determining each device's risk for failure, or, in a worse-case scenario, serious injury or death. For a cardiac device, failure is often synonymous with death. To collect as much risk data as possible and warn physicians of unforeseen dangers, the FDA instituted a requirement, in 1996, that if an adverse health event occurred in an implanted patient, the device manufacturer had to submit a Medical Device Report (MDR) describing it. In cases where the manufacturer is not available (may no longer be in business), the hospital must assume responsibility for the MDRs. Since devices are implanted in hospitals that manufacturers contract with for the procedure, and hospitals compete to keep up with the latest advances in device development, the manufacturers implore hospital administrations to pressure surgeons to follow their patients and file MDRs. To help ensure that hospitals cooperate with manufacturers, the SMDA requires the FDA to encourage hospitals to

1. Report device-related deaths to the FDA and the device manufacturer
2. Report device-related serious injuries and serious illnesses to the manufacturer, or to the FDA if the manufacturer is not known
3. Submit to the FDA on a semiannual basis a summary of all reports submitted during that period.

"Encourage" is the preferred FDA strategy because, while it has the power to invoke legal sanctions against manufacturers who do not comply with MDR regulations, the FDA does not have the same jurisdiction over hospitals. It has to rely on their goodwill and assistance, so that timely warnings may be sent to physicians with patients who carry the afflicting device. Appendix F presents some MDR cases from Orthopaedics. It includes a reporting checklist provided by the American Academy of Orthopaedic Surgeons.

By 1992 when the third pharmaceutical epoch was established, the dividing line between drugs and devices was well on its way to disappearing for an increasing number of medical products. Drug delivery was moving from simple injection or the swallowing of a pill to implantation of devices that could deliver the drugs locally. This new specialty is part of tissue engineering. In many cases the drug was not merely loaded in the delivery device; it was incorporated chemically in an absorbable/erodible scaffold composed of a material that has been programmed for control-release. Was this tissue-engineered construct a drug or a device? It is probably simplest to refer to it as a biomaterial. Biomaterials are typically treated by the FDA as devices. Biomaterial science, typically taught in bioengineering departments with a focus on implanted artificial and biological materials (called "biologics" by the FDA), now included chemically dynamic eroding implants, loaded with chemicals. Bioengineers with such biomaterial training became attractive employees to pharmaceutical companies.

12.5 FDA DEVICE CLASSIFICATION (REFER TO HTTPS:// WWW.FDA.GOV/MEDICALDEVICES/ DEVICEREGULATIONANDGUIDANCE/OVERVIEW/ FOR A COMPLETE SUMMARY OF DEVICE CLASSIFICATION CRITERIA)

The FDA defines a medical device as:

> ...an instrument, apparatus, implement, machine, contrivance, implant, in vitro reagent, or other similar or related article, including a component part, or accessory which is: recognized in the official National Formulary, or the United States Pharmacopoeia, or any supplement to them, intended for use in the diagnosis of disease or other conditions, or in the cure, mitigation, treatment, or prevention of disease, in man or other animals, or intended to affect the structure or any function of the body of man or other animals, and which does not achieve any of its primary intended purposes through chemical action within or on the body of man or other animals and which is not dependent upon being metabolized for the achievement of any of its primary intended purposes.

An implanted bioreactor carrying islets of Langerhans attached to nanomachines that stimulate them to produce insulin does not strictly adhere to this definition. But it is a device to the FDA.

For the medical device developer, a much more important FDA distinction is the device's class. Here class means "risk group". Risk group determination is a safety evaluation. It assesses the chance the device will harm the patient, and the degree to which it will have to be monitored by the FDA. There are three levels of classification, with the highest level denoting the greatest risk. At the lowest level, Class I, the developer has to provide the FDA very few data to establish that the device is safe to market. At the highest level, Class III, the developer must test the device at the cell, lab animal, and clinical levels to establish its safety. Class III devices are the costliest to develop because they must be researched the most thoroughly. Consequently, device developers try to avoid this classification if at all possible.

An important concept for understanding the classification is "General controls". If these are met by a device when a developer submits an FDA application to approve its marketing the device, the product is automatically classified as Class I. General controls are the basic provisions defined by the 1976 MDA. They include:

Ethics of Medical Product Development

1. Establishment Registration by manufacturers, distributors, repackages and re-labelers,
2. Medical Device Listing with FDA of devices to be marketed,
3. Manufacturing the devices in accordance with Good Manufacturing Practices,
4. Labeling medical devices in accordance with FDA labeling regulations,
5. Medical Device Reporting of adverse events as identified by the user, manufacturer and/or distributor of the medial device.

General controls apply to all device classes. Note that the performance of the device is not addressed in general controls. One step up, so to speak, from general controls is the *performance standards*. This is the first level requiring performance data from the applicant. These data, however, do not have to come from testing the device. They come from devices that have been approved for marketing and are *substantially equivalent* to the product being evaluated. If a device has no equivalent and no previous data allowing for risk analysis, it requires a full safety analysis before it can be considered for approval. That is, it requires supporting safety performance data all its own. This is the default or second level requiring performance data from the applicant.

Before applying, a device producer will contact the FDA to determine if the device is eligible for an exemption that would speed the approval process. At various times, such as medical emergencies (e.g. an epidemic), laws may be passed or the FDA may decide on its own to offer exemptions for a device. The fast track provision discussed below was an example of such action. If there is no exemption, the device producer must submit a Pre-Market Notification Process (510(k)) describing the device and providing data on its safety performance. The more complete the application, the faster processing of the application will be. From the 510(k) the FDA determines the device's class.

Class I Devices

These must be non-life sustaining such that their failure poses no risk to life. They require only general controls. Examples include tongue depressors, adhesive bandages, I.V. bottle stands, sunglasses.

Class II Devices

These must also be non-life sustaining. However, they must adhere to performance standards because their misuse may cause injury, and the FDA needs to compare with similar devices to assess the risk of such injury. In addition, Class II devices require special controls to cover the need for training to insure they are not misused. Under special controls one finds manuals and special labeling. Examples include: syringes, surgical masks, and powered wheelchairs. Class III devices that have been given an exemption or that are substantially equivalent to approved products qualify for this class. The equivalency decision is based on the 510(k)'s description of intended use, physical composition, and specifications of the device. To reinforce an equivalency application, the device producer will submit *in vitro* and *in vivo* toxicity study data. The FDA exemption decision is termed an *order of concurrence* or *order of non-concurrence*.

Class III Devices

Unless exempt, all devices whose failure puts the life of the patient at risk fall into this category. All the requirements for Class I and Class II devices are necessary for Class III submissions. In addition, the manufacturer must supply failure mode analysis, lab animal tests, toxicology studies, and, finally, clinical (human) studies (trials). Examples of Class III devices are as follows: heart valves, heart transplants, artificial knees—actually anything implanted surgically. Implanted tissues are biologics. Of course, a heart transplant cannot be tested for safety and efficacy because it is transferred almost directly from one body to another. But the transfer process, including extraction, storage, and the conditions for implantation must be standardized to optimize the chances the implant will survive. This process often involves specialized equipment that has been approved by the FDA for its intended use.

Once the pre-clinical study data have been submitted to the FDA, and its results approved by the FDA, the pre-clinical phase of the 510(k) is complete and the producer may submit a Pre-Market Approval Application (PMAA) that describes plans for the clinical phase of device testing. The plans must include protocols and sources of patients. To reduce the cost of research and use of lab animals, a manufacturer resubmitting a PMMA (in response to stated FDA concerns) to the FDA may combine its data with those from previous submissions. The limit for this consolidation is four PMMA submissions. Once the plans are FDA-approved, the producer must obtain IRB approval for access to patients in the institutions where the clinical trials will take place. The form for this approval is the Investigational Device Exemption (IDE). The IDE is somewhat self-contradictory, in that it is essentially a waiver to implant a device

Ethics of Medical Product Development

not yet approved for implantation. The inherent conflict of this circumstance is resolved by classifying the device as "experimental" and, therefore eligible for use in Phase I clinical trials.

Under the Medical Device User Fee and Modernization Act (MDUFMA), passed in 2002, PMAA processing was accelerated with payment of a user fee. The graph presented in Figure 12.1 shows the average time (in days) spent on an application by the FDA (A) and the applicant manufacturer (B). Their total is shown by curve C(FDA 2020). Prior to MDUFMA it was not uncommon for the process to reach 3 years.

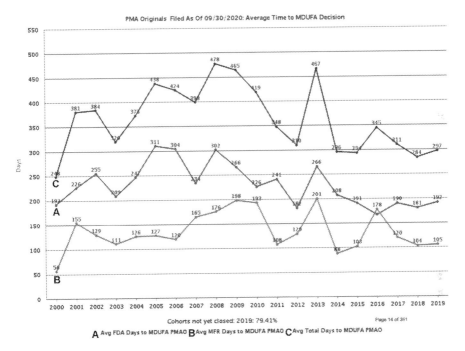

FIGURE 12.1 Graph from the FDA showing the average time it took for a Pre-Market Approval Application to be decided upon under the Medical Device User Fee Amendment Act in 2020. Downloaded from the FDA web site (page 14 of 361): file:///Users/hwinet/Downloads/4th%20Q%20FY2020%20MDUFA%20IV%20Performance%20Report%20Industry%20Meeting.pdf.

Congress under pressure from manufacturers and patients passed the FDA Modernization Act in 1997 that required the FDA to create a "fast track" (="expedited review") category for products deemed to be urgently needed. Evidence that the product is substantially equivalent to an already approved product may not exist. Nevertheless, assurances from the manufacturer that it is, are provisionally accepted by the FDA. The assumption is that substantial equivalency will be confirmed by a reduced and more quickly completed number of clinical trials. One of the risks of fast tracking is illustrated in Figure 12.2.

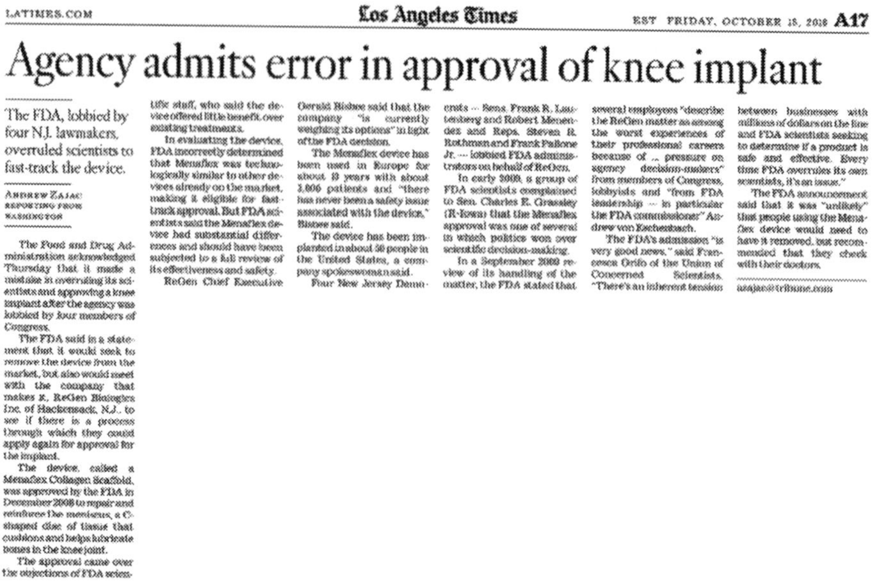

LATIMES.COM **Los Angeles Times** EST FRIDAY, OCTOBER 15, 2010 **A17**

Agency admits error in approval of knee implant

The FDA, lobbied by four N.J. lawmakers, overruled scientists to fast-track the device.

ANDREW ZAJAC
REPORTING FROM WASHINGTON

The Food and Drug Administration acknowledged Thursday that it made a mistake in overriding its scientists and approving a knee implant after the agency was lobbied by four members of Congress.

The FDA said in a statement that it would seek to remove the device from the market, but also would meet with the company that makes it, ReGen Biologics Inc. of Hackensack, N.J., to see if there is a process through which they could apply again for approval for the implant.

The device, called a Menaflex Collagen Scaffold, was approved by the FDA in December 2008 to repair and reinforce the meniscus, a C-shaped disc of tissue that cushions and helps lubricate bones in the knee joint.

The approval came over the objections of FDA scientific staff, who said the device offered little benefit over existing treatments.

In evaluating the device, FDA incorrectly determined that Menaflex was technologically similar to other devices already on the market, making it eligible for fast-track approval. But FDA scientists said the Menaflex device had substantial differences and should have been subjected to a full review of its effectiveness and safety.

ReGen Chief Executive Gerald Bisbee said that the company "is currently weighing its options" in light of the FDA decision.

The Menaflex device has been used in Europe for about 10 years with about 3,000 patients and "there has never been a safety issue associated with the device," Bisbee said.

The device has been implanted in about 30 people in the United States, a company spokeswoman said.

Four New Jersey Democrats — Sens. Frank R. Lautenberg and Robert Menendez and Reps. Steven R. Rothman and Frank Pallone Jr. — lobbied FDA administrators on behalf of ReGen.

In early 2009, a group of FDA scientists complained to Sen. Charles E. Grassley (R-Iowa) that the Menaflex approval was one of several in which politics won over scientific decision-making.

In a September 2009 review of its handling of the matter, the FDA stated that several employees "describe the ReGen matter as among the worst experiences of their professional careers because of ... pressure on agency decision-makers" from members of Congress, lobbyists and "from FDA leadership — in particular the FDA commissioner" Andrew von Eschenbach.

The FDA's admission "is very good news," said Francesca Grifo of the Union of Concerned Scientists. "There's an inherent tension between businesses with millions of dollars on the line and FDA scientists seeking to determine if a product is safe and effective. Every time FDA overrules its own scientists, it's an issue."

The FDA announcement said that it was "unlikely" that people using the Menaflex device would need to have it removed, but recommended that they check with their doctors.

azajac@tribune.com

FIGURE 12.2 Los Angeles Times article reporting one consequence of applying "fast track" to device that was neither life sustaining nor substantially equivalent to any other knee implants. Article by Andrew Zajac, courtesy of Los Angeles Times.

12.6 PRECLINICAL TESTING

Research aimed at establishing biocompatibility of both the material and its final form as a device are the best insurance of safety and efficacy prior to clinical trials. Toxicity may usually be determined with cell cultures *in vitro*. But efficacy can only be supported by testing in appropriate animal models.

For devices, testing biocompatibility in cell cultures is usually about the material. If chemicals leach from the material and are found to kill or significantly interfere with the physiology of cells, or induce immunological responses, there is no need to do further testing, as the material has been established as unsafe.

If there is concern about side effects not addressed by cell culture studies (e.g. chronic inflammatory reactions), acute experiments with animals covered by less restrictive animal welfare regulations (e.g. rats and mice) may be more appropriate and less expensive. A risk like carcinogenicity may require longer term studies.

Laboratory animal trials are crucial not just to address safety concerns. They are the most important pre-clinical window to biocompatibility, that is, to safety and efficacy, of the product. All laboratory animal studies require protocol approval from the institutions' Institution Animal Care and Use Committee (IACUC) before any testing commences.

Ethics of Medical Product Development

Even when safety is the only concern one has to be careful to use an appropriate animal model. While a dog may appear to be a better model for testing a hip replacement because it is a mammal, an emu may be the more biomechanically valid model because it is bipedal. Why might a rabbit be a poor model for testing a digestive tract device? If rats tend to form tumors far easier than humans, a material that would be optimal in humans might be prematurely discarded because it was carcinogenic in rats. Chronic studies are particularly important for assessment of biomaterial integrity and long-term effects on tissues. Bone implants are a prime example of this need because they are subject to considerable mechanical stress, and they, in turn, mechanically influence the osseous tissue in which they are imbedded.

One needs to be cautious when extrapolating lab animal results to humans. Humans may have activity levels unlike those of the animal models. Also, humans have different habits of hygiene. Whereas a lab animal may allow infection around a device that penetrates the skin, a human will keep it clean and avoid the problem. Success in demonstrating biocompatibility in laboratory animals will lead to submission of an IDE to the FDA for permission to start clinical trials. Commencement of clinical trials does not always insure an end to animal testing for a given device. If unsuspected toxicity effects appear or a need for major changes in the design becomes evident, lab animal experiments with the new design may need to be conducted to specifically address these issues. An undesirable consequence of such a sequence of events may be long delays in the time-to-market process. A need for extra testing may involve expense that would seriously impact profit margins for a product development company. It would therefore be wise for their lab director to develop a mechanism to optimize cost vs. performing sufficient lab animal experiments to avoid having to "go back to the lab".

12.7 PUBLISHING PRE-CLINICAL TEST RESULTS

In Chapter 7 we used the plan of a scientific research project to outline areas where scientific misconduct is found. The point in a project at which product development and the greater scientific community become aware of one another is the publication of a research report in a peer-reviewed scientific journal. Traditionally *Nature* or *Science* would not publish product testing articles, but they have expanded into technology, and reports about unusual capabilities of biological systems are no longer difficult to find in any issue.

As the Woo-Suk case (Chapter 8) suggests, exposure of the work to the scrutiny of peer reviewers who are often laboratory scientists allows for an evaluation process in which the evaluator may understand the subject of the report better than its authors. A number of experts in cell reproduction were skeptical of Woo-Suk's cloning techniques. When they tried to reproduce his claimed results, their skepticism was confirmed. Lack of confirmation is not proof of misconduct. There are cases in which a scientist is so adept at applying a technique that other scientists are simply not up to the challenge. The Millikan oil drop experiment seems to fall in this category (Goodstein 2010). Indeed, Woo-Suk Hwang has since achieved his goal of cloning a dog (Lee et al. 2005).

For the FDA, scientific misconduct is not merely an academic concern. If data in support of a product's safety and/or effectiveness has been falsified, lives may be at risk when it is applied. When a reviewer reads a submitted report of scientific results he/she assumes that what is presented as data is factual. Time constraints and limited resources prevent careful checking of data integrity. Reviewers are not paid to review manuscripts in science. It is a professional responsibility.

Pre-clinical studies may take place in industry, research institutes, government laboratories, or academic settings. Each will provide clues to the primary author's expertise that suggest how qualified he/she is to perform the research being reported. First, there is the reputation of the research group, and its affiliation. Have their publications been cited as standards for quality by other scientists? Second, there is the co-author list. In an academic setting pre-clinical research reports will often include the primary author's mentor. Has he/she published in highly regarded journals? Have any of the authors been convicted of scientific misconduct? The primary author and mentor are the principal defenders of the work. Other authors are present because each contributed expertise not shared by the author that was necessary for the study. Their reputations within their field of expertise serve as measures of data quality. In general, a colleague who contributes samples and is not involved in testing or interpretation of data obtained from them by the primary author is not included as a co-author because he/she is not familiar enough with the details of the study to defend it. Indeed, such a colleague may not even agree with the authors' conclusions.

After the author listing, comes the Abstract, a *concise* statement of what the study was about, its results, the authors' conclusions, and a sentence or two about its implications. Abstracts say more about the author's ability to communicate concisely than his/her scientific acumen.

The meat of the text begins with the Introduction. On its surface an introduction merely explains why the study was performed. For a scientist reporting research on a product subject to FDA approval, a statement like "We did it to cure cancer" falls to the same level of scientific bankruptcy as "We wanted to try this to see if it works", observed by this author in some submissions from engineers. In order for the writer to establish credentials as a competent scientist—on paper—he/she has to show an understanding of the **scientific basis** for the device. There should be a clear description of what medical problem the device is supposed to alleviate, if not solve. The pathophysiology underlying the problem should be included in this description. What is the history of failure to solve it in the past? Why have previous attempts failed? What is the key to a solution, and what is the rationale for it being the key? How would the device being promoted bring about the solution? What is the evidence from published scientific articles that a device like the one being promoted can perform as projected? The hypothesis is, of course, that it will.

Ethics of Medical Product Development

A Methods and Materials (M&M) section follows. In this section the author must describe all methods and materials used sufficiently to allow:

1. the specialist reviewer to evaluate their validity for obtaining the kind of data expected
2. other scientists in the field to duplicate them

In this author's experience the most deficient part of M&M is statistics. Typically, ANOVA is the model of choice, with a $p < 0.05$ for the cutoff of confidence that the hypothesis is false. A power calculation for sample size is particularly important because, as a government agency, the FDA has signed on to the NIH campaign to practice the three R's in government funded research with animals.

"Results" is usually the next section. Graphs, tables, and pictures characterize this part of the report. There are accepted conventions for discarding outliers. The most ethical approach is to include them in graphs with an asterisk. The graph legend identifies the outlier and notes that it was not used in calculating any curves. A longer explanation of the possible cause of the outlier (e.g. animal had a high temperature that day) would appear elsewhere in the results. Presentation of results should be so clear that the reviewer should be able to state the conclusions without any help.

As described in Chapter 8 the narrative will finish with "Conclusions" and "Discussion". The conclusions should deal only with the data. The discussion would be the ideal venue for selling the device. It would be judicious, nevertheless, to maintain some decorum, out of respect for the journal editors.

The final pages are the references. Rarely are there too many.

12.8 CONSIDERATIONS THAT ENHANCE SUCCESS OF CLINICAL TRIALS

Bioengineers who develop medical devices for implantation need to have a clear picture of the medical purpose of their product and the implantation process so that both may be clearly described in the 510(k) application. Assessment of potential efficacy cannot be completed by FDA scientists without a detailed understanding of the medical goal and the path the device will take to get there. Correct installation of the device cannot occur unless the surgeon understands the implantation procedure, which should include extent of surgery required, how the device may be repaired without removal, if needed, and how it may be removed safely if implantation should fail (Wathen 1999).

The FDA expects the developer to provide a protocol for removal or repair if the device malfunctions after surgery. A bone fracture plate screw may need to be removed and replaced. This biomaterial failure contingency should be provided for with spare parts and, if necessary, special instructions. An immune reaction to the device often requires removal unless the device is sustaining life. Immune suppression or replacement of the device may, then, have to be considered as options and are expected to be addressed in the 510(k) and considered in the design of the

212   Ethics for Bioengineering Scientists

product. The application is required to address the possibility that the device must be removed by describing the removal surgery and how complications such as fibrous capsules and infection will be treated.

12.9 CLINICAL TRIALS

Testing of devices and drugs in humans for FDA approval is divided into three phases.

12.9.1 PHASE I

During Phase I the product contacts human patients for the first time. Since there is a possibility for life-threatening product effects that appear only in humans, a minimum number of patients (perhaps 10–12 if the difference is expected to be great) are selected, consistent with statistical needs. Patients are monitored closely to be sure the experimental protocol is being followed. A minimum number (ideally one) of institutions are involved for the same reason. The quality of every data point is so crucial for statistical validity that selection of competent scientists may well determine the acceptance of the results by the scientific community.

One of the ethical challenges facing the developer of a life-saving product during phase I is determination of compassionate use. A device (e.g. artificial heart) or drug (e.g. anti-cancer) that has been insufficiently tested to convince any scientist of its efficacy may nonetheless be the last hope of a dying patient. Those emotionally tied to the patient as well as the patient himself may not be able to act reasonably in reaching out for a "last straw". Accordingly, they may overreact if the product increases suffering and/or accelerates death of the patient. For the manufacturer the dilemma is to weigh the positive publicity of offering the product for free, against the negative of it failing in patients not ideal for testing (e.g. they may have other pathologies that interfere with product function.)

A subject who is ideal for the restrictive needs of a phase I test is the inmate of a prison. Daily monitoring and follow-up conditions are already in place, and one can make the case that people from all walks of life are found in prisons. The ethical challenge in this case is to differentiate between limited autonomy associated with incarceration and the prisoner's basic right to autonomy as a patient. Before the National Research Act (see Chapter 10) prisoners were easily coerced into "volunteering" for product testing in order to gain "parole points" as a reward. The latter was illegal under directives of the Nuremberg Code when Dr. Southam (Hyman v. Jewish Chronic Disease Hospital) treated his prisoner subjects in 1963. But this project occurred before the National Research Act, and as has been noted, before the Nuremberg Code had been enforced in the United States. Ironically, it was being applied to prisoners by Southam under orders from Ohio prison officials but not to free patients by JCDH (Katz 1972).

The phase I protocol must be approved by the institution IRB of the principal investigator (PI). IRB approval is also required for the consent form, which must be signed by the subjects. Since the patients must be monitored closely, the PI must

Ethics of Medical Product Development

devote considerable attention to patient selection. For example, 30 years ago, hip replacements were rarely performed on patients less than 65 years because no one expected them to last more than 20 years. Being orthopedic devices, they were not required for survival, but hip pain was such a problem in the elderly, the surgery was considered warranted because it served to reduce morbidity (see glossary). Care needs to be taken also to avoid patients with complications not shared with other patients. Increasing the number of variables between research subjects is a quick path to invalidating statistical conclusions.

A termination date for data gathering is required for the protocol. In some cases, an interval between the end of data gathering and start of Phase II is included in order to allow chronic reactions such as chronic inflammation or giant cell reactions (see glossary) to play out. A full report to the FDA is, of course, necessary when the phase is completed. If the device has a sufficient impact on patient welfare, the results of Phase I may be published in peer-reviewed journals with "Preliminary Results" as part of the article title.

Physicians in this trial are often those connected with product development. Since they are usually paid for "consultation" in this context, conflicts of interest may occur.

12.9.2 PHASE II

Most of the scientifically useful data are generated during Phase II clinical trials that have greater sample sizes and longer follow-ups (keeping track of patients after surgery, e.g.). Subjects are more varied and so more reflect the population at large than those of the more controlled Phase I studies. Manufacturers usually recruit highly respected physicians as co-investigators for these trials. Financial inducements have traditionally been part of the recruitment process. Increase in pool size often requires contributions from multiple medical centers to insure patients selected fit protocol criteria. The cost of data gathering is, of course, borne by the manufacturer who must find an optimal balance between financial burden and patient sample sizes sufficient to achieve statistical validity.

As with Phase I, Phase II protocols and any changes in consent forms require IRB approval. In multicenter studies, one institute, the site of the PI, is usually chosen as principal and its protocol is sent to all the other centers for local IRB approval. This can be a time-consuming process since not all IRBs think alike. Addition of institutions and investigators to the clinical trials generates considerable administrative expense. It also provides more income to the primary institution. Another expense is the training of surgeons who have newly joined the research team in the implant procedure. A simple procedure such as implantation of a battery-powered transmitter in the fascia of a muscle requires little training. But a radically new hip usually requires that the primary institution run a surgery course for the new investigators.

Publication of results in peer-reviewed journals often occurs before their final submission to the FDA. Titles like "Three-year results of an implanted......" are typical. Since the research being reported is empirical science, it will usually not

214   Ethics for Bioengineering Scientists

appear in laboratory science journals (e.g. Annals of *Biomedical Engineering*, *Journal of Physiology*, etc.). Nevertheless, clinical journals with reputations for good science, like *The New England Journal of Medicine* can provide useful data for a causal laboratory scientist focused on physiological, rather than clinical processes.

Like Phase I trials, Phase II trials should end as near as possible to the scheduled time and with the scheduled number of patients. Also, as with Phase I trials, a time gap before commencement of Phase III trials is sometimes invoked to detect any serious long-term complications. Before the end of Phase II, the manufacturer submits accumulated data to the FDA for marketing approval. In cases where patients' lives would be threatened by late developing complications, or where there are chronic conditions not present in the patients used for Phase II, the FDA may choose to defer approval until Phase III results begin to appear. For the most part, however, marketing is approved before completion of Phase II if results are promising.

12.9.3 Phase III

It is unusual for a producer to persist marketing its product if FDA approval has not occurred by the end of Phase II. Once the device is approved, Phase III, which lasts until it is no longer needed by the patient, commences. Phase III increases patient and surgeon pools. Selection criteria for both, as a consequence, are not as strict as for previous phases. Consequently, there is a wider range of surgeon competence and risk of failure due to faulty implantation. Indeed, if full FDA approval for marketing without restrictions—except specifications for use determined by device design itself—has been obtained, the new device may be implanted by any physician. Of course, a hospital that would allow an obstetrician to implant a hip in an 80-year-old patient would be a malpractice lawyer's dream. Thus, the profession, the device manufacturer, and ethical constraints would discourage a physician from venturing into a procedure for which he/she has not been specifically trained.

12.10   PROTECTING A DEVICE OR DRUG AS INTELLECTUAL PROPERTY

By the time a product has been approved for phase II trials news of its success or failure has spread in the industry. This is particularly so if the investigators have published articles in peer-reviewed journals. Why doesn't another company that may have better manufacturing capabilities and good spies just start tooling up to market the product? If the product developer is smart enough it has retained a lawyer and filed with U.S. Patent Office to claim its drug or device as intellectual property. If any company tries to sell a copy of its product the patent owning company may sue for violation of its patent.

When a bioengineer joins a company, she must usually sign a contract that states her legal obligations to her employer and its legal obligations to her. Since the company is in business to make a profit from its products, it needs to ensure that any new ideas leading to the product's formation remain secret from competitors. Company employees are legally bound by contract to keep trade and manufacturing secrets confidential.

Ethics of Medical Product Development

215

There are two types of intellectual property rights that may be granted by the U.S. Patent and Trademark Office.

1. patents
2. trademarks

Copyrights are automatically activated with the creation of a published authored work. But additional protection may be acquired from the U.S. Copyright Office. Trade secret rights protect confidentiality of legal information that a company does not wish divulged. In many cases the information is not patentable. Common subjects are formulas, patterns, compilations, programs, devices, techniques, or processes. The protection may be provided by a signed agreement and is usually not enforceable by the U.S. government. However, many states have trade secret protection laws. The reader will recall the role of trade secrets in the Ludlum example of Chapter 4. The following description is adapted from www.uspto.gov/

In general, patents are rights that prohibit others from "making, using, offering for sale or selling the invention throughout the United States, or importing the invention into the U.S." (quote from U.S. Patent Office website). The item to be patented is classified into at least one of three categories:

1. Utility; for invention or discovery of a new and useful process, machine, article of manufacture, or composition of matter, or a new and useful improvement thereof.
2. Design; for invention of a new, original ornamental design for an article of manufacture.
3. Plant; for invention or discovery and asexual reproduction (e.g. grafting) of a distinct and new variety of plant.

A patent does not give its owner complete control over his invention. He may exclude others from making, using, or selling it, but he doesn't have the right to these actions if they are blocked by another patent.

Since its establishment in 1790, the patent office has not changed as much as, say, the NIH. Two recent patent decisions that have had major impacts on bioengineering are as follows:

1. Legislation to change patent rights eligibility from "first to invent" to "first to file" was passed by Congress in 2011 and activated in 2013.
2. The Superior Court held in Molecular Pathology v. Myriad Genetics Inc., 2013 that genetic material that differs from a naturally occurring DNA sequence simply by having been isolated from it is a not eligible for patent protection.

The second decision stems from the rule that natural phenomena are not patentable. Also, not patentable are laws of nature and abstract ideas. If a version of a natural structure is created synthetically by an inventor and is substantially different from the original it may be eligible for patent protection. This policy emerged in what is known as the "Myriad Genetics, Inc." decision of the U.S. Supreme Court (2013). In this instance the court ruled against Myriad because its DNA did not meet their substantially different standard. An account of the case may be found at www.uspto.gov/patents/announce/myriad-mayo.jsp

12.11 CRISPR PATENT CASE: REGENTS, UNIVERSITY OF CALIFORNIA V. BROAD INSTITUTE, INC.

As of this writing, this case has not exhausted appeals. The CRISPR-Cas9 system was originally developed for gene editing of prokaryotic cells by Jennifer Duodna of the University of California, and her colleagues (Jinek et al. 2012). Recall from Chapter 11 that during the adaptive immunity phase of a CRISPR-forming bacterium's response to an attacking bacteriophage, a palindromic RNA code is transcribed to form a pre-CRISPR-RNA complex that joins with a CAS nuclease to produce a CRISPR-RNA-Cas complex. One particular Cas, Cas9 was found to be effective in finding the PAM and executing the required gene editing cut, by the Duodna group, and they filed to patent it for prokaryotes in 2012. Duodna stated then that the gap between prokaryotes and eukaryotes was significant enough to be a "large bottleneck" in the quest to transfer the technique to human cells (Sherkow 2018). Nevertheless, her group achieved the desired targeting the following year (Gilbert et al. 2013). Later that same year, Feng Zhang of the Broad Institute, Inc., and his group reported CRISPR-Cas9 system editing of eukaryotic cells (Ran et al. 2013). They had also filed a patent in 2012, for the system, after Duodna. Their patent differed in that it specified that their system targeted eukaryotes. The Zhang patent was approved first (Cockbain and Sterckx 2020).

The University of California filed a complaint to the U.S. Patent Office against Broad, claiming that the latter's patent had "interfered" with their ability to execute their patent. The Patent Trial and Appeal Board (PTAB) decided against the University of California, who appealed the decision to the U.S. Court of Appeals for the Federal Circuit. The Court of Appeals confirmed the PTAB decision, concluding that there was not "substantial evidence" in the facts provided by the University of California to conclude that the technology covered by their patent was subjected to interference by the technology covered in Broad's patent. An appeal to the Supreme Court was rejected. At this writing, the University of California has 18 CRISPR-Cas9 patents (faculty in the University of California system cannot own patents connected with their positions) and Broad has more than a dozen.

While the above events were occurring in the United States, there was a parallel clash in Europe. Broad filed a number of patent applications for their system with the European Patent Office in 2013. After a long battle, a foundational component of this group of applications was revoked in 2020 (Cockbain and Sterckx 2020). The University of California has not had this problem with the EPO.

As of this writing, the University of California is struggling with the U.S. Patent Office over other rulings it contests. Meanwhile, other investigators and entrepreneurs are obtaining patents for a variety of CRISPR-Cas9 applications. The matter will probably stay newsworthy for quite some time.

Ethics of Medical Product Development 217

12.12 THE BRAVE NEW WORLD OF GENOMIC TECHNOLOGY CLINICAL RESEARCH

The amount of information and technology that floods over the patient–physician relationship is unprecedented in history. One is moved to ask: Are either of these people educated sufficiently to handle the world they must navigate in? It would seem that a useful education would have to include training in how to deal with information effectively. This chapter has presented the outlines of the new world as they apply to patients and their physicians in clinical research circumstances. Patients want the benefits of clinical research. But they can't afford all of them. Medical products companies want to provide beneficial materials. But they must profit from them to stay in business. Physicians want to deliver the best benefits to their patients. But how can they be sure that what they think is best is both safe and effective? A competent FDA is their only hope for evidence that both can be achieved with any product. But what if the product they were so sure of fails? That is the subject of the next chapter.

ENRICHMENT

1. Under what conditions is software patentable? (https://www.uspto.gov/patent)
2. What is the historical significance of the supreme court decision in Diamond v. Chakrabarty, 447 U.S. 303 (1979)? What must be demonstrated by applicant to establish uniqueness of the modification?
3. Debate. Since 2013, a number of court cases have set inventors of products against filers who obtained patents without actually inventing the product in question. They merely filed the idea to gain primacy before any competitor so that they could sell "licenses" to inventor(s) that actually developed products substantially equivalent (recall the term from FDA applications). If the inventor refuses to pay license fees to the patent owner, she is sued and has to pay penalties in addition to the fees. The defendants, who call these early filers "patent trollers", claim the practice is just a form of opportunism. In 2017 the Supreme Court ruled in TC Heartland v. Kraft Foods Group that early filer patent litigation could be brought only in states where the defendant company was incorporated or "where the defendant has committed acts of infringement and has a regular and established place of business". Since most of the suits were at this time filed in Marshall, Texas and Delaware, and few of the defendants are incorporated in Texas, it was expected that the number of patent litigation suits would decrease. However, many companies are incorporated in Delaware because of its business-friendly laws and the expected reduction in patent litigation may not be fulfilled. Some have proposed changes in the Delaware

court system to reduce patent litigation trials. Others have challenged this solution as a violation of the Supreme Court decision's intent.

Resolved: The State of Delaware should make no changes in its laws to reduce patent litigation. The problem is federal and should be solved by Congress. Besides the income in court costs is a significant contribution to the state treasury.

13 Ethics of Product Failure and the Courts

Chapter 12 turned our attention away from the voluntary act of choosing a moral vision toward the involuntary state of having to obey compulsory requirements of the law. This chapter is about the consequences of either not obeying (most cases) or being wrongly perceived of violating (silicone breast implants) medical product law.

Patients are led to assume that when the FDA approves a medical product for marketing, its manufacturer has followed the law and produced a safe and effective drug or device. Manufacturers advertise to reinforce this assumption. When the function that an implanted product, Device A, is supposed to enhance, deteriorates, or the patient becomes seriously ill, the first response has to be to stabilize her to remove her from any life-threatening danger. Tests then have to be run to pinpoint the source of the symptoms. If the pathological condition can be traced to the implant, and it is a vital implant, like a heart valve, then the device will have to be repaired or replaced. Unless repair is obvious, simple and highly likely to be enduring, replacement would be the safest option. But what would you replace the Device A with? A copy of the same device? A competing Device B? What if the affliction occurred because the device was installed incorrectly? Because quality control at the factory goofed, and let a rogue Device A pass through? Because the patient misused it (e.g. became obese while wearing a body-weight -sensitive device)? The only way one can reasonably suspect that the device itself is at fault is to learn that the same affliction has appeared in a statistically significant number of Device A-implanted patients. If so, we have to have a hunch that Device A is a failure. If hospital pathologists find evidence of inflammatory, immunological, or other pathological reaction in the vicinity of the implant, the failure case is strengthened.

The cases presented in this chapter feature patient and FDA legal response to device failure. The FDA imposes regulations defining federal legal responsibilities. This means that when the regulations are violated sufficiently, the FDA employs the Department of Justice to prosecute violators in a federal court of law. DOJ lawyers are prosecutors. The FDA is the plaintiff and the device manufacturers are the defendants. The goal of the prosecutors is to show that the defendants are liable for breaking the law. In other words to show they have liability. Plaintiffs may also be patients. They may present their cases in federal or civil courts, depending on the issue. Some cases are about professionals who produce devices being defendants being held liable by patients in court. The umbrella of legal responsibility may also include physicians who implant and maintain these devices. The need to understand liability and the legal process becomes clear when one compares the consequences of a purely ethical personal "slip" with those resulting from failure to fulfill legal

DOI: 10.1201/9781003197218-13

219

220 Ethics for Bioengineering Scientists

responsibilities. The latter case will more directly threaten a bioengineer's employer and career, particularly when their product fails.

13.1 PHASE III MONITORING OF AN FDA-APPROVED DEVICE HAS NO END DATE

Approval of a device for marketing does not end the relationship of manufacturer and FDA. As noted in Chapter 12, under the Safe Medical Devices Act (SMDA), any complications or deaths associated with the device must be reported by its manufacturer as long as it is implanted. An example of an SMDA reporting form, the MDR (Medical Device Report) recommended by one professional society is presented in Appendix F. Examine the examples of product failure that prompt such a report. Since the examples are orthopedic, one does not expect them to include fatalities. Nevertheless, deaths do occur as a secondary effect, such as a pulmonary embolism (example H in Appendix F) resulting from a thrombus formed in a vessel near an orthopedic implant; possibly as a reaction to cementing (related to the fact that the polymerizing cement generates temperatures above $50°C$.). Note that some product failures are the result of product misuse. These can be iatrogenic (the surgeons fault; examples A, C and E in Appendix F). A common example is off-label use that backfires. Sometimes the patient exceeds the limits of tolerance of the device, for example for orthopedic devices, serious obesity or strenuous exercise; as is the case in example E.

13.2 ENTER THE LAWYERS

Device failure may lead to a lawsuit. The defendant may be the manufacturer, the surgeon, or even the hospital. Rarely is a bioengineering scientist involved as a defendant in litigation about device failure. This "immunity" is partly the function of an employee bioengineer's pockets being relatively shallow. But as an inventor or the CEO of a company, a bioengineer will be unable to avoid lawyers seeking to 1) fault the design or manufacture of a device 2) fault the use of a device, or 3) challenge the claim that the device is their invention (patent infringement). A bioengineer may be on either side of these issues and may need to employ a lawyer (If a bioengineer is a whistleblower it may be wise for him/her to hire a lawyer to insure protection from retaliation.). For these reasons, for a full appreciation of the cases presented in this text and for protection of his own rights, a bioengineer needs to understand rudiments of the law.

The ultimate contractarian U.S. document defining limits or laws implementing its citizens' social contract is the Constitution. There are two kinds of divisions of the constitution each citizen needs to know about: 1) the division between state and federal governments and 2) the divisions between the branches of federal government.

The constitutionally mandated division between state and federal government is stated simply: Whatever authority the constitution does not assign the federal government belongs to the state. For example, murder is not stated as a crime in the Constitution. But it is in the constitution of every state. There are areas where the

Ethics of Product Failure and the Courts

Constitution, being a relatively short document, is not sufficiently specific or up to date to be clear about where authority lies. Can the state of California collect sales tax from a sales company that has no offices or stores in the state? As we shall see, jurisdiction for settling these issues often ends up being decided in the court of last resort, the U.S. Supreme Court.

When two or more states become involved in a litigation, the case becomes federal. Examples: a terrorist in Iowa sends a biological weapon to someone in Idaho, a toy manufactured in Arizona injures a child in Minnesota, a river polluted in Ohio flows into Missouri. These are all federal issues. There are, in fact, federal agencies that manage these issues. Respectively, they are Homeland Security, Interstate Commerce Commission and the Environmental Protection Agency.

The divisions between the branches of federal government function as follows: 1) the legislative branch creates laws; 2) the executive branch executes them, punishing those who break them through the Department of Justice (DOJ); and 3) the judicial branch decides if the actions of the other two branches or any state or—in rarer cases—individual have violated the Constitution.

Most states have roughly copied the branches of federal government. The executive branch is headed by a governor, rather than a president. There is usually a lieutenant governor in place of the federal vice-president. There is usually a state secretary rather than a secretary-of-state. As with the federal government there is usually a state attorney general, but the associated department is usually not called the DOJ. State legislatures vary somewhat. California has a senate and an assembly that are parallel with the U.S. senate and congress. But some states have only one legislative body.

It is important to know the federal judicial system in some detail in order to follow federal case histories:

1. All federal cases start in one of 94 district courts distributed around the country
2. Cases appealed from district courts go to one of 12 courts of appeal in whose circuit (region) the state in question lies (location for interstate matters is decided by the court)
3. Cases appealed from courts of appeal go to the Supreme Court if accepted. If not, the last decision becomes law.

The judicial branch in states varies considerably. As a consequence, it is often confusing to follow a case in another state. The reader needs to be aware of this discrepancy. For example, the court system of California has three court tiers: trial, district, and supreme.

1. All cases begin in one of 400 trial courts
2. An appealed case is sent to one of six district courts, each of which has up to seven divisions.
3. Cases appealed from district courts, as well as certain criminal cases from trial courts, are appealed to the state supreme court.
4. Certain cases that have constitutional implications may be appealed to a federal court of appeal or, rarely, directly to the Supreme Court.

222   Ethics for Bioengineering Scientists

One final "division" that needs to be recognized is the difference between civil and criminal law. The process of bringing a person (or group) to trial is called "litigation". In criminal law the litigator is a government prosecutor, the "litigatee" is a defendant. The litigated action of which the defendant is accused may be classified as a misdemeanor—the penalty for which may be a fine—or a felony—the penalty for which may be prison, or even capital punishment. In civil law the litigator is an individual or a group called the plaintiff and the litigatee is still a defendant. Penalties for civil defendants do not achieve the level of incarceration.

A typical litigation trial goes through the following phases

1. *Pleadings* consists of the complaint by the plaintiff and the answer to the complaint by the defendant
2. *Discovery* consists of exchanges of requested information by both parties (e.g. interrogatory, documents, subpoenas against 3rd parties). In a product liability case this would include documents associated with development of the product. Expert witnesses may be called in to interpret technical documents.
3. *Trial* is the presentation of evidence to support the two parties to a jury or judge. The verdict is the decision of the adjudicator.
4. *Appeal* is the process for a party dissatisfied with the verdict to ask a higher court to review it.

13.3   HOW DOES A DEVICE FAILURE BECOME A COURT CASE?

A tort is a wrongful act or injury for which damages are sought in a civil court. When an implanted device fails the patient suffers. If the patient is convinced that the device should not have failed given the stated risks and expectations for its success raised by the manufacturer and/or surgeon, he/she may feel a victim of a tort. Product liability laws impose legal responsibility on manufacturers of products for injuries suffered by the patient. Claiming that the manufacturer has violated its legal responsibility, the patient will hire a lawyer to litigate a civil suit claiming the manufacturer is liable to pay "damages" for this tort.

What is liability? The FDA imposes regulations that constrain specifications for manufacture of a medical device (or drug). If the specifications are not met and the product fails, severe penalties are inflicted on the manufacturer (and enforced by the DOJ). Regulations are rules set up before a device is made and are decided by a government agency. They are an expression of contractarian ethics. Medical product liability, in contrast, is patient centered because the person the tort is committed against is a patient. There is more. If, in the absence of any negligence, the product posed a physical threat to the patient at a level that required at least a warning stating the degree of risk for the danger, the company is strictly liable unless it minimizes the danger or divulges it in writing. This liability assumes the company is in the best position to correct the imperfect quality or compensate the patient for any injury it causes.

What exactly is legal negligence? Here the language gets a bit dense, but you can handle it because you know what deontological ethics is. Remember the Kantian

Ethics of Product Failure and the Courts

concept of duty? Legal negligence is a breach of the duty of care. The meaning of "care" here is a little different from its meaning in Feminist Ethics. Here it means taking care to do your best at the job for which you are responsible. In other words, negligence is conduct that falls below a standard of carefulness established by law for the protection of patients against unreasonable **risk** of harm. Negligence implies a willfulness to be sloppy. The conduct of the company more than the quality of its product is the target of a negligence or straight liability suit. Penalties reflect the seriousness of such an accusation. As might be expected, an extra burden is placed on the plaintiff(s) to demonstrate negligence.

They must show:

1. A duty is owed the patient by the manufacturer
2. A practical standard for carrying out the duty has been breached
3. As a result of the breach, the patient has been injured
4. The injury is of a sort that warrants compensation

When patients sue a company for a tort caused by one it its products, the case usually is argued before a jury whose members lack sufficient background to apply any scientific evidence in deciding for or against the claimed product failure. Indeed, in one of the cases presented later, no confirmable scientific evidence for the claimed pathological effects was presented. The professionals presenting evidence that is supposed to show cause and effect, and those who argue against them, are called "expert witnesses". Some expert witnesses have made expert witnessing a career, appearing for a fee on the side of the plaintiff or the accused in a variety of cases. Judges, in general, also lack scientific background and, therefore, no frame of reference to evaluate an expert witnesses' qualifications to make the judgments he presents. A remedy for this predicament called the "Daubert standard" was crafted after most of the silicon breast trials. It will be discussed, after they are, later. Here are some illustrative cases.

13.4 INTRAUTERINE DEVICE (IUD) THE DALKON SHIELD CASE (1971) (AFTER MAYESH AND SCRANTON 2004)

The $4.35 Dalkon Shield was a crab-shaped intra-uterine polyvinyl acetate contraceptive implant measuring about 2 × 2 cm. A monofilament string surrounded by a nylon sheath constituted the "crab tail" that extended from the uterus to the vagina, much like a tampon string. Five prongs projected from the "crab body" to secure the device on the endometrium and prevent dislodging. The shield contained cupric sulfate that was supposed to act as a spermicide (Jones et al. 1973). It was developed by a gynecologist-engineer team in response to fears of the gynecologist that chemical contraceptives posed a health danger. A.H. Robins began marketing the device in 1971. It did not report the presence of spermicides in the device. Devices were not yet regulated by the FDA but drugs were. In late 1971 patients' physicians began reporting complications, including infection and pelvic inflammatory disease, associated with the device. Robins argued that the complications were iatrogenic, caused by improper implantation by physicians. In January 1973, the first deaths associated with shields were reported. In June 1973, in response to reports in the clinical literature of

224   Ethics for Bioengineering Scientists

complications associated with the device, including pregnancy, the Centers for Disease Control and Prevention (CDC) conducted a study of IUDs involving 16,994 obstetricians and gynecologists regarding the frequency of hospitalizations, deaths, and other complications related to IUD use during a six-month period. In 1973 the Dalkon Shield, as a result of heavy advertising in popular magazines, was the most popular IUD, being used by over 2 million women. CDC researchers found that the Dalkon Shield implants were correlated with increased rates of pregnancy-associated complications, including septic pregnancies (bacterial infection of the placenta and embryo). Hospitalization was usually required for patients with these complications. In May 1974 Robins sent a letter to 120,000 physicians advising them of complications associated with the device. The following month, the medical director of the A.H. Robins Company, J.S. Templeton published a letter to the editor of the *British Medical Journal* in which he stated that the company was aware of the apparent trend of septic abortions and infections in women using the device, including several deaths. He further claimed that there was no direct evidence that the Dalkon Shield was responsible for the bacterial septic poisoning and related issues; instead, these complications were due to the general increase in use of IUDs (Templeton 1972). Later that month the A.H. Robins Company took the Dalkon Shield off the market in response to pressure from the FDA. However, they did not recall the devices that had been sold. That same year a number of articles in the journal *Obstetrics and Gynecology* reported studies showing a high frequency of septic pregnancies in patients with Dalkon Shields. In July 1975, the death count associated with the device reached 16. That same year the CDC published a study that concluded the shield posed a higher risk of abortion-related deaths than other IUDs.

Deemer v. A.H. Robins (1974) was the first Dalkon Shield lawsuit. The patient was awarded $10,000 compensatory damages and $75,000 punitive damages. Accumulation of reports of complications had convinced more patients who had suffered them to file lawsuits against A.H. Robins, such that by the end of 1975 there were enough to convince a district court judge in Kansas to consolidate them (Sobol 1991). From 1974 to 1980, following Deemer, A.H. Robins settled cases out of court, prevailing about 50% of the time. Their successes were due, in part, to their expert witnesses challenging the ability of plaintiff expert witnesses to demonstrate causality. Since the implant site had potential exposure to other sources of infection such as poor hygiene and sexually transmitted diseases, the observed complications could not be linked unequivocally to the shield. Gradually, through documents obtained in the disclosure phase of the trial, evidence came to light that A.H. Robins was aware of a phenomenon called wicking, a form of capillarity that drew fluid up the sheathed structure tailing from the head of the device, such that bacteria were drawn into the uterus from the vagina, bypassing natural antibacterial defenses (pH, macrophages, etc.) in the cervix (Sobol 1991). As noted previously, in 1976 Congress added the Medical Device Amendment to the FD&CA, motivated in part by the Dalkon Shield experience.

By October 1984, more than 400,000 lawsuits had been filed against A.H. Robins, 9, 500 of which were litigated or settled. Robins discharged a media campaign advising women implanted with shields to have them, at the company's expense, removed by a doctor. More than 4,500 medical bills were paid for the procedure. By 1985 discovery documents revealing Robins failure to warn patients about the wicking problem and histopathology micrographs showing bacteria in recovered shield sheaths were regular components of plaintiff expert witness testimony, and trial awards increased accordingly. In Tetuan v. A.H. Robins (1985) the plaintiff was awarded $9.25 million in damages. Plaintive tort claims included failure to warn, unsafe design, breach of

Ethics of Product Failure and the Courts 225

warranty, and fraud. Robins declared bankruptcy in 1985 whilst an estimated 100,000 women in the United States still had Dalkon Shields implanted. By the end of 1985, the A.H. Robins company was facing lawsuits from people in every state of the United States (and a number of other countries). In 1989 the company was sold to American Home Products who had agreed to supply most of the $2.475 billion required for a trust fund to pay outstanding claims against the Dalkon Shield (Sobol 1991).

It will be noted that no criminal charges were brought against A.H. Robins or the inventors. Because the Dalkon Shield was marketed before 1976, it was not covered by FDA regulations. Nor were there state laws that protected its users. The company was, therefore, acting within the law and could not be prosecuted by the DOJ or county district attorneys. For our purposes, the data whose integrity was compromised by non-disclosure, in this case, were the observations of wicking and the photomicrographs of bacteria in the string sheath.

13.5 *THE ARTIFICIAL HEART VALVE CASES* (AFTER MAYESH AND SCRANTON 2004)

Unlike IUDs heart valves are life-saving devices. Their failure is almost always fatal unless the patient is near a cardiac surgery facility. Of the four heart valves, the aortic needs replacement most often, followed by the mitral valve at the entrance of the left ventricle. High ejection pressures generated by left ventricle systole contribute to turbulence at the aortic valve. The resulting shear and cavitation probably contribute to its failure with age. Such failure is often the result of calcification at the base of the valve leaves. Most replacements are glutaraldehyde pretreated porcine or bovine heart valves that are providing a highly cross-linked collagen matrix. Polymeric replacements, sometimes with metal components, have been tried. If the implant lasts long enough it will also fail due to calcification-induced stiffening of the valve leaflets. In the 1970s and 1980s a series of synthetic heart valves came on the market and failed; not because of calcification but due to poor manufacturing practices that helped convince the FDA to develop a GMP protocol.

   a. *The Braunwald-Cutter caged-ball valve.* The Braunwald-Cutter valve, introduced in 1968, replaces leaves with a silastic ball (poppet) in a metal cage and was a substitute for both the mitral and aortic valves. The cage titanium struts were covered with knit Dacron tubing and the inflow ring at its base was covered with an ultrathin polypropylene mesh fabric. The coverings were assumed to reduce the chance of thromboembolism formation. At the ventricle exit, ventricular ejection pushed the ball toward the aorta, opening the valve. Aortic elastic back pressure pressed the ball against the ventricle, closing the valve. A 1977 report concluded that the poppet deformed and escaped from its cage often enough to warrant removal of the implant by five years and did not prevent thromboembolisms (Blackstone et al. 1977). Caged-ball suits began to appear in the late 1970s. Plaintiffs claimed negligence (design, manufacture and testing), breach of warrantees (expressed or implied), and strict liability. There were patients who tolerated the device. It was

226   Ethics for Bioengineering Scientists

concluded that it was effective if flow rates in the heart were low (Luk et al. 2010). Production of this device ceased in 1979.

b. *The Bjork-Shiley tilting disc valve (data from*Gott et al., 2003). The Bjork-Shiley valve was developed in 1969 with a flat Delrin disc supported by two struts of a Stellite (cobalt-chrome) ring covered with teflon. Pyrolite was substituted for Delrin in 1971 and this valve replaced 157,000 aortic and 140,000 mitral valves from then until 1986. In 1975 an enhanced flow convex disc model was introduced. A total of 86,000 of these were implanted by 1986. A seven-year study by Bjork et al. of the convex model showed strut structural failure in 12% of the implants. In 1990 the Subcommittee on Oversight and Investigations of the Committee on Energy and Commerce, U.S. House of Representatives, subpoenaed internal documents of Pfizer (who purchased rights to the both valves in 1979). Up to this time Pfizer had refused submission of these files to the FDA. Based upon the documents, the Committee concluded that strut fracture was due largely to "deficiencies in quality control procedures in the manufacturing process". Specifically, the welding process attaching the struts to the ring was "out of control", inspections were substandard and the company cut funds that would have paid for oversight of the manufacturing process. The report further alleged that Pfizer repeatedly provided misleading information to health professionals and the FDA, understating the incidence of strut fracture, to the point that the problem had been eliminated. Patients began to file lawsuits, and Pfizer settled, but required that all settlements be held in confidence. By the end of 1992 there were enough plaintiffs to warrant a class action (Bowling v. Pfizer (1992)). The courts would not, however, support product defect claims by patients whose disc valves had not failed. Plaintiffs with unbroken valves who claimed fraud, however, were more successful.

The Braunwald-Cutter valve was marketed before 1976 and so escaped FDA penalties under the Medical Devices Act of that year. The Bjork-Shiley valve, however, was marketed right after passage of the law. Nevertheless, it received minimum scrutiny because the FDA had not completed constitution of its PMA protocol. The data whose integrity was compromised by false testimony were the true incidence of valve strut failure.

13.6 *METAL-ON-METAL ASR CASE* (AFTER COHEN 2011)

Orthopedic devices rarely save lives, nor do they tend to endanger lives when they fail. It is therefore difficult to argue for acceleration of FDA orthopedic device approval based upon patient needs for survival. The DePuy (pronounced "De Pyew") Articular Surface Replacement system took advantage of a loophole in the FDA 510(k) premarketing approval process that was referred to in Chapter 12. The consequences are summarized in this case.

Ethics of Product Failure and the Courts

The original hip replacements developed in the 1940s and 1950s mimicked oil/grease-lubricated ball-and-socket hinges used in manufacturing and transportation. They were composed of metal—usually 316 L steel. Lubrication for implanted hips was assumed to be provided by the glycoproteins of synovial fluid, naturally present at joints. Wear, and to some extent corrosion, leading to metallosis (inflammation caused by metal wear particles) doomed these implants. They were replaced in 1958 by John Charnley's metal-polytetrafluoroethylene hips, which also had wear problems and were in turn replaced by metal ball-ultra high molecular weight polyethylene (UHMWPE) socket prostheses in 1962. These implants have become the gold standard for hip replacement. Some have lasted 35 years (Callaghan et al. 2009d).

In the mid-1980s, Bernard G. Weber, a Swiss Orthopedic Surgeon, published an evaluation of 1960s-implanted metal-on-metal hips like the McKee-Farrar and Sivash that had been discontinued due to unacceptably high revision rates. He found that implanted hips that did not need revision were doing well at 10 years and concluded that with appropriate adjustments metal-on-metal would be a viable option for hip prostheses (Weber 1989). He convinced Sulzer Brothers to produce the Metasul cobalt-chrome metal-on-metal total hip in 1988. In 1997, Derrick McMinn, an orthopedic surgeon at Birmingham University in the United Kingdom, convinced that cobalt-chrome would also work for joint resurfacing, introduced the Birmingham Hip. The device was manufactured by Smith & Nephew. It was a resurfacing prosthesis, as opposed to a total hip replacement. That is, it did not require cutting off the patient's hip ball, it eliminated reaming of the medullary canal, and minimized reaming of the socket. Instead, a hole was drilled in the ball apex after the articular surface was removed, and an umbrella-shaped ball cover was inserted by its handle. Both metal-on-metal hips are still being used in Europe as of this writing.

DePuy did not have a metal-on-metal prosthesis on the market in 1997 and its records show concern that the Metasul and Birmingham hips would replace its UHWWPE-metal total hip and resurfacing models in the United States. They approached two orthopedic surgeons to help them design a competitive device and strove to get it marketed as soon as possible.

It will be recalled from Chapter 12 that the FDA categorizes devices into three risk classes. The default class for any implant is Class III, which requires pre-clinical research and clinical trials. Under certain circumstances an implant may be categorized Class II. The most frequent circumstance is that they be "substantially equivalent" to devices already approved. The meaning of "substantially equivalent" has never been clarified, in great part because it contains a logical paradox. If the device is sufficiently equivalent to another that is patented by someone else, it runs the risk of patent infringement. If not, then how could it be called "equivalent", no matter what adjective precedes the term? Granting an implant Class II status while it is being evaluated for substantial equivalence is called being in the "510(k) process" and constitutes a loophole because the device may be marketed while the process is going on. The DePuy cobalt-chrome metal-on-metal ASR XL total hip and ASR resurfacing kit were marketed in Europe in 2003 and the ASR XL was allowed by the FDA to enter the 510(k) process in the United States in 2004. The ASR resurfacing kit was categorized as Class III by the FDA because the resurfacing procedure it required was not considered "substantially equivalent" to that used for non-metal-on-metal resurfacing implantations. DePuy conducted the required clinical trial but after two years the French health agency Haute Autorité reported that its patients had a 4.9% fracture rate in the femoral neck (that supports the ball). The agency concluded that there were better implants for its funding. This incidence of fracture is high for such an early

228   Ethics for Bioengineering Scientists

stage in a hip implant study. Modern hip implants usually have much lower rates through 5 years and aren't considered competitive in their market unless they reach 10 years. After a series of communications with the FDA about the disappointing results of this study, DePuy withdrew its Class III application. The ASR resurfacing kit has, therefore, never been approved by the FDA. But it continued to be employed outside the United States. The failure of the ASR had been predicted by McMinn at a 2005 meeting in Helsinki. He claimed the cup was too shallow, leading to increased wear, and the design of the kit required such accurate alignment that implantation would be too challenging for many surgeons.

In order to avoid patent infringement on the Birmingham hip, DePuy made changes in the ASR XL ball angle and size. Since they conducted no research or clinical trials they had no data to support marketing claims for either device. In order to satisfy ASTM (American Society for Testing Materials) standards, DePuy subjected the implant to hip simulator testing. This consists of rotating the implant ball under an average human's weight in its socket in a manner that simulated walking 24/7 in a serum solution. The number of rotations could be set to represent any selected number of years of wear. From 2004 to 2010 93,000 ASR XL implants were sold worldwide (about 35,000 in the United States). It was cleared for marketing in the United States in 2008. That same year the orthopedic joint registry of Australia reported that revision surgeries for failed ASR XL were occurring at an unusually high rate. In 2010 the registries of England and Wales reported a 5-year revision rate of about 13%, also unusually high. DePuy recalled the ASR in Australia in 2009 and did the same worldwide in 2010 because revision rates were multiples of other hip replacement prostheses. What caused the implant to fail? At a meeting in Dallas in 2007 one of DePuy's engineers reported that 30% of women and 7.5% of men implanted with ASR XLs had markedly raised concentrations of cobalt and chromium in their blood. The engineers blamed the implant surgeons, who happened to be members of the implant design team, for these complications. The presence of cobalt and chromium particles in blood is associated with: a) Type 1 hypersensitivity or allergic reactions (Thomas et al. 2009) and b) Type IV hypersensitivity or delayed reaction, accompanied by high levels of endothelial vascularity, necrosis, fibrin matrices, and macrophages with metal inclusions (Willert et al. 2005)—Willert et al. named this presentation Aseptic Lymphocytic Vasculitis and Associated Lesions (ALVAL). These conditions are consistent with implant loosening and significant soft tissue damage associated with pain in patients needing revision surgeries. In November 2013, the U.S. District Court in Ohio awarded about 8,000 DePuy ASR XL patients a settlement of $2.5 billion.

DePuy did not supply ASR XL data. How can there be science without data? The choice to exclude data is equivalent to saying "We were innocent of violating data integrity because we didn't present any". By allowing the ASR XL to be implanted in patients without data from clinical trials that specifically described the device marketed, DePuy was assuming safety (speculating efficacy). DePuy received FDA support to take this pathway by petitioning FDA in a 510(k) submission to treat their metal-on-metal artificial joint the same as similar devices that had been categorized as Class II, because it wasn't "high risk". The 1997 FDA Modernization Act (FDAMA) gave the FDA great leeway to conclude that if a device similar to the one in the application before them was supported by data that showed it to be "low risk" they could assume that the new device was also "low risk". The "low risk" category allows a device to be considered Class II and need minimum data

Ethics of Product Failure and the Courts

demonstrating safety and efficacy. This shortcut to Class II which is less stringent than Class III, which is normal for an implant, constitutes a loophole. Congress included this loophole in the FDAMA to accelerate processing of devices and alleviate a backlog that had been building up at the FDA.

13.7 SILICONE BREAST IMPLANT CASES (AFTER SCHLEITER 2010 AND HOOPER 2001)

Breast implants are neither life-saving nor morbidity-reducing devices. Their need is mainly psychological, and they would be considered merely cosmetic if they were not implanted so deep subcutaneously. The shape of the female human breast appears to play an aboriginal role in sexual attraction. However, it has become so socially important to both genders that industries (e.g. fashion, lingerie, entertainment, cosmetic drugs, plastic surgery) have been created to take financial advantage of the addiction. Some women seek breast augmentation even if they have no medical condition that it would alleviate. Others have had mastectomies to save their lives from the consequences of breast cancer, and the psychological devastation from both the disease and loss of an anatomical symbol of their identity, makes recreation of the original shape a mental health necessity for them.

The device, developed by DOW Corning Corp. in 1961, was a poly-dimethylsiloxane (PDMS, a silicone) elastomer-plus-fumed amorphous silica bag filled with PDMS in gel form or saline. Sometimes a highly cross-linked fibrous capsular layer (low elasticity and flexibility scar called a "contracture") would form around the bag, causing disfigurement. To prevent this complication some bags were coated with a polyurethane foam to encourage tissue ingrowth. Breast augmentation and reconstruction surgeries began in the 1960s, before passage of the MDA. By the 1990s some 2 million bags, it is estimated, had been implanted. Any implant will stimulate formation of a fibrous layer (healing scar) that marks the completion of the wound healing process initiated by the wounding procedure, surgery. Contractures are the result of overgrowth of scar tissue and may be removed by a debriding procedure. Rupture of the bags occurred occasionally. But this was not considered a design flaw. It was often caused by patient activity or mishandling of the bag during surgery. Since the number of such complications was relatively low and the Class III (so categorized by the FDA in 1988) device went on the market before clinical trials were required, the data pool for evaluating its safety and effectiveness was relatively small. Early in 1982 the FDA expressed concern about reports of scar tissue forming about the implant.

In 1982 the first product liability suit was filed against Dow Corning (Stern v. Dow Corning Inc.) in the U.S. District Court of Northern California. Stern's implants had ruptured and she testified that before and after their removal she suffered chronic fatigue and joint pains. Her physicians testified that systemic silicone had stimulated an autoimmune response. No data were presented to support this claim. Her lawyers introduced Dow Corning internal documents obtained during discovery that suggested the company was aware of bag ruptures and gel leakage. A jury awarded her $211,000

230   Ethics for Bioengineering Scientists

in compensatory damages and $1.5 million in punitive damages in 1984. The case was settled in lieu of appeal for an undisclosed amount.

In 1990 congressional hearings on the safety of breast implants commenced. The three scientific experts invited to testify before Congress were paid expert witnesses for plaintiffs in breast implant litigation cases. Not long before the hearings the NBC interview show *Face to Face with Connie Chung* broadcast a program cautioning on the dangers of silicone implants. These two events led to increased pressure on congress to take action to reduce the perceived threat. Congress pressured the FDA to investigate silicone breast implant safety. The FDA convened its General and Plastic Surgery Devices Panel to discuss the matter. The panel's members included plastic surgeons, oncologists, toxicologists, epidemiologists, immunologists, pathologists, and radiologists. The American Medical Association and other medical organizations advised the panel to oppose a precipitous ban on the implants. The panel concluded that since no controlled epidemiological studies existed that explored the relationship between silicone breast implants and systemic disease, the main regulatory problem, was a dearth of safety data. It proposed that the devices should remain on the market until clear evidence for or against their safety was obtained.

What followed the panel report was a series of liability suits against manufacturers of silicone breast implants claiming a variety of complications:

   a. Toole v. Baxter (1991) claimed increased risk of developing cancer and auto-immune disease, $5.4 million settlement
   b. Hopkins v. Dow Corning (1991) claimed connective tissue disease from ruptured implant, $7.3 million award
   c. Johnson v. Medical Engineering Corp. (MEC) (1992) claimed chronic fatigue, muscle pain, joint pain, headaches, and dizziness from ruptured implant, $25 million
   d. 3 plaintiffs v. 3 M (1994) claimed atypical lupus erythematosus, neurological impairment and/or a "silicone induced" autoimmune problem

In 1992 David Kessler, M.D., the new head of the FDA, called for a moratorium on the sale of silicone breast implants. A panic ensued amongst women with implants. On the heels of the NBC show and congressional testimony, the Kessler decision appeared to confirm the conclusion that the implant was unsafe. A number (unknown) of women had them removed. Filing of lawsuits accelerated. Finally, in 1994 21 lead lawyers and their clients were consolidated into one $4 billion class action. The 440,000 class members were not required to confirm that the implants were the cause of their ailments. At the time there were still 7,000 suits brought by women not in the class. Two effective strategies in jury trials of the plaintiff lawyers were as follows:

   a. They pointed out that Dow Corning had not performed clinical trials necessary to establish the safety of their product. The fact that silicone breast implants weren't categorized as Class III until 1988 and, therefore, Dow Corning didn't have sufficient pre-trial time to complete clinical trials, was deemed secondary to their obligation to establish product safety on their own. Company documents stressing profit motivation were used to paint Dow Corning as uncaring.
   b. They switched the testimony of their expert witnesses to highlight the plaintiff's "atypical" symptoms (see 3 M trial above). As studies like those of the Mayo Clinic (see below) began to appear in *NEJM* and other high impact journals,

Ethics of Product Failure and the Courts

plaintiff lawyers could no longer allow their paid expert witnesses to testify that silicone breast implants cause "typical" lupus and other autoimmune diseases. There was no literature evaluating atypical versions of any of these diseases. So, defendant expert witnesses could not make any scientific arguments against plaintiff testimony. Two months after the class action was finalized, a Mayo Clinic epidemiologic study appeared in the *New England Journal of Medicine* reporting no statistical correlation between silicone implants and connective tissue disease and a number of other disorders. By May of 1995 Dow Corning was facing over 20,000 lawsuits containing 410,000 claims and filed for Chapter 11 bankruptcy.

In December of 1996, Robert E. Jones, an Oregon federal judge, accepting input from a panel of scientists unconnected to implant litigation, ruled that testimony, claiming silicone implants cause disease, was inadmissible because it was scientifically invalid. Seventy claims were dismissed as part of this ruling. In the same month Sam C. Pointer, the coordinating judge for all federal silicone breast implant cases, appointed a panel of four scientists unconnected to implant litigation, an immunologist, epidemiologist, toxicologist, and rheumatologist, to evaluate scientific evidence relative to breast implant safety. He instructed them to "review and critique the scientific literature pertaining to the possibility of a causal association between silicone breast implants and connective tissue diseases, related signs and symptoms, and immune system dysfunction". After two years of testimony from scientific experts chosen by each side, including more than 2,000 documents, and a review of the scientific literature, the panel concluded that available data do not support a causal connection between silicone breast implants and defined connective tissue diseases or autoimmune diseases.

Over time, scientific evidence began to mount against causation. Epidemiology studies from the Mayo Clinic, Harvard Medical School, Johns Hopkins University, the University of Michigan, and the University of California failed to show any association between silicone breast implants and any autoimmune or "typical" disease. The term typical is used to stress the fact that the studies did not deal with "atypical" diseases because they are undefined. In 2006 the moratorium on silicone breast implants was lifted by the FDA.

What is the evidence that silicone breast implants cause disease, supplied by plaintiff expert witnesses? "Evidence" given as testimony in a U.S. courtroom is different from scientific data. In the early 1990s neither jury members nor judges had the background or resources to evaluate the credentials of an expert witness. If the witness was a physician, and had an M.D., it was assumed that she knew all about the human body. If the witness had a Ph.D. in biology, it was assumed he was a scientist who knew all about biology. Opposing lawyers could challenge the credentials of the witness, but jurors and judges rarely had the background to understand the challenges. Besides, the defendant's lawyer risked alienating a jury if he appeared to be badgering the witness. Plaintiff expert witnesses could be challenged for not being oncologists, epidemiologists, immunologists, or histologists, but they knew more about these subjects than did the judges or lay jurors, so the nuances of the challenge were lost on those passing judgment. For example, plaintiff witnesses in the silicon breast implant trials claimed that silicone is antigenic, if not directly, then by acting as an adjuvant that lowers the threshold for stimulating autoimmune responses. How could a juror or judge evaluate whether the person making this claim had the background to draw a conclusion like this? In a courtroom such testimony is evidence. It sounds plausible enough to be the subject of an actual research project. At a science meeting it would evoke demands for evidence in the form of data from lab animal experiments or epidemiological studies published in peer-reviewed journals. Introduction of Bradford Hill's criteria for empirical data type of causality to challenge plaintiff assertions would be futile in a 1990s courtroom. In the scientific community plaintiff testimony in the breast implant trials became known as "junk science". Junk science presented as evidence is the form of data integrity violation showcased in this ethics example. The term entered the jurisprudence literature in cases that followed.

13.8 EXPERT WITNESSING AND THE FEDERAL RULES OF EVIDENCE: DAUBERT V. MERRILL DOW PHARMACEUTICALS (AFTER SKAPP 2003)

One of the principle functions of a judge is deciding if evidence being presented by a witness is relevant to the issues being adjudicated. If not, it is inadmissible. The guidelines for making this determination are called the *rules of evidence*. State courts and federal courts each have their own rules of evidence and may actually disagree. The emergence of junk science in the silicone breast implant cases raised a new challenge to the rules of evidence. Can there be guidelines for determining if an expert witness is relevant to the issues? Can a general practitioner be considered an expert in immunology? If not, then the conclusions she would present must be considered no better than junk science and would be inadmissible. The case that established the first attempt by the federal courts to deal with this challenge was Daubert v. Merrill Dow. The case had nothing to do with breast implants. But its verdict was a supreme court decision and, therefore, set guidelines for all federal courts. It charged federal judges with making two determinations:

1. Is the evidence being presented scientifically valid?
2. Is the connection between the evidence being presented and the case in point valid?

Applying Daubert has become a major challenge for most judges. They are not trained in science. The reader is invited to search the curriculum of the best law school in his state and find a science course. As might be expected, one of the first opportunities to test the new rules, an appeal of a silicone breast implant case Hopkins v. Dow Corning, did not apply the rules as they were intended. Junk science was admitted by Judge Proctor Hug who didn't think the absence of published data supporting the plaintiff's testimony was an impediment to its validity. A number of states have spawned their own versions of Daubert. But the bar for successful application is still too high for most judges.

Ethics of Product Failure and the Courts   233

13.9   CAN THE FDA BE SUED?

Given the existence of loopholes in FDA regulation and the occurrence of injury from products that reached patients because of these gaps, one might expect to be able to sue the FDA when one of these products causes harm. The FDA avoids liability by making the company that produces the product fully liable. Fast-tracking of a product by the FDA is different from claiming that it is safe and effective. The action is taken because the FDA has accepted assurances by the company that the product is substantially equivalent to a product that has been fully tested. As far as the agency is concerned the fast-tracked product failed because the company was wrong in its claim that it achieved substantial equivalency. The action is also taken in response to an emergency when treatments are needed quickly to avoid a large number of deaths from a disease. Medicines for HIV and AIDS were approved in the 1990s under this condition.

Can the FDA be sued for failure of a product that it has successfully marshalled through clinical trials? No again. In fact, neither can the company that made the product. The Supreme Court decision that established this law was Riegel v. Medtronic (2008). The case involved Mr. Riegel, a heart patient in need of coronary angioplasty (surgical alteration of a blood vessel). The procedure included inserting a long flexible catheter through the left femoral artery and guiding it to the target coronary vessel. If the goal is to widen the coronary vessel, an inflatable balloon is incorporated in the tip. Riegel's cardiologist performed this procedure in 1996 with a Medtronic Evergreen balloon catheter but could not get the balloon to inflate using the recommended pressure range, so he exceeded it and the balloon burst, rupturing the vessel. Riegel almost succumbed to the consequences of a burst coronary artery. He sued Medtronic for negligence of design under state common law in New York District court and lost. His appeal to the Supreme Court was unsuccessful as they affirmed the district court decision ruling that a device that had completed clinical trials with sufficient success to win FDA approval could not by definition be unsafe. A ruling that the device is defective would result in its withdrawal, denying its benefits—confirmed by previous successes—to future patients. Riegel was followed in 2009 by a case that modified it to allow a condition where a company marketing an FDA approved Class III device could be sued. In Wyeth v. Levine, Levine, a musician who lost the use of the hand she used to play, successfully sued Wyeth Pharmaceuticals. The drug was not faulted, but the instructions for administering it by syringe were. The problem did not appear during clinical trials because technicians in the trials were trained in correct administration of the drug. The court found that for an average technician the instructions were too ambiguous and would result in more faulty administrations. The problem was resolved by changing the instructions.

Law is dynamic in the United States. By the time these words are read other court cases will have further altered the handling of medical device and pharmaceutical product torts by State and Federal courts. Changes in FDA policy will have taken place. NIH rules and punishment for scientific misconduct will have changed. Politics through Congress and state legislatures will influence all these changes. The bioengineering scientist whether generating data as a researcher, or presenting it as

234 Ethics for Bioengineering Scientists

a marketing representative, an engineer building medical products, a physician applying medical products or any of the many professionals a bioengineer can become, will face the ethical challenge of maintaining their integrity and the penal challenge of using them lawfully.

13.10 THE FUTURE OF DATA CARE

All the words that have trekked over these many pages may be cobbled into one statement: The data that bioengineering scientists are responsible for disseminating must be as truthful and comprehensive as the reporter is capable of making them, or they are not scientists. Whether this loss of identity is worth any gain from violating data integrity is a function of the bioengineer's moral vision, not necessarily evil under all moral theories. The bioengineering scientist can ensure custody of his/her identity, in any case, by adopting a moral vision that views data as clients.

ENRICHMENT

1. Senators and Representatives are pressed by lobbyists and voters to urge government agencies to rule in their favor. The politicians, in turn, depend on these pressure groups to keep them in office by voting and donating. The government agencies depend on the legislators for their funding. The agencies have no leverage in this system, unless a blatantly illegal act is performed. As a consequence, regulation circumvention rulings like "fast track" are passed, and consequences like DePuy's ASR XL occur. With this background in mind, would you be in favor of a law that allowed the FDA to be sued? Write an essay itemizing the constructive and destructive consequences of a "yes" answer.

2. Elizabeth Holmes is an entrepreneur who claims to have designed a device that can determine from a drop of blood, properties that at present require much larger blood volumes. She calls it a Theranos and commenced to try to sell it to venture capitalists in 2003. Starting in 2004, she raised money to finance its development, and built a Silicon Valley campus for this venture. By 2010 she had convinced enough in her industry to be on the verge of signing a contract to have her Theranos, now in cartridge form, administered at Walgreens. But Walgreens has never received a device that works. Her ability to persuade propelled her, by 2015, to fame and fortune, despite the lack of peer-reviewed evidence for effectiveness of her device. In October of 2015, investigative reporter John Carreyrou of the *Wall Street Journal* published a story in that newspaper that claimed Elizabeth Holmes

---

Ethics of Product Failure and the Courts

operation was a sham. In June 2018 Elizabeth Holmes and Ramesh "Sunny" Balwani were indicted by a federal judge who charged them with two counts of conspiracy to commit wire fraud and 9 counts of wire fraud. Carreyrou updated his story with a book in 2020: *Bad Blood: Secrets and Lies in a Silicon Valley Startup* (Carreyrou 2018). The trial was set to start in August of 2020, but Covid-19 delayed it. It restarted in August of 2021. Updates may be followed at https://www.justice.gov/usao-ndca/us-v-elizabeth-holmes-et-al. Since the trial is not complete, one cannot assume the defendant will be convicted. Given the possibility that she will be, the reader would gain significant insight to human character by composing an explanation for how Elizabeth Holmes got as far as she did.

References

Ackerknecht, E H. 2016. *A Short History of Medicine* (Johns Hopkins Universsity Press: Baltimore) 272pp.

Adams, B, and J Larson. 2007. 'Legislative history of the animal welfare act,' in *Animal Welfare Information Center* (U.S. Department of Agriculture: Washington, D.C.) 41: 2–7. www.nai.usda.gov/awie

Anderson, M S, M A Shaw, N H Steneck, E Konkle, and T Kamata. 2013. 'Research integrity and misconduct in the academic profession,' in M B Paulsen (ed.), *Higher Education Handbook of Theory and Research* (Springer: NY) 28: 217–256.

Anderson, R M. 1980. *Divided Loyalties* (Purdue U. Press: Lafayette) 397pp.

Armstrong, M B. 2003. 'Confidentiality: A comparison across the professions of medicine, engineering and accounting,' in J Rowan and S Jr Zinaich (eds.), *Ethics for the Professions* (Wadsworth/Thomson Learning: Belmont) 145–152.

Aslaksen, E W. 2013. 'The engineering paradigm', *International Journal of Engineering Studies*, 5: 129–154.

Axelrod, D, and D Dion. 1988. 'The further evolution of cooperation', *Science*, 242: 1385–1390.

Barry, J M. 2005. *The Great Influenza: The Story of the Deadliest Pandemic in History* (Penguin Books: NY) 546pp.

Bayles, M D. 2003. 'What is a profession?' in J Rowan and S Jr Zinaich (eds.), *Ethics for the Professions* (Wadsworth/Thomson Learning: Belmont) 58–62.

Beall, J. 2013. 'Predatory publishing is just one of the the the consequences of gold open access', *Learned Publishing*, 26: 79–84.

Bekelman, J E, Y Li, and G P Gross. 2003. 'Scope and impact of financial conflicts of interest in biomedical research', *Journal of the American Medical Association*, 289: 454–465.

Blackburn, S. 1994. *The Oxford Dictionary of Philosophy* (Oxford U. Press: NY) 408pp.

Blackstone, E H, J W Kirklin, J R Pluth, M E Turner, and G V S Parr. 1977. 'The performance of the Braunwald-Cutter aortic valve', *Annals of Thoracic Surgery*, 23: 302–318.

Blackwell, R J. 2002. 'Galileo Galilei,' in G B Ferngren (ed.), *Science and Religion* (Johns Hopkins U. Press: Baltimore) 105–116.

Bottici, C. 2008. '*Mythos* and *Logos*. A genealogical approach', *Epoché*, 13: 1–24.

Brennen, T A, D J Rothman, L Blank, D Blumenthal, S C Chimonas, J J Cohen, J Goldman, J P Kassirer, H Kimbal, J Naughton, and N Smelser. 2006. 'Health industry practices that create conflicts of interest', *Journal of the American Medical Association*, 295: 429–433.

Britannica, E. 2009. Listed editor is Augustyn A. 'Thales,' in *Encyclopedia Britannica. Encyclopedia Britannica 2009 Ultimate Reference Suite*. Chicago: Encyclopedia Britannica. www.britannica.com/biography/Thales-of-Miletus

Britannica, E. 2016. Listed editor is Augustyn, A. *Bioengineering* (Encyclopedia Britannica: Chicago).

Budinger, T F, and M D Budinger. 2006. *Ethics of Emerging Technologies* (Wiley: New Jersey) 496pp.

Bush, V. 1945. *Science The Endless Frontier*(Princeton U. Press: Princeton) 192pp.

Bynum, W E, E J Browne, and R Porter (eds.). 1981. *Dictionary of the History of Science* (Princeton U. Press: Princeton) 494pp.

238 References

Callaghan, J J, P Bracha, S S Liu, S Piyaworakhun, D D Goetz, and R C Johnston. 2009. 'Survivorship of a Charnley total hip arthroplasty', *Journal of Bone and Joint Surgery*, 91: 2617–2621.

Campbell, E G, S R Rao, C M DesRoches, L I Iezzoni, C Vogeli, D Bolcic-Jankovic, and P D Miralles. 2010. 'Physician professionalism and changes in physician-industry relationships from 2004 to 2009', *Archives of Internal Medine*, 170: 1820–1826.

Carreyrou, J. 2018. *Bad Blood: Secrets and Lies In a Silicon Valley Startup* (Vintage Books: New York) 341pp.

Chien, S. 2011. 'A brief history of the bioengineering institute of California and the UC System-wide symposia', *Annals of Biomedical Engineering*, 39: 1156–1162.

Cobert J W., Jr. 1949. 'Review of animal experimentation in infectious hepatitis and in serum hepatitis', *Yale Journal of Biology and Medicine*, 21: 335–343.

Cockbain, J, and S Sterckx. 2020. 'Patenting foundational technologies: Recent developments in the CRISPR patent struggle', *The American Journal of Bioethics*, 20: 11–12.

Cohen, A. 2017. *Imbecile: The Supreme Court, American Eugenics, and the Sterilization of Carrie Buck* (Penguin Books: NY) 432pp.

Cohen, D. 2011. 'Out of joint: The story of the ASR', *British Medical Journal*, 342: d2905–d2912.

Cohen, S. 2004. *The Nature of Moral Reasoning* (Oxford U. Press: Oxford) 432pp.

Cooper, D K C. 2017. 'Early clinical xenotransplantation experiences--interview with Thomas E. Starzl, MD, PhD', *Xenotransplantation*, 24: e12306–e12312.

Crosby, A W. 1976. 'Virgin soil epidemics as a factor in the aboriginal depopulation in America', *The William and Mary Quarterly*, 33: 289–299.

Darwin, C. 1859. *On the Origin of Species* (John Murray: London) 490pp.

Davis, M. 2009. 'Is engineering a profession everywhere?', *Philosophia*, 37: 211–225.

de Waal, F. 1997. *Good Natured* (Harvard U. Press) 296pp.

Dean-Jones, L. 2003. 'Literacy and the charlatan in ancient Greek medicine,' in H Yunis (ed.), *Written Texts and Rise of Literate Culture in Ancient Greece* (Cambridge U. Press: Cambridge) Ch. 5, 97–121.

DeVita Jr, V T, and E Chu. 2008. 'A history of cancer chemotherapy', *Cancer Research*, 68: 8643–8653.

Diamond, J. 1999. *Guns, Germs, and Steel: The Fates of Human Societies* (Norton: NY) 494pp.

Dowie, M. 1977. 'Pinto madness', *Mother Jones*, 2: 18–32.

Dyer, G S M, and M E L Thorndike. 2000. '*Quidne Mortui Vivos Docent?* The evolving purpose of human dissection in medical education', *Academic Medicine*, 75: 969–979.

Dyson, P. 2000. 'Holocaust on Trial', Public Broadcasting System, Accessed January 24. http://www.pbs.org/wgbh/nova/holocaust/experiside.html.

English, V, G Romano-Critchley, J Sheather, and A Sommerville. 2002. 'Born to be a donor?', *Journal of Medical Ethics*, 27: 384.

Faber, P. 2003. 'Client and Professional,' in Rowan J and S Jr Zinaich (eds.), *Ethics For the Professions* (Wadsworth/Thomson Learning: Belmont) 125–134.

FDA. 2020. 'PMA Originals Filed As Of 09/30/2020 Average Time to MDUFA Decision', Food and Drug Administration, Accessed June 15, 2021. file:///Users/hwinet/Downloads/4th%20Q%20FY2020%20MDUFA%20IV%20Performance%20Report%20Industry%20Meeting.pdf.

Feynman, R P. 1999. *The Pleasure of Finding Things Out* (Basic Books: NY) 270pp.

Firestein, S. 2012. *Ignorance* (Oxford U. Press: NY) 195pp.

Fox, D M. 1987. 'The politics of the NIH Extramural Program, 1937-1950', *Journal of the History of Medicine and Allied Sciences*, 42: 447–466.

Fries, R. 2005. *Reliable Design of Medical Devices* (CRC: Taylor & Francis: Boca Raton).

References

239

Gamble, V N. 1999. 'Under the shadow of Tuskegee: African Americans and health care,' in Beauchamp TL and L Walters (eds.), *Contemporary Issues in Bioethics* (Wadsworth: Belmont, CA) 78–84.

Gilbert, L A, M H Larson, L Morsut, Z Liu, G A Brar, S E Torres, N Stern-Ginossar, O Brandman, E H Whitehead, J A Doudna, W A Lim, J S Weissman, and L S Qi. 2013. 'CRISPR-mediated modular RNA-guided regulation of transcription in eukaryotes', *Cwll*, 154: 442–451.

Gilligan, c. 1982. *In a Different Voice* (Harvard U. Press: Cambridge) 216pp.

Gimpel, J. 1978. *The Medieval Machine* (Holt, Rinehart & Winston: New York) 263pp.

Goettner-Abendroth, H. 2012. *Matriarchal Societies* (Peter Lang Publishing) 533pp.

Goldman, S L. 2006. 'Science Wars: What Scientists Know and How They Know It,' in *Science and Mathematics* (The Teaching Company: Chantilly, VA).

Goodstein, D. 2010. *On Fact and Fraud* (Princeton U. Press: Princeton) 168pp.

Gorlin, R A (ed.). 1990. *Codes of Professional Responsibility* (The Bureau of National Affairs: Washington).

Gott, V L, D E Alejo, and D E Cameron. 2003. 'Mechanical heart valves: 50 years of evolution', *The Annals of Thoracic Surgury*, 76: S2230–S2239.

Gould, S J. 1997. 'The exaptive excellence of spandrels as a term and prototype', *Proceedings of the National Academy of Sciences, USA*, 94: 10750–10755.

Gould, S J. 1999. *Rocks of Ages* (Ballantine Books: New York) 222pp.

Gould, S J, and R C Lewontin. 1979. 'The spandrels of San Marco and the Panglossian paradigm: a critique of the adaptationist programme.', *Proceedings of the Royal Society of London B*, 205: 581–598.

Grimm, P. 2005. *Questions of Value* (The Teaching Company: Chantily) 154pp.

Gross, C. 2015. 'Scientific Misconduct', *Annual Review of Psychology*, 15: 4.1–4.19.

Hamilton, W D. 1964a. 'The genetical evolution of social behavior: I.', *Journal of Theoretical Biology*, 7: 1–16.

Hamilton, W D. 1964b. 'The genetical evolution of social behavior: II', *Journal of Theoretical Biology*, 7: 17–52.

Harari, Y N. 2015. *Sapiens: A Brief History of Humankind* (Harper Collins: NY) 443pp.

Harris, S H. 1994. *Factories of Death: Japanese Biological Warfare 1932-45 and the American Cover-Up* (Routledge: New York) 373pp.

Heller, J. 1972. 'Syphilis victims in U.S. study went untreated for 40 years', *N.Y. Times*, July 26.

Herkert, J R. 2005. 'Ways of thinking about and teaching ethical problem solving: Microethics and Macroethics in engineering', *Science and Engineering Ethics*, 11: 373–385.

Hill, A B. 1965. 'The environment and disease: Association or causation?', *Proceedings of the Royal Society of Medicine—London*, 58: 295–300.

Hiltzik, M. 2015. *Big Science* (Simon & Schuster: NY) 528pp.

Hockenberry, J M, P Weigel, A Auerbach, and P Cram. 2011. 'Financial payments by orthopaedic device makers to orthopaedic surgeons', *Archives of Internal Medine*, 171: 1759–1765.

Höfler, M. 2005. 'The Bradford Hill considerations on causality: a counterfactual perspective', *Emerging Themes in Epidemiology*, 2(11)9.

Hofstadter, R. 1944. *Social Darwinism iin American Thought* (George Braziller: NY) 248pp.

Holton, G. 1952. *Introduction to Concepts and Theories in Physical Science* (Addison-Wesley: Reading) 650pp.

Hooper, L L 2001. *Neutral Science Panels: Two examples of Court-Appointed Experts in the Breast Implants Product Liability Litigation* (U. Michigan Library: Ann Arbor) 120pp.

Hull, C L. 1943. *Principles of Behavior* (Appleton Century: New York) 422pp.

240 References

Hume, D. 1748. *An Enquiry Concerning Human Understanding* (Independently Published: Edinburgh) 124pp.

Ingold, T. 1998. 'The Evolution of Society,' in A.C. Fabian (ed.), *Evolution: Society, Science and the Universe* (University Press: Cambridge) 79–99.

Jinek, M, K Chylinski, L Fonfara, M Hauer, J A Doudna, and E Charpentier. 2012. 'A progammable dual RNA-guided DNA endonuclease in adaptive bacterial immunity', *Science*, 337: 816–821.

Jones, R W, A Parker, and M Elstein. 1973. 'Clinical experience with the Dalkon Shield intrauterine device', *British Medical Journal*, 3: 143–145.

Juengst, E, M L McGowen, J R Fishman, and R A Settersten. 2016. 'From "Personalized" to "Precision" medicine: The ethical and social implications of rhetorical reform in genomic medicine', *Hastings Center Report*, 46: 21–33.

Kant, E. 1998. *Critique of Pure Reason* (Cambridge U. Press: Cambridge) 785pp.

Katz, J. 1972. 'The Jewish Chronic Disease Hospital Case', in J Katz (ed.), *Experimentation with Human Beings* (Russell Sage Foundation: NY) Ch. 1: 9–65.

Kennedy, D. 2006. 'Editorian retraction', *Science*, 311: 335–336.

Kennerly, S W, M E Walton, T E J Behrens, M J Buckley, and M F S Rushworth. 2006. 'Optimal decision making and the anterior cingulate cortex', *Nature Neuroscience*, 9: 940–947.

Larson, E J. 2002. *The Theory of Evolution: A History of Controversy* (The Teaching Company: Chantily).

Lassman, T C. 2005. 'Government science in postwar America: Henry A Wallace, Edward U. Condon, and the transformation of the National Bureau of Standards, 1945-1951', *Isis*, 96: 25–51.

Lee, B C, M K Kim, G Jang, H J Oh, F Yuda, H J Kim, M H Shamim, J J Kim, S K Kang, G Schatten, and W S Hwang. 2005. 'Dogs cloned from adult somatic cells', *Nature*, 436: 641.

Lee, J. 2003. 'Innovation and strategic divergence: An empirical study of the U.S. pharmaceutical industry from 1920 to 1960 ', *Management Science*, 49: 143–159.

Lee, T L, and M D Ermann. 1999. 'Pinto "Madness" as a flawed landmark narrative: An organizational and network analysis', *Social Problems*, 46: 30–47.

Leicester, H M. 1956. *The Historical Background of Chemistry* (Dover Publications, Inc.: NY) 260pp.

Lindberg, D C. 2002. 'Medieval science and religion', in G B Ferngren (ed.), *Science and Religion* (Johns Hopkins U. Press: Baltimore) Ch. 5: 57–72.

Lopez, C-A. 1993. 'Franklin and Mesmer: an encounter', *Yale Journal of Biology and Medicine*, 66: 325–331.

Löwy, I. 2011. 'Historiography of biomedicine', *Isis*, 102: 116–122.

Luk, A, K-D Lim, R Siddiqui, S Gupta, B W Gilbert, S E Fremes, and J Butany. 2010. 'A Braunwald-Cutter valve: a mitral prosthesis at 33 years', *Cardiovascular Pathology*, 19: E39–E42.

MacArthur Clark, J. 2008. 'Alternative research and practice supported by international veterinary professionals', *AATEX*, 14: 21–27.

Malerba, F, and L Orsenigo. 2001. "Innovation and market structure in the dynamics of pharmaceutical industry and biotechnology: Towards a history friendly model." In *DRUID (Danish Research Unit for Industrial Dynamics) Nelson and Winter Conference*. Aalborg.

Marchalik, D, and A Jurecic. 2015. 'We, the animals', *Lancet*, 386: 2132.

Marquès-Bonet, T, O A Ryder, and E E Eichler. 2009. 'Sequequencing primate genomes: What have we learned?', *Annu. Rev. Genomics Hum. Genet*, 10: 355–386.

References   **241**

Martin, B. 2007. 'Unnecessary Cardiac Procedures II', University of Wollongong, Accessed May 22, 2017. www.uow.edu.au/~bmartin/dissent/documents/health/tenet_reddingupdate.html.

Martinson, B C, M S Anderson, and R de Vries. 2005. 'Scientists behaving badly', *Nature* 435: 1662–1663.

Matfield, M. 2002. 'Animal experimentation: The continuing debate', *Nature Reviews Drug Discovery*, 1: 149–152.

Mayesh, J P, and M F Scranton. 2004. 'Legal aspects of biomaterials', in B D Ratner, A S Hoffman, F J Schoen and J E Lemons (eds.), *Biomaterials Science* (Elsevier: San Diego) 797-804.

McCoy, T. 2015. 'The Disneyland measles outbreak and the disgraced doctor who whipped up vaccination fear', *Washigton Post*, 01/23/15.

McCullough, D. 1977. *The Path Between the Seas* (Simon & Schuster: NY) 698pp.

Mcpherson, C W, and S F Mattingly (eds.). 1999. *50 Years of Laboratory Animal Science* (American Association for Laboratory Animal Science: Memphis) 174pp.

Menn, S. 1992. 'Aristotle and Plato on God as Nous and as the Good', *The Review of Metaphysics*, 45: 543–573.

Millar, D, I Millar, J Millar, and M Millar. 1996. *The Cambridge Dictionary of Scientists* (Cambridge U. Press: Cambridge) 387pp.

Morens, D M, J K Taubenberger, H A Harvey, and M J Memoli. 2010. 'The 1918 influenza epidemic: Lessons for 2009 and the future', *Critical Care Medicine*, 38: 1–21.

Mukherjee, S. 2011. *The Emperor of All Maladies: A Biography of Cancer* (Simon & Schuster: NY) 592pp.

Munsey, R R. 1995. 'Trends and events in FDA regulation of medical devices over the last fifty years', *Food and Drug Law Journal*, 50: 163–177.

Murphy, T F (ed.). 2004. *Case Studies in Biomedical Research Ethics* (MIT Press: Cambridge, MA) 340pp.

NAS, Committee on Science Engineering and Public Policy. 2009. *On Being a Scientist* (National Academy of Sciences: Washington) 63pp.

New, M I. 1993. 'Pope Joan: a recognizable syndrome', *Transactions on American Clinical and Climatological Association*, 104: 104–122.

Newton, L H. 2004. *Ethics in America: Study Guide* (Annenberg/CPB: Upper Saddle River) 243pp.

Nix, E. 2017. 'The infamous, 40-year Tuskegee study', A+ENetworks, Accessed Jan.22.

Nordenskiöld, E. 1928. *The History of Biology* (Tudor: NY) 654pp.

Orfanos, S D. 2006. '*Mythos* and *Logos*', *Psychoanalytic Dialogues*, 15: 481–499.

Parker, S. 2019. *A Short History of Medicine* (Penguin Random House: London) 400pp.

Parodi, A, D Neasham, and P Vineis. 2006. 'Environment, population, and biology: a short history of modern epidemiology', *Perspectives in Biology and Medicine*, 49: 357–368.

Peake, J B, J S Morrison, M M Ledgerwood, and S E Gannon. 2011. 'The defense department's enduring contributions to global health,' in *Report of the CSIS Global Health Policy Center*. Washington: Center for Strategic and International Studies.

Pence, G E. 1995. 'The Tuskegee study,' in G E Pence (ed.), *Classic Cases in Medical Ethics* (McGraw-Hill: New York) 463–469.

Perl, E D. 1998. 'The demiurge and the forms: A return to the ancient interpretation of Plato's *Timaeus*', *Ancient Philosophy*, 18: 81–92.

Perri, A. 2016. 'A wolf in dogs clothing: Initial dog domestication and Pleistocene wolf variation', *Journal of Archeological Science*, 68: 1–4.

Peterson, J C, and D Farell. 1986. *Whistleblowing: Ethical and Legal Issues in Expressing Dissent* (Kendall Hunt: Dubuque) 48pp.

Phillips, M T, and J A Sechzer. 1989. *Animal Research and Ethical Conflict* (Springer-Verlag: New York) 251pp.

Pickstone, J V. 2011. 'Sketching together the modern histories of science, technology and medicine', *Isis*, 102: 123–133.

Popper, K R. 1959. *The Logic of Scientific Disovery* (Hutchinson: London) 493pp.

Principe, L M. 2002. "Course Guidebook: History of Science: Antiquity to 1700." In. Chantilly, VA: The Teaching Company, 3 Parts 175pp.

Ran, F A, P D Hsu, J Wright, V Agarwala, D A Scott, and F Zhang. 2013. 'Genome engineering using the CRISPR-Cas9 system', *Nature Protocols*, 8: 2281–2308.

Reiss, S. 2004. 'Multifaceted nature of intrinsic motivation: The theory of 16 basic desires', *Rev. Gen. Psychol.*, 8: 175–193.

Requena-Carrión, J, and R S Leder. 2009. "The natural history of the Engineering in Medicine and Biology Society from a modern perspective." In *31st Annual International Conference of the IEEE EMBS*. Minneapolis: IEEE.

Reynolds, T S. 1991a. 'The engineer in 19th century America.' in T S Reynolds (ed.), *The Engineer in America* (U. Chicago Press: Chicago) Overview: 7-26.

Reynolds, T S. 1991b. 'The engineer in 20th-century America.' in T S Reynolds (ed.), *The Engineer in America* (University of Chicago Press: Chicago) Overview: 169–190.

Robbins, J (ed.). 1999. *The Pleasure of Finding Things Out. The Best Short Works of Richard P. Feynman* (Basic Books: New York).

Rodwin, M A. 1994. 'Patient accountability and quality of care: Lessons from medical consumerism and the patients' rights, women's health and disability rights movements', *American Journal of Law and Medicine*, 20: 147–168.

Rosen, G, A Byrne, J Cohen, E Harman, and S Shiffrin. 2018. *The Norton Introduction to Philosophy* (W.W. Norton & Co.: NY) 1312pp.

Ross, S. 1962. 'Scientist: The story of a word', *Annals of Science*, 18(2): 65–88.

Rothman, D J. 1991. *Strangers at the Bedside* (Basic Books: New Brunswick) 313pp.

Rowan, J. 2003. 'The moral foundation of employee rights.' in J Rowan and S Jr Zinaich (eds.), *Ethics for the Professions* (Wadsworth/Thomson Learning: Belmont) Ch. 3: 90–96.

Rowan, J, and S Jr Zinaich. 2003. *Ethics for the Professions* (Wadsworth: Australia) 445pp.

Russell, W M S, and R L Burch. 1959. *The Principles of Humane Experimental Technique* (C.C. Thomas: Springfield, IL) 238pp.

Salsman, J, and G Dellaire. 2016. 'Precision genome editing in the CRISPR era', *Biochemistry and Cell Biology*, 95: 187–201.

Schleiter, K E. 2010. 'Silicone breast implant litigation', *American Medical Association Journal of Ethics*, 12: 389–394.

Schoen, E J, P A Lewis, and J S Falchek. 2012. 'Conflicted research: Medical scientists on the payroll', *Southern Law School Journal*, 22: 269–304.

Sherkow, J S. 2018. 'The CRISPR patent decision didn't get the science right. That doesn't mean it was wrong.', New York Law School, Accessed May11. https://digitalcommons.nyls.edu/fac_other_pubs/363.

Shivayogi, P. 2013. 'Vulnerable population and methods for their safeguard', *Perspectives in Clinical Research*, 4: 53–57.

Shorey, P, and Plato. 1953. *Plato's Republic* (Harvard U. Press) v. 2 592pp.

Sidell, F R, E T Takafuji, and D R Franz (ed.). 1997. *Medical Aspects of Chemical and Biological Warfare* (Office of Surgeon General, U.S. Army: Washington) 721pp.

SKAPP. 2003. "Daubert: The Most Influential Supreme Court Ruling You've Never Heard Of." In *Project on Scientific Knowledge and Public Policy*, edited by Tellus Institute. Cambridge, MA: Tellus Institute 24pp.

Smith, A G R. 1972. *Science and Society in the Sixteenth and Seventeenth Centuries* (Science History Publications: NY) 216pp.

Smith, R R, and Lodder. 2013. 'When does a nanotechnology device become a drug?', *Journal of Developing Drugs*, 2: 1–2.

References

Sobol, R B. 1991. *Bending the Law: The Story of the Dalkon Shield Bankrupcy* (Universithy of Chicago Press: Chicago) 408pp.

Sontheimer, E J, and R Barrangou. 2015. 'The bacterial origins of the CRISPR genome-editing revolution', *Human Gene Therapy*, 25: 413–424.

Stearns, S C. 1987. 'Introduction.' in S C Stearns (ed.), The Evolution of Sex and Its Consequences (Springer: Basel) 15–32.

Stevenson, A (ed.). 2010. *Oxford Dictionary of English* (Oxford U. Press: Oxford) 2112pp.

Supady, J. 2020. 'Ancient Greek medicine during Hellenistic Age and the Roman Empire', *Health Promotion & Physical Activity*, 2: 28–34.

Swain, D S. 1962. 'The rise of a research empire, NIH, 1930-1950', *Science*, 138: 1233–1237.

Templeton, J S. 1972. 'Pharmacologically active I.U.D.s', *British Medical Journal*, 2: 633.

Thomas, P, L R Braathen, M Dorig, J Aubök, F Nestle, T Werfel, and H G Willert. 2009. 'Increased metal allergy in patients with failed metal-on-metal hip arthroplasty and peri-implant T-lymphocytic inflammation', *Allergy*, 64: 1157–1165.

Walker, L, H LeVine, and M Jucker. 2006. 'Koch's postulates and infectious proteins', *Acta Neuropathol.*, 112: 1–4.

Waterlow, S. 1982. *Nature, Change, and Agency in Aristotle's Physics* (Oxford U. Press: NY) 269pp.

Wathen, R L. 1999. 'Multiphasic device testing.' in A F von Recum (ed.), *Handbook of Biomaterials Evaluation* (CRC: Taylor & Francis: Boca Raton) 839–848.

Watson, J D. 2005. 'Foreword.' in J D Watson (ed.), *Darwin: The Indelible Stamp* (Running Press: Philadelphia) vii–xiv.

Waxman, H A. 2005. 'The lessons of Vioxx—drug safety and sales', *New England Journal of Medicine*, 352: 2576–2578.

Weber, B G. 1989. '[Polyethylene wear and late loosening of a total prosthesis of the hip joint. New perspectives for metal/metal pairing of the capsule and head] in German', *Der Orthopade*, 18: 370–376.

White, R D. 2003. 'Former heart patients sue Tenet', *L.A. Times*, August 16.

WHO. 2014. "Global Alert and Response." In. Geneva. Switzerland: World Health Organization.

Willert, H G, G H Buchhorn, A Fayyazi, R Flurey, M Windler, G Koster, and C H Lohmann. 2005. 'Metal-on-metal bearings and hypersensitivity in patients with artificial hip-joints: A clinical and histomorphological study', *J. Bone Jt. Surg. A*, 87: 28–36.

Woodward, J, and D Goodstein. 1996. 'Conduct, misconduct and the structure of science', *American Scientist*, 84: 479–490.

Worboys, M. 2011. 'Practice and the science of medicine in the nineteenth century', *Isis*, 102: 1–9-115.

Working, R. 2001. 'The trial of unit 731', *The Japan Times*, June 5, 2001.

Yücel, M, C Pantelis, G W Stuart, S J Wood, P Maruff, D Velakoulis, A Pipingas, S F Crowe, H J Tochon-Danguy, and G F Egan. 2007. 'Anterior cinculate activation during stroop task performance: A PET to MRO coregistration study of individual patients with schizophrenia', *American Journal of Psychiatry*, 159: 251–254.

Glossary

3R's of animal research	replace animals with alternative where feasible. Reduce the number of animals used to a statistically valid minimum. Refine experiments to minimize animal stress.
19-nor-17a-ethynyltestosterone	the active component of the Djerassi contraceptive pill.
510(k)	the application to the FDA for pre-market approval to start the process of seeking approval for a device.
actual duty	the final decision, in Rossian deontology, of which duty takes priority, when faced with conflicting duties.
act-utilitarianism	version of utilitarianism associated with Bentham, according to which the measure of the value of an act is the amount by which it increases general utility or happiness. An act is to be preferred to its alternatives according to the extent of the increase it achieves, compared to the extent the alternatives would achieve. An action is thus good or bad in proportion to the amount it increases (or diminishes) general happiness, compared to the amount that could have been achieved by acting differently. Act utilitarianism is distinctive not only in the stress on utility, but also in the fact that each individual action is the primary object of ethical evaluation.
adaptationism	the evolutionary notion that traits that are naturally selected are those best adapted so far, for the environment in which an organism resides.
affinity relationship	a client–professional relationship in which trust arises from the two participants belonging to the same social group; i.e. religion, race, gender, family, nationality, etc.
"after the fact" regulation	using the Department of Justice to restrict a food or medical product after it has been found to be unsafe in humans, rather than having it tested by the FDA before marketing.
agency relationship	a client–professional relationship in which the professional may advise but has minimal responsibility for advising about or implementing decisions.
alchemy	from the Arabic for "The Chemistry". Early chemistry, occupied with transmutation.
allocative efficiency	the degree to which goods are traded in such a way that both the giver and the receiver feel they have benefited.
allogeneic	for transplants: from a nongenetically identical member of the same species.
altruism	unselfish consideration of, or devotion to the well-being of others.*

(Continued)

Altruism equation	the mathematical form of Hamilton's rule in sociobiology.
amicus curiae	"friend of the court" information from someone who is not part of the case.
analytic	logically true or necessary, or reducible by definition to logical truth.*
ancient period	the historic age from 15,000 to 2,500 years ago.
animal magnetism	the name Francis Mesmer gave to the electromagnetic field created by his generator that he claimed had curative powers.
animal rights	legal obligations owed to nonhuman animals.
Animal Welfare Act	the law listing regulations for the treatment of animals used in laboratory animal research (AWA).
anterior cingulate cortex	a region of the brain hypothalamus which evidence suggests is crucial for learning the value of actions.
anthropomorphic	assuming that nonhuman animals can think like humans.
Aristotelianism	the belief in the secular philosophy of Aristotle that focused on how we gain knowledge of the world.
ALVAL	Aseptic Lymphocytic Vasculitis and Associated Lesions. An inflammatory condition associated with the DePuy metal-on-metal hip implant.
Astrolabe	a device used in navigation that measured distances and objects in the night sky.
Asus	Babylonian healers who were familiar with herbal potions an other empirical treatments for ailments.
autism	a developmental neurological disorder causing difficulty with social interactions and communication.
autogeneic	for transplants: from a genetically identical source.
autoimmune response	activation of the adaptive immune system to attack host(self) epitopes.
automatic train control system	a traffic regulating program, used with subways that coordinates train speeds and door closings. part of BART (ATC).
autonomy	the power to make moral choices and be self-governing; an ethical principle based on the union of rationality and freedom.*
autonomy competence (patient)	the degree to which a patient is mentally able to be autonomous.
axiology	that field of philosophy devoted to the study of value.‡
axiom	a claim accepted as a premise without proof and from which are derived theorems.‡
Bacillus anthracis	the causative bacterium for anthrax.
Bayh-Dole Act of 1980	law that made it lawful for universities that developed products from government funded research to patent and profit from them.
Belmont Report	a report generated by the National Commission for the Protection of Human Subjects of Biomedical and Behavioral Research that proposed all research using

Glossary

247

	humans demonstrate respect for persons, beneficence and justice.
beneficence	an ethical principle of helping others wherever possible; active goodness, kindness, or charity.*
Big Science	scientific enterprise that takes place in large laboratories, with large research teams, and at great expense.
biologics	Implanted devices products produced by a living things.
Biologics Control Act	a 1902 law that banned the use of contaminated biologics.
bioreactor	a device that carries living cells that perform a biological function.
Black death	Bubonic plague. Caused by the bacterium *Yersinia pestis*.
blinded	In research, the group of human subjects who are not allowed to sense the stimulus being measured or know the information to which other groups are exposed.
bloodletting	a medical procedure thought to prevent disease by opening a vein and allowing it to drain blood for a specified time. Phlebotomy
bonding	a form of attracting behavior stimulated by receptive actions between primates.
Bonobos	apes, closely related to humans, who form matriarchal societies.
Bradford Hill's criteria	nine conditions that must be met if data correlation is to be considered strong enough to suggest a causal connection. If they are met, medical policy, dependent on their being met, should be activated.
Braunwald-Cutter caged ball valve	an artificial heart valve with a silastic ball in a metal cage.
Bubonic plague	Black plague.
cardiac catheterization	an angiogram procedure during which a long catheter is inserted in the femoral artery and guided to a coronary artery.
Cas nuclease	one of nucleic acid hydrolyzing enzymes use by CRISPR.
Cas9	the most successful editing nuclease to partner with CRISPR.
case control study	a retrospective epidemiological study of at least two populations, usually one with a particular condition and another without it, serving as a control. The goal is usually to find an agent highly correlated with the first population and absent in the control (e.g. tobacco for smokers vs its absence in nonsmokers).
categorical imperative	an ethical requirement that binds anybody, regardless of his or her inclinations. It could be represented as, for example: 'Tell the truth! (regardless of whether you want to or not)'. The core moral principle of Kant's ethics: Act only such that you could will the maxim of your action to become a universal law.

(Continued)

248 Glossary

causal science — the scientific approach that seeks an understanding of the natural world.

causation — the process by which effect is philosophically linked to cause.

Challenger — the NASA space shuttle that exploded on January 28, 1986, killing all its passengers.

Chi-square test — a measure of the "goodness-of-fit" of the predicted frequency of an event or other data measure to the actual measured values.

Cholera epidemic, London, 1854 — the event that caused John Snow to develop epidemiology.

chronic inflammation — an inflammatory response that lasts much longer than normal healing.

Chronic studies — research of biological events that last over long periods of time.

civil court — The trial venue in which disputes are settled. Not concerned with crimes, as are criminal courts.

Class I devices — nonlife sustaining medical devices that are not in a position to pose a serious threat to the patient.

Class II devices — unless substantially equivalent to approved devices, nonlife sustaining medical devices that could be a threat to the patient if misused.

Class III devices — all devices whose failure puts the life of the patient at risk.

Classical period — 2,500 to 1,600 years ago, covering the Greek and Roman empires.

cloning — growing a living thing from pieces of an existing living thing, thereby making a duplicate.

Clostridium — a genus of bacteria with a number of harmful species.

collective — by, Characteristic of, or relating to, a group of individuals, especially a public group such as social class or a whole society.*

collision price — the total amount that the collision of one of their cars would cost the company. Used in risk analysis by Ford in the Pinto case.

community — any organization that exercises limited political authority over a small region, such as a town or village; in ethics, a pattern of life where collective demands and interpersonal relations are as important as individual goals and choices.*

community standards — the baseline reference for acceptable behavior in any group/community.

Compound atom — a concept of John Dalton before "molecule" devised. The structure formed by combining two or more atoms.

Condemnation of 1277 — an inquisition-type document, testifying to 219 propositions, in conflict with the bible and attributed to Aristotle, that had been illegally discussed in the universities.

confidentiality — severely limiting dissemination of information about an individual

Glossary

249

conflict of interest	a situation wherein there is a risk that professional decisions regarding a primary **interest** will be unduly influenced by a secondary **interest.**
conflict resolution	one of the social mechanisms of group dynamics that diffuses internal conflict within the group.
confounding variable	a parameter in a complex system that varies in an unpredictable manner making it difficult to quantify events in the system's behavior so as to see a pattern.
congenital malformation	a physical defect that has been present since birth.
consent form	the questionnaire for an informed consent.
consequential moral theory	any theory of ethics that holds that the moral value of an action is determined entirely by the consequences of that action.‡
contractarian ethics	a moral theory that is focused on a hypothetical agreement about how to behave; is concerned with original positions to be taken in setting up the agreement.
contractual relationship	a client-professional form if relationship based on a formal agreement that specifies the role of each participant.
contingent attributes	chance human conditions which determine circumstance into which one is born.
contraindications	applications for which the medicine in question should not be used for safety reasons.
controlled experiment	an experiment that has a cohort not exposed to the experimental treatment.
controlled-release	drug release at a constant rate, usually slowly.
conversion liability (in law)	in biotechnology: The technical law term for the unauthorized use of one person's property in a way that causes him loss; as was alleged in Moore v. University of California Regents.
copyright	the exclusive legal right, given to an originator or an assignee to print, publish, perform, film, or record literary, artistic, or musical material, and to authorize others to do the same.
correlation	the degree to which two variables are related. They may not be causally related however as in the case where a number of events occur at the same time but are caused by one common event.
corroboration	subject a hypothesis to tests that have failed to disproved it.
counterfactually causal	a Bradford Hill concept that states that a relationship between an agent and an effect can be identified with this term in place of it being strictly causal, for medical purposes.
course of treatment	the directions that should be followed for treating a patient for a given condition.
COVID-19	the influenza caused by the SARS-CoV-2 virus.

(Continued)

COX-2	Cyclooxygenase-2, an enzyme that catalyzes the Arachidonic Acid cascade, leading to inflammation.
craftsmen	individuals who performed jobs usually listed as "crafts".
criminal proceedings	trials for those accused of being felons.
criminally liable	subject to be tried as a felon.
CRISPR	a segment found in the genome of some bacteria that consists of Clustered-Regularly-Interspaced-Short-Palindromic-Repeats.
CRISPR RNA	the transcribed form of CRISPR created by the host cell (in the case of the attacked bacterium) during adaptive immunity or created in the lab artificially.
CRISPR RNA-Cas system	the attack form of CRISPR, with the Cas marker for any Cas nuclease.
CRISPR-Cas9 system	the attack form of CRISPR, with Cas9 that is most common for gene editing.
Critique of Pure Reason	the attack of Emmanuel Kant on the logic of "knowing" just because it has been achieved by reason.
cronyism	the practice of directing one's business to one's friends rather than choosing the best product or service.
Cruelty to Animals Act, 1876	the first British laws regulating treatment of nonhuman animals.
curve-fitting	a statistical technique for developing the curve-generating function that best expresses the observed relationship of two measures. e.g. Time and concentration, Dose and height, etc.
Dalkon Shield	an intrauterine device marketed by A.H. Robins in 1971.
Daubert	a reference to a Supreme Court decision in 1993, Daubert v. Merrill Dow, in which criteria were set up for deciding how federal judges are to determine if an expert witness's testimony is relevant to the case at hand.
Darwinism	a theory of organic evolution developed by Charles Darwin and others stating that biological species develop from pre-existing species through the natural selection and accumulation of hereditary variations in individual organisms.**
deafferented limbs	limbs that have had severe damage to their afferent nerves.
deductive reasoning	a pattern of reasoning that deduces a conclusion by strictly logical means. Deductive reasoning is characteristic of mathematics.‡
De Humani Corporis Fabrica	Andreas Vesalius' anatomical publication that corrected Galen.
Demigod	a human with god-like character.
Demiurge	a Platonic spiritual entity responsible for creation of the universe.
deontological ethics	any moral theory that holds that morality is determined by moral principles above and beyond the considerations of consequences. Any moral theory that admits a source of

Glossary

251

	morality beyond (or in addition to) consideration of consequences, however, will also count as deontological.[‡]
De Revolutionibus Orbium Coelestium, 1543	the publication of Copernicus that postulated a heliocentric universe.
descriptive	used to designate a claim that merely reports a factual state of affairs, rather than evaluating or recommending a course of action.[‡]
determinism	the position that all events are determined and, thus, could not have been otherwise.[‡]
Dialogue on the Two Chief Systems of the World, 1632	the publication of Galileo confirming the conclusions of Copernicus.
ding an sich"	German for "thing in itself" the Kantian concept that he said could never be known.
Diploid state	usually of cells. Having a full complement of chromosomes/genetic material, as is found in somatic cells.
directed beneficence	producing good by improving other people's virtue, intelligence or pleasure.
discovery	in law. The exchange of information requested by the two opposing lawyers prior to trial.
Disputation	a formal academic debate. Part of the scholastic method.
distributive justice	the ethical principle that is concerned with the fair allocation of privileges, duties, and goods within a society in accordance with merit, need, work, or other agreed upon criteria.[*]
doctrine of the mean	Aristotelian stipulation that virtues are habits that are expressed at midlevel between deficiency and excess.
Dogmatics	Greek physicians who based their medicine on reasoning more than observation.
duty	behavior required by moral obligation, whether or not it will make anyone happier, or make us better people.[*]
duty of care	the responsibility to take utmost care in the design and manufacture of a medical device to optimize its safety and efficacy.
dyadic level conflict resolution	conflict resolution between two individuals, the simplest level; the other levels are national and international.
Ebola virus	a filovirus that is highly contagious and deadly, being fatal in at least 40% of the cases.
ECPD Canons of Ethics	Engineers' Council for Professional Development Ethics code that stresses fidelity to the public, one's employers and clients.
editorial retraction	a disowning of a work that has been published in a journal by the editorial staff. It has the effect of cancelling the validity of the work.
efficacy	in parlance of the FDA, ability to perform the function for which it was designed.

(Continued)

egoism ethics	the position that it is ethically right to act only so as to maximize one's own self-interest.[‡]
ELF	Environmental Liberation Front. An animal rights group classified as terrorist by Homeland Security.
empirical statements	factual assertions about the world and our physical environment, verifiable by controlled observation. Experiment, or direct sense experience; usually opposed to theoretical statements.*
empirical science	investigation of the natural world only to the point of high correlation for the purpose of solving problems.
empirical data	a confirmed observation.
Empiricism	the philosophy that knowing must be based on sensory input.
Endless Frontier	Vannevar Bush's hopeful epithet for the future of science.
The enlightenment	the period of European thought characterized by the emphasis on experience and reason, mistrust of religion and traditional authority, and gradual emergence of the ideals of liberal, secular and democratic societies.***
environmental pressure	in evolutionary theory, the challenges to their existence presented to every living organism.
epidemiology	the statistics of association that is the basis for predicting the occurrence of one variable from the incidence of another. The association relationship of the two variables tends to occur more often than chance would explain. An association that has been demonstrated to be epidemiologically established at a high level of statistical confidence is more valid than an anecdotal association.
Epistêmê	scientific knowledge that focuses on explaining. "how come".
Epistemism	a moral theory that places increase of knowledge as the highest priority.
epistemology	the field of philosophy concerned with the theory of knowledge.*
ethical egoism	the belief that the only principle you should use to guide your life is the principle of advantage to yourself.*
ethics	the study and evaluation of human conduct in light of moral principles.*
etiology	the development of or the study of the development of a particular diseased state
eugenics	a theory of applied science, popular during the early-20th century, that sought to improve the human race by encouraging breeding by supposedly superior individuals and discouraging breeding by supposedly inferior ones.**
Eukaryotes	organisms containing cells with nuclei and having DNA-based genetics.
European translation movement	a quest (1125-1200) in Latin Europe to translate ancient Greek philosophical works for use in the universities being developed by Charlemagne.

Glossary

evidence-based medicine	medical practice grounded in the latest scientific evidence.
evolution, organic	the scientific theory that new species evolve from pre-existing species through gradual change rather than being abruptly created.**
evolutionary psychology	the study of animal behavior evolution for clues to the sources of human social behavior.
executive branch	the branch of the government assigned the carrying out of laws.
experimenting ON"	using the subject for testing. Purely empirical, not science.
Extramural research	performing research outside the company.
fabrication of data	creation of false data where there were none before.
falsifiable hypothesis	a prediction that can be directly disproven.
failure to warn	A company is liable if they have evidence that theirs is an unsafe product, and fail to warn owners.
False Claims Act	law that protects insurance companies from fraudulent claims.
falsification of data	alteration of data to fit predictions.
FCA award	award to whistleblowers for revealing false claims to insurance companies.
FDA Modernization Act of 1997	required the FDA to expedite review of products deemed to be urgently needed. Fast tracking.
Federal Food, Drug and Cosmetic Act 1938	FDA could enforce regulations for interstate products. Devices subject to regulation. Drugs could not be misbranded or adulterated.
feeblemindedness	used as a target for nonvoluntary sterilization in a number of states.
felony	a crime often involving violence and punishable by imprisonment.
Feminist Ethics—the Ethics of Care	moral theory based on recognition of differences between males and females.
fertile crescent	a roughly crescent-shaped region which runs from Europe to East Asia through India.
fidelity	faithfulness, support.
fiduciary	involving confidence or trust; a fiduciary obligation is one arising out of trust.*
fiduciary relationship	a client-professional association built on trust, usually secured with a financial agreement.
Fisher's ANOVA	ANalysis Of VAriance. A statistical tool for determining how significant is the difference between measured data and predicted data.
fissioning	splitting of a population into two or more groups upon reaching a triggering size.
Food and Drug Act, 1906	the first legislation defining the role of what was to become the FDA. It required manufacturers to identify the ingredients of their products.

(Continued)

Glossary

fundamental drives	hunger, Thirst, Sex, Avoidance of pain.
future productivity losses	part of the calculation of the monetary value of risk of causing death by a product.
game theory	mathematical models for strategy in human interactions.
gender neutral moral theory	any moral theory that either considers both male and female values or neither's.
general controls	FDA-defined basic characteristics of a device that show the manufacturer is prepared for the evaluation process. They are: 1. Registration of manufacturer in their industry. 2. Listing with FDA of intention to be market device. 3. Confirm device manufactured with GMP. 4. Confirm device labelled according to FDA regulations. 5. Confirm promise and/or record of filing MDRs.
Genome editing	changing the configuration of DNA in living cells using a genetic engineering technique.
Genome sequencing	determining gene sequence in an intact genome.
genomic technology epoch	suggested title for present historical period.
Germ Theory of Disease	Any disease that depends on the growth and reproduction of an invading organism, was caused by infection with that organism, and was not spontaneous.
giant cell reactions	Indicators of a foreign body, giant cells are formed by merging of macrophages that have not been successful in eliminating the invader.
Göbekli Tepi	An anthropological site that is yielding evidence that not all agricultural societies transitioned from hunter-gatherers.
good manufacturing practices	a requirement of the FDA for devices (GMP).
Grassley-Kohl Sunshine Act 2009	an amendment to the Patient Protection and Affordable Care Act that requires public reporting by medical product manufacturers of any annual payments to physicians totaling $100.
gross national product	an economic indicator of the worth of commercial production by a nation for a year (GNP).
group value	a condition for morality development within a species that is driven by dependence on social groups for finding food or defense against enemies and predators.
Guanxi	a form of Chinese cronyism.
Guide for Laboratory Animal Facilities and Care	a publication from NIH that instructed lab personnel in the care and use of lab animals.
guide RNA	an accessory to Cas 9 that is crucial for its editing function.
Guilds	craftsman groups parallel to the societies of professionals.
Hamilton's rule	a statement of the relationship between kinship and altruism; also known as the Altruism equation.
Haploid cells	cells with one member of each chromosome pair, such that they have half the chromosomes of a diploid cell.
Haploid evolution	the sexual component of evolution, starting with formation of the first haploid cells.

Glossary

health-care providers	physicians, nurses, technicians, psychological and social workers that provide care to patients.
Health Information Portability and Accountability Act, 1996	the first comprehensive federal law pertaining to privacy of electronically accessible patient information (HIPAA).
Health Research Extension Act, 1985	directs all institutions receiving HHS funding to develop programs for reporting research fraud (changed to "scientific misconduct" the following year).
Helsinki declaration	a list of recommendations and guidelines for physicians conducting biomedical research involving human subjects that was developed by the World Medical Association.
heteronomy	lack of moral freedom or self-determination; control by others.*
hominid	a primate of a family of upright-walking, relatively large-brained animals of which modern humans is the only surviving species.**
Homo erectus	potential hominid ancestor. Extant 2 million years ago.
Human Genome Project, 2003	mapped the human gene sequence.
humane	with minimum stress and pain (in reference to animal treatment).
Humanist	during the Italian Renaissance it meant unity with nature and was religious. Modern version more atheistic and pro-science activist.
hunger	one of the animal basic drives.
hypothesis	an educated guess.
Iatrogenic	physician caused.
imperative	an act that must be carried out; a duty.*
inductive	a type of argumentation that arrives at a generalization regarding an entire class of things on the basis of observations regarding smaller samples from that class.‡
Industrial Revolution, 1750–1850	(dates controversial). the practical fruits of The Enlightenment are applied as manufacturing changes society.
informed consent	a term used in medical ethics to indicate the patient's approval of a procedure or treatment, based on possession and understanding of all relevant information.*
infringed	broken. Usually said of a trust. In ethics it is an obligation, like confidentiality, that is not fulfilled.
initial obligation of commitment to a client	This is an obligation that a professional is required to fill. The two most basic are autonomy and confidentiality. There is also the serving of a client who has no alternative help. A physician in isolation with a sick person. A lawyer with a defendant who has no defense lawyer.
Institutional Review Board	committee of the institution at which FDA approved devices are implanted, and which must take responsibility for all surgeries (IRB).

(Continued)

Glossary

integrity of the data — a quality of data that ensures it is as representative of what it reports as is humanly possible.

intellectual property — original forms of expression or ideas, for which the right to control belongs to an individual; includes patents, copyrights, trademarks and trade secrets.

interfered — with respect to patents, the claim that one patent has inhibited the ability of another patent to function.

intraocular lens — an implant that replaces the eye lens.

intrinsic value — the value that something has in itself, rather than as a means to something else.[‡]

investigational device exemption — an application to the FDA for permission to conduct clinical trials on a device that has not yet been approved for marketing. Application must first be approved by institution(s) in which the trials will take place.

Italian Renaissance, 1400–1650 — considered to be the "official" Renaissance. Marked by upheavals in the church and flourishing of art.

Jigokudani Park — a nature park in Japan where Mozu lived.

judicial branch — the government branch that determines if an act is "just", as defined by the Constitution.

Julius Rosenwald Foundation — the charity that funded the Tuskegee Project.

Junk science — in jurisprudence, scientific terminology and usage that is not scientifically valid for the issue at hand.

justice — right action: the principle that demands that we subject our actions to rule and that the rule be the same for all.[*]

justice, kinds of — as defined by contractarianism, there are two kinds, distributive and retributive. Distributive concerns the just distribution of benefits and burdens. Retributive concerns balancing of injustices.

Kantian deontology — Kant's version of Deontological moral theory. Proposes strict application of rules relating to duty.

kickbacks — an unrecorded payment, similar to a commission, to a person who has facilitated a transaction.

Koch's postulates — the criteria for establishing that a particular organism is the cause of a particular disease.

laissez faire — an economic and social doctrine that believes in human progress through rugged individual effort unfettered by governmental intervention in the economy or charitable welfare programs.[**]

Latin Europe — in history, the part of Europe that spoke Latin in the Middle Ages.

Latin West — in history, the part of Europe that conquered most of the world, from the 15th century on.

law — an authoritative system for governing human conduct by rules.[*]

legal negligence — a breach of the deontological duty of care.

Glossary

legal responsibilities	the responsibilities defined by regulations, usually of the FDA.
legislative branch	the branch of government that creates and changes laws.
level of confidence	in statistics, level of trust that a falsifiable hypothesis has been disproved.
Levin-Grassley act of 1989	offered limited protection to whistleblowers from retribution. Covered only federal agencies.
liability	a measure of a defendant's vulnerability to legal recovery of damages by a plaintiff; includes negligence unless limited to strict liability.
libertarian	a person who gives priority to the principles of individual liberty and freedom of thought and of action, no matter how unwise the choice may seem to others.*
limbic	region at the posterior cerebral cortex associated with motivation.
litigation	the act of arguing a dispute in civil court.
Little climatic optimum	warming of the climate in Europe, around 750, that is associated with a jump in population and conversion of religious centers into centers of learning.
locator gene	a marker in the genome adjacent to a CRISPR cluster.
logic	the field of philosophy concerned with the validity of argument* and considered the highest form of reasoning.
logical positivism	the philosophy that knowledge based on experience alone—empiricism—is meaningless because perception introduces error into observations; and induction alone cannot lead to understanding. Instead, one must construct a base of conclusions resulting from logical (causal) analyses of data gathered under controlled conditions/experiments, the design of which is based on our understanding of the natural world.
logical statements	formal statement. Statements derivable from definitions, which can be verified by a formal procedure drawn from the definitions that govern the field in question; includes the entirety of mathematical discourse. True formal statements are analytic.*
logos	the Greek concept of knowledge of the natural world and how it is attained.
long-term good	the measure for the goal of rule utilitarianism.
loyalty	in ethics, the principle of fidelity or allegiance to an overarching concept, such as a government, belief, person, country or other principle.*
lymphokine proteins	a secreted protein that has the function of stimulating lymphocytes.
macroethics	the ethics of social issues and policy (as opposed to individual behavior).
maleficence	Seeking to do harm or evil.

(Continued)

Glossary

mean — moderate actions or attitudes appropriately chosen between two extremes; identified with virtue.*

means to an end — a description of how one may view other people in terms of their use. A Kantian concept.

mediated reconciliation — form of involvement of members of a community in resolving conflicts. Consists of encouraging the members of the conflict to resolve.

Medieval period, 400-1400 — marked by rise of Christianity and Islam.

metallosis — inflammatory response to metal particles.

microethics — ethics involving individual decisions as opposed to political policy.

Middle Ages — see Medieval period.

misdemeanor — a legal misdeed that is less serious than a felony.

mitigating factors — considerations that may alter a professional misconduct trial decision.

MMR vaccines — trivalent vaccines for measles, mumps and rubella.

MO cell line — the lymphokine-producing cells harvested from John Moore by David Golde and turned into a profitable lab tool by the latter.

modeling — the formation of a structure analogous to the reality being represented. The structure may be physical or mathematical, as in a function that is capable of being represented by a curve.

molecular genetics — the study of the function of nucleic acids as components of the genome.

***Molecular pathology v. Myriad Genetics Inc.*, 2013** — a patent protection dispute between two companies that found that genetic material with the same DNA sequence as natural material, but having the distinction of having been isolated is not patentable.

moral — pertaining to principles or considerations of right and wrong behavior or good and bad character.*

moral agent — an individual who is capable of acting morally.

moral contract — a commitment to act according to some moral theory, as in an obligation.

moral law — some theories of ethics see the subject in terms of a number of laws. The status of these laws may be that they are the edicts of a divine lawmaker, or they are truths of reason knowable *a priori*.

moral theory — the behavioral guide for ethics derived from a particular philosophy.

morality — a doctrine or system of ideas concerned with imperatives, duties, or right conduct.*

moral virtues — in Aristotle's philosophy, those virtues associated with ethical action.‡

moral vision — how one is motivated to act in accordance with his/her values.

Glossary

259

moral vision, descriptive	a moral vision directed by a specific set of rules, e.g. religious commandments.
moral vision, prescriptive	a moral vision developed through philosophical reasoning.
moral voice	an Ethics of Care concept that proposes that people should make ethical decisions following conversations with other people.
morbidity	degree of disease or pain in an individual (extreme case is "mortality").
Morrill Act	federal law establishing grants to colleges for engineering programs.
mortality	tendency to die; when used in relation to a disease or product, it is the tendency/risk for either of these to be associated with death.
Mozu	a female macaque with a congenital malformation of no hands nor feet who elicited altruistic behavior from fellow macaques.
mythos	the Greek concept of knowledge from the non-natural world and how it is attained.
nationalism	a consequential moral theory in which the nation's needs are paramount.
natural causes	events that are due to phenomena from the natural world.
natural law	a body of law arising out of nature, which governs human society; may function independently or in addition to societal law.*
natural selection	a scientific theory separately derived by Charles Darwin and Alfred Russell Wallace that accounts for organic evolution through the higher reproductive rates of individuals in a species that possess and inheritable variation rendering them better able to survive in their environment.**
natural philosophy	a worldly outlook that presents the endpoint of understanding nature.
negative duty	the obligation to not change the default position of a moral theory. For example, keep a confidence.
negative eugenics	improve the gene pool by discouraging the reproduction of individuals with "undesirable" genes.
negligence	in law, the failure to exercise the degree of care required to avoid foreseeable injury.‡
Neo-Darwinian synthesis	a theory of evolution that sees a species as an array of similar individuals containing a range of genetic variations that can be acted on by natural selection to generate shifts in gene frequencies such that new species can result, especially in isolated populations or in response to environmental changes.**
Neosalvarsan	an arsenic-containing drug used against syphilis.
nepotism	the practice of hiring one's relative rather than choosing the most qualified candidate for the job.

(Continued)

260 Glossary

noncontrol component of autonomy the part that refers to one's freedom to do what one chooses to do, or at least to act without coercion or restraint.

non-maleficence avoidance of doing harm or evil.*

normative used to designate a claim that is evaluative in nature or recommends a course of action.‡

Novum Organum, 1620 the seminal publication of Francis Bacon, explaining the application of inductive reasoning to understanding nature.

nuclease a digestive enzyme for nucleic acids.

Nuremberg Code the ethical declaration crafted by Ivy and Alexander after the Nuremberg "doctors" trial.

objective considered by rational minds to be real, true, or valid; observable or verifiable; based on interpersonal truth; opposed to "subjective".*

obligation (vs. duty) a service owed by one individual to another as a result of an agreement between the two, or a promise.

off-label use application of a drug or device for a condition not indicated in its instructions.

off-target effects unexpected results of drug or device application on a body structure or function not projected to be involved in the procedure.

On the Origin of Species, 1859 the seminal work of Charles Darwin, explaining organic evolution.

ontology the component of a philosophy concerned with what exists and how it came to be.

Order of concurrence FDA decision to grant a device an exemption.

Order of nonconcurrence FDA decision to not grant a device an exemption.

over-ridingness the state of moral reasons taking precedence over nonmoral reasons in a decision.

P value a statistical measure of confidence that a difference is significant.

paleomedicine medicine practiced in paleolithic times.

Palindromic codes code sequences that read the same when flipped horizontally.

paradox an argument or statement that seems to contradict itself, yet may be true.*

patent a government authority or license conferring a right or title to an invention for a set period, (includes the sole right to exclude others from making, using, or selling the invention).

patent infringement violation of the lawful restrictions against copying an invention.

Patent Trial and Appeal Board the panel that judges challenges to decisions by the U.S. Patent Office (PTAB).

paternalism in ethics, the principle of caring for and controlling the behavior of subordinates (workers, patients, citizens) in a fatherly fashion, for their own good.*

Glossary

261

pathology	abnormal changes in or the study of abnormal changes in the body and their causes.
Patient Self Determination Act, 1990	formalizes the right of a patient to refuse treatment (PSDA).
peaceful arbitration	a "higher level" community's social process for resolution of disputes.
Pearson's chi-square	a statistical method for evaluating scatter of data that requires large samples for validity.
peer reviewers	scientists with expertise in the field of the information being reviewed.
peer-reviewed publication	a report that has been evaluated by peer reviewers.
Performance standards	data from examination of the device being evaluated or others substantially equivalent that indicate its potential performance capability.
Philosophiae Natarulis Principia Mathematica	the seminal work of Sir Isaac Newton.
philosophy	critical reflection about fundamental beliefs and questions about life and death. Includes metaphysics, epistemology, logic, ethics and aesthetics.*
Piltdown Man	the subject of a classic scientific fraud.
Placebo	a control substance. A nonactive replacement for the drug or device being tested in an experiment.
plagiarism	theft of another's words, work or ideas for the purpose of presenting them as one's own.
plaintiffs	the parties in a lawsuit making the complaint.
Platonists	followers of Plato's philosophy. In medicine, physicians who based their decisions on reasoning more than on observation.
Pleistocene ice age	a geologic era lasting from 2.6 million to 11,700 years ago.
Polydimethylsiloxane	a silicone used in breast implants (PDMS).
Polymethylmethacrylate	an acrylic used to make intraocular lenses and as a bone cement (PMMA).
Polyurethane foam	a polymer used as a coating on breast implants.
population genetics	the study of the distribution of genes in a population.
population tendency	an unsuccessful measure used by Francis Galton to evaluate whether a given population was advancing or retreating eugenically.
positive duty	Deontological concept that promotes discarding the default position of a duty, and making the change. e.g. betray a confidence.
positive eugenics	encouraging "desirable" couples to produce more children.
positivism	the philosophy that all knowledge is based on what is "positively given" that is without speculation or introduction of unnatural causes; the underlying philosophy of modern science.
power calculation	calculation to determine sample/cohort sizes.

(Continued)

Praeses	the master teacher in a scholastic disputation.
pre-CRISPR RNA	the transcribed molecule with a palindromic code that is joined with a Cas nuclease to form a mature CRISPR RNA-Cas complex.
Pre-Market Approval Application	an application that follows an approved 510(k) and describes plans for the clinical phase of device testing (PMAA).
precedent	judgment that is accepted as automatic for determining judgments in similar cases.
precedent-setting verdict	a decision that includes a written opinion that is deemed so definitive that it becomes a precedent.
precision	repeatedness. Measuring technique so accomplished that it produces the same data under the same conditions each time.
precision medicine initiative	campaign with goal of precise classification of diseases in terms of specific molecular causal factors.
prescriptive	based on rules already established.
prima facie	depending on the situation.
primary goods	conditions desired by any rational person regardless of their contingent attributes.
principle of indeterminacy	One cannot determine the speed and position of a particle simultaneously. Foundation for uncertainty of science.
prisoner's dilemma	in game theory, a two-person game in which each player seeks to optimize his or her advantage.[‡]
privacy	the ability of the individual to keep large portions of his or her life away from the observation of others; the control of personal space.[*]
product liability	strict liability applied to products.
Prokaryotes	cell-based organisms with no distinct nuclei. e.g. bacteria.
protective factors	a counter to risk factors; these may range from body defenses to products that reduce the risk of disease.
Protestant Reformation	challenge of Protestants against the Catholic Church in 1517.
protocol	the design of an experiment (Typically used in place of "Materials and Methods" when referring to experiments involving humans).
protomorality	apparent moral behavior in nonhumans.
protospacer-adjacent motif	a chemical pattern that follows a DNA sequence that is receptive to editing by Cas9 (PAM).
pulmonary embolism	formation of a clot in the lungs.
punitive damages	an addition to actual damages, in a tort trial, that are awarded if the jury finds the defendant guilty of willful misconduct.
quantitative experimentation	a characteristic of engineering science that borrows from the nonphilosophical aspects of laboratory research, to focus on measurement, often without the guidance of hypotheses.
R_0	average distance between people at which the germ is infective.

Glossary 263

rationalist interpretation of autonomy the belief that the real rational interests of the individual correctly express his autonomy, and to the extent that the individual happens to choose against these interests, to that extent he is deceived.

rationality the capacity to consider abstract concepts, use language, think in terms of categories, classes, and rules; the ability to evaluate situations accurately and to choose appropriate means to cope with them*. At a lower thought level than reason.

Ratio of benefit to cost a crucial value in allocative efficiency. If you optimize these ratios sufficiently in manufacturing, you achieve allocative efficiency, and you cannot be sued for negligence. Standard was established in *U.S. vs. Carol Towing* 1947. Was used by Ford in their Pinto case, Grimshaw vs. Ford Motor Co., 1981.

reason ordered problem solving by drawing a conclusion from a set of premises. At a lower thought level than logic.

reciprocal altruism one individual benefits another without receiving compensation until after some delay and there is no requirement that benefit and compensation are of equal value.

reciprocity one of the animal behaviors that indicate proto-morality.

recombinant DNA DNA formed by combining DNA from two species.

Recombination exchange of chromosome segments by two chromosomes, or parts of the same chromosome, if sufficiently separated.

reconstruction an important procedure in the historical sciences (particularly geology and astronomy) that allow for solving the mystery of how an event took place.

reductionism the belief that humans are capable of total understanding of the natural world in terms of physics and chemistry.

relativism characterized by the notion that no point of view is more correct than any other; in matters of policy and ethics, the belief that there is only subjective (personal) opinion and no objective (interpersonal) truth.*

relativization using our own intuitions of adequate freedom and reason as the measure of the case before us.*

Responden a student participant in a scholastic disputation, who responds to the master.

retributive justice in ethics, the principle of justice that is concerned with punishing an individual for his or her actions.*

revision surgery definition is not settled, according to the NIH. A surgery following an initial surgery. For the FDA, the crucial definition involves correcting a problem with an implant. Such an event would negatively impact the record of the device.

Rickettsia typhi the causative agent for typhus.

(Continued)

Riegel	a reference to the *Riegel v. Medtronics* supreme court case. A product safety case, involving bursting of a Medtronic Evergreen balloon catheter being used for coronary angiography. Established that FDA could not be sued for product safety issue if product had been approved.
risk	the chance of suffering harm or loss.
risk/benefit analysis	the assessment of potential risk as it relates to potential benefit, of an act.
risk factors	treatments or behaviors that affect the chance of the recipient suffering harm or loss.
rule-utilitarianism	an indirect version of utilitarianism, which applies to institutions or groups in the form of rules of conduct.
Safe medical devices act 1990	provides the FDA with power to check a device's design, pre-production, for obvious safety violations (SMDA).
safety and efficacy	the two qualities of a device regulated by the FDA.
Sandoz Pharmaceuticals Corporation	one of the defendants in the Moore vs. Regents of the University of California case.
Sarbanes-Oxley Act, 2002	an amendment to the Levin-Grassley Act that added penalties for retribution against whistleblowers and increased the latter's' rewards.
scholasticism	a filter on observations of the natural world requiring that they be interpreted to enhance the "glory of God".
secular	limited to the natural world.
selfish genes	a version of neo-Darwinian evolution theory that sees genes (rather than individual organisms) as the basic unit of selection, such that organisms evolve as a means to facilitate the survival of their genes, which can account for seemingly altruistic behavior by individuals on behalf of their kin.**
sexual harassment	generating, in a social situation, unwelcome and inappropriate behavior with a sexual element.
significant	a statistical concept: At a level of confidence that allows accepting the falsifiable hypothesis to be falsified.
Singapore Statement on Research Integrity	"Research findings have integrity if they can be trusted by researchers who will learn from and build on those findings; by practitioners who will base decisions on them; and by funders, institutions and publishers whose credibility is linked with the results they support and promote".
skeptics	Greek physicians who challenged the possibility of thoroughly solving any medical problem.
skin lice	Humans have three species: body, head and pubic lice. They are useful in Anthropology because they are found on ancient bodies.
social contract	an agreement which brings a society into being and regulates the relations between the members of the society with each other and with their government.*

Glossary

265

social Darwinism	a loosely defined term used by critics to ridicule any late-19th century social and economic policies and practices that assumed human progress came through a competitive "survival-of-the-fittest" process among individuals.**
socially distanced	an infection prevention protocol to keep people beyond R_0 during an epidemic.
sociobiology	the view that Darwinian theories of evolutionary biology, featuring a competitive struggle for survival among individuals and successful reproductive strategies for individuals, provide a basis for understanding societal behavior patterns of individuals, including those of humans.**
Somatosensory	the receptor part of the nervous system that focuses on perception of impulses carried by afferent neurons. The research of Edward Taub was focused on the perception of pain.
speciesists	individuals who favor one species over all others. Used by animal rights advocates against those who employ nonhuman animals.
spermicide	sperm toxin. Used in some forms of contraception.
spiritualism	a belief system that accepts supernatural existence.
Splenectomy	removal of the spleen.
standard of care	the expected minimum quality of practice for a licensed physician as it relates to his/her patients.
Standards for Privacy of Individually Identifiable Health Information	a set of regulations for handling of electronically accessible patient information that the Health and Human Services Department added to HIPAA in 2002.
statistical correlation	a linkage in time and place between two variables, that if high enough should be subjected to Bradford Hill's criteria for a causal connection.
statistical method for hypothesis testing	the most common application of statistics in scientific research papers. The method of choice is commonly Fisher's ANOVA.
statistically significantly different	usually means the P value was low enough to reject the null hypothesis.
statutes	government-generated laws.
stipulates	presents as undisputed evidence.
strict liability	defendant vulnerability, without the burden of negligence, to legal recovery of damages for producing a defective product that has harmed the plaintiff.
subjective	based on personal opinion, rather than universal or certifiable conditions; opposed to "objective".*
subjective relativism	the assertion that since ethics is subjective, any discussion of it is useless, because the listener will end up choosing the parts he likes and ignoring the rest.

(Continued)

substantially equivalent	sufficiently similar to an approved product that it poses no safety concerns beyond those of the approved product.
Survival of the fittest	a slogan used by Herbert Spencer in his social Darwinism model to explain the success of business tycoons, like the robber barons.
syllogism	deductive logical scheme of a formal argument; consisting of a major premise, a minor premise, and a conclusion.*
sympathy-related traits	a group of traits that are expressed, according to de Waal in an animal with proto-morality.
synthetic statements	statements that put together in a new combination, two ideas that do not initially include or entail each other.*
synthetic RNA complex (crRNA + tracrRNA)	a synthesized molecule that attaches to a Cas nuclease and helps guide it to the editing target.
T-lymphocyte	T cell. These are key to recognizing antigenic epitopes as part of adaptive immunity. The CD4 T cell seeks the MHC Class II complex on the surface of antigen presenting cells, where it learns the identity of the antigen.
Tarasoff v. University of California Regents	a classic case that set a precedent for not infringing confidentiality.
targeted research	research that is committed to curing selected diseases.
Taub incident	the attack on Edward Taub by PETA that first publicized the animal rights movement.
technê	knowledge of the craftsman, the "how to" of solving a problem.
teleological	end-directed; teleological theories evaluate or explain something in terms of the end toward which it is aiming.‡
Thalidomide	a sedative/morning sickness drug that had the side effect of producing congenitally deformed babies.
theology	the philosophical basis of a religion.
Thromboembolisms	blood clot plugging of a blood vessel by a dislodged thrombus from another site.
Title VII, 1991	part of the Civil Rights Act that prohibits employment discrimination based on race, color, religion, sex and national origin.
tort	any private or civil wrong (due to strict liability or negligence) for which a civil suit can be brought; breach of contract is an exception.
trade mark	any word, name, symbol, or design, or any combination thereof, used in commerce to identify and distinguish the goods of one manufacturer or seller from those of another, and to indicate the source of the goods.
trade secrets	a procedure or object used in the manufacture of a product, that the manufacturer wishes to keep secret.
translational clinical science	the kind of clinical research that leads to clinical application.
transmutation	the conversion of one element into another.

Glossary

267

trephines	devices for cutting holes in bone.
Treponema pallidum	the bacterial causative agent for syphilis.
truth professionals	professionals who solve problems for people, the solutions being sufficiently final to constitute "truths".
Tuskegee Syphilis study	a classic ethics case, in which the patients were allowed to live with the disease untreated, and were lied to about the procedures performed on them.
Uniform Health-Care Information Act, 1988	provided safeguards for patient information, even restricting subpoena power. (UHCIA).
ultimate truth	the endpoint of complete understanding of the universe.
universality	applicability to all individuals in similar situations.
universal maxim	a general truth, basic principle, or rule of conduct, often expressed as a proverb or saying.*
utilitarian ethics	a moral theory that focuses on consequences; concerned with theoretical decision-making procedures involving measurements of happiness; one's motivation for an action is irrelevant.
value judgment	a judgment that assigns good or evil to an action or entity.*
variance	data scatter.
Variola	the virus that causes smallpox.
veil of ignorance	in the work of Rawls, the metaphorical description of the barrier against using special concerns in order to assess principles of justice. The veil of ignorance defines the original position. It is as if the parties have to contract into basic social structures, defining for example the liberties that their society will allow, and the economic structure it will recognize, but not knowing which role in the society they themselves will be allocated. Only if a social system can rationally be chosen or contracted into from this position, does it satisfy the constraints of justice.
ventromedial frontal region	a region in the limbic part of the brain. Significant because it was damaged by the nail that went through Phineas Gage's head.
Vibrio cholerae	the bacterium that causes cholera.
Vioxx	an anti-inflammatory drug with serious side effects that was marketed by Merck, who lied about its tendency to cause myocardial infarctions.
virtue ethics	the moral theory of Aristotle that stressed virtuous people serving as models for forming a moral vision.
virtuous habit	the tendency to exhibit a particular virtue.
vivaria	living quarters for laboratory animals.
whistleblowing	testifying to a government authority about a wrongdoing by any government or government-licensed agency or by any product manufacturer.
Wyeth	reference to *Wyeth v. Levine* supreme court case.

(Continued)

xenogeneic	re transplants: donor from another species.
Yellow fever	a virus-caused disease that is spread by the mosquito *Aedes aegypti*.
Yersinia pestis	the bacterium that causes bubonic plague.
ZMapp	a triple antibody drug against the Ebola virus disease, made by Mapp Biopharmaceutical.

*From "Ethics in America" accompanying guidebook (Newton 2004)

**From "The theory of Evolution: A History of Controversy" accompanying guidebook (Larson 2002)

‡ From "Questions of Value" accompanying guidebook (Grimm 2005)

***From "Oxford Dictionary of Philosophy" (Blackburn 1994)

Appendix A Suggested Format for Class Debates

Two positions will be established. The "PRO" position will present arguments that will give bioengineers maximum freedom to practice as they wish. The "CON" position will impose restrictions on bioengineering practice. For example, PRO in the debate about when a zygote is a person might be "at birth". This position could make it legal to use pre-birth embryos for experiments and stem cells. The CON position might be "at fertilization". Such a position could make it illegal to use a human embryo for harvesting or experiments.

Each debate team will consist of five members. The moderator will state the background and summary of positions. Pro-1 will present pro-position arguments. Con-1 will present con-position arguments. The Con-2 and Pro-2 will critique the pro and con arguments respectively. Moral theories will be applied where appropriate.

The goal of the debates is to appreciate opposing points of view for controversial issues and practice applying moral theories to the ethical problems raised.

All positions and debate choices will be determined by a random selection process. The debater may be assigned a viewpoint to which he/she is opposed.

The debate experience involves developing a logical argument for a particular point of view. The viewpoint of the debater is, therefore, irrelevant. One of the goals of any scholarly debate is to understand a viewpoint to which one disagrees. Accordingly, the richest learning experience in a debate occurs when a debater has to argue the view point to which he/she is personally opposed. Therefore, any exchange of debate assignments will be considered equivalent to cheating and subject to the appropriate honor code penalty.

DEBATE PANEL EVALUATION (Rating for four debates)

#	SUBJECT	MOD	PRO #1	CON #1	PRO #2	CON #2	TOTAL
1							
2							
3							
4							

HOW TO RATE

1. Each participant may earn a rating up to ten units
2. The maximum values for each category are

CATEGORY	MODERATOR	DEBATOR
Clarity of presentation sound	1	2
Clarity of presentation subject matter		2
Subject knowledge		3
Ability to keep speakers on time	2	
Ability to present background while setting the stage	2	
Focuses on subject without wandering		3
Ability to summarize arguments presented	3	
Maintained order while encouraging contrary opinions	2	

Appendix B Informed Consent

Downloaded from: https://www.nhlbi.nih.gov/files/docs/clinical-reseach-guide-consent-template.doc

INFORMED CONSENT FORM FOR HUMAN RESEARCH EXAMPLE

(As you read, consider whether its complexity is at an eighth grade level as required by federal law)

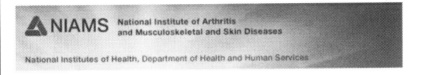

CLINICAL RESEARCH

Updated September 10, 2007

This sample patient consent form serves as an example to guide investigators who intend to conduct research with human subjects. The intent of the document is not to suggest required wording or format but rather to provide categories and level of detail that are pertinent to many studies.

OBSERVATIONAL STUDY CONSENT FORM

Clinical Center
  Principal Investigator
  24-Hour Contact

If you are able, you may choose to participate in this observational study entitled (title). The purpose of the study is to look at the relation between lifestyle factors and health, as well as quality of life. If you decide to join the study, you will be asked to complete questionnaires, have a physical exam, and provide blood samples. This study will look at the role of several health habits (e.g., physical activity and diet) and exam results (such as blood pressure and body weight), as well as factors measured in the blood sample. The investigators will look at how these factors affect risks of heart disease, cancer, general health, and quality and length of life.

272 Appendix B Informed Consent

Purpose of the Observational Study

The main purpose of this Observational Study is to learn more about the causes of disease in the selected population. The clinical staff has determined that you are eligible to join this part of the study.

Reasons for the Observational Study

Examples: There are several major diseases that women may get as they get older. Breast cancer is the most commonly occurring major cancer in women. Cancers of the colon and rectum are the third most common major cancers in women. Heart disease is the most common cause of death in women aged 50 to 79 years. If we could prevent these diseases, women could expect to live longer and healthier lives.

What Will You Be Doing?

If you decide to take part in the study, you will be followed for about 20 years. During this follow-up period, you will be contacted by mail each year. You will be asked to complete health update questionnaires and mail them back to the clinic. These questionnaires should take about 30 minutes to complete.

You will also receive a newsletter each year, informing you of news about the study and general information about health for women your age.

You will be invited to return to the clinic every 4 years. Before that visit, you will be mailed some forms, including the questionnaires to complete and bring with you to the clinic visit. At that visit, clinical staff will:

- Review the questionnaires you completed.
- Record the names (and possibly dosages) of medications you are taking currently.
- Measure your pulse, blood pressure, height, weight, and the distance around your hips and waist.
- Measure bone density in your hip and spine. This test is painless and takes about 30 minutes.
- Give you questionnaires to complete about yourself and your lifestyle.
- Draw about 3 tablespoons of blood for laboratory tests. For 12 hours prior to the blood test, you will not be able to exercise vigorously, eat, or drink anything except water and your regular medications. For one hour prior to the test, you will not be able to smoke.
- Ask you to provide a urine sample (about 1 tablespoon) which will be stored for laboratory tests at a later date.

Abnormal findings of the following clinic tests will be reported to you or your doctor. Some of the blood and urine will be stored for purposes of future research studies specifically related to your disease. These studies may involve testing for the presence of genes (DNA) and investigations of blood factors (e.g., antibodies or novel inflammatory proteins) that may influence the risk of getting disease, the risk

Appendix B Informed Consent

of having a severe form of the disease, and the chance of responding to treatment. These blood tests will not replace your usual medical care and results will not be available for your medical care (e.g. your cholesterol will not be reported to you or your doctor). Research studies require only looking at all lab results together, and individual results will not be available.

I consent to such uses _____ (patient initials)

I do not consent to such uses _____ (patient initials)

BENEFITS AND RISKS

There may be no direct benefit to you for participating in this study. By taking part in this study, you may help to increase scientific knowledge about (e.g., the prevention of breast cancer.)

Blood Draw

There is a small risk with the process of drawing blood. You may feel a little discomfort as the needle goes through the skin. There may be some bruising at the site where blood is drawn. Pressing hard on the spot for 1 or 2 minutes after the needle is removed will help to prevent a bruise. Very rarely, the arm may become infected. Occasionally people feel lightheaded or even faint when their blood is drawn. If you feel faint, tell the person drawing your blood and she/he will have you lie down until the feeling goes away.

Bone Density Measurement

The bone density measurement involves a small amount of radiation. Small amounts of radiation may have potential harm, but the risk is difficult to measure and is probably very small. The total radiation from the bone density measurements is less than 4% of the natural background radiation a person receives living in a typical American community for one year. It is about the same radiation as three coast-to-coast airline flights from the east to the west coast.

Urine Sample

Providing a urine sample involves no risk.

COSTS

The tests, procedures, and visits that are a part of this study will cost only your time and travel. Any test or procedure that would normally be billed to your insurance company, Medicare, or Medicaid will be billed to those sources. If you do not have sources to pay for tests and procedures, the study will pay these costs.

The study clinical center has not set aside funds to pay for any health conditions that you may develop, and will not pay for any health problems or conditions that might occur during the course of this study. These might be covered by your usual insurance, Medicare, or Medicaid. You will not be paid back for any wages lost from taking part in this study. You will not be paid for being in the study.

274   Appendix B Informed Consent

CONFIDENTIALITY

All of your study records will be kept confidential to the extent required by law. Your personal identity will not be revealed in any publication or release of results. If a health condition is detected during this examination, you will be told about it and the information will be given to your doctor or clinic. Only staff at [name of clinical site], the Clinical Coordinating Center, FDA and the sponsor, NIH, will have access to your medical records for the purpose of study wide mailings, as well as maintaining and updating your study records. Study records will be kept indefinitely for analysis and follow-up. This study is authorized by Privacy Act 42 United States Code 241.

RIGHT TO WITHDRAW

Your decision to join in this study is voluntary. You may quit at any time, for any reason, without notice. We hope you will take part for the entire time of the study because we will use all of this information to draw correct conclusions. If you decide to leave the study, we hope to be able to contact you yearly to see how you are doing. If you decide to leave the study, it will not affect your regular medical care.

VOLUNTARY CONSENT

If you have any questions about any aspect of the study or your rights as a volunteer, a staff member will be on hand to answer them before you sign this consent form. Additionally, if you have any questions about you rights as a participant in this study, please call (name) in the Institutional Review Board Office of [Clinical Center] at [phone number]. If you have any questions at any time, you may call: [Clinical Center name and phone number] or any of the investigators listed at the beginning of this form. Before you sign this form, please ask any questions on any part of this study that is unclear to you.

OTHER INFORMATION

Your joining is important to the success of this study. In order for this study to be valid, you should not join other health studies where you would be assigned at random (like the flip of a coin) to receive a medication, special test, or special treatment.

If any test suggests that a health problem needs further study, you will be sent back to your doctor or clinic, who will evaluate the need for further study. Copies of reports and hospital records of your doctor's follow-up may be requested by the institution and become part of your study record at [Clinical Center]. Whether or not you choose to join, your medical care or your medical insurance coverage will not be affected. The study does not replace your usual medical care.

If you are unable to complete the follow-up forms, the clinic staff may contact your spouse, close relative, or friend for updated information about your health. If

Appendix B Informed Consent

you move, and we are not able to find you, we may try to locate you through nationally available records, such as social security.

INVESTIGATOR'S STATEMENT

I have provided an explanation of the above research program. The participant was given an opportunity to discuss these procedures, including possible alternatives, and to ask any additional questions. A signed copy of the consent form has been given to the participant.

_____

Signature of Principal Investigator or Designee   Date

PARTICIPANT STATEMENT

I certify that I have read, or had read to me, and that I understand the description of the Observational Study. I have asked and received answers to all my questions about the study. I voluntarily consent to join the study. I understand that I may quit the study at any time. I understand that I may ask further questions at any time and that I will receive a copy of this signed consent form for my records. I have had an opportunity to carefully review the Informed Consent form and ask questions about it.

_____

Signature of Participant   Date

_____

Signature of Witness   Date

Appendix C Advance Health Care Directive Example

 Downloaded from: https://leginfo.legislature.ca.gov/faces/codes_displaySection.xhtml?lawCode=PROB&sectionNum=4701.

State of California PROBATE CODE
Section 470

4701. The statutory advance health care directive form is as follows:

Advance Health Care Directive

(California Probate Code Section 4701) Explanation

You have the right to give instructions about your own health care. You also have the right to name someone else to make health care decisions for you. This form lets you do either or both of these things. It also lets you express your wishes regarding donation of organs and the designation of your primary physician. If you use this form, you may complete or modify all or any part of it. You are free to use a different form.

Part 1 of this form is a power of attorney for health care. Part 1 lets you name another individual as agent to make health care decisions for you if you become incapable of making your own decisions or if you want someone else to make those decisions for you now even though you are still capable. You may also name an alternate agent to act for you if your first choice is not willing, able, or reasonably available to make decisions for you. (Your agent may not be an operator or employee of a community care facility or a residential care facility where you are receiving care, or your supervising health care provider or employee of the health care institution where you are receiving care, unless your agent is related to you or is a coworker.)

Unless the form you sign limits the authority of your agent, your agent may make all health care decisions for you. This form has a place for you to limit the authority of your agent. You need not limit the authority of your agent if you wish to rely on your agent for all health care decisions that may have to be made. If you choose not to limit the authority of your agent, your agent will have the right to:

277

> a. Consent or refuse consent to any care, treatment, service, or procedure to maintain, diagnose, or otherwise affect a physical or mental condition.
> b. Select or discharge health care providers and institutions.
> c. Approve or disapprove diagnostic tests, surgical procedures, and programs of medication.
> d. Direct the provision, withholding, or withdrawal of artificial nutrition and hydration and all other forms of health care, including cardiopulmonary resuscitation.
> e. Donate your organs, tissues, and parts, authorize an autopsy, and direct disposition of remains.
>
> Part 2 of this form lets you give specific instructions about any aspect of your health care, whether or not you appoint an agent. Choices are provided for you to express your wishes regarding the provision, withholding, or withdrawal of treatment to keep you alive, as well as the provision of pain relief. Space is also provided for you to add to the choices you have made or for you to write out any additional wishes. If you are satisfied to allow your agent to determine what is best for you in making end-of-life decisions, you need not fill out Part 2 of this form.
> Part 3 of this form lets you express an intention to donate your bodily organs, tissues, and parts following your death.
> Part 4 of this form lets you designate a physician to have primary responsibility for your health care.

After completing this form, sign and date the form at the end. The form must be signed by two qualified witnesses or acknowledged before a notary public. Give a copy of the signed and completed form to your physician, to any other health care providers you may have, to any health care institution at which you are receiving care, and to any health care agents you have named. You should talk to the person you have named as agent to make sure that he or she understands your wishes and is willing to take the responsibility.

You have the right to revoke this advance health care directive or replace this form at any time.

* * * * * * * * * * * * * * * *

PART 1 POWER OF ATTORNEY FOR HEALTH CARE

DESIGNATION OF AGENT: I designate the following individual as my agent to make health care decisions for me:

_____

(name of individual you choose as agent)

_____

(address)   (city)   (state)   (ZIP Code)

_____

Appendix C Advance Health Care Directive Example

_____

(home phone)   (work phone)

_____

OPTIONAL: If I revoke my agent's authority or if my agent is not willing, able, or reasonably available to make a health care decision for me, I designate as my first alternate agent:

_____

_____
(name of individual you choose as first alternate agent)

_____
(address)   (city)   (state)   (ZIP Code)

_____
(home phone)   (work phone)

_____

OPTIONAL: If I revoke the authority of my agent and first alternate agent or if neither is willing, able, or reasonably available to make a health care decision for me, I designate as my second alternate agent:

_____

_____
(name of individual you choose as second alternate agent)

_____
(address)   (city)   (state)   (ZIP Code)

_____
(home phone)   (work phone)

_____

AGENT'S AUTHORITY: My agent is authorized to make all health care decisions for me, including decisions to provide, withhold, or withdraw artificial nutrition and hydration and all other forms of health care to keep me alive, except as I state here:

_____

_____
_____
_____
(Add additional sheets if needed.)

_____

WHEN AGENT'S AUTHORITY BECOMES EFFECTIVE: My agent's authority becomes effective when my primary physician determines that I am

280 Appendix C Advance Health Care Directive Example

unable to make my own health care decisions unless I mark the following box. If I mark this box □, my agent's authority to make health care decisions for me takes effect immediately.

AGENT'S OBLIGATION: My agent shall make health care decisions for me in accordance with this power of attorney for health care, any instructions I give in Part 2 of this form, and my other wishes to the extent known to my agent. To the extent my wishes are unknown, my agent shall make health care decisions for me in accordance with what my agent determines to be in my best interest. In determining my best interest, my agent shall consider my personal values to the extent known to my agent.

AGENT'S POSTDEATH AUTHORITY: My agent is authorized to donate my organs, tissues, and parts, authorize an autopsy, and direct disposition of my remains, except as I state here or in Part 3 of this form:

_____

_____

_____

_____

(Add additional sheets if needed.)

_____

NOMINATION OF CONSERVATOR: If a conservator of my person needs to be appointed for me by a court, I nominate the agent designated in this form. If that agent is not willing, able, or reasonably available to act as conservator, I nominate the alternate agents whom I have named, in the order designated.

PART 2 INSTRUCTIONS FOR HEALTH CARE

If you fill out this part of the form, you may strike any wording you do not want.

END–OF–LIFE DECISIONS: I direct that my health care providers and others involved in my care provide, withhold, or withdraw treatment in accordance with the choice I have marked below:

a. Choice Not to Prolong Life
I do not want my life to be prolonged if (1) I have an incurable and irreversible condition that will result in my death within a relatively short time, (2) I become unconscious and, to a reasonable degree of medical certainty, I will not regain consciousness, or (3) the likely risks and burdens of treatment would outweigh the expected benefits, OR

b. Choice To Prolong Life

Appendix C Advance Health Care Directive Example

I want my life to be prolonged as long as possible within the limits of generally accepted health care standards.

RELIEF FROM PAIN: Except as I state in the following space, I direct that treatment for alleviation of pain or discomfort be provided at all times, even if it hastens my death:

_____

_____

_____

(Add additional sheets if needed.)

_____

OTHER WISHES: (If you do not agree with any of the optional choices above and wish to write your own, or if you wish to add to the instructions you have given above, you may do so here.) I direct that:

_____

_____

_____

(Add additional sheets if needed.)

_____

PART 3 DONATION OF ORGANS, TISSUES, AND PARTS AT DEATH (OPTIONAL)

☐ Upon my death, I give my organs, tissues, and parts (mark box to indicate yes). By checking the box above, and notwithstanding my choice in Part 2 of this form, I authorize my agent to consent to any temporary medical procedure necessary solely to evaluate and/or maintain my organs, tissues, and/or parts for purposes of donation.

My donation is for the following purposes (strike any of the following you do not want):

a. Transplant
b. Therapy
c. Research
d. Education

If you want to restrict your donation of an organ, tissue, or part in some way, please state your restriction on the following lines:

If I leave this part blank, it is not a refusal to make a donation. My state-authorized donor registration should be followed, or, if none, my agent may make a donation upon my death. If no agent is named above, I acknowledge that California

282 Appendix C Advance Health Care Directive Example

law permits an authorized individual to make such a decision on my behalf. (To state any limitation, preference, or instruction regarding donation, please use the lines above or in Section 1.5 of this form).

PART 4 PRIMARY PHYSICIAN (OPTIONAL)

I designate the following physician as my primary physician:

_____

_____
(name of physician)

_____
(address)   (city)   (state)   (ZIP Code)

_____
(phone)

OPTIONAL: If the physician I have designated above is not willing, able, or reasonably available to act as my primary physician, I designate the following physician as my primary physician:

_____

_____
(name of physician)

_____
(address)   (city)   (state)   (ZIP Code)

_____
(phone)

* * * * * * * * * * * * * * * *

PART 5

EFFECT OF COPY: A copy of this form has the same effect as the original.

SIGNATURE: Sign and date the form here:

_____

_____   _____
(date)   (sign your name)

_____   _____
(address)   (print your name)

_____

Appendix C Advance Health Care Directive Example

(city)   (state)

STATEMENT OF WITNESSES: I declare under penalty of perjury under the laws of California (1) that the individual who signed or acknowledged this advance health care directive is personally known to me, or that the individual's identity was proven to me by convincing evidence, (2) that the individual signed or acknowledged this advance directive in my presence, (3) that the individual appears to be of sound mind and under no duress, fraud, or undue influence, (4) that I am not a person appointed as agent by this advance directive, and (5) that I am not the individual's health care provider, an employee of the individual's health care provider, the operator of a community care facility, an employee of an operator of a community care facility, the operator of a residential care facility for the elderly, nor an employee of an operator of a residential care facility for the elderly.

First witness   Second witness

(print name)   (print name)

(address)   (address)

(city)   (state)   (city)   (state)

(signature of witness)   (signature of witness)

(date)   (date)

ADDITIONAL STATEMENT OF WITNESSES: At least one of the above witnesses must also sign the following declaration:

I further declare under penalty of perjury under the laws of California that I am not related to the individual executing this advance health care directive by blood, marriage, or adoption, and to the best of my knowledge, I am not entitled to any part of the individual's estate upon his or her death under a will now existing or by operation of law.

(signature of witness)   (signature of witness)

PART 6 SPECIAL WITNESS REQUIREMENT

The following statement is required only if you are a patient in a skilled nursing facility—a health care facility that provides the following basic services: skilled nursing care and supportive care to patients whose primary need is for availability of skilled nursing care on an extended basis. The patient advocate or ombudsman must sign the following statement:

Statement of Patient Advocate or Ombudsman

I declare under penalty of perjury under the laws of California that I am a patient advocate or ombudsman as designated by the State Department of Aging and that I am serving as a witness as required by Section 4675 of the Probate Code.

_____

(date)   (sign your name)

(address)   (print your name)

(city)   (state)

_____

   (Amended by Stats. 2018, Ch. 287, Sec. 1. (AB 3211) Effective January 1, 2019.)

Appendix D Research Misconduct Policy Example

UCLA POLICY 993

Permission: Vice Chancellor Roger Wakimoto

UCLA Policy 993: Responding to Allegations of Research Misconduct

ISSUING OFFICER: Executive Vice Chancellor

RESPONSIBLE OFFICE: Office of Research Administration

EFFECTIVE DATE: June 16, 2006

SUPERSEDES: UCLA Policy 993, dated 7/1/1998 and UCLA Procedure 993.1, dated 7/1/1997

I REFERENCES

1. UC Policy on Integrity in Research, June 19, 1990;
2. UCLA Policy 910, Management of Contract and Grant Projects;
3. Code of Federal Regulations, Title 42, Part 93: Public Health Services Policies on Research Misconduct, as modified, effective June 16, 2005.).

II DEFINITIONS

Initial Assessment: Initial evaluation of allegations of Research Misconduct by the Research Integrity Officer.

Inquiry: Preliminary information gathering and fact-finding to determine whether an allegation of Research Misconduct warrants an Investigation.

Investigation: The formal development of a factual record and the examination and evaluation of that record to determine if Research Misconduct has occurred and, if so, to determine the responsible person(s).

Research: A systematic experiment, study, evaluation, demonstration or survey designed to develop or contribute to general knowledge (basic Research) or specific knowledge (applied and demonstration Research) by establishing, discovering, developing, elucidating or confirming information about or the underlying mechanism relating to, causes, functions or effects.

Research Integrity Officer: The institutional official at UCLA responsible for coordinating campus actions taken in response to allegations of Research Misconduct. At UCLA, the Vice Chancellor for Research (VCR) serves as the Research Integrity Officer, except that the Vice Chancellor, Academic Personnel shall serve instead of the VCR if, in a particular Research Misconduct Proceeding, the VCR has a conflict of interest.

286 Appendix D Research Misconduct Policy Example

Research Misconduct: Fabrication, falsification, or plagiarism in proposing, performing, or reviewing Research, or in reporting Research results. It does not include honest error or differences of opinion.

- **Fabrication** is making up data or results and recording or reporting them.
- **Falsification** is manipulating Research materials, equipment or processes, or changing or omitting data or results, such that the Research is not accurately represented in the Research Record.
- **Plagiarism** is the appropriation of another person's ideas, processes, results, or words, without giving appropriate credit but not a dispute among collaborators about authorship or credit.

Research Misconduct Investigator: A person designated by the VCR to assist in conducting a Research Misconduct Proceeding.

Research Misconduct Proceeding: Any formal University action (or other action by a Research Sponsor with regulatory responsibility) related to an allegation of Research Misconduct, including but not limited to an Initial Assessment, Inquiry, or Investigation.

Research Record: The record of data or results that embody the facts resulting from Research, including but not limited to Research proposals, laboratory records (both physical and electronic), progress reports, abstracts, theses, oral presentations, databases, internal reports, and journal articles, as well as any documents and materials provided to the Research Sponsor or to UCLA, or its employees, by a Respondent in the course of a Research Misconduct Proceeding.

Research Sponsor: A governmental or non-governmental entity that funds Research (such as the Public Health Service, the National Science Foundation, or the American Cancer Society) or has oversight responsibility for Research Misconduct, such as the Office of Research Integrity of the U.S. Department of Health and Human Services (ORI).

Respondent: The person or persons against whom an allegation of Research Misconduct is directed or who is the subject of a Research Misconduct Proceeding.

III GENERAL POLICY

UCLA is committed to maintaining the integrity of scholarship and Research and to fostering a climate conducive to Research integrity in accordance with the University's Policy on Integrity in Research. Such integrity includes not just the avoidance of wrong doing but also the rigor, carefulness, and accountability that are hallmarks of good scholarship. All persons engaged in Research at UCLA are responsible for adhering to the highest standards of intellectual honesty and integrity. Faculty and other supervisors of Research have a responsibility to create an environment that encourages those high standards through open publication and discussion, emphasis on quality of Research, appropriate supervision, maintenance of accurate and detailed Research procedures and results, and suitable assignment of credit and responsibility for Research.

Appendix D Research Misconduct Policy Example

UCLA assumes primary responsibility for: 1) assessing allegations of Research Misconduct; 2) conducting Inquiries and Investigations; 3) reporting the results to Research Sponsors as required; 4) determining and implementing disciplinary action as appropriate; 5) cooperating with Research Sponsors, such as ORI, during Research Misconduct Proceedings and assisting in administering and enforcing any federal administrative actions imposed upon UCLA or persons at UCLA; 6) having in place an active assurance of compliance with ORI; and 7) taking reasonable steps to ensure the cooperation of Respondents and others at UCLA with Research Misconduct Proceedings.

Some practices (including but not limited to matters involving misuse of University funds, facilities and resources, use of human subjects, confidentiality, authorship, conflicts of interest, conflicts of commitment, misuse of animals, etc.) are not Research Misconduct, but may be violations of other University policies, such as the Code of Faculty Conduct, the UCLA Student Code of Conduct, or Personnel Policies for Staff Members.

This policy is intended to satisfy the requirements of the U.S. Department of Health and Human Services (DHHS), and other federal agencies. However, this policy also applies to all Research conducted under the responsibility of UCLA, whether or not the Research is supported by an external sponsor.

IV PROCEDURES

A APPLICABILITY

This policy is applicable to all individuals with an appointment or formal affiliation with UCLA, including: faculty; staff; postdoctoral scholars; visiting scholars; graduate students engaged in the preparation of Masters or Ph.D. theses; and students (either graduate or undergraduate) while satisfying requirements (such as paid or unpaid internships in Research laboratories or summer employment incidental to their student status) or while supported by funds from Research training grants, except that it does not apply to a student's classroom actions such as assignments.

This policy does not apply to a faculty member's classroom actions such as the preparation and presentation of classroom lectures, examinations or websites. Scholarly activities that do not fall specifically within the definition of Research remain governed by the Faculty Code of Conduct and other University of California and UCLA policies.

B ALLEGATIONS OF RESEARCH MISCONDUCT

Any individual (whether faculty, staff, student, or individual outside the University community) may report, either orally or in writing, suspected Research Misconduct against one or more persons. Such an allegation should normally be addressed to the Respondent's chair, director, or dean. Whoever receives such an allegation shall promptly notify the Research Integrity Officer (the Vice Chancellor for Research (VCR)).

C Initial Assessment

Upon receiving an allegation of Research Misconduct, the VCR shall promptly make an Initial Assessment to determine whether the alleged facts are: 1) within the definition of Research Misconduct; 2) sufficiently serious, credible and specific so that potential evidence of Research Misconduct may be identified; and 3) within the limitation period.

If the VCR determines that these criteria have been met, the VCR shall initiate an Inquiry, as provided in IV.F below, and shall:

- if the Respondent is an academic appointee, notify the Vice Chancellor, Academic Personnel who may temporarily stay any pending personnel action involving the Respondent;
- if the Respondent is a student, notify the Dean of Students, who may temporarily withhold a diploma or transcript, with concurrent notice to the Dean of the Graduate Division in the case of a graduate student;
- if the Respondent is a postdoctoral scholar or visiting scholar, notify the appropriate academic dean, with concurrent notice to the Dean of the Graduate Division; and
- if the Respondent is a staff member, notify the Assistant Vice Chancellor – Campus Human Resources.

If the VCR determines that an Inquiry is not warranted, the case will be closed, although the matter may be referred to other campus officers, as appropriate.

Notice to Respondent. Whether or not an Inquiry is initiated, within a reasonable time and no later than the commencement of an Inquiry, if any, the VCR shall notify the Respondent of the allegation in writing, and reference this policy.

Limitation Period. No Inquiry shall be initiated if the allegation of Research Misconduct is received more than six years after the alleged misconduct occurred, unless 1) for potential benefit, the Respondent has continued or renewed any incident of alleged Research Misconduct through the citation, re-publication or other use of the Research Record at issue; 2) the alleged Research Misconduct would possibly have a substantial adverse effect on the health or safety of the public; or 3) the allegation was made prior to June 16, 2005, the date on which the current Public Health Service regulations became effective.

D Securing of Evidence

With the assistance of a Research Misconduct Investigator, representatives from Audit & Advisory Services, Campus Counsel, and/or the Inquiry Committee (see IV.F, below), the VCR shall take reasonable and practical steps to obtain custody of, inventory, and securely sequester all Research Records and evidence required to conduct the Inquiry and Investigation. This may include either data on instruments that are shared among a number of users or copies of that data, provided that those copies are substantially equivalent to the evidentiary value of the instruments.

Appendix D Research Misconduct Policy Example

1. At each stage of these proceedings, those responsible for conducting the Inquiry and Investigation shall notify the VCR when and if additional evidence is identified that needs to be secured and retained hereunder.
2. The Respondent shall receive copies of, or reasonably supervised access to, the Research Record to prepare a response and to continue Research.
3. The VCR shall securely maintain such data and evidence as well as the records of the Inquiry and Investigation Committees for seven years after the completion of a UCLA Research Misconduct Proceeding, unless custody of the records has been transferred to a Research Sponsor or a Research Sponsor has notified UCLA that the records are no longer needed.

E GENERAL STANDARDS FOR COMMITTEES AND ADMINISTRATORS

In appointing persons to conduct an Inquiry (see IV.F, below) or Investigation (see IV.G, below), the VCR shall assure, to the extent practicable, that such persons: 1) have appropriate scholarly expertise and 2) do not have any unresolved personal, professional, or financial conflicts of interest with the complainant. Respondent or principal witnesses involved in a Research Misconduct Proceeding, although they may be members of the Respondent's, complainant's or witness' departments, schools or disciplines and may have collaborated with any of them in the past.

The VCR and the members of the Inquiry and Investigation Committees shall assure a thorough, competent, objective, and fair Inquiry and Investigation. A Committee may investigate more than one Respondent.

An Inquiry or Investigation Committee is under a continuing obligation to identify and secure any unsecured evidence relevant to the Inquiry or Investigation and to so notify the VCR under IV.D, above.

Confidentiality. To the extent possible, UCLA and all participants in Research Misconduct Proceedings shall limit disclosure of the identity of Respondents and complainants to those who need to know, provided that this limit is consistent with a thorough, competent, objective, and fair Research Misconduct Proceeding and with law. Except as may otherwise be prescribed by applicable law and University policy, and as necessary to conduct Research Misconduct Proceedings, confidentiality must be maintained for any records or evidence from which Research subjects may be identified.

Settlement. At any time during or after an Initial Assessment, the VCR may settle, in writing, and close a Research Misconduct Proceeding, after consultation with the appropriate campus administrators and with a Research Sponsor if required, and subject to any UC policies on settlement agreements.

F CONDUCTING AN INQUIRY

Following a decision to initiate an Inquiry (see IV.C, above), the VCR shall appoint an Inquiry Committee consisting of one or more persons to conduct preliminary information gathering and fact-finding with respect to the allegations. With the concurrence of the VCR, this Committee may ask the Research Misconduct Investigator or Campus Counsel for assistance.

290　　　Appendix D　Research Misconduct Policy Example

The following table lists the sequential actions to be taken in conducting an Inquiry and the person(s) with responsibility for each action:

RESPONSIBILITY	ACTION
VCR	Appoints an Inquiry Committee of one or more persons.
Inquiry Committee	Engages in preliminary information gathering and fact-finding. If, based upon that fact-finding, the Committee determines that: 1) there is a reasonable basis for concluding that the allegations fall within the definition of Research Misconduct, and (2) the allegations may have sufficient substance, then the Committee shall recommend to the VCR that an Investigation is warranted.
	Prepares a draft Inquiry report that includes: the name and position of the Respondent; a description of the allegations; the basis for determining whether to recommend that the Respondent's alleged actions warrant an Investigation; and a description of any extramural support for the Research at issue (e.g., the proposal, grant or contract number, or publications that cite such support).
	Forwards a copy of this draft Inquiry report to the VCR for transmittal to the Respondent who may return written comments within two weeks.
VCR	May provide comments as to whether the Committee's actions and draft Inquiry report conform to this policy and transmits the comments (if any) of the Respondent and VCR to the Inquiry Committee.
Inquiry Committee	Within 60 days of its appointment (unless the VCR concurs in writing that the circumstances warrant an extension of time), considers any comments provided by the Respondent and VCR, and submits to the VCR its Inquiry report with the Respondent's comments attached.
VCR	Within two weeks of receiving the Inquiry report, decides whether to accept the Committee's determination as to whether an Investigation is warranted.
	Sends a copy of the Inquiry report and the VCR's written determination to the Respondent, along with references to this policy and the policies on Research Misconduct of the Research Sponsor (e.g., PHS Policies on Research Misconduct, 42 CFR Part 93).

G Conducting an Investigation

1 Appointment of Committee

Within 30 days of the determination that an Investigation is warranted, the VCR shall appoint an Investigation Committee to determine whether Research Misconduct has occurred. The VCR shall so notify the Respondent.

In appointing an Investigation Committee, the VCR shall consult with 1) the appropriate chair, director, or dean and 2) if the Respondent is an academic appointee, the Chair of Charges; if a staff member, the Assistant Vice Chancellor – Campus Human Resources; if a student, the Dean of Students; or, if a postdoctoral scholar or visiting scholar, the appropriate academic dean.

The composition of an Investigation Committee shall be as follows:

Appendix D Research Misconduct Policy Example

- If Respondent is a member of the Academic Senate, the Committee will consist of three members of the University of California Academic Senate, or more if warranted in the view of the VCR, and at the discretion of the UCLA Academic Senate Charges Committee, a representative designated by that Committee.
- If Respondent is an academic appointee who is not a member of the Academic Senate, a staff member or a student, the Committee will consist of two or three members of the University of California Academic Senate, or more if warranted in the view of the VCR. The VCR has the discretion to appoint an additional member from the respondent's peer group (non-Senate academic appointee [e.g., professional researcher, adjunct faculty, visiting scholar or post-doctoral scholar]; staff or student).

2 Investigation

The Investigation Committee shall take reasonable steps to: ensure an impartial and unbiased Investigation; comply with IV.D & E, above; diligently pursue all significant and relevant issues and leads; ensure that the Investigation is thorough and sufficiently documented; and examine all relevant Research Records and evidence, including evidence of additional allegations of Research Misconduct and evidence reasonably identified by the Respondent.

During the Investigation, the Respondent shall have the right to be represented, but the right of the Respondent and a representative to attend meetings of the Committee is limited to those times when the Respondent is being interviewed. If the Respondent elects to have legal counsel, Campus Counsel will also be invited to participate.

An Investigation Committee must complete its work, including the formal development of a factual record and the preparation of and transmittal to the VCR of its preliminary and final reports within 120 days of its appointment. The VCR may extend that time period, provided that a Research Sponsor, if it so requires, has assented in writing.

The following table lists the sequential actions to be taken in conducting an Investigation and the entity with responsibility for each action:

RESPONSIBILITY	ACTION
Investigation Committee	Interviews each Respondent, complainant and other available persons who have relevant information, including witnesses reasonably identified by the Respondent.
	Each interview shall be recorded or transcribed, a copy of which shall be provided to the interviewee for annotation and correction, which in turn shall be included in the record of the Investigation.
	With respect to papers, proposals, grant applications and the like at issue, all co-authors shall be deemed to have relevant information, and co-authors may offer as evidence any of their statements (to journals, in personnel actions, and the like) regarding their individual responsibility for the Research Record.

(Continued)

292   Appendix D   Research Misconduct Policy Example

RESPONSIBILITY   **ACTION**

Considers the arguments and evidence submitted by the Respondent.

If new allegations arise that were not addressed by the Inquiry or the initial notice to the Respondent, notifies the VCR who shall so notify the Respondent in writing.

With the concurrence of the VCR, may ask a Research Misconduct Investigator or Campus Counsel for help in information-gathering and presenting evidence.

Prepares a preliminary Investigation report for the VCR that should include:

- The specific allegations being considered in the Investigation and a list of all allegations made;
- Identification and summaries of the Research Records and evidence reviewed, as well as identification of evidence taken into custody but not reviewed;
- For each allegation, a finding of whether Research Misconduct occurred, whether it involved Falsification, Fabrication, or Plagiarism, and whether it was intentional, knowing or in reckless disregard of the facts; and a summary of the facts and analysis that support each such finding, including a consideration of any explanation by the Respondent;
- For each allegation, identification of all Research Records that need to be corrected or retracted;
- For each allegation, a description and documentation of extramural support and known applications or proposals for support, including the proposal, contract or grant number, Research Sponsor, or publications listing extramural support.

VCR

Provides the Respondent with a copy of the preliminary Investigation report and a copy of, or supervised access to, the evidence upon which it is based.

May prepare written comments for the Committee on whether its actions and preliminary Investigation report conform to this policy.

Respondent

Within 30 days, may submit to the VCR a written response to the preliminary Investigation report for transmittal to the Committee and provide oral testimony and argument before the Committee.

Investigation Committee

Within 120 days of its appointment, unless otherwise extended for good reason by the VCR in writing, submits to the VCR an Investigation report that: satisfies the criteria for the preliminary Investigation report set forth above; takes into account the Respondent's response; and attaches to it the Respondent's written response.

3   Evidentiary Requirements for Findings of Research Misconduct

A finding of Research Misconduct requires that 1) there be a significant departure from accepted practices of the relevant Research community; 2) the misconduct be committed intentionally, knowingly, or recklessly; and 3) the allegation be proven by a preponderance of the evidence.

Evidence of Research Misconduct may include showing, by a preponderance of the evidence, that both: (1) the Respondent had Research Records and intentionally,

Appendix D Research Misconduct Policy Example

knowingly or recklessly destroyed them, had the opportunity to maintain them but did not do so, or maintained them and failed to produce them to the VCR in a timely manner; and (2) such actions constitute a significant departure from accepted practices of the relevant Research community.

The Respondent has the burden of going forward with and proving by a preponderance of the evidence: any and all affirmative defenses raised, proof of honest error or difference of opinion; and any mitigating factors relevant to a decision to impose administrative sanctions following a Research Misconduct Proceeding.

Preponderance of the evidence means proof by information that, compared with information opposing it, leads to the conclusion that the fact at issue is more probably true than not.

H VCR's Determination of Research Misconduct

The following table lists the sequential actions to be taken subsequent to the submission of an Investigation report and the person(s) with responsibility for each action:

RESPONSIBILITY	ACTION
VCR	Determines whether to accept all or part of the Investigation report, and its findings, which determination shall constitute, solely for the purpose of satisfying its responsibility to Research Sponsors, UCLA's determination as to whether Research Misconduct has occurred.
	Forwards to Research Sponsor(s), as appropriate: said determination; a copy of the Investigation report (with any necessary redactions); and notice of any pending or completed related administrative actions.
	Upon finding that Research Misconduct has occurred, forwards that determination and a copy of the Investigation Committee report (with any necessary redactions) to the:
	Vice Chancellor, Academic Personnel, and the Charges Committee of the Academic Senate, and thereby files charges in accordance with APM-016 and UCLA Academic Senate Manual, Appendix XII, if the Respondent is a member of the Academic Senate;
	• Vice Chancellor, Academic Personnel for appropriate action under APM-150, if the Respondent has an academic appointment but is not a member of the Academic Senate;
	• Office of the Dean of Students (and, in the case of a graduate student, the Graduate Division) for appropriate action, if the Respondent is a student;
	• Dean of the Graduate Division for appropriate action under APM 390, if the Respondent is a postdoctoral scholar; or
	• Assistant Vice Chancellor – Campus Human Resources for appropriate action in coordination with the authorized organization head, if the Respondent holds a staff or management position.

(Continued)

294   Appendix D Research Misconduct Policy Example

RESPONSIBILITY ACTION

Following the completion of an aforementioned disciplinary process, ensures that appropriate retractions and corrections of the Research Record have been completed.

If requested, makes reasonable efforts to protect or restore the positions and reputations of: 1) persons alleged to have engaged in Research Misconduct but against whom no determination of Research Misconduct is made; and 2) any complainant, witness, Committee member, or other person involved in Research Misconduct Proceedings who has acted in good faith, in order to counter potential or actual retaliation against them.

For the purposes of this policy, retaliation means an adverse action against someone (including a complainant, witness or Committee member) taken on account of that person's good faith participation in a Research Misconduct Proceeding.

Good faith means having the belief in the truth of one's allegation or testimony, which belief a reasonable person in the position of complainant or witness could have based on the information known by that person at the time; knowing or reckless disregard of information that would negate the allegation or testimony is inconsistent with acting in good faith. As applied to a member of either an Inquiry Committee or an Investigation Committee, good faith means cooperating with the Research Misconduct Proceeding by carrying out the duties assigned with impartiality; participating in a Proceeding involving a complainant, Respondent, or principal witness with whom the committee member has a personal, professional, or financial conflict of interest that is not disclosed to the VCR is inconsistent with acting in good faith.

I   VCR's Other Notification Responsibilities

- Advises a Research Sponsor, as required by Federal Regulations or Research Sponsor policy: 1) of a finding of an Inquiry Committee that an Investigation is warranted; 2) of the findings of an Investigation Report, of the VCR's determination whether Research Misconduct occurred, and of pending or completed University actions resulting from those findings; and 3) of information requested by ORI or other Research Sponsors.
- Notifies ORI, or other Research Sponsors as required, before closing a case if an Inquiry or Investigation ends prior to completion because: the Respondent has admitted guilt; a settlement has been reached with the Respondent; or for any other reason, except the closing of a case at the Initial Assessment or Inquiry stage on the basis that an Investigation is not warranted.
- As required, immediately notifies a Research Sponsor at any time during Research Misconduct Proceedings if there is reason to believe that any of the following conditions exist: the health or safety of the public is at risk; there is an immediate need to protect human subjects or animals; federal resources or

Appendix D Research Misconduct Policy Example

interests are threatened; Research activities should be suspended; there is reasonable indication of a possible violation of civil or criminal law; federal action is required to protect the interests of those involved in the Research Misconduct Proceeding; UCLA believes that, because the Research Misconduct hearing may be made public prematurely, notice would afford the Federal government the opportunity to take appropriate steps to safeguard the evidence and protect the rights of those involved; or the Research community or public should be informed.

- Advises a Research Sponsor, pursuant to its requirements, of such other information as it may lawfully request.

V ATTACHMENTS

A OTHER RELATED POLICIES, PROCEDURES, AND RESOURCES

ISSUING OFFICER
/s/ Daniel M. Neuman

Executive Vice Chancellor

Questions should be directed to the Contact for the Responsible Office identified at the top of this procedure.

Administrative Policies & Compliance Office
· 2255 Murphy Hall · Mail Code 140501 · (310) 825-9116

Appendix E Significant Events in the History of Experimentation With Human Subjects

Significant Events in the History of Experimentation With Human Subjects
Compiled by: R. Ensminger Courtesy of: WellnessJourneys
original website: http://www.mnwelldir.org/docs/history/experiments.htm
replaced by www.wellnessjourneys.org

1718	George I offers free pardon to any inmate of Newgate Prison who agrees to be inoculated with infectious small pox in variolation experiment.
1796	Edward Jenner injects healthy eight-year-old James Phillips first with cowpox then three months later with smallpox and is hailed as discoverer of smallpox vaccine.
1803	First consultation with peers by a physician, Percival, before starting a new therapeutic procedure.
1845-49	Marion Sims, the "Father of Gynecology" in the United States, conducts gynecological experiments on slaves in South Carolina.
1865	French physiologist Claude Bernard publishes "Introduction to the Study of Human Experimentation," advising: "Never perform an experiment which might be harmful to the patient even though highly advantageous to science or the health of others."
1874	Cincinnati physician Roberts Bartholow conducts brain surgery experiments on Mary Rafferty, a 30-year-old domestic servant dying of an infected ulcer.
1891	Prussian State legislates that a treatment for tuberculosis cannot be given to prisoners without their consent.
1892	Albert Neisser injects women with serum from patients with Syphilis, infecting half of them.
1896	Dr. Arthur Wentworth performs spinal taps on 29 children at Children's Hospital in Boston to determine if procedure is harmful.
1897	Italian bacteriologist Sanarelli injects five subjects with bacillus searching for a causative agent for yellow fever.
1900	Walter Reed injects 22 Spanish immigrant workers in Cuba with the agent for yellow fever paying them $100 if they survive and $200 if they contract the disease.
1906	Dr. Richard Strong, a professor of tropical medicine at Harvard, experiments with cholera on prisoners in the Philippines killing thirteen.
1915	U.S. Public Health Office induces pellagra in twelve Mississippi prisoners. All the prisoners are, however, volunteers and after the experiment they are cured (with proper diet) and released from prison.

(Continued)

298 Appendix E Significant Events in the History of Experimentation

1919–22	Testicular transplant experiments on five hundred prisoners at San Quentin.
1931	1. Germany issues "Regulation on New Therapy and Experimentation" while 75 children die in Lubeck, Germany from pediatrician's experiment with tuberculosis vaccine.
	2. In America, Dr. Cornelius Rhoads, under the auspices of the Rockefeller Institute for Medical Investigations, infects human subjects with cancer cells. He later goes on to establish the U.S. Army Biological Warfare facilities in Maryland, Utah, and Panama and is named to the U.S. Atomic Energy Commission. While there, he begins a series of radiation exposure experiments on American soldiers and civilian hospital patients.
1932	The Tuskegee Syphilis Study begins.
1935	The Pellagra Incident. After millions of individuals die from Pellagra over a span of two decades, the U.S. Public Health Service finally acts to stem the disease. The director of the agency admits it had known for at least 20 years that Pellagra is caused by a niacin deficiency but failed to act since most of the deaths occurred within poverty-stricken black populations.
1938	Japanese immunologist Ishii Shiro ("Dr. Ishii") conducts experiments with anthrax and cholera on Chinese prisoners in Ping Fan.
1939	Third Reich orders births of all twins be registered with Public Health Offices for purpose of genetic research.
1939–45	Dr. Ishii begins "field tests" of germ warfare and vivisection experiments on thousands of Chinese soldiers and civilians.
1940	Four hundred prisoners in Chicago are infected with Malaria in order to study the effects of new and experimental drugs to combat the disease. Nazi doctors later on trial at Nuremberg will cite this American study to defend their own actions during the Holocaust.
1941	Sterilization experiments at Auschwitz.
1941–45	Typhus experiments at Buchenwald and Natzweiler concentration camps.
1942	1. Harvard biochemist Edward Cohn injects sixty-four Massachusetts prisoners with beef blood in U.S. Navy-sponsored experiment.
	2. High altitude or low-pressure experiments at Dachau concentration camp.
	Chemical Warfare Services begins mustard gas experiments on approximately 4,000 servicemen. The experiments continue until 1945 and made use of Seventh Day Adventists who chose to become human guinea pigs rather than serve on active duty.
1942–43	1. Bone regeneration and transplantation experiments on female prisoners at Ravensbrueck concentration camp.
	2. Coagulation experiments on Catholic priests at Dachau concentration camp.
	3. Freezing experiments at Dachau concentration camp.
	4. Phosphorus burn experiments at Buchenwald concentration camp.
	5. In response to Japan's full-scale germ warfare program, the United States begins research on biological weapons at Fort Detrick, MD.
1942–44	U.S. Chemical Warfare Service conducts mustard gas experiments on thousands of servicemen.
1942–45	1. According to congressional hearings held in Washington, D. C., in September 1986, former American POWs were among Ishii's experimental subjects.
	2. Malaria experiments at Dachau concentration camp on more than twelve hundred prisoners.
1943	1. Epidemic jaundice experiments at Natzweiler concentration camp.

Appendix E Significant Events in the History of Experimentation

	2. Refrigeration experiment conducted on 16 mentally disabled patients who were placed in refrigerated cabinets at 30° Fahrenheit, for 120 hours, at University of Cincinnati Hospital., "to study the effect of frigid temperature on mental disorders".
1944	1. Manhattan Project injection of 4.7 micrograms of plutonium into soldiers at Oak Ridge.
	2. Seawater experiment on 60 Gypsies given only saltwater to drink at Dachau concentration camp.
	3. U.S. Navy uses human subjects to test gas masks and clothing. Individuals were locked in a gas chamber and exposed to mustard gas and lewisite.
1944–46	University of Chicago Medical School professor Dr. Alf Alving conducts malaria experiments on more than 400 Illinois prisoners.
1945	1. Manhattan Project injection of plutonium into three patients at Billings Hospital at University of Chicago.
	2. Malaria experiment on 800 prisoners in Atlanta.
	3. Project Paperclip is initiated. The U.S. State Department, Army intelligence, and the CIA recruit Nazi scientists and offer them immunity and secret identities in exchange for work on top secret government projects in the United States.
	4. "Program F" is implemented by the U.S. Atomic Energy Commission (AEC). This is the most extensive U.S. study of the health effects of fluoride, which was the key chemical component in atomic bomb production. One of the most toxic chemicals known to man, fluoride, it is found, causes marked adverse effects to the central nervous system but much of the information is squelched in the name of national security because of fear that lawsuits would undermine full-scale production of atomic bombs.
1946	1. U.S. secret deal with Ishii and Unit 731 leaders cover up of germ warfare data based on human experimentation in exchange for immunity from war-crimes prosecution.
	2. Opening of Nuremberg Doctors Trial.
	3. Patients in VA hospitals are used as guinea pigs for medical experiments. In order to allay suspicions, the order is given to change the word "experiments" to "investigations" or "observations" whenever reporting a medical study performed in one of the nation's veteran's hospitals.
1946–53	Atomic Energy Commission and Quaker Oats-sponsored study of Fernald, Massachusetts residents fed breakfast cereal containing radioactive tracers.
1946–74	The Atomic Energy Commission authorized a series of experiments in which radioactive materials are given to individuals in many cases without being informed they were the subject of an experiment, and in some cases without any expectation of a positive benefit to the subjects, who were selected from vulnerable populations such as the poor, elderly, and mentally retarded children (who were fed radioactive oatmeal without the consent of their parents), and also from students at UC-San Francisco. In 1993, the experiments were uncovered and made public. In 1996, the United States settled with the survivors for 4.9 million dollars.
1947	1. Judgment at Nuremberg Doctors Trial including ten-point Nuremberg Code which begins: "The voluntary consent of the human subject is absolutely essential".
	2. Colonel E.E. Kirkpatrick of the U.S. Atomic Energy Commission issues a secret document (Document 07075001, January 8, 1947) stating that the agency will begin administering intravenous doses of radioactive substances to human subjects.

(Continued)

300   Appendix E Significant Events in the History of Experimentation

	3. The CIA begins its study of LSD as a potential weapon for use by American intelligence. Human subjects (both civilian and military) are used with and without their knowledge.
1949	1. Intentional release of iodine 131 and xenon 133 over Hanford Washington in Atomic Energy Commission field study called "Green Run".
	2. Soviet Union's war crimes trial of Dr. Ishii's associates.
1949–53	Atomic Energy Commission studies of mentally disabled school children fed radioactive isotopes at Fernald and Wrentham schools.
1950	1. Department of Defense begins plans to detonate nuclear weapons in desert areas and monitor downwind residents for medical problems and mortality rates.
	2. In an experiment to determine how susceptible an American city would be to biological attack, the U.S. Navy sprays a cloud of bacteria from ships over San Francisco. Monitoring devices are situated throughout the city in order to test the extent of infection. Many residents become ill with pneumonia-like symptoms.
	3. Dr. Joseph Stokes of the University of Pennsylvania infects 200 women prisoners with viral hepatitis.*
1951	Department of Defense begins open air tests using disease-producing bacteria and viruses. Tests last through 1969 and there is concern that people in the surrounding areas have been exposed.
1951–60	University of Pennsylvania under contract with U.S. Army conducts psychopharmacological experiments on hundreds of Pennsylvania prisoners.*
1952	Henry Blauer injected with a fatal dose of mescaline at Psychiatric Institute of Columbia University per secret contract with Army Chemical Corps.
1952–74	University of Pennsylvania dermatologist Dr. Albert Kligman conducts skin product experiments by the hundreds at Holmesburg Prison; "All I saw before me," he has said about his first visit to the prison, "were acres of skin".*
1953	1. Newborn Daniel Burton rendered blind at Brooklyn Doctor's Hospital during study on RLF and the use of oxygen.
	2. U.S. military releases clouds of zinc cadmium sulfide gas over Winnipeg, St. Louis, Minneapolis, Fort Wayne, the Monocacy River Valley in Maryland, and Leesburg, Virginia. Their intent is to determine how efficiently they could disperse chemical agents.
	3. Joint Army-Navy-CIA experiments are conducted in which tens of thousands of people in New York and San Francisco are exposed to the airborne germs *Serratia marcescens* and *Bacillus glogigii*. The germs and chemicals used by the Army and Navy posed known health risks before and during the time of testing.
	4. CIA initiates Project MKULTRA at 80 institutions on hundreds of subjects. This is an 11-year research program designed to produce and test drugs and biological agents that would be used for mind control and behavior modification. Six of the subprojects involved testing the agents on unwitting human beings.
	5. A declassified CIA document dated 7 January 1953 describes the experimental creation of multiple personality in two 19-year-old girls.

> These subjects have clearly demonstrated that they can pass from a fully awake state to a deep hypnotic-controlled state by telephone, by receiving written matter, or by the use of code, signal, or words, and that control of those hypnotized can be passed from one individual to another without great

Appendix E Significant Events in the History of Experimentation

difficulty. It has also been shown by experimentation with these girls that they can act as unwilling couriers for information purposes.*

1953–57	Oak Ridge-sponsored injection of uranium into eleven patients at Massachusetts General Hospital in Boston.*
1953–70	U.S. Army experiments with LSD on soldiers at Fort Detrick, Md.*
1955	The CIA, in an experiment to test its ability to infect human populations with biological agents, releases a bacteria withdrawn from the Army's biological warfare arsenal over Tampa Bay, Fl.
1955–58	Army Chemical Corps continues LSD research, studying its potential use as a chemical incapacitating agent. More than 1,000 Americans participate in the tests, which continue until 1958.*
1956	1. U.S. military releases mosquitoes infected with Yellow Fever over Savannah, GA and Avon Park, Fl. Following each test, Army agents posing as public health officials test victims for effects.
	2. Dr. Albert Sabin tests experimental polio vaccine on 133 prisoners in Ohio.*
1958	LSD is tested on 95 volunteers at the Army's Chemical Warfare Laboratories for its effect on intelligence. 1958–1960
1958–60	Injection of hepatitis into mentally disabled children at Willowbrook School on Staten Island in an attempt to find vaccine.*
1958–62	Spread of radioactive materials over Inupiat land in Point Hope, Alaska in Atomic Energy Commission field study code named "Project Chariot".
1959–62	Harvard Professor Henry A. Murray conducts psychological deconstruction experiment on 22 undergraduates including Theodore Kaczynski, the result of which, at least according to writer Alton Chase, may have turned Kaczynski into the Unabomber.*
1960	The Army Assistant Chief-of-Staff for Intelligence (ACSI) authorizes field testing of LSD in Europe and the Far East. Testing of the European population is code named Project THIRD CHANCE; testing of the Asian population is code named Project DERBY HAT.
1962	1. Thalidomide withdrawn from the market after thousands of birth deformities blamed in part on misleading results of animal studies; the FDA thereafter requires three phases of human clinical trials before companies can release a drug on the market.
	2. Injection of live cancer cells into elderly patients at Jewish Chronic Disease Hospital in Brooklyn.*
	3. Stanley Milgram conducts obedience research at Yale University.
1962–80	Pharmaceutical companies conduct phase one safety testing of drugs almost exclusively on prisoners for small cash payments.*
1963	1. NIH supported researcher transplants chimpanzee kidney into human in failed experiment.
	2. Linda MacDonald was a victim of Dr. Ewen Cameron's destructive mind control experiments in 1963. Dr. Cameron was at various times president of the American, Canadian, and World Psychiatric Associations. He used a "treatment" which involved intensive application of these brainwashing techniques; drug disinhibition, prolonged sleep treatment, and prolonged isolation, combined with ECT (Electro Convulsive Therapy) treatments. The amount of electricity introduced into Linda's brain exceeded by 76.5 times the maximum amount recommended. Dr. Cameron's technique resulted

(Continued)

	in permanent and complete amnesia. To this day, Linda is unable to remember anything from her birth to 1963. As recorded by nurses in her chart, she didn't know her name and didn't recognize her children. She couldn't read, drive, or use a toilet. Not only did she not know her husband, she didn't even know what a husband was. A class action suit against the CIA for Dr. Cameron's MKULTRA experiments was settled out of court for $750,000, divided among eight plaintiffs in 1988.*
1963–73	Dr. Carl Heller, a leading endocrinologist, conducts testicular irradiation experiments on prisoners in Oregon and Washington giving them $5 a month and $100 when they receive a vasectomy at the end of the trial.*
1964	World Medical Association adopts Helsinki Declaration, asserting "The interests of science and society should never take precedence over the well-being of the subject".
1965–66	1. CIA and Department of Defense begin Project MKSEARCH, a program to develop a capability to manipulate human behavior through the use of mind-altering drugs. 2. University of Pennsylvania under contract with Dow Chemical conducts dioxin experiments: prisoners at the Holmesburg State Prison in Philadelphia are subjected to dioxin, the highly toxic chemical component of Agent Orange used in Viet Nam. The men are later studied for development of cancer, which indicates that Agent Orange had been a suspected carcinogen all along.*
1966	1. CIA initiates Project MKOFTEN, a program to test the toxicological effects of certain drugs on humans and animals. 2. U.S. Army dispenses *Bacillus subtilis* variant niger throughout the New York City subway system. More than a million civilians are exposed when army scientists drop light bulbs filled with the bacteria onto ventilation grates. 3. Henry Beecher's article "Ethics and Clinical Research" in *New England Journal of Medicine*. 4. U.S. Army introduces *Bacillus glogigii* into New York subway tunnels in field study. 5. NIH Office for Protection from Research Risks ("OPRR") created and issues Policies for the Protection of Human Subjects calling for establishment of independent review bodies later known as Institutional Review Boards.
1967	1. British physician M.H. Pappworth publishes "Human Guinea Pigs," advising "No doctor has the right to choose martyrs for science or for the general good". 2. CIA and Department of Defense implement Project MKNAOMI, successor to MKULTRA and designed to maintain, stockpile and test biological and chemical weapons.
1968	CIA experiments with the possibility of poisoning drinking water by injecting chemicals into the water supply of the FDA in Washington, D.C.
1969	Dr. Robert MacMahan of the Department of Defense requests from congress $10 million to develop, within 5 to 10 years, a synthetic biological agent to which no natural immunity exists.
1971	Dr. Zimbardo conducts Psychology of Prison Life experiment on students at Stanford University.*
1973	Ad Hoc Advisory Panel issues Final Report of Tuskegee Syphilis Study, concluding "Society can no longer afford to leave the balancing of individual rights against scientific progress to the scientific community".
1974	National Research Act establishes National Commission for the Protection of Human Subjects and upgrades OPRR Policies to Regulations to be known as "The Common Rule".

Appendix E Significant Events in the History of Experimentation

1975	HHS promulgates Title 45 of Federal Regulations titled "Protection of Human Subjects," requiring appointment and utilization of IRBs.
1976	National Urban league holds National Conference on Human Experimentation, announcing "We don't want to kill science but we don't want science to kill, mangle and abuse us".
1977	Senate hearings on Health and Scientific Research confirm that 239 populated areas had been contaminated with biological agents between 1949 and 1969.
1978	Experimental Hepatitis B vaccine trials, conducted by the CDC, begin in New York, Los Angeles and San Francisco. Ads for research subjects specifically ask for promiscuous homosexual men.
1979	National Commission issues Belmont Report setting forth three basic ethical principles: respect for persons, beneficence, and justice.
1980	The FDA promulgates 21 CFR 50.44 prohibiting use of prisoners as subjects in clinical trials shifting phase one testing by pharmaceutical companies to non-prison population.
1981	Leonard Whitlock suffers permanent brain damage after deep diving experiment at Duke University.
1987	Supreme Court decision in United States v. Stanley, 483 U.S. 669, holding soldier given LSD without his consent could not sue U.S. Army for damages.
1990	1. More than 1500 six-month-old black and Hispanic babies in Los Angeles are given an "experimental" measles vaccine that had never been licensed for use in the United States. The Center for Disease Control later admits that parents were never informed that the vaccine being injected to their children was experimental.
	2. The FDA grants Department of Defense waiver of Nuremberg Code for use of unapproved drugs and vaccines in Desert Shield.
1991	1. World Health Organization announces CIOMS Guidelines which set forth four ethical principles: respect for persons, beneficence, nonmalfeasance, and justice.
	2. Tony LaMadrid commits suicide after participating in study on relapse of schizophrenics withdrawn from medication at UCLA.
1994	Senator John D. Rockefeller issues a report revealing that for at least 50 years the Department of Defense has used hundreds of thousands of military personnel in human experiments and for intentional exposure to dangerous substances. Materials included mustard and nerve gas, ionizing radiation, psychochemicals, hallucinogens, and drugs used during the Gulf War.*
1995	1. U.S. Government admits that it had offered Japanese war criminals and scientists who had performed human medical experiments salaries and immunity from prosecution in exchange for data on biological warfare research.
	2. Dr. Garth Nicolson uncovers evidence that the biological agents used during the Gulf War had been manufactured in Houston, TX and Boca Raton, Fl and tested on prisoners in the Texas Department of Corrections.
1998	Three children die at St. Jude Children's Hospital in Memphis during participation in clinical trial for acute lymphoblastic leukemia.*
1999	1. Veterans Administration shuts down all research at West Los Angeles Medical Center after allegations of medical research performed on patients who did not consent.
	2. OPRR shuts down research at Duke University because of inadequate supervision of human subject experiments...

(*Continued*)

304   Appendix E Significant Events in the History of Experimentation

3. One-year-old Gage Stevens dies at Children's Hospital in Pittsburgh during participation in Propulsid clinical trial for infant acid reflux.*

4. 18-year-old Jesse Gelsinger dies after being injected with 37 trillion particles of adenovirus in gene therapy experiment at University of Pennsylvania. His death triggers a reevaluation of conflicts of interest in human subject research.*

2000   University of Oklahoma melanoma trial halted for failure to follow government regulations and protocol. OPRR becomes Office of Human Research Protection ("OHRP") and made part of the Department of Health and Human Services.

2001
1. Biotech company in Pennsylvania asks the FDA for permission to conduct placebo trials on infants in Latin America born with serious lung disease though such tests would be illegal in the United States.

2. Ellen Roche, a 24-year-old healthy volunteer, dies after inhaling hexamethonium in an asthma study at Johns Hopkins Medical Center. OHRP shuts down all research at Hopkins for four days.

3. Elaine Holden-Able, a healthy retired nurse, dies in Case Western University Alzheimer's experiment financed by the tobacco industry.*

2003   FDA reports that, for the past four years, experiments on cancer patients were conducted at Stratton Veterans Affairs Medical Center by Paul Kornak who had no valid medical license and who repeatedly altered data and committed numerous violations of the protocols.

*It was not clear from the description if a human consent form was signed before these experiments.

Appendix F Examples of Medical Device Report Incidents

Examples of Medical Device Report Incidents (Used with permission of AAOS).

THE SAFE MEDICAL DEVICES ACT OF 1990: USER FACILITY REPORTING

AMERICAN ACADEMY OF ORTHOPAEDIC SURGEONS
60th Annual Meeting
February 18 - 23, 1993
San Francisco, California

SAFE MEDICAL DEVICES ACT TASK FORCE
COMMITTEE ON BIOMEDICAL ENGINEERING

A. Seth Greenwald, D.Phil. (Oxon)
J. David Blaha, M.D.
James Hundley, M.D.
Richard Pelker, M.D.
Michael Rock, M.D.

Purpose:

- To explain the responsibilities of orthopaedic surgeons in identifying orthopaedic device problems as required by the Safe Medical Devices Act of 1990.
- To seek the opinions of Academy members in defining what device information and clinical circumstances realistically assist an understanding of these problems.

What is the Safe Medical Devices Act of 1990?

The Safe Medical Devices Act of 1990 is a Law enacted by Congress on November 28, 1990 with the intent of assuring that medical devices entering the market, including those used in orthopaedic procedures are:

- Safe and Effective
- Monitored so that FDA learns quickly about serious device problems
- Quickly removed if they are defective

What does the Act mean for Orthopaedists?

The act requires that medical device user facilities report to the FDA and manufacturers device problems which cause or contribute to the death, serious illness or serious injury of a patient.

Orthopaedists practicing in hospitals, nursing homes, ambulatory surgical or outpatient treatment facilities are required to identify device problems.

To comply with these requirements, the orthopaedist must supply information identifying the device and the circumstances under which the problem developed.

How is this information collected?

Each user facility has designated an individual, usually a Risk Manager, who is responsible for the formulation of incident reports and correspondence with the FDA and device manufacturer.

To facilitate the process the FDA has developed an Incident Report Test Form shown on the back page.

What safeguards are there for the Orthopaedist who identifies a problem?

Under the Freedom of Information Act, any report is available for public disclosure purged of confidential details.

FDA has no interest in the identity of the patient or the facility staff members making the report, and this information is not requested in the Incident Report Test Form.

The Act further states that reports are not admissible into evidence nor can they be used in any civil action involving private parties unless the facility, or individuals, including the physician making the report knew that the information was false.

How does the FDA intend to use the information collected?

- Gain *insitu* experience into the numbers, types, severity and longevity of orthopaedic devices giving rise to clinical problems.
- Provide preemptory information on device failures that can assist an early decision to recall a defective product.
- Collect information relevant to a determination of the anticipated service life of orthopaedic devices.

Exactly which device problems need to be reported?

The regulation defines an injury as an event where medical or surgical intervention was required to preclude impairment of a body structure or function. This definition potentially includes a broad range of orthopaedic procedures.

The AAOS through the Safe Medical Devices Act Task Force is working with the FDA to define the scope and specifics of orthopaedic device complication reporting. The case scenarios which follow typify a range of these events.

Appendix F Examples of Medical Device Report Incidents

EXAMPLE EVENT DESCRIPTIONS

Case A PATELLA FAILURE IN TKA

This 76 year old osteoarthritic patient demonstrates persistent pain with patella subluxation six years following a cementless TKA.

At revision polyethylene failure is noted along with marked reactive synovitis and gross tissue discoloration resulting from metal debris.

At the time of implantation this device was cleared by the FDA for cemented use only.

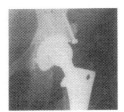

Case B MODULAR ACETABULAR CUP FAILURE

Ten month radiograph of a 50 year old patient who experienced left hip pain four months following THA for degenerative joint disease.

At revision liner separation was confirmed. The retrieved components demonstrate polyethylene fracture and significant galling of the cup interface attributed to six months of continued ambulation following the onset of hip pain.

At the time of implantation this particular porous coated acetabular component was approved for cementless application and was subsequently removed from clinical use.

Case C SPINAL FIXATION FAILURE

A 62 year old female patient underwent revision decompression combined with L3-Sacrum fusion to correct therapy resistant back pain with sciatica. Luque pedicle instrumentation with bone graft was used.

The patient enjoyed a pain free interval. Although the screws were properly placed at the time of implantation, subsequent x-rays revealed backing out of the screws in conjunction with progressive pain and sciatica. Four years later a third surgery was necessary to provide the fusion enough stability for consolidation.

Currently posterior spinal stabilization using pedicle screw and plate instrumentation is under clinical investigation and has not been cleared by the FDA for this application.

EXAMPLE EVENT DESCRIPTIONS

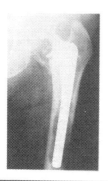

Case D PARTICLE DISEASE RESULTING IN HIP REVISION

This 50 year old, 200 lb osteoarthritic male patient demonstrates marked mid to distal shaft osteolysis four years following cementless HG hip arthroplasty. Subsequent subsidence and pain resulted in revision surgery.

Particle disease resulting from small intracellular polyethylene debris visualized under polarized light microscopy is thought to be an associated cause of this failure.

Titanium mesh devices of this type have recently been reclassified by the FDA for cementless application.

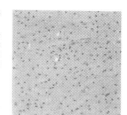

Case E FAILED ARTIFICIAL LIGAMENT

A 16 year old male patient underwent primary ACL replacement using a Gortex ligament prosthesis. Two years following implantation, rupture of this device occurred as a consequence of trauma sustained while playing football.

At revision fraying, abrasion and strand rupture of the ligament are noted. Histologically giant cells with foreign body incorporation are observed under polarized light.

This ligament device is cleared for marketing by FDA only for use in patients with previously failed intra-articular reconstructions.

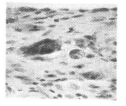

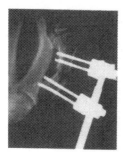

Case F THREADED PIN FAILURE

A 58 year old male patient underwent a lengthening procedure of the first metacarpal following a crush injury which resulted in amputation of the thumb and index finger.

A half frame lengthening device employing four threaded pins for fixation was utilized. After 30 days of continuous distraction, breakage of one of the proximal pins and subsequent loosening of the other resulted in a loss of interface stability required for bony consolidation.

The use of external fixators for lengthening procedures are allowed to be marketed by the FDA.

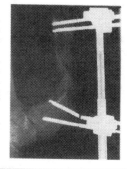

Appendix F Examples of Medical Device Report Incidents

EXAMPLE EVENT DESCRIPTIONS

Case G LONG TERM BROKEN FEMORAL STEM

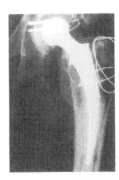

A 50 year old farmer had implantation of cemented total hip arthroplasty because of disabling symptoms of osteoarthrosis. Thirteen years later he had sudden onset of upper thigh pain associated with activity.

Fifteen years after initial surgery, the prosthesis was replaced. At surgery the acetabular component was firmly fixed as was the distal part of the femoral component. There was wear of the polyethylene, some metal debris near the broken stem and significant osteolysis at the proximal part of the femur.

Cemented THA prostheses have been cleared for marketing by FDA.

Case H PULMONARY EMBOLUS

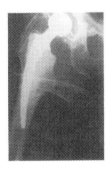

A 67 year old retired coal miner had implantation of a cemented total hip arthroplasty for disabling symptoms of osteoarthrosis. On the third postoperative day he complained of severe pleuritic chest pain, shortness of breath and haemoptysis. Ventilation perfusion scan showed a high probability of pulmonary embolus.

He was treated with heparin and had significant wound hematoma without nerve compression symptoms or infection. Anticoagulation was converted to Coumadin and continued for 6 months. Ten years after replacement he maintains a good result.

Cemented THA prostheses have been cleared for marketing by FDA.

Epilogue:

This information has been developed to acquaint Academy members with user facility reporting requirements relating to orthopaedic device complications called for in the Safe Medical Devices Act of 1990.

A further purpose of the Academy's Task Force is to work with the FDA in the development of a Guidance Document specifically related to orthopaedic device complications.

To this end the Task Force welcomes further comment which may be sent to Candice Croft, Ph.D., Staff Liaison at the Academy Office.

310 Appendix F Examples of Medical Device Report Incidents

Reproduced with permission from Kirkpatrick JS et al. Adverse Event Reporting-An FDA Requirement What, When, Who & How_**Presentation at: 2010 American Academy of Orthopaedic Surgeons Annual Meeting, March 2010, New Orleans, LA.**

Index

Note: Page numbers in *Italic* refer to figures; and in **bold** refer to tables

A.H. Robins, 223–225, 250
abortion, 61, 64, 95, **131**, 198, 224
academic senate, 69, 290–293
act utilitarianism, 50–55, 71, 79–80, 108, 121
actual duty, 55–56, 245
adaptationism, 41, 43, 245
Advanced Health Care Directive, 130
affinity form, 92–93
agency form, 89–90
AIDS, 193, 196, 233
alchemy, 10, 245
Alexander, Leo, 169, 176, 260
Alhazan (Ibn al-Haytham), 9
allocative efficiency, 108, 245, 263
alpha females, 38
altruism equation, 37, 41, 47, 53, 55, 92–93, 160,
    246, 254
AMA standards group, 126
American Association for Laboratory Animal
    Science (AALAS), 163
American Association of Engineering Societies
    (AAES), 110–111
American Cancer Society, 187–188, 286
American Institute of Electrical Engineers Code of
    Ethics, 109
American Medical Association (AMA), 26, 48,
    111, 133, 148, 174, 193, 198
American Society for Testing Materials
    (ASTM), 228
American Society of Civil Engineers, 19, 110
American Society of Mechanical Engineers, 110
American style of engineering, 103
anesthesia, 24, 164–165, 183
animal liberation, 159, 164
Animal Liberation Front (ALF), 165
animal models, 24, 161, **161**, 184–185, 208–209
animal rights, 159–161, 164–167, 246, 252,
    265, 266

animal stress, 162, 245
Animal Welfare Act, 160, 164, 172, 246
antibacterials, 181, 224
antibiotics, 137, 173, 182–183
antisepsis, 24, 183
Arab physicians, 11
Archimedes, 7
architecture, 7–9, 31–32, 114
Aristotle, 5–8, 12, 58, 60, 75, 119, 124, 158, 246,
    248, 251, 258, 267
army engineers, 103
artificial heart valve, 225–226, 247
artificial selection, 45
artificially assisted reproduction, **131**
Aseptic Lymphocytic Vasculitis and Associated
    Lesions (ALVAL), 228, 246
ASR XL, 227–228, 234
astrolabe, 9, 246
Asus, 3, 246
Atomic Energy Commission, 104, 298–301
authorship, 146–147, **147**, 287
autism, 154–155, 246
autoimmune response, 229–232, 246
automatic train control system (ATC), 111, 246
autonomous individual, 34, 94, 121
autonomy, 56, 77–79, 85, **86**, 94–95, 104, 119–131,
    131, 132, 147, 169, 179, 191, 198,
    212, 246, 255, 260, 263; rationalist
    model, 121–122, 263; right to,
    124, 212
Avicenna, 9, 11–12

baboon, head injury experiments, 165, organ
    donors, 166
Bacillus anthracis, 175, 246
Bacon, Francis, 15–17, *16*, 139, 260
Bacon, Roger, 12
bacterial resistance, 137

311

Index

BART case, 110–112, 246
Bayh-Dole Act, 1980, 191, 246
Beall, Jeffrey, 152
Beecher, Henry K., 178, 302
Belmont Report, 178–179, 246, 303
beneficence, 55, 73, 79, 179, 247, 251, 303
Bentham, Jeremy, 49–51, 121, 245
Bernard, Claude, 159, 297
Big Science, 28–29, 104, 143, 247
biological warfare, 163, 174–175, 298, 301, 303
biological weapons, 175, 221, 298
Biological Weapons Convention of 1972, 175
biologics, 201, 204, 206, 247
biomedicine, 129, 184
bioreactor, 204, 247
Bjork-Shiley heart valve, 226
black death, 11, 247; *see also* bubonic plague
bloodletting, 23, 247
Bradford Hill's criteria, 2, 186, 232, 247
Brahe, Tycho, 15
Braunwald-Cutter caged ball valve, 225–226, 247
breach of confidentiality, 125
breach of fiduciary duty, 77, 80
breach of warranty, 224–225
bribes, 114
bubonic plague, 11, 13, 175, 247, 268
Bush, Vannevar, 117, 182, 252
Buxtun, Peter, 171–172, 180

cardiac catheterization, 128, 247
cardiovascular card, 201
Cases for ethics study: ASR-XL Hip, 227–228,
234; BART Engineers, 110–112, 246;
Bjork-Shiley valve, 226; Braunwald-
Cutter valve, 225–226; Challenger
Engineers, 87, 112–113, 115, 248;
Covid-19 (fictitious example), 125;
CRISPR-Cas9, eugenics (fictitious
example), 64; curative, 134–135;
Dalkon Shield, 223–225, 250; Darsee,
John, 143, 153–154, 156; Daubert vs
Merrill Dow, 223, 232, 250;
Endovascular Technologies, 97–101;
Gennarelli, Thomas A., 165;
Grimshaw v. Ford Motor Co, 105–109,
263; Holmes, E. (Theranos), 234–235;
Hwang, Woo-suk, 153, 155–156, 210;
Hyman v. Jewish Chronic Disease
Hospital, 187–188, 212; Ludlum
(fictitious example), 70–75; Molecular
Pathology vs Myriad Genetics Inc,
215, 258; Moore v. Regents University
of California, 75–80, 96, 129, 249,
258, 264; Nazi Concentration Camp
experiments, 45, 170–175, 180, 298,
299; Novartis and U.C. Berkeley,
190–191; Piltdown Man, 152; Ping
Fan experiments, 170, 174–175, 298;
Regents University of California vs
Broad Institute Inc, 216; Riegel v.
Medtronic, 233, 264; Sergios, Paul
(AIDS), 196–197; sexual harassment
(fictitious example), 85; Silicone breast
implants, 217, 229–232; Starzl,
Thomas, 166; Summerlin, William,
154, 156; Tarasoff v. Regents
University of California, 96–97, 126,
266; Taub, Edward, 160–161, 164,
167, 265, 266; Tuskegee Syphilis
study, 170–172, 174, 176, 178–179,
180, 256, 267, 298, 302; U.S. v.
Carroll Towing, 108; U.S. v. Sell,
123–124; U.S. v. Tenet Healthcare
Corp, 127–128; Vioxx, 195–196,
200–201, 267; Wakefield, Andrew,
154–155, 156; Wyeth v. Levine,
233, 269
Cas9, 64, 134–135, 194, 216–217, 247, 250, 262
categorical imperative, **49**, 54–56, 73–74, 247
causal component, 186
Centers for Disease Control (CDC), 171–172,
224, 303
Challenger, 87, 112–113, 115, 248
Charlemagne, 10, *11*, 252
Charnley, John, 196, 227
chemotherapy, 181, 196, 202
chi-square test, 138–139, 248, 261
cholera epidemic, 24, 175, 248, 267, 297, 298
civil court, 219, 222, 248, 257
Class I devices, 204–206, 248
Class II devices, 205–206, 248
Class III devices, 204–206, 248; devices that have
been given an exemption, 205
client education, 94
client trust, 93–95
clinical research, 29, 117, 178, 181, 183, 185–187,
188–189, 191, 197, 210, 217, 227, 266,
271, 302
clinical trials, 98, 129, 184, 189, 193–196,
206–209, 211–214, 227–233, 256,
301, 303
"clinically proven", 130
cloning, 131, 153, 166, 209–210, 248
Code of Ethics, 38, 56, 72–75, 104, 109, 111,
126–127, 141–142
Collision Price, 107t, 108–109, 248
community standards, 85, 248
compassionate use, 212
Condemnation of 1277, 12, 248
confidentiality, 94–97, 111, 125–126, 128, 131,
148, 215, 248, 255, 266, 274, 287, 289;
may be infringed, 95

Index

313

conflict of interest, 97, 127, 129, 131, 149, 150–151, 155, 181, 190–191, 194–195, 249, 285, 294
conflict resolution, 40, 249, 251
confounding variable, 105, 162, 249
consent form, 76–79, 120, 124, 130, 169, 187–188, 191, 212–213, 249, 271, 274–275, 304
constraint-induced movement therapy, 161
contraception, 64, 131, 265; contraceptive pill, 184, 245
contractarian moral theory, 77, 92, 119; contractarianism, 56–58, 61, 74, 85, 91, 179, 256
contractual form, 91–92
controlled experiment, 19, 249
conversion liability, 77, 80, 249
Cooper Committee, 202
copyrights, 114, **147**, 215, 249, 256
correlation coefficient, 26
corroborate, 18, 25, 28, 138, 144, 162
counterfactually causal, 186, 249
course of treatment, 118, 120, 249
COVID-19, 81, 125, 235, 249
craftsmen, 3–4, 7, 14, 17, 25, 250, 254, 266
criminally liable, 113, 250
CRISPR-Cas9, 64, 135, 194, 216, 250
Critique of Pure Reason, 18, 22, 250
cronyism, 114, 250, 254
Cruelty to Animals Act, 162, 250
Cumming, H.S, 171, 174
curve-fitting, 23, 250

Dalkon Shield, 223–225, 250
Dalton, John, 24–25, 248
Darsee, John, 143, 153–154, 156
Darwin, Charles, 23–24, 26, 37, 41–43, 45, 142, 250, 259–260
Darwinism, 24, 26, 250
data curves, 138
data integrity, 1, 15, 83, 87, 137–138, 172, 210, 228, 232, 234, 256
data scatter, 19, 23, 138, 267
Daubert v. Merrill Dow, 223, 232, 250
De Humani Corporis Fabrica, 13, 159, 250
De Revolutionibus Orbium Coelestium, 14, 251
de Waal, Frans, 38–39, 40–41, 266
deafferented limbs, 160, 250
deductive reasoning, 7, **7**, 15–16, 21, **21**, 28, 63, 139, 250, 266
Deer, Brian, 155
demiurge, 7–8, 250
deontological ethics, 48, **49**, 52, 56, 59–60, 64, 72–73, 79–80, 85, 94–96, 119, 125, 179, 245, 250–251, 256, 261

Department of Defense, 165, 177, 181, 185, 300, 302–303
Department of Justice (DOJ), 1, 113, 128, 182, 193, 200, 219, 221–222, 225, 245
Department of the Navy, 25
Depression, The, 104, 117, 162, 170
Descartes, Rene, 15–17
descriptive statements, 46, 251, 259
desires, human, 34, 34–35, **35**, 40, 50, 94, 121
determinism, 18–20, 27, 251
device-related deaths, 203
device-related serious injury, 203
Dialogue on the Two Chief Systems of the World, 15, 251
Diamond, Jared, 2, 158
ding an sich, 18, 20, 27, 251
directed beneficence, 55, 73, 251
disclosure (legal), 110, 224–225
discovery for trial, 222, 224, 229, 251
disputation, 12, 251, 262–263
distributive justice, 58, 251, 256
doctrine of the mean, 60, 75, 124, 147, 251
dogmatics, 5, 251
Dowie, Mark, 107–109
drug development, random screening approach, 183–184, 192
duty, deontological, 53–56, 71, 77, 79–80, **86**, 95–97, 110–111, 121, 125–126, **132**, 147, 177, 223, 245, 251, 255–256, 259–261, 298
duty of communication, 147
dyadic level, 40, 251

Ebola virus, 22, 251, 268
Ehrlich, Paul, 181
Einstein, Albert, 18, 26
empathy, 40
empirical scientist, 20, 138
empiricism, 2–4, 17, 20, **21**, 22, 24, 129, 169, 252, 257
Endovascular Technologies, 97–101
engineering education, 11, 14, 19, 117
Engineers' Council for Professional Development (ECPD) Canon of Ethics, 109–110, 251
environmental liberation front (ELF), 165, 252
environmental pressure, 40–41, 60, 252
epidemiology, 2, **21**, 24–25, 31, 45, 105, 129, 189, 231, 248, 252; risk assessment, 113
epistêmê, 7, 252
ether, 159
ethical analysis strategy, 69–70
ethical business practice, 113–114, 84
ethical genes, 33–44
ethics of Care *see* feminist ethics
etiology, 22, 252

Index

314

eugenics, 45–46, 64, 174, 180, 194, 252, 259, 261
European Patent Office (EPO), 216
European translation movement, 10, 252
evidence-based medicine, 117, 253
evolutionary psychology, 35–38, 43–44, 160, 167, 253
experiment design, 139, 141–142, **144**, 150, 162, 169, 177, 183–184, 187, 209, 257, 262
experimentals, 23, 189
experimenting ON a subject, 169, 253
expert witnesses, 222–224, 230–232, 250

fabrication, 143, **146**, 154, 203, 253, 285, 286, 292
facilitated a transaction, 114
failure is our teacher, 138
False Claims Act, 128, 253
falsifiable hypotheses, 24, 30, 33, 162, 189, 253, 257, 264
falsification, 143–144, **146**, 154, 253, 285–286, 292
fast track, 233
FDA: animal models, 24, 161, **161**, 184–185, 208–209; biologics, 201, 204, 206, 247; Class I devices, 204–206, 248; Class II devices, 205–206, 248; Class III devices, 204–206, 248; devices that have been given an exemption, 205; compassionate use, 212; Cooper Committee, 202; device-related deaths, 203; device-related serious injury, 203; expedited review, 207; fast track, 233; FDA Modernization Act of 1997, 207, 228, 253; Federal Food and Drug Act, 201, 253; Food, Drug and Cosmetic Act, 93, 253; Food Security Act, 164; general controls, 204–205, 254; good manufacturing practices (GMP), 202, 205, 254; infomercial, 119, 200; Institutional Review Board, 130, 178–179, 186, 188, 192–193, 206, 212–213, 255, 303; Investigative Device Exemption, 206, 209; Medical Device Report (MDR), 100–101, 203, 220, 254, 305–310; Medical device user fee amendment (MDUFA), 207; Medical device user fee and modernization act (MDUFMA), 207; Medical Devices Amendments, 193, 202, 204, 224, 229; order of concurrence, 206, 260; order of non-concurrence, 206, 260; performance standards, 205, 261; Pre-Market Approval Application (PMAA), 206–207, 262; Pre-Market Notification Process (510(k)), 205–211, 226–228, 245, 262; quack medicines, 201; Safe medical devices act (SMDA), 203, 220, 264; safety and efficacy data for drugs, 184
FDA Modernization Act in 1997, 207, 228, 253
Federal Food, Drug and Cosmetic Act, 93, 253
felony, 113, 184, 222, 253, 258
fetus, 123, **131**, 134, 188
Feynman, Richard, 87, 112–113, 142, 151, 152
fidelity, 55, 73, 79, 109, 251, 253, 257
fiduciary form of relationship, 93–94, 124
fiduciary obligation, 87, 253
Fisher, Ronald, 28, 138–139, 253, 265
Fisher's ANOVA, 138–139, 211, 253, 265
Fleming, Alexander, 137
Food and Drug Act, 201, 253
Food Security Act, 164
Ford Pinto, 105–109, *106*; *see also* Grimshaw, Richard
Franklin, Benjamin, 15
fraud, 98, 113, 123, 127–128, 141, 143, 153, 155–156, 177, 187–188, 225–226, 235, 253, 255, 261, 283
free will, 94–95
fundamental drives, 34, 254

Gage, Phineas, 42, *42*, 267
Galen, 6, 9, 11, 13, 17, 159, 250
Galileo Galilei, 15–17, 24–25, 251
Galton, Francis, 19, 26, 45, 261
game theory, 37, 254, 262
gender discrimination, 61
gene editing, 64, 194, 216, 250
gene therapy, 131, 304
Genentech, 184, 192
general controls, 204–205, 254
genetic engineering, 45–46, 64, 68, 131, 166, 183, 199, 254
genetic engineering of crops, 199
Genetics Institute, 76–77
Gennarelli, Thomas, 165
genome sequencing, 117, 254
genomic technology epoch, 193–194, 254
germ theory of disease, 24, 129, 184, 254
Gilded Age of Research, 183
Gilligan, Carol, 61–63, *62*
Golde, David, 76–80, 258
Good Manufacturing Practices (GMP), 202, 205, 254
Grassley-Kohl Sunshine Act, 195–196, 254
Grassley, Senator Charles, 111–112, 195–196, 254, 257, 264
gravity, 5, 18, 26, 70
Grimshaw, Richard, 105–108, 263
grooming, 38, 92

Index

Guanxi, 114, 254
Guide for Laboratory Animal Facilities and Care, 163, 254
guilds, 14, 254

H1N1 influenza epidemic of 1918, 25
Hamilton, William, 37–38, 41, 47, 62, 92, 114, 160, 246, 254
Hamilton's rule, 37, 38, *41*, 62, 114, 246, 254; *see also* altruism equation
happiness score calculation, 51, **51**, 53, 71
Harvey, William, 17, 96, 169, 185
Health Information Portability and Accountability Act (HIPAA), 126, 255, 265
Health Research Extension Act, 143, 255
Heisenberg, Werner, 27–28, *27*, 138
Helsinki Declaration, 33–34, 37, 178, 255, 302
herbal potions, 3, 246
heteronomous, 94
Heyday of Drug Development, 183, 189–190
Hill, Bradford, 2, 181, 186–187, 232, 247, 249, 265
Hippocrates, 6, 11, 127
HIV *see* AIDS
Human Genome Project, 117, 193, 255
humanist, 12, 14, 15, 32, 255
Hume, David, 18, 22
Hwang, Woo-suk, 153, 155–156, 210
Hyman, William A., 187, 212

Ibn al-Haytham (Alhazan), 9
Ibn Sina (Avicenna), 9–11
individually tailored medicine, 118
inductive logic, 15–16, 19, **21**, 139, 255, 260
Industrial Revolution, 3, 10, 17, 18–23, 23–27, 103, 181, 255
infomercial, 119, 200
informed consent, 77, 79, 80, 120, 122–124, 126, 130, 176, 187–188, 197, 249, 255, 271–276
infringed, 93, 95–96, 217, 220, 227–228, 255, 260
Institute for Ethics, 127
Institute for Laboratory Animal Resources (ILAR), 163
Institute of Electrical and Electronic Engineers (IEEE), 111
Institute of Industrial Engineers, 110
Institutional Animal Care and Use Committee (IACUC), 164, 208
Institutional Review Board (IRB), 130, 178–179, 186, 188, 192–193, 206, 212–213, 255, 303
intellectual property (IP), 114, 214–215, 256
intraocular, 182–183, 256, 261
intrauterine device (IUD), 223–225, 250
Investigational Device Exemption (IDE), 206, 209

Ishii, Shiro, 174, 298–299
Italian Renaissance, 12–16, 255, 256
Ivy, Andrew, 169, 176, 260

Jenner, Edward, 129, 170, 184, 297
judges, lack of scientific background, 223, 231–232, 250
judicial branch, 58, 221, 256
Julius Rosenwald Foundation, 170, 256
junk science, 232, 256

510(k) process, 205–211, 226–228, 245, 262
Kant, Emmanuel, 18–19, 22, 27, *54*, 250–251; Kantian deontology, 53–56, 256
Kepler, Johannes, 15
kickbacks, 114, 256
Koch, Robert, 24, 129, postulates, 24, 256
Kohl, Senator Herbert, 195–196, 254

lab animal research, 35, **161**, 167
last chance procedures, 166
least squares, 23
legal negligence, 222–223, 256
leukemia, 76, 78, 80, 303
level of confidence, 28, 162, 257, 264
Levin-Grassley act of 1989, 111–112, 257, 264
liability, 31, 64, 77, 80, 96, 106, 113, 200, 219, 222–223, 225, 229–230, 233, 249, 257, 262, 265–266
liable for damages, 106, 165, 222, 224, 230, 259, 262, 265, 303
libertarian autonomy model, 121–122, 134, 257
limbic, 43, 257, 267
logical positivists, 19–20
logos, 4–7, 14, 18, 257
long-term good, 51, 257
Louis, P.C.A., 23

macroethics, 46, 68, 257
magic bullets, 181
malpractice, 23, 90, 119, 124, 128, **132**, 214
Manhattan Project, 29, 104, 299
maximum utility, 49
means to an end, 54, 79, 95, 179, 258
measles, 154–155, 258, 303
mediated reconciliation, 40, 258
Medical Device Amendments (MDAs), 193, 202, 204, 224, 229
Medical Device Report (MDR), 100–101, 203, 220, 254, 305–310
Medtronic Evergreen balloon catheter, 233, 264
Mendel, Gregor, 24, 26
Merck & Co., 195, 200–201, 267
Mesmer, Francis, 18–20, 129, 246
metallosis, 227
microethics, 46, 68, 258

316
Index

Military Academy at West Point, 103
military engineer, 7
Mill, John Stuart, 49, *50*
MO cell line, 76, 258
Molecular Pathology v. Myriad Genetics Inc.,
    2013, 215, 258
Moon, Chae Hyun, 128
Moore, John, 75–80, 96, 129, 249, 258, 264
Moore, Lawrence, 96
moral vision, 32, 46, 59, 61, 63, 67, 83, 85, 219,
    234, 258–259, 267
moral voice, 62, 259
Morrill Act, 103, 259
Mozu, 38–39, 256, 259
Mukherjee, S., 29, 202
mythos, 4–7, 14, 19, 259

NASA engineers, 112
National Cancer Institute (NCI), 29
National Commission for the Protection of Human
    Subjects of Biomedical and Behavioral
    Research (NCPHSBBR), 178–179
National Institute of Biomedical Imaging and
    Bioengineering (NIBIB), 30
National Institutes of Health (NIH), 29–30, 84,
    117–118, 143–144, 146, 149, 153–154,
    160, 163–164, 178, 183, 192, 200, 211,
    215, 233, 301–302
National Research Act (NRA), 178–179
National Science Foundation (NSF), 30, 143, 184,
    192, 286
National Society of Professional Engineers,
    104, 111
natural law, 20, 259
natural selection, 23–24, 26, 37, 40–43, 45, 60,
    134, 179, 250, 259
negative duty is keeping the confidence, 96, 259
negligence, 106, 108, 127, 222, 225, 233, 256,
    259, 263, 265, 266
neo-Darwinism era, 26, 259, 264
neosalvarsan, 170, 181, 259
nepotism, 114, 259
Newton, Isaac, 17–19, 25–26, 261; laws, 17, 19,
    25, 261
NIH Committee on Scientific Conduct and
    Ethics, 143
NIH Office for Protection from Research Risks
    (OPRR), 165, 178, 302–303
NIH Office for Research Integrity (ORI), 146
19-nor-17a-ethynyltestosterone, 184, 245
normative, 5, 40, 47, 260
Norwich College, 103
Novartis, 191
Novum Organum, 15, 260
nuclease, 134–135, 194, 216, 247, 250, 260,
    262, 266

Nuremberg Code, 176–179, 212, 260, 299, 303
Nuremberg trials, 45, 176–177

Occupation, Safety and Health Administration
    (OSHA), **86**, 90
off-label use, 189, 260
off-target effects, 135, 194, 260
Office of Naval Research, 183
Office of Scientific Research and Development
    (OSRD), 117, 182
On the Origin of Species, 23, 43, 260
opponen, 12
optimize product design, 113
optimize the interface, 113
oral consent, 187
order of concurrence, 206, 260
order of non-concurrence, 206, 260
organ selling, 68
outliers, 140, 211
overridingness, 69

p value, 28, 138, 254, 260, 265
Pacheco, Alex, 160–161
Pasteur, Louis, 28, 129, 159, 169, 184–185
patent, infringement, 220, 227–228, 260; Patent
    Trial and Appeal Board (PTAB), 216,
    260; rights eligibility, "first to
    file", 215
paternalism form, 90–91, 121, 130, 260
patient's rights, 124
peaceful arbitration, 40, 261
Pearson's chi-square, 26, 138–139, 261
penicillin, 137, 171–172, 182
People for the Ethical Treatment of Animals
    (PETA), 160–161, 266
performance standards, 205, 261
persons as ends, 54
Philosophiae Naturalis Principia Mathematica,
    18, 261
Physicians' Desk Reference (PDR), 190
Piltdown Man, 152, 156, 261
plagiarism, 143, **144**, 145, **146**, 261, 286, 292
plaintiffs, 96, 106, 111, 128, 219, 225–226, 230,
    261, 302
planetary motion, three laws, 15
Plato, 4–8, 15, 34, 250, 261
Platonists, 5, 261
Poddar, Prosenjit, 96
polydimethylsiloxane (PDMS), 229, 261
polymethylmethacrylate (PMMA), 206, 261
polyurethane foam, 229, 261
Popper, Karl, 28, *28*
population genetics, 26, 45, 261
positive duty is the infringement, 96, 261
positivists, 19–20, 261
Powelson, Harvey, 96

Index

317

power calculation, 139, 211, 261
Pre-Market Approval Application (PMAA), 206–207, 262
precedent-setting verdict, 68, 75–79, 262
precision medicine, 118–119, 193, 262
prescriptive, 40, 46, 259, 262
prima facie, 49t, 55–56, 73, 94–95, 111, 262
principle of indeterminacy, 27, 262
prisoner's dilemma, 37, 262
Product Safety Commission, 74
professional, 74, 83, 88–97, 119, 133, 141, 155, 210, 255
professional fiduciary, 93–94
proprietor engineers, 103
proto-morality, 39–40, 43, 263, 266
Public Health Service, (PHS), 26, 170–172, 180, 187, 290
Public Policy Perspectives: Ethical Standards, 110
punitive damages, 106, 224, 230, 262

quack medicines, 201

Rawls, John, *57*, 58, 267
reciprocal altruism, 39, 263
reciprocity, 40, 263
recombinant DNA, 184, 263
Redding (CA) Medical Center, 127–128
reductionism, 18–19, 24, 27, 263
Reed, Walter, 25, 297
regulation after the fact, 182, 245
Rensselaer Polytechnic, 103
reparation, 55
research fraud, 141, 143, 155, 255
Respect for Persons, 179, 247, 303
responden, 12, 263
retribution, 71, 85, 112, 257, 264
Rickettsia typhi, 175, 263
Riegel v. Medtronic, 233, 264
risk assessment, 19, 22, 25, 105, 113, 153, 188
risk factors, 25, 262, 264
risk/benefit analysis, 108–109, 264
Roman classical engineers, 6–7
Ross, W.D., 55–56, 60, 73, 83, 245
Rousseau, Jacques, 44, 58, 121
Royal Society of London, 17, 151
Russell, W.M.S., 163

Safe Medical Devices Act (SMDA), 203, 220, 264
safety, 21, 31, 35, 65, 69, 74–75, **86**, 97, 100, 103, 105–106, 109–114, 126, 167, 184–193, 197–210, 228–231, 249, 251, 264, 266, 288, 294, 301
safety and efficacy data for drugs, 184
St. Augustine, 8, *8*, 12
Sandoz Pharmaceuticals Corporation, 77, 264

Sanger, Frederick, 183
Sarbanes-Oxley Act, 2002, 112, 264
scholasticism, 8, 12, 15, 264
Scientists' Code of Ethics, 142
Secretary of Health and Human Services (HHS), 143
sexual harassment, 61, 85, 264
Singapore Statement on Research Integrity, 141, 264
Singer, Peter, 159–160, 164, 166
skeptics, 5, 264
Snow, John, 24, 248
social contract, 47, 56–58, 74, 158, 220, 264
social Darwinism, 26, 43, 45, 265, 266
social engineering, 45
socialized medicine, 29
socially distanced, 81, 265
Society for the Prevention of Cruelty to Animals (SPCA), 159, 162
Southam, Chester, 187–188, 212
speciesists, 159, 265
Spencer, Herbert, 26, 43, 266
Standard of Care, 118–119, 123–124, 127, 184, 189–190, 265
Standards for Privacy of Individually Identifiable Health Information, 126, 265
Stanley, William, 103, 301, 303
Starzl, Thomas, 166
statistical correlation, *21*, 231, 265
statistically significantly different, 162, 219, 265
strict liability, 225, 257, 262, 265, 266
Student's t test, 138
subjective relativism, 63, 265
Summerlin, William, 154, 156
Sunshine Act *see* Grassley-Kohl Sunshine Act
surrogate motherhood, 64, **131**
survival of the fittest, 43, 265–266
synthetic dyes, 181
synthetic RNA complex (crRNA+tracrRNA), 134, 194, 266

T-lymphocyte, 76, 196, 266
Tarasoff v. Regents, U. Calif, 96–97, 126, 266
targeted research, 181–183, 266
Taub incident, 160–161, 164, 266
technê, 7, 14, 266
Templeton, J.S., 224
Tenet Healthcare Corp, 127–128
Thales of Miletus, 4
thalidomide, 178, 266, 301
The Canon of Medicine, 9
The Enlightenment, *3*, 13, 17, 44, 159, 169, 252
The Principles of Humane Experimental Technique, 163
thirst, 34, 137, 254
three R's, 211

318   Index

tissue engineering, 203–204
Title 45, Part 46 of the U.S. Department of Health
     and Human Services Code of Federal
     Regulations, 130, 303
Title VII, 85, 266
tort, 43, 222–224, 233, 262, 266
total hip replacement, 227
trade secrets, 70–75, 114, 215, 256, 266
trademarks, 215, 256
translation movement: Arabic, 7–9;
     European, 10, 252
translational clinical science, 117, 266
transmutation, 10, 245, 266
transplantation, 52, 95, **132**, 134, 154, 166, 174,
     188, 206, 245, 246, 268, 281, 298, 301
Treponema pallidum, 170, 267
truth profession, 2, 5, 20, 25, 27, 30–31, 56, 104,
     118, 137–138, 141, 190, 267
Tuskegee Syphilis study, 170–172, 174–180, 256,
     267, 298, 302

U.S. Foreign Corrupt Policies Act, 114
uncertainty, 27, 96, 138, 262
Uniform Health-Care Information Act (UHCIA),
     125, 267
universal maxims, 54, 59, 267
using patient "FOR an experiment", 169

vaccines for measles, mumps and rubella (MMR),
     154–155, 258
variance, 138, 253, 267

Variola, 170, 267, 297
veil of ignorance, 58–61, 74, 92, 179, 267
venture capitalists, 184, 234
Vesalius, Andreas, 13–14, *13*, 159, 250
Vibrio cholerae, 175, 267
Vioxx, 195–196, 200–201, 267
virtuous habit, 60, 267
Vitruvius, Markus, 7
voice (Feminist Ethics), 61–62, 81, 259

Wakefield, Andrew, 154–156
Walker-Smith, John, 154–155
Weldon, W.F.R., 19
whistleblower, 71, 73–74, 111, 128, 151, 172,
     220, 253, 257, 264
Wilson, E.O., 37
workplace, 61, 83–85
World Medical Association, 178, 255, 302
wound healing, 1, 138, 163, 185, 229
WWII, 29, 45, 104, 117, 129, 162, 170–179,
     181–183
Wyeth v. Levine, 233, 267

xenogeneic transplants, **132**, 154, 166, 268
yellow fever, 25, 181, 268, 297, 301

Yersinia pestis, 175, 247, 268

zero, 9
Zmapp, 22, 268

Printed in the United States
by Baker & Taylor Publisher Services